Building and Integrating Virtual Private Networks with Openswan

Learn from the developers of Openswan how to build industry-standard, military-grade VPNs and connect them with Windows, Mac OS X, and other VPN vendors

Paul Wouters
Ken Bantoft

BIRMINGHAM - MUMBAI

Building and Integrating Virtual Private Networks with Openswan

First published: February 2006

Production Reference: 2090306

Published by Packt Publishing Ltd.
32 Lincoln Road
Olton
Birmingham, B27 6PA, UK.

ISBN 1-904811-25-6

www.packtpub.com

Cover Design by www.visionwt.com

Credits

Authors
Paul Wouters
Ken Bantoft

Reviewers
Michael Stelluti
Tuomo Soini
Nate Carlson
James Eaton-Lee

Technical Editor
Richard Deeson

Editorial Manager
Dipali Chittar

Development Editor
Louay Fatoohi

Indexer
Abhishek Shirodkar

Proofreader
Chris Smith

Production Coordinator
Manjiri Nadkarni

Cover Designer
Helen Wood

About the Authors

Paul Wouters has been involved with Linux networking and security since he co-founded the Dutch ISP Xtended Internet back in 1996, where he started working with FreeS/WAN IPsec in 1999 and with DNSSEC for the .nl domain in 2001.

He has been writing since 1997, when his first article about network security was published in *Linux Journal*. Since then, he has written mostly for the Dutch spin-off of the German *c't* magazine, focusing on Linux, networking, and the impact of the digital world on society.

He has presented papers at SANS, OSA, CCC, HAL, BlackHat, and Defcon, and several other smaller conferences.

He started working for Xelerance in 2003, focusing on IPsec, DNSSEC, Radius, and training delivery.

Ken Bantoft started programming in 1988, and successfully avoided it as a full-time job until 2002. Before that, he opted instead to focus on Unix, Networking, and Linux integration.

Beginning at OLS2002, he started working alongside the FreeS/WAN project, integrating various patches into his own fork of its code—Super FreeS/WAN, which is now known as Openswan.

He currently lives in Oakville, ON, Canada, with his wife Van, two cats, and too many computers.

Ken started working for Xelerance in 2003 where he works mostly on IPsec, BGP/OSPF, Asterisk, LDAP, and Radius.

Acknowledgements

Over a year ago, we wrote a proposal for an Openswan book. Without knowing about this proposal, Louay Fatoohi of Packt Publishing asked us if we were interested in publishing just such a book. We are very happy with the result of that collaboration.

We would like to thank everyone who is or has been part of the Linux IPsec and Openswan communities, without whom neither Openswan nor this book would have been possible.

Many thanks to John Gilmore for founding the FreeS/WAN Project, and to XS4ALL for hosting it. Many people contributed to FreeS/WAN, but we would like to especially thank Hugh Daniel, Michael Richardson, Hugh Redelmeier, and Richard Guy Briggs.

The FreeS/WAN and Openswan community contributed some important features. Thanks to Andreas Steffen of StrongSec for the X.509 patches, JuanJo Ciarlante for the original ALG patches that included AES, Mattieu Lafon of Arkoon Systems for the NAT-Traversal patches, and Hendrik Nordstrom of MARA Systems for the Aggressive Mode patches.

Further thanks are due to Rene Mayrhofer of Debian and Robert-Jan Cornelissen of Xtended Internet as early adopters of Openswan. Xtended Internet also graciously hosted the Openswan servers for two years.

We are especially grateful to Herbert Xu for his tremendous work on integrating Openswan with the Linux 2.6 NETKEY stack, and Michael Richardson for maintaining and enhancing `tcpdump`.

Thanks also to Jacco de Leeuw for his excellent work on documenting L2TP, and Nate Carlson for his elaborate X.509 configuration guide. They have invested a large amount of time in helping the community with Openswan configuration.

Everyone knows how important a cute logo is, but the logo that Nana Manojlovic spontaneously gave us surpasses even the penguin. Thank you Nana!

And of course, thanks to all the Linux distributions that have included Openswan in their packages. You have truly caused the widespread use and acceptance of Openswan.

Over the course of a year, quite a few people have helped to create this book. Many thanks to Louay Fatoohi and Richard Deeson of Packt Publishing. This book would have been filled with errors, had it not been for our reviewers, Tuomo Soini, Nate Carlson, and James Eaton-Lee. Extra praise goes to Mike Stelluti who, without ever having touched a Linux computer, went through the book verifying every single command, which included setting up and testing entire X.509, L2TP, and UML setups from scratch. And a special thanks goes to Michael Richardson for writing the section on debugging Openswan using `tcpdump`.

Paul Wouters and Ken Bantoft

First and foremost, I would like to thank my family. My parents, Frans and Reina, for getting that Apple][+ that started my interest in computers back in 1983, despite the fact that they did not allow me to have a modem, which I worked around by ordering my own phone line in 1992. My sister Silvia, her husband Gerwin, their kids and Annie van de Zwaluw. I would not be whom I am today without you.

Thanks to John Viega for convincing me I can and should write a book, and thanks to Xelerance for giving me the time to write it. Thanks to Robert-Jan Cornelissen and Xtended Internet for allowing me to deploy DNSSEC and IPsec all over the network even before the IETF has reached consensus, and thanks to Olaf Kolkman and Miek Gieben for their work on DNSSEC.

Thanks to Hugh Daniel whose super power can fix anything mechanical and break everything digital and to John Gilmore for many pleasant yet passionate discussions. I will bring you widespread OE!

Thanks to the Cypherpunks (Ian, Nikita, Len and Lucky), the CCC, and of course the Hippies From Hell - especially Ariane, Patrice, Ruedi, Kristel, Hinde, Dave, Rop, Barry, Marcel, Lucia, and the wonderful people at the PH kade whose parties resulted in many new dear friends.

Thanks to some of my scattered friends around the globe - Aaron, Ambrese, Joanna, Jeff & Ping and the other BlackHat folk, my MUD friends Emeradii, Perrin, Ayres and Carol who is now worth 17 books.

Many thanks to Irene and her colleagues of Coffee Company. I still miss the best coffee in the world.

Thanks to Liz for many lunches while writing the book. Thanks to Aldert for letting me deploy Wifi and IPsec on HAL2001, and our continued friendship ever since. Many thanks to Vesna, you were so much more then just a housemate, confidante, light of the party, or mole. But you should have opened door #3. And thanks to Nana for a warm friendship and of course our beautiful Openswan logo. Your tattoo befits you.

Thanks to Antony, not only for our many pleasant conversations, but also for "lending" me your ibook on which a large part of this book was written and on which we are currently porting Openswan to MacOSX. Remember friendships are not binary.

Karin Spaink. Eight years ago I asked you at HIP'97 if I could take your picture. Now, I can hardly remember not knowing you. Part of my daily confidence comes from knowing that you are only a phone call away.

Zenon Pannoussis. I failed in only letting reason dictate my feelings for you. You have far outranked any friendship I have ever had. No, let me finish. I like you. And if you insist, I have 1,709,098 words in 4120 emails from you to objectively back up those subjective feelings. Even religion only needs 791,328.

Naomi Rae Estreicher. Thank you for our wonderful time together, and for letting me work on my book from your place for many months. I never felt so loved in my life as when you exclaimed "I can't believe you're here". I hope to continue viewing Battlestar Galactica with you, it wouldn't be the same without your company.

Yella Cremer. It took five years, but then I found a passion burning in me with unprecedented intensity. I did not only gain a continuous craving for sushi. You are simply irresistible. How did I get any writing done in those months you lived with me?

And finally thanks to everyone who still dared to ask me "How's the book going?". I sincerely hope asking was as painful as answering was :)

Paul Wouters

I'd like to thank: My father, who put a computer in front of me 20 years ago, and who has supported my digital addiction for all those years; My wife Van, who puts up with the large amount of hardware in the basement, and the power bills it generates; Kyle Schustyk, with whom I set up my first IPsec tunnel; Jim Alton, Alex Bichuch, and Rob Rankin who kept me busy building VPNs for various people; Michael Richardson—without his ROT13-encrypted party invitation I'd have never starting hacking IPsec code; Sam Sgro, with whom a bet started Super FreeS/WAN, which in turn begat Openswan; D. Hugh Reidelmier, who still answers any C question I have.

Ken Bantoft

About the Reviewers

Michael Stelluti is completing his studies in Computer Science and has been an intern at Xelerance Corporation since 2005. As part of the Xelerance support group, Michael reproduces client environments in the labs and also moderates the Openswan mailing lists. To relax, he enjoys watching Battlestar Galactica with a pint of Guinness well in hand. Michael currently resides in Kelowna, British-Columbia, in Canada.

Tuomo Soini is one of the founders of Foobar Oy (Inc.), a Linux software and services company in Finland deploying Openswan IPsec networks and other Internet services. He lives with his wife and three kids at countryside in south Finland.

Nate Carlson is currently a full time systems administrator for Internet Broadcasting, and also does occasional Linux consulting on the side. He's been using IPSec under Linux since the early FreeS/WAN days, and has written a popular guide on using Windows XP in a RoadWarrior configuration.

He lives near Minneapolis, Minnesota with his wonderful wife Tiffany. He can be reached via his website, www.natecarlson.com

James Eaton-Lee works as an Infrastructure Security Consultant for a firm whose clients range from small businesses with a handful of employees to multinational banks. He has formerly worked for an Internet Service Provider and at a call center, as well as providing independent consultancy in the areas of forensics and security.

James has extensive experience of traditional and IP telephony, as well as how these technologies can be integrated into existing IT infrastructure. He has been involved in a variety of work in his present role, ranging from simple IT and infrastructure work for small clients to security work across infrastructure comprising thousands of servers for a large bank. He is a strong advocate of the relevancy of open-source and free software, and—wherever appropriate—uses it for himself and his clients.

Table of Contents

Preface

With the widespread use of wireless networking and the integration of VPN capabilities in most modern laptops, PDAs, and even cellular phones, there is a growing desire for encrypting more and more communications to prevent eavesdropping. Can you trust the coffee shop's wireless network? Is your neighbor snooping on your WiFi network? Or are your competitors perhaps engaged in industrial espionage? You might need to send confidential information to your office while on the road or on board a ship, or perhaps you just want to securely access your MP3s at home. IPsec is the industry standard for encrypted communication, and Openswan is the de facto IPsec implementation for Linux.

Whether you want to connect your home network with your laptop when on the road, or you need an industrial-size, military-strength VPN infrastructure for a very large organization, this book will assist you in setting up Openswan for those needs.

The book will take you through the process of designing, building, and configuring Openswan as your VPN gateway, covering these topics with the detail and depth of explanation you would expect from key members of the Openswan development team. You should note that Openswan is not restricted to only Linux clients, but can support all common operating systems such as Microsoft Windows and Mac OS X. Furthermore, you will look at some common interoperability examples for third-party hardware, from vendors such as Cisco, Check Point, NetScreen, and others.

As official developers of the Openswan code, the authors give you the inside view on essential techniques. This book includes the latest developments and upcoming issues. With their experience in answering queries from users on the mailing lists since the creation of Openswan, and its predecessor FreeS/WAN, the authors are authority figures well known and respected by the community. They know the ins and outs of a wide range of setups, and also know the caveats and pitfalls that can obstruct successful Openswan deployment.

What This Book Covers

Chapter 1 presents the historical context of IPsec and Openswan, and discusses the legal aspects involved with using and selling cryptography tools such as Openswan.

Chapter 2 explains in non-mathematical terms how the IPsec protocols work. It is written especially with the system administrator in mind, and will appeal to both cryptographic experts and beginners alike.

Chapter 3 contains all you need to know to install Openswan on any of the major Linux distributions. It covers installation from binary packages, as well as how to build Openswan from source. It also guides you through the features your kernel needs to support, and helps you choose between the two IPsec stacks currently available – KLIPS and NETKEY.

Chapter 4 is a step-by-step tutorial on how to configure the most common type of Openswan VPN connections. These include net-to-net, host-to-net, roaming users (roadwarriors), and head office to branch office connections. This chapter also investigates common scenarios, such as Cisco implementations using Aggressive Mode, and XAUTH with Openswan as the IPsec client.

Chapter 5 introduces IPsec authentication using X.509 Certificates. It explains how X.509 certificates work, how to generate them for Linux, Windows, and Mac OS X clients, and how to set up your own Certificate Authority.

Chapter 6 explains the Openswan feature known as **Opportunistic Encryption (OE)**. This visionary technology allows automatic host-to-host encryption for machines without any specific configuration by the end user. Using OE, anyone can use IPsec protected connections to your servers without even realizing it.

Chapter 7 digs right down to the packet level and discusses common problems that you might face on your IPsec gateway. These include special firewalling rules, handling broken IPsec implementations, and various MTU-related issues that can occur.

Chapter 8 discusses IPsec from the perspective of the two most popular end-user operating systems: Microsoft Windows and Apple Mac OS X. This chapter will help you decide between X.509 Certificates and the less complex L2TP. It includes a detailed guide on how to set up L2TP on your Openswan VPN server, and explains how to configure X.509 or L2TP on your Microsoft Windows or Apple MacOSX clients. We also look at the pros and cons of some commonly used third-party software packages that work with Openswan.

Chapter 9 deals with getting Openswan to properly interoperate with third-party IPsec VPN servers such as Cisco, Check Point, NetScreen, WatchGuard, and various other common modem/router appliances.

Chapter 10 explores how to use IPsec to encrypt local traffic on an intranet. It specifically focuses on 802.11 wireless connections, but it applies in general to all types of LAN. It discusses Xelerance's IPsec WaveSEC software, as used to encrypt the wireless networks at IETF, BlackHat, and DefCon.

Chapter 11 discusses advanced Openswan techniques, such as how to set up a robust fail-over VPN Openswan server, and how to deal with the bottlenecks that large enterprise deployments can experience, as well as how to handle BGP and OSPF using IPsec and Openswan.

Chapter 12 is the distillation of two years of end-user support on the public mailing lists. The chapter shows the solutions to common problems that you can encounter in your IPsec setup. This is a chapter that you will come to rely on to help you through the hiccups of real-world deployment.

Appendix A discusses some bleeding-edge Linux kernel issues, known security vulnerabilities, and bugs, as well as upcoming features for end-users and developers.

Appendix B provides a tutorial in networking basics to provide a firm grounding in relevant TCP/IP concepts and principles that are essential for a good understanding of your network.

Appendix C lists helpful online resources for Openswan users, and *Appendix D* lists IPsec-related RFC documents.

What You Need for This Book

You only need a Linux box and a network to install and run Openswan. Testing some of the configurations discussed in the book would require other machines running different operating systems and/or other VPN appliances.

Conventions

In this book, you will find a number of styles of text that distinguish between different kinds of information. Here are some examples of these styles, and an explanation of their meaning.

There are three styles for code. Code words in text are shown as follows: "We can include other contexts through the use of the `include` directive."

A block of code will be set as follows:

```
version 2
config setup
    # klipsdebug=none
    # plutodebug="control parsing"
    nat_traversal=yes
```

When we wish to draw your attention to a particular part of a code block, the relevant lines or items will be made bold:

```
version 2
config setup
    # klipsdebug=none
    # plutodebug="control parsing"
    nat_traversal=yes
```

Any command-line input and output is written as follows:

```
# sudo "/Applications/Utilities/Keychain Access.app/Contents/MacOS/Keychain Access"
```

New terms and **important words** are introduced in a bold-type font. Words that you see on the screen, in menus or dialog boxes for example, appear in our text like this: "clicking the Next button moves you to the next screen".

Warnings or important notes appear in a box like this.

Tips and tricks appear like this.

Reader Feedback

Feedback from our readers is always welcome. Let us know what you think about this book, what you liked or may have disliked. Reader feedback is important for us to develop titles that you really get the most out of.

To send us general feedback, simply drop an email to feedback@packtpub.com, making sure to mention the book title in the subject of your message.

If there is a book that you need and would like to see us publish, please send us a note in the SUGGEST A TITLE form on www.packtpub.com or email suggest@packtpub.com.

If there is a topic that you have expertise in and you are interested in either writing or contributing to a book, see our author guide on www.packtpub.com/authors.

Customer Support

Now that you are the proud owner of a Packt book, we have a number of things to help you to get the most from your purchase.

Errata

Although we have taken every care to ensure the accuracy of our contents, mistakes do happen. If you find a mistake in one of our books—maybe a mistake in text or code—we would be grateful if you would report this to us. By doing this you can save other readers from frustration, and help to improve subsequent versions of this book. If you find any errata, report them by visiting http://www.packtpub.com/support, selecting your book, clicking on the **Submit Errata** link, and entering the details of your errata. Once your errata have been verified, your submission will be accepted and the errata added to the list of existing errata. The existing errata can be viewed by selecting your title from http://www.packtpub.com/support.

Questions

You can contact us at questions@packtpub.com if you are having a problem with some aspect of the book, and we will do our best to address it.

1
Introduction

No one shall be subjected to arbitrary interference with his privacy, family, home or correspondence, nor to attacks upon his honor and reputation. Everyone has the right to the protection of the law against such interference or attacks.

—Universal Declaration of Human Rights, article twelve

Before we look at how to use Openswan to secure and protect your communications, we will first go over a little of the history of cryptography, and the reasons why we are now able to discuss and use a technology that was until recently considered a vital military secret. Three important events made this possible: the creation of the Internet, the (re)invention of public key cryptography, and the creation of free-to-use software.

Another important issue we will cover in this chapter is the legal side of using Openswan. While the creators of Openswan grant everyone the right to use the product, some governments have additional laws governing cryptography. Before you use, give, or sell Openswan, you should make sure it is legal for you to do so. Though the authors are no lawyer, we hope this chapter will provide enough information for you to properly consider this aspect.

The Need for Cryptography

The history of cryptography and therefore the history of IPsec and Openswan involve some level of politics.

Privacy

Today, a lot of what we do is logged somewhere. Our cellphone companies keep a database of where we have been and whom we talked to. Some countries, not only totalitarian regimes or theocracies, but Western democracies as well, are implementing data retention laws to force ISPs to store a copy of everything their customers do for anything from a number of years to indefinitely. Companies gather massive amounts of data using discount cards and RFIDs, turning citizens into statistical consumers. Certain well-known companies have been known to employ the tactics of spyware and viruses, deliberately infecting customers' PCs with rootkits to monitor their activity, and even control what they can do with their own computers, all in the name of anti-piracy.

If you play the online game of World of Warcraft, every title bar your computer displays, including subjects and recipient names of your emails, will be sent to the vendor, Blizzard, to ensure you "do not cheat" in the game. Governments have made secret deals with printer vendors such as Canon, who secretly implemented a 'fingerprint' on pages produced by their color printers in almost invisible yellow dots that encode the printer's serial number, as well as the date and time the page was printed. Anonymity and privacy has never been so far away. Neighbors can easily watch what you do on your wireless network at home. We are leaving our digital footprints everywhere, for better or worse. The Big Brothers (and even more little ones) are here to stay. Everyone needs to take their precautions. They should, and now can, use strong cryptography.

However, this freedom for the good guys also means that organized crime, petty thieves, vandals, frauds, and terrorists can use cryptography. This fact is often cited by governments to justify regulations to limit the use of cryptography for private citizens and to increase surveillance. Unfortunately, the "privacy versus security" argument is a persuasive one, although it is in our opinion a fallacy at best, and a deliberate misrepresentation at worst. The argument is framed with manipulative questions such as, "Would you be willing to sacrifice some privacy to increase your security against terrorism?" However, the truth is that privacy and security are separate issues. One need not be sacrificed for the other.

We will never be able to hide the information needed for terrorists to do harm, but we can show potential terrorists what a true free world has to offer. And a free world is not one where governments and corporations look at and predict all your steps along the way so they can manipulate, intervene, or maximize profits. Privacy is essential to what makes us individuals. It is a Human Right.

Security

Cryptography does not just provide privacy; it also provides security. Using cryptography we can ensure that we are talking to whom or what we intend, whether it is a person or an ATM machine. We can ensure that no one else is eavesdropping on us, and that no one else is pretending to be us. By encrypting data, we prevent information leakage. We protect against manipulation of our data stream. The security works both ways. We can trust them, and they can trust us. Security gives us integrity.

A History of the Internet

The Internet was, in fact, not invented by Al Gore. If one could bestow the invention of the Internet onto a single person, this person would be Jon Postel. However, he is not considered as the inventor of the Internet. By most, he is considered the first Guardian of the Internet.

The key to the Internet's success is that these millions of computers are able to communicate to one another without disrupting the communications of other computers trying to accomplish the same thing. At the core of that success is the **Internet Protocol (IP)**. Another essential part of the Internet is the lack of central control, and the absence of any third-party approval—be it governmental or corporate—before one may communicate.

Holding the Internet Together

The Internet is an international network. It is not owned by any organization. And though some governments would like to believe otherwise, it is not under the control of any national or international governmental body either. No single individual or company dictates how the Internet should be run or evolve, and no single restrictive non-free patented technology is necessary to communicate using the Internet. For this to continue, many parties need to agree on protocols, and on top of that, need to recognize and adhere to these protocols. These protocols usually have many options, which all parties communicating need to agree upon. Compare this to the 'car driving' protocol, where everyone agrees to stop for a red light, and to continue on a green light.

These formal registrations used to be maintained by one man, Jon Postel. The task was later delegated to a more formal group of technology people, the Internet Assigned Number Authority, IANA. In 1998 the US Department of Commerce (DoC) released two policy documents that called for the creation of a new body to govern these core functions of the Internet, which led to the creation of the **Internet Committee for Assigned Names and Numbers**, **ICANN**.

The Creation of ICANN

ICANN's creation was not very well received internationally, as it gave the US full control over the *root* of the Internet. As such, worldwide engineers largely ignored this non-technical political organization. An attempt was made to gain more widespread acceptance by reforming ICANN. Though this process started in 1998, it took years to complete. A famous Green Paper and White Paper with recommendations were written, leading to a Memorandum of Understanding (MoU) between ICANN and the DoC.

The 'ICANN at large' program, which allowed every individual to participate with ICANN and elect three board members, took two years to set up and was launched in 2000.

Two of these newly elected directors—Karl Auerbach, a legal scholar and Internet veteran who had been involved with the Internet before the Internet Protocol existed and Andreas Mueller-Maguhn from the German hacker community Chaos Computer Club—tried to get a true reform going but they were instantly blocked by the directors that had not been elected by the public. They were not even allowed to see the books of the organization they represented, and for which they were formally held responsible for.

The **Electronic Freedom Frontier** (**EFF**), a digital rights organization, assisted Auerbach so he could sue the Board of Directors in 2002. After he won the case, ICANN squirmed until finally a judge ordered ICANN to allow all the directors to see the books. However, while ICANN stalled handing out this information, it changed its own rules and more or less fired the At Large elected directors instead. It was pretty much apparent that ICANN was to be kept a US-only affair, and the international Internet community responded in a way that became typical of the Internet. It started to collectively maneuver around ICANN.

ICANN Bypassed

ICANN was supposed to handle three separate tasks: protocol registrations, IP address allocation, and **top-level domain (TLD)** management.

Protocol registrations are really done by the IETF and IANA, and ICANN just stamps its approval. It completely lacks the skill or desire to interfere with this process.

The IP address allocation is really done by the **Regional Internet Registries (RIRs)**, which are pro-actively ignoring ICANN completely. This became painfully obvious when the three major RIRs, ARIN (for North America and South America), RIPE (for Europe, Africa, and the Middle East), and APNIC (Asia and the Southern Pacific), set up the **Number Resource Organization (NRO)**. They no longer acknowledged ICANN as the central authority for handing out IP allocations to the RIRs. It was nothing less than a coup d'état.

The Root Name Servers

For technical reasons, there should not be more than thirteen name servers for any given domain, including the *root*. Otherwise, a DNS query answer would not fit into a single UDP packet, greatly delaying the answer of DNS requests. These name servers, eleven in the US and two in Europe, were historically placed at locations with the best Internet connectivity. They were run by volunteers, often at the big universities. When ICANN formally received control, they only actually got control of one of these root name servers, the so called 'A' root server, although this is the ultimate master root server. The other twelve servers are set up to pull data from the 'A' server. The 'A' server is currently run for ICANN by Verisign.

The reliance of the entire Internet on only thirteen servers has been a major concern for those involved in Internet design. A new protocol was created, called ANYCAST. In essence, it allows an IP address to exist at multiple places at once, and a computer requesting that IP address will be directed to the nearest ANYCAST IP address. The most important non-US root server, 'K', is run by RIPE-NCC, the operational branch of RIPE. Using ANYCAST, it currently resides in multiple places, including the two biggest conglomerations of Internet connections, LINX in London and the AMSIX in Amsterdam. An important side effect of ANYCAST was that the international community is no longer as dependent on the 11 of the 13 root servers that are based in the US and which are still in large part formally under government control. It has greatly reduced ICANN's influence over the root. The 'K' root server is a prime candidate to split off from the 'A' server if for some technical or political reason such a change becomes necessary.

Running the Top-Level Domains

ICANN is left with only the top-level domain management. This task is perhaps the most politically loaded task, and not as technologically neutral as handing out IP addresses or Internet protocol numbers or running the root name servers.

There are two kinds of TLDs, country code TLDs ("cc:tld") and generic TLDs ("gtld"). The cc:tlds are fairly straightforward. There are already international ISO procedures for this. Every country receives a two or three letter representation. The US has 'us', the Netherlands has 'nl', and China has 'ch'. These translate one to one to the top-level domains, .us, .nl, and .ch respectively.

ICANN has no real say in this matter either. Whether Taiwan is recognized as a separate country or as a Chinese province, for instance, is not something that ICANN or even the US government will have the final say on.

What's left under ICANN's control is management of the generic top-level domains. The most common ones are .com, .net, and .org. ICANN created a few more, such as .info, .biz, and .museum. But after the 'dot com' hype was over and Internet stock lost its magic (and power), no one was really interested in these obscure generic TLDs. For a few years, no new ones were created. Then in mid-2005, ICANN was about to approve the top-level domain .xxx for adult websites. The US Department of Commerce, under pressure from the religious-influenced Bush administration, forbade ICANN from doing this, for the first time using their formal control over ICANN.

The issue threw the public spotlight onto the government's influence over ICANN. There was a national and international call for a truly independent body to take its place, perhaps UN-based. Whether such politics will have any real technical effect on the Internet is not known, but it is not unthinkable that the *root* as we know it now will cease to exist, to be replaced by several new roots, under the control of various international organizations.

One thing that is clear is that Internet governance is set to change, affecting the creation of new top-level domains and the creation or deletion of cc-tlds. The creation of .biz and .info has been largely ignored on the Internet as a whole, and a similar fate is to be expected for the newly approved .mobi domain, a domain intended for mobile phone content. Some see these domains as milk cows for ICANN. Even Tim Berners-Lee, inventor of the World Wide Web, was strongly opposed to this domain, as it broke a fundamental paradigm of the Web, namely that content should have a proper device-neutral markup so that any device can decide how best to display the information. The .eu domain, originally planned for EU organizations, will soon be opened for everyone, but whether it will become an alternative for .com is unknown. Lastly, we should not forget the grassroots community that was responsible for creating the Internet. The technicians still have a remarkable influence envied by the political powers.

History of Internet Engineering

Those people involved in the birth of the Internet never talk about the Internet as having been 'invented', as it was not. It was engineered by many people. It incorporates many, now standard, protocols for communicating in many different but specific ways, suitable for a wide range of different applications. The creation of the Internet was not only a breakthrough on the technological front, it was also a tremendous breakthrough sociologically. It all started with a handful of people meeting in a single room to talk about how to connect their computer networks, and grew to become an international ad hoc effort with the least amount of formal and official structure possible. In short, it was a meeting of technicians, not a meeting of politicians.

The Internet Engineering Task Force (IETF)

The fact that no formal organization is responsible for the design and development of the Internet does not mean that the Internet is in a perpetual state of chaos and near collapse. On the contrary, the Internet functions with extreme reliability, made possible by the ad hoc organization of the IETF, the Internet Engineering Task Force. And what makes this even more unique is that the

IETF does not exist. There is no legal entity called IETF. The IETF solely works by the existence of two processes and a mantra.

The mantra that describes the goals of the IETF is concrete and precise: Consensus and running code. The two processes that make this possible are the mailing lists that are organized in 'working groups', and the quarterly gatherings of people at IETF conferences around the world, which give everyone and anyone, even those not backed by a large organization, a chance to attend a few meetings per year. Anyone can join a working group mailing list and become part of this process. There are no fees involved. The conferences are usually sponsored by vendors of networking equipment, and cost about $1500 to attend. These fees are to recover the rent of the conference facilities and administrative costs.

People attend and speak at the IETF as individuals, and not on behalf of their employer. In fact, many IETF regulars have switched jobs repeatedly without letting it impact their work within the IETF.

RFCs—Requests For Comments

The procedure followed by the IETF is relatively simple. When some people identify a need for a new protocol to solve some technical issue, they can form a working group. They pick a chairman, and set up one or more mailing lists. They create a charter that formulates the problem and then discussion on the mailing lists and at IETF conferences proceeds until the working group reaches a consensus on the design. This process generally sees the working group publish several draft documents. At some point, a working implementation will be written by someone, some group, or vendor with a specific interest in the new protocol. Once the working group is confident enough that no flaws can be found in the protocol, and when those claims are backed by at least two independently written functioning (interoperating) implementations of the drafted protocol, it will be submitted to the **Internet Engineering Steering Group (IESG)**. This group consists of individual experts who have proven their knowledge and skills over a prolonged time at the IETF. They are expected to be very knowledgeable, and capable of confirming the working group's claims. For certain essential core protocols, the process might also involve the Internet Architecture Board, another group of IETF veterans.

Once this group gives its approval to the new protocol, the draft protocol needs to be assigned a unique identifier. Historically, though now somewhat badly, named, this official registration is called a **Request For Comments**, or **RFC**. Furthermore, there are usually options or parameters of the new protocol that need some kind of central registration as well. These will receive their unique registrations in one of the IANA registers. For example, the list of ports used by certain protocols such as HTTP or SMTP is such a register.

This process of finalizing is done by the **RFC Editor**. The first RFC Editor was Jon Postel, but nowadays the RFC Editor is actually a small group of varying people. The RFC Editor will stamp the new protocol with its final official RFC registration number. Vendors who have not yet implemented the draft protocol can now go and implement the final RFC-specified implementation. Sometimes, vendors get together in *bake off* events. There, they will test their implementation with those of other vendors, to see if they interoperate correctly. Once they do, the new protocol is ready to be included in their new equipment or software.

This is exactly the same procedure that the IPsec protocols went through, before becoming RFCs. Due to the complexity of IPsec, there are over 20 RFCs describing the various parts of the protocols. An overview of those can be found in Appendix D.

IETF and Crypto

At some point, even in the old days of the first RFC Editor, Jon Postel, it became clear that the IETF had to take a stance on security, cryptography, and whether or not its protocols should have backdoors or key escrow built in. Some people noticed that the RFCs had skipped one particular RFC number, the number 1984. In August 1996, the IETF released RFC 1984, expressing the view of the IETF on cryptography and key escrow. The IETF strongly opposed any backdoors or key escrow feature in its protocols. Any attempt to make a protocol weaker just to assist a government in online surveillance was considered extremely dangerous. This was not a political opinion, but purely motivated by technological reasoning. The IETF would not hamper its protocol design. An excerpt from RFC 1984:

> The Internet Architecture Board (IAB) and the Internet Engineering Steering Group (IESG), the bodies which oversee architecture and standards for the Internet, are concerned by the need for increased protection of international commercial transactions on the Internet, and by the need to offer all Internet users an adequate degree of privacy.
>
> Security mechanisms being developed in the Internet Engineering Task Force to meet these needs require and depend on the international use of adequate cryptographic technology. Ready access to such technology is therefore a key factor in the future growth of the Internet as a motor for international commerce and communication.
>
> The IAB and IESG are therefore disturbed to note that various governments have actual or proposed policies on access to cryptographic technology that either:
>
> (a) impose restrictions by implementing export controls; and/or
>
> (b) restrict commercial and private users to weak and inadequate mechanisms such as short cryptographic keys; and/or
>
> (c) mandate that private decryption keys should be in the hands of the government or of some other third party; and/or
>
> (d) prohibit the use of cryptology entirely, or permit it only to specially authorized organizations.
>
> We believe that such policies are against the interests of consumers and the business community, are largely irrelevant to issues of military security, and provide only a marginal or illusory benefit to law enforcement agencies, as discussed below.
>
> The IAB and IESG would like to encourage policies that allow ready access to uniform strong cryptographic technology for all Internet users in all countries.

RFC 1984 has been complemented by RFC 2804, *Policy on Wiretapping*, where the IETF announced its stance that wiretapping had no place in the protocol standards, and should be achieved using alternative means. This position was not based on a consensus of political opinion, but was based purely on technical arguments.

The War on Crypto

In the late eighties, with the increased use of the Internet, then still mostly limited to governments, military, big corporations, and universities, the friendly nature of the Internet and its old trust in everyone was disappearing. Protocols such as Telnet and FTP that used plaintext passwords were becoming a big problem. The Internet was becoming too big to trust.

Everyone was further abandoning expensive secure private leased lines in favor of cheaper Internet connections, just as now people are switching from classic phone lines to Voice over IP telephony. These things all need security and they need privacy. In other words, they needed cryptography.

Dual Use

Cryptography has always been enshrouded in secrecy. What started as the art of concealing a secret has now bloomed into protecting secrets out in the open in plain view of everyone, using near-unbreakable mathematical formulae. Of course, the early adopters of these technologies were the military, but in the 70s it became clear that companies would need cryptography, and today just about everyone is communicating using electronic means, and has a need for privacy.

Researchers at IBM invented DES, the Digital Encryption Standard, and the NSA gave in. They allowed American companies to use DES, and even suggested that IBM slightly change its new encryption scheme, to make the protocol far more robust against a certain attack than it would have otherwise been.

Public Cryptography

One by one, all inventions made secretly within the military were being re-invented by non-military cryptanalysts. And new algorithms and ciphers were being designed at universities and private companies. Rivers, Shamir, and Adelman invented RSA public key encryption. In 1976 Diffie and Hellman came up with a technique which has become known as **DH key exchange**, enabling the safe exchange of public keys. Unbeknownst to them, the technique had already been discovered a few years earlier by Malcolm J. Williamson of GHCQ, the British version of the NSA, who kept it secret. Phil Zimmerman wrote PGP, the first simple-to-use encryption program for the PC. And in 1994 Bruce Schneier published his book on the once-secret science of cryptography, completely letting the genie out of the bottle. The book, *Applied Cryptography* (John Wiley & Sons, 1995, ISBN 0-471-11709-9), quickly became the standard work for anyone who needed or wanted to learn and understand cryptography.

The Escrowed Encryption Standard

Under the Clinton administration, the US government adopted a strategy of containment to control the spread of unbreakable cryptography. The idea was to allow a broken cryptography standard to be used by the general public, with a built-in backdoor for governmental use. The Escrowed Encryption Standard, with its now infamous Clipper Chip, was signed into law in 1994.

The Clipper Chip was designed by the NSA and implemented the Skipjack algorithm, which contained a backdoor accessible to the US government. Perhaps not surprisingly, few foreign entities embraced this crippled security. Other governments and organizations, especially in Europe, were working hard on making unbreakable crypto, and in the end the US Government gave into pressure and the Clipper Chip never saw the light of day.

Export Laws

Encryption methods not requiring the Clipper Chip were still legal for US companies and citizens, but in order to try to prevent everyone else from using cryptography, cryptography was classed as munitions, an item on the list of controlled weapons and resources that may not be exported to other countries without explicit government permission. Cryptography was treated exactly the same way as nuclear bombs.

But the export laws could not prevent the world from obtaining cryptographic software independently. The European countries still do not recognize software patents, meaning encryption algorithms patented in the US can be freely used by anyone outside the US. This included the RSA and IDEA algorithms, both used by the PGP software, though Phil Zimmerman never actually licensed RSA for this.

Other countries, especially Europe and Israel, were working hard to catch up with the US. Companies from these countries were free to sell strong cryptographic software to the US, but US companies were not getting the government permission they needed to export their products outside the US. The result was that many products existed in two versions: a US version, with full encryption, which usually meant 128-bit encryption, and an international version, which was usually limited to 40-bit encryption. This was most visible when Netscape invented the **Secure Socket Layer (SSL)**, a method allowing a browser to talk securely to a web server without anyone being able to eavesdrop on the content of the communication. This was essential for doing business on the Internet, allowing users to give a web server their credit card information with the confidence that it could not be read by an unauthorized party.

Netscape had to release two browser versions, one with 40-bit encryption and one with 128-bit encryption. But since its browser program was freely downloadable, it was impossible for Netscape to restrict the 128bit version to the US alone, but it still needed to make some effort in order to comply with the US export laws. It was not really practical to stop the spread of the 128-bit encryption version of their browser. People mirrored the software in Europe, others wrote software to tweak the 40-bit version to enable its 128-bit encryption that was built into the software binaries.

The Linux Debian distribution started a non-US branch, which contained the cryptographic software, and only non-US Debian download sites could have this software. Cryptography in the Linux kernel existed for a while as a separate patch on a non-US site, www.kerneli.org.

Pressure from researchers at universities in the US increased. With help of the EFF, Prof. Bernstein, then still a graduate student at Berkeley, sued the US government in 1995, claiming that talking about cryptography was a right protected by the First Amendment. He followed up with another lawsuit in 2002 claiming that "it's inexcusable that the government is continuing to interfere with my research in cryptography and computer security." But while Bernstein was fighting to liberate crypto, someone else had found a loophole in the law.

The Summer of '97

The munitions laws that restricted cryptography were focused on software. Bernstein was suing the US government so he would be able to teach cryptography in his classes. But exporting paperwork, such as research material, was never covered by the export restrictions. Two groups of hackers, the Dutch 'Hacktic' group and the San Francisco 'Cypherpunks', took on a project and printed the entire source code of the PGP program, with checksums on every page.

They then took this stack of paper and flew to The Netherlands to an open-air hacker event called 'Hacking In Progress'. They scanned the papers, ran character recognition software on them, manually fixing letters that were not read correctly, aided by the checksum printed on each page. At the end of the five-day event, the PGP source code had been reconstructed in digital form. PGP had now been legally exported from the US.

The export laws came under more and more pressure, mostly from US companies who were crippled in selling their software abroad. They could still only sell crippled 40-bit encryption outside the US, and nobody wanted it, since a lot of European software with strong cryptography had become commercially available. Then the EFF put the final nail in the coffin of weak crypto.

The EFF DES Cracker

In a basement room of John Gilmore in San Francisco, a machine was built, the DES Cracker. It consisted of a Linux machine that acted as console for a large array of specially-designed DES cracking chips. The costs, including all R&D, were $250,000. On July 18 1998, it took 'Deep Crack' only three days to crack RSA Laboratory's 'DES Challenge II'. On January 19 1999, it cracked the 'DES Challenge III' in 22 hours. The previous record on that challenge had taken 56 hours using 100,000 PCs worldwide. The US government could no longer claim that DES was good enough for encryption. A few months later it became clear why the US government wanted the international community to use weak crypto.

Echelon

In April 1999, Duncan Campbell, a British journalist, handed over his report entitled *Interception Capabilities 2000* to the Director General for Research of the European Parliament. Campbell reported that, after years of research all over the world, he had uncovered the existence of Echelon, a massive top-secret network of interception capabilities built and operated by the US and the UK, aimed at their allies in Europe. Tension between Europe and the US rose. Accusations of industrial espionage were highlighted in a case where US airplane manufacturer Boeing underbid the European Airbus in a very large contract, apparently after having inside information handed to it by the NSA.

The End of the Export Restrictions

In 1999, the US finally relaxed the export laws covering cryptography. Under License Exception TSU pursuant to 15 C.F.R. Section 740.13(e), cryptographic software could now be exported freely to anyone in the world, with the exception of the Usual Suspects (Iran, Iraq, Cuba, and a few other countries). It allowed the publication of cryptographic software on the Internet, even if it meant that people from those blacklisted countries could download it as well. But there is an emergency break. Formally, to this day, the President of the United States can still at any time issue a decree that limits or bans the export and use of cryptography.

Though this seems a great concession, it was merely the formalization of the existing situation. A new phenomenon had given rise to an immense amount of cryptographic software being available on the Internet, following something started in 1984 by a former MIT graduate, Richard Stallman.

Free Software

Richard Stallman wanted to share his software with others. He wanted to continually improve the software, and share these improvements. However, no vendors were interested in giving away their software; they wanted to sell many copies to everyone. In 1982 Stallman began to write alternative software from scratch—software that everyone was allowed to copy and modify as they saw fit. He wrote various key tools that we now take for granted, as part of his 'GNU: Gnu's Not Unix' project. He wrote the GNU C compiler, GNU make, Emacs, and much more. In 1985 he founded the *Free Software Foundation*.

He had rewritten most of the tools that came with the commercial Unix operating systems; all he needed was the core of the system itself, the kernel. As it turned out, Linus Torvalds from Finland had just written that part and released his Linux kernel on 25 August 1991. The GNU project tools, together with the Linux kernel, provided a completely free operating system for the first time ever. In parallel with that, another Unix operating system, the AT&T BSD code, was being rewritten. Though the source code was available, it still came with restrictions, and you needed to buy a license from AT&T. NetBSD released its first distribution in April of 1993, which contained no AT&T code. Around the same time, another BSD variant, FreeBSD, was also released.

The GPL

The BSD variants allowed anyone to do whatever they wanted with the code, with the provision that an acknowledgment in the form of a copyright statement be visible in all products that used BSD code, a requirement that was eventually dropped as well. However, GNU software came with a strong philosophy. Though both the BSD people and the GNU people wanted to share their software with others, and collectively improve software and allow everyone the freedom to run, distribute, and change that software, the fundamental difference was that those in the GNU camp wanted to ensure that these freedoms would not be lost in the future. They wanted to prevent someone taking their code, and releasing an improved version that was licensed under non-free terms.

For this purpose, Richard Stallman created the **GNU Public License (GPL)**, which applied copyright in a completely different way than usual. Normally, people use copyright to prevent their works from being distributed without their consent. The GPL copyright statement, also called

copyleft, aimed to ensure that freely available source code could only be used in programs that also offered the same freedom to use, modify, and redistribute the source code. As they explain it in the preamble to the GPL:

> To copyleft a program, we first state that it is copyrighted; then we add distribution terms, which are a legal instrument that gives everyone the rights to use, modify, and redistribute the program's code *or any program derived from it* but only if the distribution terms are unchanged. Thus, the code and the freedoms become legally inseparable.

This is usually expressed within the community in the phrase, "Free as in freedom, not beer", referring to the difference between free and gratis. Free beer is great, but it's a different kind of free to free as in freedom. It is perfectly legal to sell software covered under the GPL. In fact, GPL software now powers many small appliances, ranging from wireless access points, to phones, to specialized industrial computers. Sometimes, vendors take GPL code, use it, and refuse to give the source code to someone asking for it. Several court cases have now upheld the license conditions of the GPL, and most infringing vendors quickly settle out of court because they know they would lose. Vendors that have produced source code in response to lawsuits on GPL violations include Cisco/Linksys, TomTom, Fujitsu-Siemens, Asus, Sitecom, Edimax, and Belkin. Another huge court case, between the SCO group and IBM, is ongoing, with SCO claiming that IBM stole code, which IBM then released under the GPL. To date, all of SCO's claims have been disproved by both the free software community at large, and more importantly, the court. However, the case is still underway and SCO has yet to come up with verifiable proof. The outcome of this court case is expected to firmly confirm the legal standing of the GPL in court.

Free as in Verifiable

Especially for cryptography, it is essential that the code is free. One can never trust a cryptographic machine whose internal workings are unknown. Because it is impossible to detect whether such a black box is doing something subtly bad, such as leaking key information, or using a set of bad or predefined random numbers, either of which would fundamentally undermine the security of the encryption in a completely undetectable way.

> One should never, under any circumstances, trust cryptographic software without having the source code of the software to verify the absence of insecure or malicious code.

Even now, many governments do not even have the source code of their own digital tapping rooms, and they are at the mercy of certain vendors and the governments of those vendors.

The Open Source Movement

The term **open source software** is often used when talking about free software. It was coined by Eric Raymond to make free software more appealing to corporations. It was believed that the term *free* was misinterpreted by commercial companies to mean *gratis*, which was believed to be a reason why many companies shied away from such free software. It was also thought to have an image of being *free and unsupported*. A myriad of free and open source licenses have now appeared, as each vendor's lawyers want its license to be phrased slightly differently for a certain legal reason.

The History of Openswan

While the IETF was still busy designing the IPsec protocols, entrepreneur John Gilmore founded the FreeS/WAN Project. S/WAN stands for Secure Wide Area Network. The ultimate goal of the project was to make IPsec the default mode of operation for the entire Internet. Version 1.0 was released for Linux in April of 1999 under the GPL license and worked on the Linux 2.0.36 kernel.

In effect, the Presidential decrees on crypto export meant that should an American touch the Free/SWAN code, the US government could legally restrict its use to whomever they wanted. For this reason, Gilmore barred any American from ever coding for the project, running it entirely outside of the US from Canada and Europe. No patches from Americans were ever accepted.

This became a major problem when end users really wanted the kernel code of FreeS/WAN (**KLIPS**) to be merged into the mainstream Linux kernel. First of all, Linus Torvalds, the original programmer and current maintainer of the Linux kernel as a whole, has a policy of keeping politics from entering into the kernel, so code with such restrictions would never be permitted. On top of this problem, the maintainer of the network subsystem of the Linux kernel, Dave Miller, was an American. Thus, KLIPS never made it into the mainstream kernel, and FreeS/WAN never got included in the popular Red Hat Linux distributions. This situation lasted for a few years during which users had to patch their kernel manually to add IPsec support, and compile their own FreeS/WAN software. Later on the project shipped binary packages for Red Hat (RPMs) to make IPsec deployment relatively easy.

Meanwhile, although Gilmore's project was widely used as a VPN solution, the intention to encrypt the entire Internet was failing. It seemed that the project was not succeeding in its political goal, even though FreeS/WAN was widely deployed to increase the privacy and security of military organizations and Fortune500 companies.

IETF Troubles over DNS

To encrypt the entire Internet using IPsec, through a method dubbed **Opportunistic Encryption (OE)**, it was necessary that a certain DNS record be added for FreeS/WAN support. Purists at the IETF did not want applications to use DNS, and worse, DNS itself was long overdue for an overhaul to add cryptographic security to it, but the process of drawing up this new **DNSSEC** protocol has been one of the slowest projects coming out of the IETF and was only released as RFC 4034 and RFC 4035 in March 2005. On top of these DNS issues, OE faced more and more problems due to the wide deployment of NAT, a method for connecting multiple computers using 'internal-only' IP addresses behind a single computer with a single *real* Internet-connected IP address. IPsec however, was more and more necessary after wireless networking took off, and the WiFi encryption standards were broken one after the other.

Super FreeS/WAN

The rigorous views of the FreeS/WAN project were extremely problematic. Its political leanings drew it away from the real-world demands for certain VPN features and IETF standards implementation. Most notably, the refusal for inclusion of the X.509 patch, written by Andreas Steffen, a computer science research professor at the University of Applied Sciences Rapperswil in Switzerland, and the NAT-Traversal patch written by the French security company Arkoon, made a "stock FreeS/WAN" release next to useless for most *real-world* VPN usage, something the FreeS/WAN Project was not too concerned about since X.509 was deemed inferior compared its own DNS-based OE. This was because it was only really offering privacy to businesses rather than everyone on the Internet.

The non-DNS-based authentication method in IPsec using X.509 Certificates was becoming further entrenched because of Windows support. If someone wanted IPsec to support their Windows users, they would now need to download FreeS/WAN, download a few patches, patch the FreeS/WAN code, patch the kernel, compile the kernel IPsec module, and then compile the rest of the non-IPsec kernel modules and install all of the compiled components. And since there was no coordination between the patch maintainers and the FreeS/WAN maintainers, the patches were breaking continuously when new versions of FreeS/WAN or the Linux kernel were released. It was a very difficult process for someone not familiar with FreeS/WAN. This resulted in the creation of Super FreeS/WAN by one of the authors of this book (Ken Bantoft) to provide an easy-to-use patched version of FreeS/WAN that had all of the features people needed for VPNs and interoperability. However, maintaining Super FreeS/WAN was becoming harder and harder.

The Arrival of Openswan

The lack of out-of-the-box IPsec code for the Linux kernel was becoming a big problem for users setting up VPNs, and there were members of the FreeS/WAN project who wanted to work on a solution. In the summer of 2003, European volunteers and some members of the FreeS/WAN project—led by Paul Wouters, one of the authors of this book—met and talked to Gilmore at the Chaos Computer Club summer camp near Berlin. The foundation of the fork was laid, and in November of that year, Openswan was released by Xelerance, a newly founded company for the continued development of a free IPsec implementation for Linux.

Openswan's main mission was to cater more to the commercial world, while still keeping the FreeS/WAN ideals alive. This new code-fork also released the FreeS/WAN Project to stick even more strongly to its philosophies, and the next FreeS/WAN version removed support for AH and Transport Mode, two hardly used modes of IPsec, even though that completely broke interoperability with Microsoft Windows 2000 and XP. In April 2003, the end of the FreeS/WAN Project was announced and the last version of FreeS/WAN, with KLIPS support for the Linux 2.6 kernel, was released. In the next year, Openswan expanded and became the de facto IPsec implementation for Linux in practically all Linux distributions.

NETKEY

While this was happening, the lack of native IPsec support in Red Hat was a big problem for Linux distributions aimed at the enterprise market. They decided to code their way out of this problem by porting the IPsec code from another free operating system, FreeBSD. At this point, many kernel hackers also worked for Red Hat, so inclusion in the kernel would come naturally. Their adaptation of the KAME IPsec code from the BSD resulted in the Linux kernel NETKEY code.

Red Hat initially used the somewhat limited Racoon userland IPsec software in combination with the NETKEY code, but Openswan was added in version 3 of the Fedora Core distribution when Red Hat realized the political constraints of the FreeS/WAN Project did not apply to Openswan.

Further Reading

This book is not about politics. Software should not be about politics. If you are interested in these historical and political matters, we can recommend some excellent books that deal with these subjects.

Firstly, the following table lists some very useful non-fiction guides:

Crypto: how the Code Rebels Beat the Government—Saving Privacy in the Digital Age Steven Levy, Diane Pub Co, ISBN 0-7567-5774-6.	This book gives an excellent overview of the history and politics surrounding modern cryptography and software. (Another book by Levy, 'Hackers', gives a similar overview for computer technology in general.)
Secrets and Lies: Digital Security in a Networked World Bruce Schneier, Hungry Minds Inc, ISBN 0-471-45380-3.	This book talks about the true and false claims and thoughts behind using cryptography.
Database Nation : The Death of Privacy in the 21st Century Simpson Garfinkel, O'Reilly, ISBN 0-596-00105-3.	This book shows the danger of the information age and the massive collecting of the digital bits of our lives and the mistakes made with this data.
Cracking DES: Secrets of Encryption Research, Wiretap Politics and Chip Design Electronic Frontier Foundation, O'Reilly, ISBN 1-56592-520-3.	The story behind the building of the DES Cracker machine.

And if you want some engaging bedtime reading, try the books on the following list:

1984 George Orwell, Penguin Books Ltd, ISBN 0-14-012671-6.	A classic you should have read by now.
True Names Vernor Vinge, Tor Books, ISBN 0-312-86207-5.	A story about anonymity written before the Internet was invented.
Fahrenheit 451 Ray Bradbury, Voyager, ISBN 0-00-718170-1.	The classic about information restriction.
Cryptonomicon Neal Stephenson, Arrow, ISBN 0-09-941067-2.	A story about information 'havens' and the use of crypto. (Another recommended book by Stephenson is *The Diamond Age*.)

Using Openswan

If reading about the politics and license issues has made you nervous about the legality of your use of Openswan, do not worry. The following section will explain the legalities of Openswan, though you should not read this section as a replacement for the advice of a skilled lawyer. Treat it more as the basic information you would supply to your lawyer to determine your specific case.

If you are in doubt whether or not it is legal for you to use Openswan, consult a lawyer!

Copyright and License Conditions

Openswan is based in large part on FreeS/WAN. The copyright of that code lies with the respective developers, who all released their code under the GNU Public License. All the patches to FreeS/WAN are copyright of the respective authors and released under the GPL. New Openswan code written by Xelerance is copyright of Xelerance, and is also released under the GPL.

The GPL does not discriminate against use. Anyone is encouraged to use this software as they see fit, whether for a homebrew VPN or a nuclear power plant. As programmers, we, the authors of this book, believe that we do not have the skills, nor should we have the authority, to distinguish rebels from freedom fighters or insurgents from dissidents. We provide the tools; it is society's responsibility to provide the ethical framework. Should we limit our own freedom to grow out of fear that someone might use our software for something bad? Should we never have picked up those stones to make tools because some of us would use them as weapons? Should the toolmaker dictate what goals are righteous? If we limit the use of our cryptography to certain people, how much different would that be from the movie studios telling us in which country, using what vendors and software we can play our purchased movie? Should your car agree with your destination? Precisely some of these concerns about individual freedoms were originally behind the project to bring IPsec to the Linux kernel.

Writing and Contributing Code

Since Openswan is released under the GPL, any modifications or additions to the code that are distributed will have to be released under the same license, the GPL. Though you could also release modifications under a BSD license, as soon as the code is incorporated into Openswan, it is (as the BSD license allows) re-released under the GPL. Failure to comply to the GPL will mean that you no longer have the legal right to use or distribute Openswan at all.

Though at first this might seem simple and straightforward, but there can be some additional hassle. What if you just received a patch to Openswan from a vendor under a **Non Disclosure Agreement (NDA)**? Are you allowed to publish this patch? Probably not, as you would be violating the NDA with the vendor and be in violation of your contract, a civil offense. Of course, in this (unfortunately not so hypothetical) case, the vendor is actually violating the GPL and could be sued by any of the copyright holders of Openswan even if they have no business relationship with the vendor. The vendor has also committed a civil offense. The third party clause in the GPL guarantees that copyright holders can sue whoever is responsible for violations without having been a victim of that violation personally. If a copyright holder who has signed an NDA finds that the copyright has been violated, the copyright holder—whether it is a company or an individual—could probably sue since a contract can never be used as a protection scheme against a civil offense.

It is therefore important to realize that if you distribute GPL code in binary-only form, and you cannot release the source code—for instance, because you yourself bought the code as binary-only—you are still violating the GPL, and you can be sued and restrained from using Openswan in your products by a court. So those who are thinking of implementing certain hardware IPsec accelerators for Openswan, of which they cannot redistribute the patches, should definitely have a long talk with their lawyers.

Legality of Using Openswan

If you release a new product based on Openswan (or any other GPL software for that matter), you are quite free to ship Openswan on the CD of your new product—as long as you meet the GPL license requirements such as supplying the Openswan source code to any interested party.

However, there might be other laws that apply to you. Different countries have varying legal requirements, since many countries consider cryptography as munitions, as a weapon. So even though the copyright holders of Openswan say you can use it, your government, or a completely other government or international body, might deem that you may not use it. So the first thing to do is to check whether your own government allows you to use cryptography.

A survey in 1999 by the **Electronic Privacy Information Center** (**EPIC**) found the following countries limit the use of cryptography by their own citizens: Belarus, China, Israel, Kazakhstan, Pakistan, Russia, Saudi Arabia, Singapore, Tunisia, Vietnam, and Venezuela. France and Belgium were on this list for a long time, and the US allow their citizens to use cryptography, but if it is used to commit an offense, the use of cryptography itself is an offense on its own. Countries on this list probably also restrict or ban the import of cryptographic software.

You should also be aware that some Western governments are considering a ban on crypto as part of anti-terrorist measures, so be sure to get up-to-date information from your government.

International Agreements

Apart from national law, whether or not you may use or export cryptography also depends on international treaties that countries adhere to. International treaties that may apply to your country are the 1886 Bern Convention on copyrights (though it was last amended in 1979), the 1995 Wassenaar Arrangement on the export restrictions of munitions to 'Evil Regimes', amended in 1998 to get an additional section on cryptography guidelines, and the European Union Dual-Use Export laws. Then there are also recommendations and guidelines from the Organization for Economic Cooperation and Development (OECD), the European Union, the G-7/G-8, the Council of Europe, the Organization for Security and Co-operation in Europe (OSCE but also sometimes called OVSE) and perhaps the UN Security Council has issued a specific resolution boycotting your country from receiving munitions, which would include cryptographic software.

Probably the most relevant international agreement is the Wassenaar Arrangement, which has a special exemption in the *General Software Notes, entry 2*, for software which is in 'the public domain'. The use of public domain should probably be interpreted as "readily available at no cost". This would seem to include Openswan.

The list of restricted countries varies between the various international agreements, partially as a result of the Wassenaar Arrangement that dictated the individual countries are responsible for implementing the Arrangement in local law. Sometimes, a country is not completely banned, but a separate export license is required before you can export cryptography to those restricted countries. The list of restricted countries at this point probably includes Cuba, Iran, Iraq, Libya, North Korea, Sudan, Syria and strangely enough international organizations such as the United Nations. But again, the implementation of the Wassenaar Arrangement varies from country to country, so check the export laws of your own country.

For example, the following countries have listed extra restrictions on top of the Wassenaar Arrangement: Australia, France, New Zealand, Russia, and the US.

The Wassenaar Arrangement website has a convenient list of countries and contact information for their respective government departments that deal with export.

So far, we have only covered the *receiver* of the cryptographic software. But there is also law that applies to the export of cryptographic software in the country of the *sending* party.

International Law and Hosting Openswan

Xelerance is a company incorporated under Canadian law. Distribution of the code happens from servers located in the Netherlands, therefore Dutch export law applies. Xelerance still needs to adhere to export restrictions on crypto code. It is legal to export cryptographic code from Canada to The Netherlands.

Xelerance does not own the copyright on all the code in Openswan. We can only speak for the parts that are copyrighted by Xelerance. But as far as we know, no separately copyrighted code by US individuals or companies is included. And even if some lines were written by US citizens, Canadian law seems to dictate that software is *Canadian* if more than 50% of the code has been written by Canadians, a requirement that Openswan easily satisfies.

Xelerance, however, cannot be held responsible for where the code is exported to, since the code is free software. The Netherlands and Canada signed the Wassenaar Agreement, which exempts 'public domain' software. The Netherlands also complies with the European Union Dual-Use Export laws. As far as we know, we are not violating any export laws, meaning that whoever downloads Openswan cannot be accused of assisting in an export violation.

Unrecognized International Claims

Certain countries claim jurisdiction even outside their national borders. Most notably, France claims the right to regulate information on foreign servers, Italy assumes jurisdiction over sites directed to an Italian audience, and the US reserves the right to prosecute offenses against American interests according to US law irrespective of where they take place.

You may want to consider the possibility that you can be sued or prosecuted in another country. Additionally, if you are physically in a country other than the Netherlands when you download our software, you are probably subject to that country's jurisdiction anyway.

Patent Law

On 1 June 2001, WIPO members adopted the Patent Law Treaty. However, software patents are not universally recognized. Specifically, software patents are not recognized in The Netherlands or Canada. However, US patents may in some circumstances be enforced in Canada. Since US patents cover things such as prime numbers, Openswan would likely be considered in violation of a few software patents in the US. There are at least two known US software patents covering concepts used in Openswan.

The first patent relates to NAT-Traversal, and has been patented by SSH Communications. However, they have given the IETF the following statement:

> SSH Communications Security Corp hereby makes it known that it will not assert any claims in any patents issued in any country based on
>
> —the Finnish patent application FI974665 or any patent application listing the same as a priority application; or
>
> —the US patent application 09/333,829 or any patent application listing the same as a priority application,
>
> —against any party that makes, uses, sells, imports, or offers for sale a conforming implementation of an IETF standards-track specification of an IPSec NAT traversal module.
>
> This statement is limited in that SSH Communications Security Corp does not give any rights to incorporate NAT traversal technology covered by patents of SSH Communications Security Corp in implementations for any other protocols other than the IETF standards-track IPSec protocols.

Interestingly, this might actually be a benefit for the community. Microsoft cannot play 'embrace and extend' techniques unless it buys out SSH. And technically, Apple has no license to use the NAT-Traversal patent since it incorrectly implements the IETF NAT-traversal specification.

A second patent involves the DH groups and their numbers, which seem to have been patented. Information about this is unclear, and it is unlikely to be ever enforced.

A number of patents related to Elliptic Curve Cryptography are still valid (in the US only).

Expired and Bogus Patents

In 1997 the Diffie-Hellman key exchange patent and the Knapsack (and probably all public key cryptography methods) patent expired. The RSA patent expired on September 20, 2000. In 2001 a patent on Exponentiation Cryptographic Apparatus and Method expired.

There are also a lot of blatantly bogus patents that could theoretically be used against Openswan users. In 2002 for example, five years after the start of the FreeS/WAN Project, Safenet was awarded a patent that covers 'Extending cryptographic services to the kernel space of a computer operating system'. Patents like these only prove the absurdity of software patents.

Useful Legal Links

http://www.freeswan.org/freeswan_trees/freeswan-1.5/doc/exportlaws.html

The above site provides a good overview of cryptography export laws.

http://www.wassenaar.org/

Information on the Wassenaar Arrangement, covering national export controls.

http://www.gnu.org/philosophy/wassenaar.html

Further notes on the Wassenaar Arrangement.

http://www.wipo.int/treaties/en/ip/berne/

The Berne Convention on copyright.

http://www.efc.ca/pages/doc/crypto-export.html

This document provides a summary of Canada's export controls on cryptographic software. This is relevant to all Openswan users, as Openswan is developed in Canada.

http://rechten.uvt.nl/koops/cryptolaw/index.htm

A survey of existing and proposed laws and regulations on cryptography in Europe. This is relevant even if you are outside of the EU, as Openswan is hosted on a Dutch server.

http://trade-info.cec.eu.int/doclib/html/118992.htm

EC Regulation 1504/2004 for the control of exports of dual-use items and technology.

http://europa.eu.int/comm/trade/issues/sectoral/industry/dualuse/index_en.htm

This page provides a detailed description of dual-use goods and EU legislation on them.

http://europa.eu.int/comm/trade/issues/sectoral/industry/dualuse/faqs.htm

Frequently asked questions and background on the EC Regulation on export control of dual-use goods.

http://trade-info.cec.eu.int/doclib/html/118993.htm

Report to the EU Parliament and Council on the implementation of EU Regulation 1334/2000 on dual-use items and technology.

http://cr.yp.to/patents.html

A list of US patents relating to cryptographic software.

http://www.nosoftwarepatents.org/

The home-page of a campaign against the further legalization of software patents.

Summary

It might not come as a surprise that people involved with cryptography often also have strong political views on freedom, privacy, and civil rights. It is easy, even tempting, to wander from the realm of technology into the realm of politics. These issues are the cause for the formation of groups such as The **Electronic Frontier Foundation (EFF)**, **European Digital Rights (EDRI)**, the **Foundation** for **Information Policy Research (FIPR)**, and IPJustice, as well as more informal groups such as the free software and open source movements, the Cypherpunks, Groklaw, Politech, 2600 Magazine, the CCC, Hacktic/HfH, and many more.

All these groups have reached the same conclusion. Cryptography is a strong tool that can be used and abused by governments, criminals, businesses, and individuals. Cryptography has become an essential part of daily life, and should not be limited to the military. It is essential to freedom, something the FreeS/WAN Project believed strongly in. They have created the foundation for widespread use of IPsec to ensure privacy for many, ranging from NATO to Greenpeace. Openswan continues to provide those means for everyone. And the remainder of this book will help you accomplish the same.

Esther Dyson, member of the President's Export Council Subcommittee on Encryption and board member of the EFF, formulated these believes in a powerful concise matter:

> Encryption...is a powerful defensive weapon for free people. It offers a technical guarantee of privacy, regardless of who is running the government...It's hard to think of a more powerful, less dangerous tool for liberty.

2

Practical Overview of the IPsec Protocol

The focus of this chapter is on the cryptographic theories and IPsec protocols you need to know about as a system administrator. We will not look at detailed mathematical formulas but instead will explain the basics of cryptography so that you can understand the key management and packet processing performed by the IPsec protocols. References to all the appropriate RFCs and drafts are in the appendix, so those who want to dive deep into the mathematical core of cryptography can do so.

A Very Brief Overview of Cryptography

Normal IP packets consist of the IP header and the IP data, or payload. The IP header contains information about where the packet came from, where it should be going to, what kind of (sub-) protocol the packet has, the size of the packet, the time-to-live (TTL, sometimes called hopcount), some option bits that tweak little things, and finally an extra verification number, called the checksum. The checksum is a simple addition of all numbers in the IP packet. If one number gets accidentally changed during transmission, the checksum will be different, allowing the packet to be recognized as 'broken'.

IP Header		Payload
Source Address: 195.10.157.17 Destination Address: 12.110.110.204 Protocol: 6	**TCP Header** Source Port: 22 Destination Port: 32783 RSS TTL	SSH Data
A normal IP packet		

For instance, this packet could be a UDP packet, in which case the protocol field in the IP header would have the value 17. It has a source and destination IP address, and a source port and destination port, since the UDP protocol uses ports. Within the header, there is a checksum that can be used by routers to see if the packet has been mangled. If so, the packet is dropped. Even though the checksum detects mangling that happens by accident, it is not sufficient to protect against the packet being altered, since if someone wants to change a packet, they can simply calculate what the new checksum needs to be and alter that as well. To protect against malicious packet tampering, one needs to have a stronger method for verifying the packet than a simple checksum. This is where cryptographic functions come into play. Instead of a simple checksum that everyone can generate, we need to add some kind of cryptographic checksum that only the sender and receiver know how to make and verify.

Valid Packet Rewriting

There is, however, a catch with this idea of a checksum that can only be made and checked by sender and receiver. As transmitted packets travel across the network, they are not immutable and some items in the IP header can change quite legitimately.

Probably the most important is the time-to-live (TTL). When a packet is passed along by a router, it must decrease its TTL value by 1. If that value would become 0, the packet has traveled over too many hops and is dropped. A special control packet, using the ICMP protocol, is sent back to the sender notifying it of the lost packet. The whole idea of TTL is to ensure packets don't travel in loops on the Internet for ever.

Other parts that may be changed are those that handle quality-of-service issues. Some networks may treat certain types of packets as less important, by giving such packets a lower priority. They can set QoS bits in the header to indicate these policies to their devices.

Ciphers

Ciphers and algorithms are the two main types of cryptographic functions used with IPsec. A cipher is nothing more than a deterministic scrambling scheme. If you have an unencrypted value X (the **plaintext**) and you push it through a **cypher box**, you get a scrambled text Y (the **ciphertext**). The sizes of the plaintext and the ciphertext are the same.

An often-used toy cipher is called **ROT13**. The ROT13 cipher works like this: Replace all letters with the letter 13 spaces further in the alphabet. If you get to Z, continue counting at A. If we put 'ABC' through this cipher, we could get 'NOP'. If we put 'NOP' through our ROT13 cipher, we would get 'ABC'.

The problem is that the security of our cipher lies in the secrecy of it. Anyone who knows, or works out, how our secret cipher works, is able to decipher all our messages. It is very dangerous to rely on the secrecy of a cipher. You cannot ask a lot of people (mathematicians or cryptanalysts) whether your cipher is good without betraying your secret. And cryptography is deemed too difficult for a single person to securely invent in their basement.

A more common type of cipher is one where the cipher method is not a secret, and is known to everyone, but the cipher takes two inputs instead of one. One input is the plaintext, and the other input is a secret only known by the two parties involved. This secret is called a **key**, in this case a secret key. The cipher mangles the plaintext with the key and the result is the ciphertext. The receiver uses the same key and the ciphertext as input to the cipher to recreate the plaintext. This is called a **symmetric cipher**. Because of the use of a secret key, we do not need to keep the cipher secret. We only need to keep our key secret. And if someone steals our key, we can just decide on another key to use; we do not have to throw away the cipher.

DES, 3DES, and AES

The first cipher to enter widespread use throughout the world was **DES**, the **Digital Encryption Standard**. It was designed by IBM in the seventies, and slightly (but crucially!) modified by the NSA. Since then, computers have become much more powerful and DES is no longer secure against a **brute force attack**. This is an attack where all possible keys are tried on the ciphertext until the attacker stumbles upon the plaintext when they happen to use the right key.

Most installations using DES switched to **triple-DES (3DES)** years ago. Recently, the Rijndael cipher was chosen as the successor for DES, also called the **Advanced Encryption Standard (AES)** by the National Institute of Standards and Technology (NIST) in the US.

Algorithms

The cryptographic algorithms used with IPsec are mathematical one-way functions. A one-way function, like a cipher, takes an input and produces an output, but unlike a cipher, you cannot use the output and any other function to obtain the input. Hence the name 'one-way'. In IPsec terminology, these are often called the algorithms.

These types of algorithms are frequently used to make secure checksums for data. Again, the security of the algorithm does not lie with its secrecy, but in the fact that it is next to impossible to modify the input in such a way that it produces the same output. Algorithms that create a much shorter output than input are called **hash functions**. The two most commonly used hash algorithms are **Message Digest 5 (MD5)** and **Secure Hashing Algorithm 1 (SHA1)**.

Recently a lot of media attention has focused on how MD5 and SHA1 have been hacked or broken. The truth is slightly less worrying. Researchers have found 'collisions' in these functions, which means that someone could find another plaintext that has the same MD5 or SHA1 hash as the original plaintext. However this does not mean it's possible to swap the plaintext with any other arbitrary plaintext at will. The implementation in IPsec uses a sequence number scheme called HMAC, which makes it even harder to find the proper alternative plaintext that would pass the MD5 or SHA1 algorithm.

> MD5 and SHA1 are still safe algorithms to use for IPsec, but if a newer algorithm becomes available and you can use it, it is recommended to switch. A likely candidate for inclusion in the near future is SHA-256 or SHA-512.

Uniqueness

One way eavesdroppers could still manipulate a secure communication would be to capture valid communication, and even though they cannot read this captured communication, to resend it. Since these resent packets are valid, digitally encrypted packets, they will pass the checks for proper authentication. This might disrupt the secure communication, or trigger other responses. This is called a **replay attack**. One way to avoid it is to add a counter to all the packets before running them through the cipher. Every time the counter is used, it is increased. This way, a replayed packet can be correctly identified as an old packet, and can be discarded.

Public-Key Algorithms

Of course, using a secret key is a Catch 22 situation. If you could communicate the secret key securely, you would not need a new form of encrypted communication to begin with. The solution to this problem was invented by Diffie and Hellman around the time DES was introduced. Without going into too much mathematical detail, the idea is to generate two very large numbers and use a one-way function in such a way that using one of the numbers as input to the function gives a ciphertext, but if you have the second large number, you can actually reverse the one-way function. This second number is a so-called 'trap door'.

The first large number you can give away to everyone, and is called the **public key**. The second number is your **private key**, and no one but you should know it. People can use the public key to encrypt a message that only you can decrypt with the private key.

Exchanging Public Keys

If two parties (by convention known as Alice and Bob) have never securely exchanged each other's public key, then they have a problem to solve before they can communicate. How do they know that they are talking to the person that they think they are talking to? How can each be sure that they are not talking to a 'man in the middle'? A man in the middle (often called Mallory) is someone who pretends he is Bob to Alice, and pretends he is Alice to Bob.

Digital Signatures

This public key encryption scheme can even be extended. Using a more complex algorithm, such as RSA or DSA, the private key can also be used to create a digital signature. The principle of a digital signature is similar to that of a handwritten signature. The assumption is that only the person represented by the signature is able to produce a correct signature. If your signature appears on a piece of paper, and it matches the reference signature that is on file that you have made in the past in the presence of a notary or bank employee, then it is assumed that only you could have written that signature, so therefore you signed that piece of paper. For a digital signature, the same assumption is used. Anyone with the public key can verify a digital signature, but only the person with the private key can make it.

Diffie-Hellman Key Exchange

The **Diffie-Hellman (DH)** key exchange allows you to exchange a secret key over a public channel, and thereby gain privacy no matter who listens in on this DH key exchange.

In essence, the DH key exchange guarantees privacy; that is, you can be sure you are only talking to *one* other person. However, the public channel used for the DH key exchange could be manipulated. What if Alice just did a DH key exchange with Mallory instead of Bob, because Mallory is trapping all communications to Bob? DH key exchange is certainly valuable, but it does not address how to authenticate the other party, to ensure you are not talking (privately) to a man-in-the-middle (**MITM**).

Avoiding the Man in the Middle

There are two ways out of this problem. One is to use someone else, with whom Alice and Bob already have a trust relationship, as a mediator. This is called a **Trusted Third Party (TTP)**. The TTP can send them an encrypted message only they can read in order to prove the identities of Alice and Bob to each other. The communication with the TTP cannot be forged by a man-in-the-middle because Alice and Bob already have a trust relationship.

The second solution for Alice and Bob is to do an 'out-of-bound' communication that is either trusted, or for which it is trusted that an attacker is not able to perform a MITM attack on *both* channels of the communication. For example, one way for Alice and Bob would be to call each other by phone, and read the keys aloud. If Alice and Bob have talked to each other before, they will recognize their voices and trust what those voices are saying. Of course, this is very much prone to errors, so a common method is to run a secure hash function over the public keys that Alice and Bob have sent to each other, and only read the short output of that hash function. This output is called the **fingerprint**.

There is actually a third 'better than nothing' solution, which is called a 'leap of faith'. Since it is very unlikely that upon their first communication, an attacker is already trying a MITM attack, both Alice and Bob accept the public keys as true and store them. Any later communication uses these keys. This leap of faith method is frequently used with the SSH program. When trying to connect to a new machine with an unknown public key, the SSH client informs the user of that fact, shows the user the fingerprint, in case an out-of-bound verification is needed, and then stores the key for future use. If the remote public host key changes, or an attacker is trying a MITM attack, the SSH program complains loudly.

Session Keys

Common cryptographic systems do not use the private key to encrypt or sign. Instead, they sign and encrypt a new key, called the session key. This key is used to encrypt the bulk of the data, but is discarded after some relatively short time. The advantage here is that using session keys protects your communication even in the case where all your encrypted communication is logged and at some point your private key is compromised. Since the session keys have long since been destroyed after their use, having the private key will not enable someone to decrypt all previous communication since even the holder of the private key does not have the old session keys any more. This is called **Perfect Forward Secrecy (PFS)**.

Crypto Requirements for IPsec

In conclusion, we need a strong cryptographic checksum to protect the integrity of our packets using a symmetric cipher. This cipher will be keyed by a session key, which we need to exchange after we have achieved privacy using a DH key exchange, and have authenticated each other based on trusted public key encryption.

We want to add a digital signature to as much of the packet as we can. That is, we want a digital signature that covers all the IP headers that don't change plus the data (payload) of the packet. Since there is no space in the original TCP or UDP headers, we will have to define a new IP protocol. And it turns out we don't have just one, but two new IP protocols: **Authenticated Header (AH)** and **Encapsulated Security Payload (ESP)**.

We also learned that we need a clever system to exchange session keys based on public key systems. The protocol in the IPsec suite that is used for that is called the **Internet Key Exchange (IKE)**.

These protocols are explained in depth later in this chapter.

IPsec: A Suite of Protocols

There is not a single IPsec protocol. IPsec is in fact a collection of standards (and drafts, because the IETF process is very slow) that all deal with using cryptography to ensure authenticity and in almost all cases to also guarantee confidentiality of the content of the IP packets. Most of the standards documents contain details of the cryptographic ciphers and algorithms used. The intent of this chapter is to cover what you need to know from a practical point of view, without going into all the details and design decisions.

The IPsec protocols can be split into two main categories: **packet handling** and **trust relationship management**. Packet handling is usually done by the operating system kernel itself, since it requires speed, efficiency, and low latency that are easier to offer at the low-level processing of the kernel.

The trust relationship management is not as time sensitive, since it only happens at the start and at the refresh intervals of an IPsec connection, which is usually about once an hour. It is also a very complex process, requiring a lot of very complex code that is much better done outside the kernel, as a regular program running on the computer.

Kernel Mode: Packet Handling

The kernel deals with the individual packets sent and received by the computer. This is sometimes called the **forwarding plane**. It involves turning *normal* IP packets into *secure* IPsec packets, carrying out encryption, decryption, signing, encapsulation, and decapsulation of the packets. These techniques all involve changing and verifying packets, and are normally performed by the kernel.

Authentication Header (AH)

Authentication Header (RFC 2404) is the first new network protocol that was introduced. It received IP protocol number 51. (Other examples are the TCP protocol, IP protocol 6, and the UDP protocol, IP protocol 17. On a computer running Linux, you can find a list of IP protocols in /etc/protocols). Don't be misled by the name: AH does not just authenticate the header of an IP packet, but authenticates the data (payload) as well as parts of the header.

When two machines are configured with secret keys to communicate using the AH protocol, they agree on a unique number identifying the connection. This number is called the **Security Parameter Index (SPI)**.

The machines then set the **Sequence Number (SN)** to 0. For each packet that is to be sent, the SN is increased by one to prevent replay attacks. In a replay attack, a malicious listener intercepts an encrypted packet, and without being able to read that captured data, resends it over and over again. Without the SN, the two computers that are communicating with encryption would not be able to distinguish a genuine packet from a copy of a previous packet, since the cryptography checks will be satisfied by the replayed packet. After all, it was a valid packet. The SN prevents these attacks, because now the packet can be correctly identified as an old retransmitted packet, and discarded.

A cryptographic checksum is then calculated for the packet, using a hashing algorithm, usually MD5 or SHA1, using a secret key that only the sender and receiver know. This cryptographic checksum is called the integrity check value (ICV). The SPI, SN, and ICV form the important part of the AH header. The SN and ICV together with the hash are also called the **HMAC** (for keyed **Hash Message Authentication Code**). The term HMAC actually refers to the specific method used to calculate the ICV, but colloquially the result is sometimes called the HMAC.

The rest of the header consists of various administration pointers for these header parameters within the packet. This packet is then sent to the other IPsec endpoint. Upon receiving the packet, it also calculates the ICV for the packet using its own copy of the secret key. If the calculated ICV matches the ICV stored in the received packet, the packet is authentic. The IPsec header of the packet is then removed, leaving a regular IP packet which can then continue on into the kernel like any other unencrypted packet. If the ICV does not match, for instance because a NAT device rewrote the IP address, or some host on the way changed any data in the packet, the packet is discarded by the kernel before any application gets to see the malicious or broken packet.

AH only provides authentication and does not encrypt the payload. Anyone who can sniff the AH packets can see who is communicating with whom, and what they are saying. However attackers cannot change or inject any packets, since they cannot forge the ICV in the packets since they do not have access to the secret key used to compute the ICV that assures packet integrity.

The source and destination address are part of the data protected by AH, so they cannot be spoofed. But neither can they be rewritten by a NAT device without causing the packet to be discarded as invalid, because the rewriting does not match the computer AH HMAC. Therefore, AH does not work together with NAT. This can be seen as a feature or as a bug, depending upon your threat model.

Since AH on its own does not offer encryption, it is hardly used at all.

Encapsulated Security Payload (ESP)

ESP is a much more useful new protocol of the IPsec suite. It received protocol number 50. Its job is not only to authenticate the packet, like AH, but also to add a security policy to the packet, and optionally encrypt it. So it has some of the same properties as AH, such as the SPI, SN, and ICV. For the decryption of the packet content, both ends need to have the secret key with which the packet has been encrypted, and can be decrypted. You can use ESP without encryption by using the NULL encryption. The protocol header is different to accommodate the additional encryption settings and some padding, which is necessary due to the way some ciphers work.

Originally ESP provided no authentication, so if you wanted integrity and privacy, you would build an IP packet in ESP in AH. ESP now provides for authentication as well, in a very similar form to AH. So now you either use ESP with authentication or you have an AH header around the ESP header. In practice however, the ESP implementations do not allow ESP without authentication, so the ESP in AH construct of packets is no longer used.

The only reason AH is separate from ESP is because of the US export restrictions that were in effect when they were devised.

Transport and Tunnel Mode

There are two modes for IPsec connections. One is called transport mode, the other is called tunnel mode. **Transport mode** is only used for communication between two hosts. There is only one IP header, and the protocol header within the IP header (such as TCP or UDP) is protected. In transport mode, the goal is to safely transport the packet itself. In other words, the packet itself is the payload. In **tunnel mode**, there is a clear distinction between the transport packet and the payload, which is a complete packet in its own right. An entire IP packet, with its own full IP header, forms the payload of a newly created IPsec packet. On top of that, there is an additional IPsec policy that dictates what kinds of packets are allowed to travel over a tunnel mode connection. You could call this a built-in *ingress firewall*.

You can compare this with cars. Transport mode equates to simply driving a car from one place to the other. Tunnel mode is more like driving the car onto a train, which then takes the car to its destination, where the car is unloaded again. You would need to obtain a valid train ticket for your car to be allowed to be put on the train.

The only time transport mode is still useful today is when you perform your own encapsulation, as it saves another layer of IP header, or about 20 bytes per packet. This is the case for Microsoft's LT2P protocol, which uses PPP encapsulation.

The reason for the existence of both modes is now mostly historic. **Host-based** stacks would like to get rid of tunnel mode, because it can be done with transport mode, but third-party IPsec stacks that put themselves between the operating system and the user, also called **bump in the stack**-based stacks, would like to get rid of transport mode because it can be done with tunnel mode.

Choosing the IPsec Mode and Type

In almost all cases, you will use ESP in tunnel mode. This is what people call a **Virtual Private Network (VPN)**. ESP allows you to encrypt your packets as well as authenticate them, and tunnel mode means that you can connect not only a single host to another single host, but also that you can hook up subnets to subnets. And you can even hide the source and destination addresses of those packets, since in tunnel mode the entire packet, including source address, destination address, and port are encrypted. Even if you are setting up a host to host connection, you should use tunnel mode, so that all the IP options of the packets can be encapsulated and encrypted. In fact, two well known people in the cryptography world, Bruce Schneier and Niels Ferguson, have argued for AH and transport mode to be got rid of altogether.

> ESP tunnel mode offers all the options you could want at a cost of a very few bytes per packet at the most.

The only time we will use transport mode in this book is when we're discussing how to set up Microsoft L2TP, or **Layer 2 Tunneling Protocol**.

Some people might be tempted to use AH in an effort to reduce the CPU load of some IPsec connection, for example if they believe that their network is already encrypted safely. People with WiFi networks who encrypt using the (very weak) WEP encryption regularly try to disable IPsec encryption because the CPU on most WiFi equipment is not very powerful. We feel we must stress the point that most of these vendor-made encryption protocols are broken sooner rather than later. And even if they are not broken yet, those protocols have not withstood the years of public scrutiny and research that the IPsec protocol has had. Don't be too clever. Do not try to be too efficient. Stick to ESP with tunnel mode, unless you are trying to do L2TP interop with Microsoft.

> Do not use Authenticated Header (AH) or Transport mode. Only use Encapsulated Security Payload (ESP) in Tunnel mode. This is the most secure solution from a cryptographic point of view.

The Kernel State

The kernel needs to manage the IPsec connections it has been made aware of, and it does this mainly through **Security Policies (SP)**. These determine which packets need or do not need processing. For example, one important rule is: Never accept unencrypted traffic from a host for which we have an established, working IPsec connection. Another rule could be: If we do not have an established IPsec connection for this host, an attempt should be started to establish one before allowing this packet through. Security Policies are stored in the **Security Policy Database (SPD)**.

Furthermore the kernel has to keep track of all IPsec connections and their corresponding parameters, such as SPI, mode, cryptographic keys, and SPs that apply to it. All this information for a single IPsec connection is called an **IPsec Security Association (IPsec SA)**. This is a unidirectional concept. Two are required for packets to flow in both directions.

You can have multiple IPsec SAs between two endpoint hosts, since you can have different policies. For example, one IPsec SA could describe an IPsec connection using ESP and tunnel mode between the two hosts, while a second IPsec SA could describe an IPsec ESP tunnel mode connection between machines on the subnets behind the IPsec hosts. You could even limit the range of ports allowed on such a connection if you wanted to. These IPsec SAs are stored in the **Security Association Database (SAD)**.

The SPD and SAD work together almost like a firewall. An IPsec packet that is received has to match an SPI in the SAD, or the packet is dropped (as dictated by an SPD entry). If a matching SPI is found for an authenticated packet, once the IPsec packet is successfully decrypted using ESP, the source and destination address and ports are checked with the policy that belong to this IPsec SA. If the packet matches the policy, it is allowed to enter the *normal* networking path of the kernel. But if the decrypted packet has an unexpected source address, for example 127.0.0.1, the packet does not match the IPsec SA policies and will be dropped.

Encryption Details

Apart from the policies, the IPsec SA also contains the agreed stream cipher to use. There is a wide variety of stream ciphers that can be used, but the most common ones are AES and 3DES. Single DES (or 1DES) is sometimes still used but is really far too weak for modern use and it is very strongly discouraged.

Currently SHA1 and MD5 are used as secure hashing algorithms. Which ciphers and hash functions are available depends on the specific kernel implementations. MD5's lifespan is limited at this point, as it is showing some cracks, but HMAC usage of MD5 has not yet been attacked. It was designed to work despite this possible form of attack, which involves finding 'collisions'.

Manual Keying

So far we have seen what happens when two trusted parties want to exchange authenticated and encrypted data. But how do they establish this trust relationship when they are on the other side of the world?

One could send an encrypted email, or talk over a (presumably) secure telephone to exchange a secret key, known as **manual keying**, and then enter this key into the kernel manually where it can be used for the cryptographic functions of that IPsec SA.

Manual keying is not recommended. Not only is it hard to set up, it is invariably never touched again by the system administrator, and the key-life becomes indefinite, making it more susceptible to a brute force attack. Also, once the secret key is compromised, all past intercepted communication can be decrypted using it. Manual keying has no replay protection.

> Manual keying is strongly discouraged, so much that the authors will not explain how to set it up in this book. Those who, against better judgment, want to use manual keying should read the relevant parts of the manual that comes with Openswan.

Final Note on Protocols and Ports

A common mistake is that people who are configuring firewalls think that AH and ESP are *port numbers*. They then write ACCEPT rules for ports 50 and 51 and think this will cause IPsec packets to be allowed to pass. But this is wrong. AH and ESP are IP protocols, just like TCP, UDP and ICMP are IP protocols. They are not ports. And like ICMP, the AH and ESP protocols do not themselves have ports.

Usermode: Handling the Trust Relationships

The other aspect is the creation of a trust relationship between hosts on the Internet. This is also called the **control plane**. It involves the creation of a secure communication channel and the exchange of cryptographic keys. It also involves many choices and options and a lot of state information. This part is usually implemented in a process that runs on the OS continuously listening for requests for new IPsec connections. Programs that listen for incoming connections are typically called **daemons**.

These two layers—the userland daemon and the kernel IPsec stack—talk through a special socket interface, usually the PF_KEY interface. Most of the RFCs in the IPsec protocol suite are not actually about packet handling, but about these trust relationships. Handling packets is a relatively straightforward process. A packet comes in, matches a ruleset, is transformed into an IPsec packet, and is sent on.

But handling a whole range of different kinds of trust relationships becomes very complex very quickly. This is one of the reasons why manual keying is so discouraged. Keys need to be destroyed and renewed regularly, and this task is not something a system administrator should do every hour. Instead, a trust relationship is established by other means, and session keys are agreed on and loaded into the kernel by a special daemon. This daemon will talk using the Internet Key Exchange (IKE) protocol.

The IKE Protocol

The IKE protocol is a very complex protocol, and involves many difficult cryptographic operations, and requires even more options to be exchanged between two hosts who want to communicate via IPsec. IKE is therefore always implemented as a userland process. IKE operations can be roughly split in two parts, or **phases**.

Phase 1: Creating the ISAKMP SA

Phase 1 deals with obtaining privacy through a Diffie-Hellman key exchange, which ensures there is no eavesdropper. Next, the two hosts perform an out-of-bound verification of the other based on the type and content of the ID they receive, to prevent a man-in-the-middle attack. The type of ID can vary, but it will be based on IP address, hostname, email address, or ASN.1 Distinguished Name (DN).

ID Type	Typical Example
ID_IPV4	193.110.157.77
ID_FQDN	lists.openswan.org
ID_USER_FQDN	user@openswan.org
DER_ASN1_DN	C=CA,L=Toronto,O=Xelerance ,CN=lists.openswan.org, E=paul@xelerance.com

The out-of-bound verification can happen in various ways. One can use a PreShared Key (PSK), but much better is to use public key cryptography, such as RSA, to prove one's identity. These raw RSA keys can come from a PGP-signed email. Or the keys can come from DNS, preferably protected by DNSSEC to prevent attacks on the DNS, or they can come from X.509 certificates signed by a mutually trusted third party, a so-called Certificate Agency (CA). If one person is setting up both ends, it is of course possible to use Secure Shell (ssh or scp) to set up raw public RSA keys on both machines.

What is important to realize is that phase 1 needs to convey the identity of the remote host, and the host that receives the supposed identity from a remote host should have some way of verifying that claim. If phase 1 is successful, the two hosts have established an **Internet Security Association Key Management Protocol Security Association (ISAKMP SA)**. This is often called a **Phase 1 SA**.

This exchange will also state whether the identification is based on PSK or RSA public keys. Because this information is exchanged very early on in the negotiation, these decisions need to be made very quickly. This actually hampers certain situations where it is not clear what type of exchange is requested in the first few packets. One such difficult situation is a client using PSK on a dynamic IP address, which is not recommended for precisely this reason.

The ISAKMP SA also needs to be re-negotiated at regular times to prevent overusing a single cryptographic session key.

Main Mode
Establishing a successful phase 1 connection requires a few packets to be sent and received before the ISAKMP SA is established. This normal method is called **Main Mode**. However it has the longest latency, because it involves sending and receiving several packets one after the other. These packets set up a full Diffie-Hellman key exchange, before sending any information about the requested IPsec connection. Because of these extra packets, it is both the safest mode of operation, and the most flexible, since both parties can safely and privately request options, and when the other end denies a certain request, a less favorable but still acceptable alternative option can be tried.

Aggressive Mode
Some vendors wanted a faster mode, where less packets would be needed, so that the overall latency to establish a phase 1 ISAKMP SA would be shorter. This mode is called **Aggressive Mode**, and to reduce the number of packets needed, this mode requires that some CPU-intensive

tasks involving the Diffie-Hellman key exchange are already done before the first packets are sent and received. The problem is that this leads to an easy denial-of-service attack: just sending bogus initial Aggressive Mode packets to a host can bring it to a grinding halt.

Main Mode versus Aggressive Mode

A bigger vulnerability in Aggressive Mode is that to reduce the number of packets sent, the hash of the PreShared Key is transmitted before encryption has been enabled. These packets can be captured, and a brute force or dictionary attack can be run against them, for instance using a program such as ikecrack. In Main Mode however, this hash is sent only after the encryption has been enabled.

With Aggressive Mode, there is also no way to negotiate the most favorable options. The initial packet has to have all the right options in the request, or the remote end will have no choice but to say "I cannot do this." When combined with XAUTH, a man-in-the-middle attack becomes possible, and even trivial when the attacker is a valid VPN client on the network.

The limitation of negotiation of options has another drawback. Imagine that at some point in the future, the one cipher you had hard-coded into all your configurations for Aggressive Mode has been broken by a clever cryptographer. You now have to reconfigure all your clients, while if Main Mode had been used, all you would have to do would be to disallow that one broken cipher on the gateway, and the Main Mode negotiation would just pick another of the ciphers that it supports.

> Avoid using Aggressive Mode since it is known to be unsafe in certain deployments, and restricts the flexibility of your configurations.

Phase 2: Quick Mode

When the ISAKMP SA is established, 'Phase 2' can start. This is also called 'Quick Mode'. Phase 2 involves creating key material for the 'IPsec SA'. That is, the key material that the program needs to communicate to the kernel for use in the IPsec SA.

Phase 2 also involves agreeing many cryptographic parameters, such as which ciphers and algorithms to use, and how long a session key may be used for, but also further information, such as for which source and destination addresses the IPsec SA will be valid. Of course it also contains which 'transform' to use, that is, which kind of protocol to use (AH or ESP) and which mode (Transport or Tunnel mode). The IPsec SA information is communicated from the userland process to the kernel using a PFKEY socket. This IPsec SA is then stored in the SAD.

> The term Quick Mode is ambiguous. Some refer to a Phase 2 SA to mean the IPsec SA, but throughout the book we will use the term IPsec SA for this purpose.

Perfect Forward Secrecy (PFS)

Another option that is strongly recommended, but not available on all IPsec products, is **Perfect Forward Secrecy** (PFS). This is also negotiated and must be agreed upon by both ends for phase 2 to complete successfully.

PFS ensures that even if your current private key is compromised, all past communication that has been sniffed and stored cannot be decrypted with this private key. It works by using a session key that is discarded after use.

VendorIDs

To make it easier to work around bugs in certain IPsec implementations, one option introduced is VendorID. It identifies the vendor, device, and sometimes even the firmware version. VendorIDs can assist in debugging a certain IPsec connection, but of course they can also pose a security risk. You might not want to announce a VendorID of a known vulnerable device for instance. If you are accepting IPsec negotiations from dynamic IPs (roadwarriors), you might have a rogue client attempting to connect, and you would give out the VendorID before you have determined this client cannot authenticate with you and should be denied. By then it might already be too late.

Multiple VendorIDs can be sent. Usually VendorIDs are strings which are hashed using MD5, which has a few advantages. First, you have to know the original string to understand the MD5 hash, so it is harder for information to leak. Second, it makes all the VendorIDs equally long in size (96 bits), which greatly simplifies the programming effort, as 96 bits happens to be the length of the md5sum output. Every parameter space in IKE has private-use values and in order to avoid conflicts among vendor-proprietary extensions, the VendorID is used to qualify whose private use it is. It has also turned out to be useful for public extensions, options that span multiple or all vendors. For example, the capability to do ESPinUDP encapsulation, to break through NAT (called IPsec NAT-Traversal), is advertised using a VendorID.

Some vendors send proprietary extensions and information through additional VendorIDs, most notably Nortel, Cisco, and Microsoft. Since we often only know the MD5 hashes, we have no idea what some of these VendorIDs actually signify.

Dead Peer Detection (DPD)

DPD is an addition to the IKE protocol, also using VendorIDs to see if the remote IPsec gateway is still up. This is done by sending and responding to **probe packets** over the ISAKMP SA. It works much like the ping command, but is not supported by all vendors, being notably absent from Microsoft's built-in IPsec client. This is somewhat unfortunate, since DPD would be most useful on roaming end-user laptops.

ModeConfig

ModeConfig is an extension to the IKE protocol for *interactiveness*. One peer can ask the other peer for something and get an answer back. This can be a username, a password, an IP address, an IP address assignment (via DHCP), policies of the tunnel, or cryptographic token responses such as SecureID.

XAUTH

XAUTH is a custom authentication extension to the IKE protocol to work around various operational issues when deploying IKE. It is actually implemented with ModeConfig and VendorIDs, and provides for an additional user and password identification. This user/password scheme can include onetime passwords, SecureID tokens, or hooks to other authentication mechanisms such as Radius, PAM, or LDAP.

XAUTH is often combined with Aggressive Mode, and the combination is vulnerable to a man-in-the-middle attack, because it uses a 'group password', and in general it is always a bad idea to share secret credentials with others. How secret is a secret that a whole group knows? It is expected that IKE version 2 will incorporate all the extra features of XAUTH without the problems that surround it.

> Even though we do not recommend XAUTH, it is often the only way to get an IPsec connection into the big corporate networks.

X.509 Certificates

X.509 is a method of packing up cryptographic keys with an identity or other options and then digitally signing the bundle. Though people like to believe X.509 is the only way to use public key authentication, this is not the case. For example, DNSSEC-based raw RSA keys are another secure method for combining one's identity with a key.

The X.509 extensions to IKE move the IPsec authorization more to a **Public Key Infrastructure (PKI)** system. You have Certificate Agencies (CA) who can sign X.509 certificates for people or computers, which can then be used to permit or deny access to a VPN. X.509 certificates offer various options that can be set, tightly controlling their validity. X.509 is very popular in larger organizations.

Both IPsec hosts have the CA certificate and their own X.509 certificate, which includes their own private key belonging to the public key in the certificate. When they connect, they exchange their X.509 certificates, and verify the signature. If they have the proper CA certificate installed, they can each validate the other's identity. Then they can use each other's public RSA key from that certificate. The 'trusted third party' here, preventing the man-in-the-middle attack, is the CA, the certificate for which both ends already have installed.

The NAT Problem

Network Address Translation, NAT, is a classic example of a good hack gone bad. It proved to be so incredibly useful for so many people that NAT is not going to go away any time soon. The original reason for NAT was to hook up more networks and hosts behind fewer IP addresses, to hold off the end of the world when the IPv4 address space would run out.

Internal IP addresses of the network are translated on the fly by the NAT gateway. The NAT gateway swaps, or translates, the source address and source port of the packet for its own actual public address and another port that is free.

Usually NAT devices try to keep the same source port, but that is not always possible. Multiple clients in its local network could be using the same source port. It also remembers the destination address and keeps a list of these mappings ready. When a response comes in from a remote machine, which thinks that the NAT device itself sent the packet, the NAT device reverses the packet rewriting. It will look up the remote IP address, see which internal client belongs to this connection, and swap its own IP address in the packet it just received for the internal client's address (and port).

We have looked at a similar network scenario to this already, the man-in-the-middle attack. Only at that time, we were talking about a malicious man in the middle, and not a friendly one. The problem is, of course, that IPsec peers cannot tell the difference.

One important feature (or limitation, depending on your point of view) is that a computer behind a NAT gateway can only initiate a connection to the outside world. The outside world cannot initiate a connection to a specific computer, since any connections from the outside to the *original* sender of the IP packet would just end up at the NAT device, since its IP address is the IP address that ended up as source address in the outgoing packet. When the NAT gateway receives a packet for a new connection, it will not be able to determine to which of the clients behind it should send the packet and it will be dropped.

The situation is further complicated by combining NAT with port-forwarding. For instance, one can put a web server behind a NAT device, and forward all HTTP packets that arrive on port 80 to the web server's internal IP on port 80. People have even used NAT to implement failover or load balancing solutions.

There are NATs that can only handle TCP and UDP. Most NAT routers can handle ICMP as well, but the IP protocol has 256 different protocols. Many consumer NAT routers do not support these other IP protocols, such as IPsec ESP or Multicast.

NATworks

People saw additional use for these NATed networks. They were much easier to deploy than the various SOCKS proxies. NAT, combined with transparent proxies, proved an excellent way to centrally control web browsing and caching within big companies. Additionally, machines with vulnerable software were no longer susceptible to being probed and taken over from the Internet, since the Internet couldn't reach those machines behind the NAT gateway.

However, NAT has been overused in recent years. Every company now claims their network is their *own private* network, and thus justifies using private IP space and a NAT gateway. Unfortunately, this is often an excuse to keep more control in their network, force a proxy or even a portal login site, and simply reduces the cost for deploying proper IP-space networks. Many *public* networks are now really just big private networks. The new GPRS and many WiFi networks especially suffer from this problem.

At the other end of the spectrum are the home users. Because many end-user ISPs give their customers only one IP address, NAT is used for home networks on a massive scale.

Passing Clients Through

As the big corporations switched from leased lines to VPNs, and broadband at home became commonplace, end users behind a NAT device became more of a problem. Usually the end-user machine has some fixed internal IP address, and at home, only one person would be using any VPN connection. So some NAT devices simply remember which internal client generated the first IPsec packet, and when IPsec answers come from the Internet, they simply translate these packets to that single IP address. On some devices, you would have to configure this single address manually. This option of the even friendlier man in the middle is called **IPsec passthrough support**.

Unfortunately, it is both severely limiting in its requirement of a single client inside the NAT, and is also usually completely broken. IPsec and NAT just don't go together very well, since IPsec protects the packet integrity, and NAT mangles the packets and thus destroys integrity. A new standard was necessary, and many IETF drafts have been issued and implemented. The results of all these drafts are what we now call **IPsec NAT-Traversal support**, or **NAT-T**. In January 2005 these drafts were finally released as RFC 3947 and RFC 3948.

NAT-Traversal

NAT-T is an addition on top of the IPsec protocol to detect a NAT device in between the two endpoints. It basically works by the clients telling each other what they believe their IP address is. The other end can then compare what the client thinks with what it sees. If it is different, the remote end is being NATed. It will then inform the other end of this unfortunate situation. Once both ends have found out and agreed that a NAT router would likely mangle or drop IPsec packets, the two sides will encapsulate each IPsec packet in a UDP packet. A NAT device can handle simple UDP packets, translating the outer IP address, without touching what is inside the packet, which in this case happens to be a full IPsec packet, which of course contains another complete packet in its payload.

At the other end, the IPsec peer will just discard the outer IP address, and take the payload and decapsulate it. The resulting IPsec packet, having survived any possible network mangling, can then be authenticated, verified, decrypted, and processed just like any normal IPsec packet.

NAT-T and IPsec Passthrough

Routers supporting **IPsec passthrough** sometimes recognize these IPsec in UDP packets and will try to attempt some passthrough-type operations on those packers. This almost always breaks NAT-T because at the very least, the SPI is changed by these routers, so they themselves can keep state of the connections.

That is why IPsec passthrough is no longer a feature you want to have on a NAT device. Unfortunately, especially vendors of NAT devices that do not support IPsec natively seem to like the sound of IPsec passthrough support, so they keep this feature in their products. But with all the major IPsec stacks now supporting full NAT-T, this feature breaks a lot more than it saves.

> Always and without any exception, disable IPsec passthrough support. If you have not yet bought the device supporting IPsec passthrough, put it back on the shelf.

NAT-T Intricacies

When NAT is involved, IPsec needs to talk to an entity that is not the current IP address, since the current IP address is not that of the client, but of the NAT device. NAT-T uses the subnet-to-subnet method of connecting. So in the case of a roadwarrior for instance, where you would normally see a host-to-subnet connection from a public IP address, you now establish a subnet-to-subnet tunnel, where the roadwarrior's local subnet is its own internal IP address. This is how the packets can still reach the roadwarrior's internal IP address, while still being part of an IPsec connection with a different IP address as endpoint. And the encapsulation of this connection in UDP causes it to move through the NAT device without being mangled.

Of course, having an IP packet inside an IP packet can cause some other side-effects. Most importantly, the size of the inner packet may need to be reduced a little to prevent fragmentation. If the packet you are trying to encapsulate is at the **Maximum Transmission Unit (MTU)** size, then you need to break it in two, since the IPsec header takes up some additional space. You need to encapsulate that one packet in two packets, and the receiver needs to perform the reverse procedure. MTU issues become important when using NAT-T, often because networks using NATs involve tunneling in some form or other, and not all the MTU values of those networks and tunnels will be the same.

NAT-T is a nifty solution but remember to treat it as better than nothing. If you can avoid it, it is in your interest to do so.

NAT-T's Hard Limit

There is one important case when NAT-T cannot possibly work: when the remote network you are trying to connect to is using the same private IP-space as your own local NAT network. An IP address cannot be at both ends of the tunnel. To prevent these IP address clashes, it is wise to choose small networks for both subnets to reach through VPN, as well as choosing small networks behind the NAT router.

For example, choosing 10.0.0.0/8 as an office network is very bad practice, because it depletes the entire 10.*.*.* address space. If an IPsec client is trying to connect from behind a NAT, which is very likely to be either in the 10.0.0.0/8 address space or in the 192.168.0.0/16 address space, there is a large chance of conflicting IP addresses.

Therefore, when configuring your routers, you should avoid the obvious choices and default ranges used by many WiFi products and ADSL routers. These common ranges include 10.0.0.0/24, 10.0.1.0/24, 192.168.0.0/24, and 192.168.1.0/24. Instead, pick something semi-random, such as 10.54.10.0/24.

Summary

This chapter has provided a brief overview of the principles behind the IPsec protocol. You can find a list of applicable IPsec RFCs in the appendix of this book which can give you a deeper insight into the technological and cryptographic details surrounding IPsec. But if you understood the gist of this chapter, then you know enough to actually deploy IPsec. In the next chapter, we will discuss installing Openswan.

3
Building and Installing Openswan

This chapter will describe how to build and install Openswan. It will discuss some design decisions that need to be made, and then guide you through the process of building and installing Openswan:

- Choosing a Linux distribution
- Picking an IPsec stack: KLIPS or NETKEY?
- Using existing source or binary packages
- Compiling and installing Openswan from source
- Optionally patching your kernel for NAT-Traversal and KLIPS

Some of the decisions that must be made before beginning the installation of Openswan depend on the precise use of Openswan and the type of IPsec connections it will need for your specific scenario. A choice of kernel, distribution, and of IPsec kernel stack will then need to be made.

Linux Distributions

The choice of distribution is really a personal one. Security is not a product, but a process. The decision of which Linux distribution to use is not a decision that depends solely on the quality of a vendor's boxed Linux distribution with respect to its VPN capabilities. It also depends on how the system administrators, who are the ones that will need to work with the security product, will interact with that product.

If you install a highly secure Linux distribution that your system administrators do not understand, then your VPN server will likely not be maintained very well. As a result, your once highly secure VPN gateway will acquire security holes. It is important to pick a distribution that the system administrators who will need to maintain it are comfortable with. If that distribution does not support IPsec, you can still add it by building your own Linux kernel and by building Openswan from source code.

If you are completely new to Linux, pick a more popular distribution such as Red Hat, Fedora Core, or SuSE. If you come from the BSD world, you would probably prefer Debian. In the following sections, we give a few details about the advantages and disadvantages of the most commonly used distributions.

Red Hat

Although Red Hat distributions do not come with Openswan out of the box, both source and binary RPM packages of the latest versions of these distributions are available from the Openswan website. Fedora Core distributions come with Openswan pre-installed.

> Openswan is well tested on the free Red Hat distributions: Red Hat Linux 7.x and 9, and the Fedora Core distributions.

It might be tempting to buy a commercial Red Hat distribution, such as **Red Hat Enterprise Linux (RHEL)**, but for IPsec this can be a bad choice. RHEL3 (which comes in various flavors, such as Advanced Server, Work Station, and Enterprise Server) uses a mixture of code from the 2.4 and 2.6 kernel. It will complicate your choice of stack immensely, since this mixture of code contains known bugs in IPsec as it was merged in from an older (broken) 2.6 kernel. The appearance of 2.6 code in the 2.4 kernel also prevents you from patching that kernel to switch from the broken code to the code shipped with Openswan. And patching your kernel will likely void your support and warranty on the system, probably one of the major reasons to buy a RHEL system to begin with. We do not recommend using these hybrid kernel systems. RHEL4, however, comes with a modern 2.6 kernel, which should work as well as a normal 2.6 kernel.

There are two closely-related free Linux distributions available that are based on RHEL, but are not released or supported by Red Hat. They are called White Box Linux and Centos. White Box Linux is based on RHEL3 and therefore has the same problems mentioned above. Centos version 4 is based on RHEL4, and should work fine with Openswan.

Debian

Thanks to Rene Mayrhofer of the Debian Project, the Debian distribution has been one of the early adopters of Openswan, and ships with a stable and recent version of Openswan. If you have experience with Debian, then this distribution is a very good choice. Debian has its own way of building kernels, but it is very easy to build kernels for Debian based on the stock kernels released by Linus Torvalds as well.

SuSE

SuSE is also a good choice for Openswan. Just be aware that versions prior to SuSE Linux 9.2 might be running their IPv6-modified version of FreeS/WAN. This means that you cannot replace the FreeS/WAN package with Openswan without also changing the kernel package to match the new software. SL9.2 and higher do not have this problem.

Slackware

This is one of the oldest Linux distributions around. Unfortunately, it shows. There is no advanced package manager, just a small utility called `pkgtool` that untars an archive, and does not perform any dependency checks. Currently, there is no Openswan package, so you will have to compile and install your own package and rebuild your own kernel.

Slackware still uses a BSD-like start-up scheme. It has no concept of 'services', and the IPsec service file that is executed on all other distributions will not be installed or called on Slackware. Instead, you will need to manually edit a file in `/etc/rc.d/rc.*`, such as `rc.inet` or `rc.local`, and add the command:

```
ipsec setup start
```

All the usual properties of a real service are not supported. One of those properties detects when Openswan is first started and generates a new IPsec key for the host if one doesn't already exist. On Slackware, this command will have to be run manually:

```
# ipsec newhostkey --output /etc/ipsec.secrets
```

We do not recommend you use Slackware, even if it is currently your favorite distribution.

Gentoo

Gentoo is a distribution that is quite different to any other Linux distribution. To install Gentoo, you bootstrap it with a minimum system that includes a C compiler. This mini system then downloads various source packages and literally builds your entire machine from source. Instead of installing the OS from precompiled packages, you compile your entire system yourself. If you are installing a full system, the compilation might take days.

To add a certain package on Gentoo, you *emerge* it. Emerging a package will download, compile, and install the package.

Gentoo uses its own method for compiling new kernels, called **gen-kernel**, though as with Debian, it is still very easy to build the kernel in the standard way. There is an Openswan (userland) package available for emerging, but be aware that the kernel and the userland must work well together.

Gentoo unfortunately has seen a lot of problems in the past with IPsec support. It seemed there was not enough communication between the kernel developers and the FreeS/WAN / Openswan maintainer for Gentoo. In practice this meant that the Gentoo *swan packages have never properly worked. We were also fairly unsuccessful in reporting bugs to Gentoo. Of course, this might all have changed, since Gentoo is under very active development.

But in general, Gentoo users are expected to be experienced Linux users. Unless you are already a Gentoo user, this would be very poor choice.

Linux 'Router' Distributions

There are many mini Linux distributions that focus on just offering router and firewall functionality. Examples of these are Smoothwall, LEAF, IPCOP, vpnX, and Astaro. Some offer add-on packages for existing Linux distributions, such as Webmin. Sites such as freshmeat.net provide dozens of these firewall add-on packages and mini distributions to choose from.

The free mini distributions tend to lack in features and often fail to keep up to date with IPsec (and other important firewall features in general). A lot of them never made the transition from the 2.2 to the 2.4 Linux kernel. Some are still using **ipchains** instead of **iptables**, and their user interface often leaves much to be desired.

Commercial Linux firewalls, such as Astaro, have the advantages that come with a support department. If you have the budget, these distributions can be worth it.

If you are going to pick a mini-router distribution, we still recommend you to first experiment with a full-blown Linux distribution and IPsec, so that when you switch to the mini-distribution, you can tell the difference between IPsec configuration errors, and errors caused by the GUIs of the mini distribution.

Deciding on the Userland

Openswan has the most versatile and feature-rich IKE daemon called Pluto. It has been written from the ground up with security in mind. Even though people are easily confused when reading the log messages, they are nonetheless extremely precise. Pluto is very pedantic and will refuse to process or accept anything malformed. It has even been used as a reference implementation when testing commercial IKE daemons.

Pluto

Every night, the Openswan project runs a nightly regression test suite on all of the code, including Pluto. If a code change breaks any functionality, it is automatically reported the next day on the nightly mailing list. There are also tests that check whether packets that should have been dropped have actually been dropped. Other tests check for bogus X.509 certificates, insecure CA chains, NAT traversal functionality, Dead Peer Detection, and many more tests. The test suite is shipped with the source code in the testing subdirectory.

Anyone can run the test suite on their own systems, and it is a very useful tool if you are writing your own patches or extensions for Openswan. See Chapter 12 for more information about the regression test suite.

Pluto features robust restarting in case of unexpected failure. This way, a single bug that would crash Pluto won't bring down your entire VPN.

These are all very critical issues. Having access to a VPN means having access to the innermost sanctum of an organization. Not having access to remote places can be very annoying, especially if someone has to drive for a few hours to repair or restart a VPN server.

Pluto has an impressive list of features:

- Simple yet advanced methods for the configuration of tunnels
- Fully RFC-compliant (AH, ESP, transport and tunnel mode)
- Full NAT-Traversal support
- Opportunistic Encryption (based on public keys in DNS/DNSSEC) with DHCP integration
- Advanced roadwarrior support (clients on dynamic IP)
- The ability to execute customized scripts on a per-user or per-tunnel basis
- Raw RSAsig keys (public keys are specified directly)
- Advanced X.509 certificate usage, CAs, and intermediate CA processing
- Dynamic Certificate Revocation List (CRL) fetching using FTP, HTTP, or LDAP
- Dead Peer Detection
- XAUTH server and client support
- Aggressive Mode support for compatibility
- ModeConfig support
- Pluggable Authentication Module (PAM) support
- Windows L2TP over IPsec Transport mode support
- Interop with many non-standard commercial implementations (hard- and software)
- Implementation of all publicly known VENDOR-ID options
- Smartcard and other hardware token support (SecureID, eToken, and others)
- Support for large scale deployment (thousands of simultaneous tunnels on simple PC hardware)
- Very portable source code, ported to many Linux platforms (MIPS, ARM, Sparc, Alpha) ranging from Linux 2.0 to the latest, 2.6, and Windows 2000/XP; ports to BSD and MacOSX planned
- Works with multiple IPsec stacks (currently KLIPS and NETKEY)

Racoon

Racoon is much harder to configure than Pluto. For Pluto, you only need to know and specify the high-level information to enable the VPN, such as IP addresses of the endpoints and subnets, and the authentication method used. Pluto will take care of converting those into low-level kernel data structures. You do not even need to know what they are. With Racoon, you will need to configure most of these low level data structures, such as SPDs and SPIs, yourself.

Another major drawback of Racoon is that it needs to be completely restarted if you want to add or remove a tunnel definition, making it unsuitable for large-scale deployment. Imagine adding a tunnel and then restarting a thousand IKE connections when you restart Racoon. This will quite likely overload the VPN server to the point of failure. Racoon seems to be mostly used for simple host-to-host static VPN tunnels.

Racoon is not as well tested as Pluto. Ralf Spenneberg, an IPsec consultant from Germany, has carried out extensive testing on various IKE daemons, and found several large holes in Racoon that have been present in the Racoon code for many years.

Apparently Racoon also has a tendency to forget established SAs, causing a lot of unnecessary re-key events. This would also complicate large scale deployment.

Isakmpd

Isakmpd originally comes from OpenBSD, and is not really used on Linux although a Debian port exists. There is some sparse information available if you use a search engine such as Google, but we do not know of any large scale isakmpd deployment on Linux.

More Reasons to Pick Pluto

Pluto is the default IKE daemon in Debian, SuSE, Mandrake, Gentoo, and all Linux-based embedded solutions we have encountered. Red Hat and Fedora distributions are still using Racoon, though Pluto is available for those distributions too.

Configuring Racoon is explained in Chapter 8. We will assume the Openswan IKE daemon will be used. Otherwise, you would not be reading this book.

Choosing the Kernel IPsec Stack

A more difficult choice is that of the IPsec kernel stack. There are currently three IPsec stacks in use, the most widely deployed being KLIPS. The upcoming alternative is the NETKEY stack, which is currently included in the 2.6 kernel. NETKEY is a rewrite from scratch of KAME. NETKEY can be used with the traditional KAME userland tool Racoon, which has been ported to Linux and is called **ipsec-tools.** The third commercially deployed stack is the USAGI stack, a patched KLIPS stack that adds IPv6 support to the IPsec code and was mostly used by SuSE Linux, Germany's biggest Linux distribution.

There are a few other obscure IPsec stacks out there, but these are mostly scientific experiments or personal hobby projects, and have not gotten any large scale deployment or extensive scrutiny from the Open Source community. They should clearly not be used for production environments where money or lives are at stake.

KLIPS, the Openswan Stack

KLIPS was the first available IPsec stack for Linux. Early versions ran on Linux 2.0, and the latest version runs on anything between 2.2 and 2.6. It is the only Linux IPsec stack that has been in use for over a year; in fact, it has been in use for over five years. It has a very strong solid reputation in the IPsec community, and was considered the de facto interop test platform by many commercial vendors. If KLIPS didn't talk to your proprietary IPsec hardware, you had done something wrong.

KLIPS got a major rewrite between FreeS/WAN version 1.99 and version 2.x. Some of its functions had grown far too big and were re-factored. The 2.x code also introduced the regression testing system. Every single feature of KLIPS was tested in a nightly regression test suite. The 2.x version was also the base for Openswan 2.x.

ipsecX Interfaces

Since KLIPS pre-dates the netfilter code in the Linux kernel, it had to find another way to hook into the kernel and the network stack. The solution creates virtual devices, the ipsecX devices, and applies a routing trick to send packets into these virtual devices. The advantage is that the flow of packets is very clear. An encrypted packet comes in on the ethX device. It is detected that this is an IPsec packet, and it is sent to the KLIPS code to be processed. KLIPS decrypts the packet, and puts the decrypted packet on the ipsecX device. Thus the packet traverses all the Linux iptables (or ipfwadm /ipchains on older kernels) once per interface, allowing separate firewall rules to be made for the encrypted and the decrypted packet. This makes writing firewall rules very easy and is considered to be one of KLIPS' major features.

First Packet Caching

Another important feature is the caching of network packets for which it is known that an IPsec tunnel needs to be created. Because of this caching, tunnels can be easily brought up and down without any packet loss. Now packet loss in general is not much of a problem, but losing the first few packets will give you a substantial delay. If you are at home, and fire up the website of your company's internal web server, you do not want to always wait ten seconds while your packets are dropped because your first browser packet triggered the IPsec negotiation, which is still being negotiated as your browser sends more packets that are just being dropped.

Proper packet caching is essential for Opportunistic Encryption, where IPsec tunnels are set up on the fly depending on the received packets, as we will discuss later in Chapter 6.

Path MTU Discovery

Another feature of KLIPS is that it supports full **Path MTU discovery** (RFC 1191). Path MTU discovery describes a method for determining the Maximum Transmission Unit of a packet.

In the early days of the Internet, a lot of strange non-standard devices or communication lines were used to hook up machines. Some of them were as slow as 300 baud. Buffers to store network packets would be small, so some devices had to send a lot of small packets instead of fewer bigger packets. Of course mainframes had far less problems with big packets, and didn't want to send lots of smaller ones. Competing technologies in the LAN, such as token ring, Ethernet, DECnet, LAT, and other technologies such as serial cables, all had a different standard packet size that could be received and transmitted. The packet size was not as uniform as it is today, when most people use 1500 byte Ethernet frames.

Path MTU discovery finds the largest packet size that can be handled by all the intermediary routers between two computers. The initiating computer will start sending small packets, but once they are received correctly on the other side, will increase its packet size incrementally. At some point, either that other end, or a machine in the middle that is just relaying the packets on, will get a packet it cannot send further because it is too big. It will drop the packet and send a notification back to the sending host. This is an ICMP 'Destination Unreachable' packet which contains a message saying "Datagram Too Big". The sending computer will receive that ICMP packet, read the 'Next-Hop MTU' value, and use that (smaller) packet size instead. If the path between the two computers changes, and another hop in the chain can't receive a certain size packet, the same process will start again with that host. And just once in a while, the sending computer will increase the packet size just in case the limiting computer in the middle has vanished.

Firewalls and Path MTU

Unfortunately, in January 1997, the Internet was hit by something that came to be known as the Ping of Death. A bug in the networking code for processing certain incoming packets, most notably ICMP ping request packets, could crash the operating system. This bug was found in the reference code for fragmentation handling, code that had been copied into a wide range of commercial and open source operating systems. Almost all operating systems were affected: Sun, Microsoft, Novell, HP, Digital, SCI, IBM, some BSDs, and Linux.

Since these ping packets are a type of ICMP packet, a lot of system administrators decided to block all types of ICMP packets. And since Path MTU discovery depends on the ICMP Destination Unreachable packet, it was broken when these packets were dropped by the Internet at large. This is the main reason that IPv6 no longer implements Path MTU discovery. But since most computers on the Internet are now connected by ethernet, this limitation does not cause too many problems. At least, that was true until the commercial battle for broadband access began.

A lot of technologies were rolled out for broadband, and most of them worked by tunneling packets one way or another. The complexity of cable and DSL networks and their tunneling mechanisms, such as Microsoft's PPTP, PPPoE (A hack to pretend ethernet is just like an analog phone line), PPPoA (similar, involving ATM instead of ethernet), and various other types of tunneling protocols used by ISPs introduced a lot of tunnels within tunnels. Suddenly, packet size became variable again, and Path MTU discovery once more became an important issue. VPNs are used to connect two remote ends of the Internet. These connections will travel through many ISP networks, often a consumer-grade cable or DSL network. Therefore, broken Path MTU discovery greatly impacts on IPsec connections. Unfortunately, NETKEY does not support this properly.

KLIPS' Downside

KLIPS is not included in the official Linux kernel. As such, many people automatically dislike or distrust KLIPS. Often, the system administrator is already trying something new, IPsec, and does not want to make things any harder than they are already, for instance by having to add code and build their own custom kernel. Compiling KLIPS into your kernel has been made very easy, however, so don't be too quick to discard it as an option. Remember that KLIPS has been in use for about ten years and has proven itself to be extremely stable. NETKEY on the other hand is brand new. It looks very promising, but it hasn't seen large scale deployment yet.

That said, you might not have a choice. KLIPS has no IPv6 support, and unless you are willing to run the unmaintained SuSE version of KLIPS, you will need to use NETKEY if you need IPv6.

Another drawback of KLIPS is that routing hack to receive packets from the kernel. On a KLIPS machine, you can see routes going into ipsecX devices. If these routes are deleted or vanish, packets are no longer being processed by KLIPS. This happens mostly in scenarios where the physical interface is changed, for instance if a PC card or USB network device is added or removed from the system. However it also happens when PPP or PPTP sessions restart, which can happen regularly on DSL or GPRS connections. Most of this can be addressed using custom updown scripts. In the future, these kind of *hotplug* devices should be better supported.

NETKEY, the 2.6 IPsec Stack

This relatively new IPsec stack is based on the KAME stack from the BSD world. It is not a direct port, but it uses the same API, so the same software that runs on a BSD can be used to run it on Linux (The Racoon daemon or the isakmpd daemon). Because of the various back ports of this stack to the 2.4 kernel, one should not call this 'the 2.6 stack'. Other suggestions for names have been made, such as '26sec' or 'native' stack. Throughout the book, we will call this the NETKEY stack, since the configuration option for this stack is CONFIG_NET_KEY.

The NETKEY stack is under heavy development, which can be considered both good and bad. It supports both IPv4 and IPv6. It does not support first packet caching and still seems to have a little bit more of a problem with Path MTU discovery.

NETKEY also hooks into the networking code differently. Packets are intercepted by the IPsec stack after they are received on the physical ethX interface, and magically reappear on the same device in decrypted form. Packets that are being sent appear only in encrypted form. This complicates iptables-based firewall rules and can be confusing when using tcpdump to debug IPsec connections.

This interception also creates problems when using NAT and IPsec on the same machine, since the packet does not traverse through all the iptables as expected. Unencrypted packets never travel the POSTROUTING table. The netfilter **patch-o-matic** set of patches contains fixes for this, but they are being tested and are not yet ready for inclusion in the kernel.

Finally, NETKEY has another problem in how it implements the state of IPsec tunnels and the matching of known IPsec tunnels. Where KLIPS sorts its tunnels like a routing table, meaning it uses the most specific match first, NETKEY sorts based on destination for the incoming packets, and based on source for the outgoing packets. This results in a strange match on most generic first. This causes problems for a setup where a local IP range used by teleworkers (for instance 192.168.1.0/24) is part of a bigger range used by the entire company (like 192.168.0.0/16). With KLIPS you can define one tunnel for this setup, but with NETKEY you need to poke holes to avoid having the local IP nodes being considered on the other end of the tunnel.

Most people agree that this will become the default IPsec stack to use on Linux, but there is a clear demand for the features of KLIPS to be added to NETKEY. For Linux 2.6, you have a choice of either KLIPS or NETKEY. Hopefully, the good sides of both will merge into one stack that is even better.

The USAGI / SuSE IPsec Stack

The USAGI patch to add IPv6 to KLIPS was rejected by its maintainers, because it consisted of a crude cut-and-paste job. A lot of the code from KLIPS had been copied, renamed and had IPv6 features added to it. This was considered to be an unmaintainable hack that would have duplicated code all over the place. SuSE, however, had a strong need for IPv6, and reluctantly integrated the USAGI patch into KLIPS. Now, just like most other distributions, SuSE is moving towards NETKEY for its IPv6 functionality, so don't count on anyone maintaining this stack.

This stack is obviously a poor choice, unless you need IPv6-based IPsec, and you need it immediately, and you cannot use the Racoon IKE daemon with NETKEY. Some people have managed to get Openswan to run with IPv6 using NETKEY. Though this is not yet officially supported, there is a clear interest in this functionality, and it's possible that at some future time, perhaps by the time you are reading this, Openswan will officially support IPv6 using NETKEY.

Making the Choice

The following table summarizes our recommendations for the decision-making process:

Distribution	Pick a general purpose distribution that you (or your colleagues) are most familiar with, or pick a dedicated commercial distribution.
Userland	Use Openswan's Pluto.
IPsec stack	If you are forced to use an ancient 2.0/2.2 kernel: KLIPS
	if you are still using 2.4 kernels: KLIPS

	if you are using 2.6 kernels:
	  Production grade VPN's: KLIPS
	  Teleworkers: KLIPS
	  You want or need IPv6: NETKEY
	  Simple static tunnels: NETKEY

GPL Compliance and KLIPS

Once in a while, we are contacted by people who want to add some newer feature of Openswan to an old FreeS/WAN version. There is only one reason people ask us this question, and that is because they are stuck with a patch (sometimes misleadingly called *reference code*) to support some foreign piece of hardware that the vendor supports. The vendor has decided that its code may not be released to the public (the person contacting us will be under NDA) and the job of porting that ancient patch on modern Openswan versions is just too daunting for the person contacting us.

We cannot help in such a case, because the vendor is violating the GNU Public License. By reselling such a patched version of FreeS/WAN or Openswan, the person buying these hardware products with patch is also violating the GPL. The only way out of this is for the hardware vendor to release their patch under the GPL license. We can then consider integrating their work into Openswan.

Binary Installation of the Openswan Userland

Linux distributions use different package management software. Most commercial distributions use the Red Hat Package Manager (RPM). These include Red Hat, Fedora, SuSE, and Mandrake. Debian uses the Advanced Package Tool (APT). For small devices, IPKG is often used. Gentoo Linux uses something called emerge.

The drawback of RPMs has been that figuring out the necessary dependencies was left to the user. If package A needed package B, you would only find out when you tried to install package A, and it refused because you didn't have package B. Once you downloaded package B and tried to install both of them, it might complain about package C.

On Debian, you can use apt to figure out these dependencies for you. On Fedora, you can use yum do to a more automated RPM-based install. There is also apt-rpm, which brings the apt command structure from Debian to RPM-based systems. YAST for SuSE automatically handles dependencies for you as well.

Below we will explain the rpm and the apt commands for package management. If you use yum, you can often use the apt arguments with the yum command. If you use apt-rpm, you can follow the instructions we give for apt literally. If you use a distribution with another package manager, you will need to consult its documentation.

Checking for Old Versions

Before you install any new binary package of Openswan, you should make sure no previous version of FreeS/WAN, Super FreeS/WAN, or Openswan is installed.

On RPM-based distributions, use:

```
# rpm -qa | grep swan
```

On Debian-based distributions, use:

```
# dpkg --list | grep swan
```

As a result of the rename that happened between FreeS/WAN, Super FreeS/WAN, and Openswan, it is better to remove an old version before trying to install Openswan, since dependencies might not realize that Openswan is a replacement for the installed *swan package. To remove any existing packages, use:

```
# rpm -e freeswan
```

On Debian-based distributions, use:

```
# apt-get remove freeswan
```

Installing the Binary Package for Openswan

Fetching the latest version of Openswan can be automated by your package manager. Normally an update or upgrade command can be used to fetch the list of latest versions of software. If you use an RPM-based system without automatic update facility, you can download the updates manually from your distribution's FTP server (or mirror). You can also check to see if the Openswan project is releasing binary RPMs for your distribution at one of the following locations:

```
ftp://ftp.openswan.org/openswan/binaries/
```
```
http://www.openswan.org/code/
```

After you have downloaded Openswan, you should use GPG to verify the package integrity, and that your download is in fact from a trusted source. All Openswan packages are signed with OpenPGP. You should import the GPG key from a public keyserver, or download it from the Openswan website:

```
# wget http://www.openswan.org/code/openswan.signingkey.asc
```

Ideally, you would first verify the key. For instance you could add it to your personal PGP keyring and check the signatures. You should see a few signatures from Xelerance employees on the key, which in turn should be signed by well-known people in the security community. Once you have faith in the key, install it for use within the distribution. On RPM-based distributions this is done with:

```
# rpm --import openswan.signingkey.asc
```

Currently there are some issues using rpm and gpg to import certain keys, seemingly related to the type of key used, and the versions of rpm and gpg that are installed. Therefore it is not always possible to properly verify the signature of an RPM package signed by the Openswan team.

Next, you can validate the package has not been compromised:

```
# rpm --checksig -v openswan-2.4.5-1.i386.rpm
```

Finally, to install the latest version on RPM-based distributions, use:

```
# rpm -Uhv openswan-2.4.5-1.i386.rpm
```

Debian packages are not signed, so we will just have to have faith and install the package:

```
# apt-get install openswan
```

> If you are going to use NETKEY, the ipsec-tools package should be installed.

This might seem odd, since the ipsec-tools package contains Racoon, another implementation of IKE (and in some way a competitor to Openswan). The reason for this is that NETKEY uses the KAME PF key API to talk to the kernel. This API has not yet fully been merged into Openswan, so Openswan still uses the setkey binary from the ipsec-tools package in a few of the scripts to talk to the kernel, though these have now mostly been replaced by ip xfrm commands.

Building from Source

It is possible to build Openswan from source packages, thereby automating much of your custom compile. This can be especially useful when binary packages of the latest Openswan release have not yet been released for your distribution. It is also useful if you are using your own RPM-based distribution. On Debian systems, the following commands build a package from source, and fetch all necessary build dependencies:

```
# apt-get build-dep openswan
# apt-get -b source openswan
# dpkg -i openswan.deb
```

Using RPM-based Distributions

Before we are ready to compile our own RPMs, we need to make sure some of the development packages are installed on our system.

Often, development RPMs contain the include files necessary for using a certain library, so you do not need to install the development package just to use the binary software. If you do want to compile your own software that uses a certain library, you will need to install the development package for that library as well. The exception to this is SuSE, which includes the header files for a library with the regular binary package.

On RPM-based systems, these packages are usually called xxx-devel where xxx corresponds to the package name.

To compile Openswan and possibly recompile the kernel, you will need at least:

Package name	Description
kernel-source (Red Hat Linux 7/8/9 and Fedora Core 1/ 2/ 3)	Despite what the name suggests, this is a binary package and not a source package. You only need this is you are rebuilding the kernel.
kernel-devel (Fedora Core 4 and up)	The kernel source package for FC4.
gmp-devel	GNU math precision library header files.
rpm-devel	This is only needed if you want to build RPM packages for Openswan or KLIPS.
gcc	The GNU C compiler.
make	The GNU make package for interpreting Makefiles.
lex or flex/bison	Used for creating and interpreting grammar.
glibc-dev / glibc-devel	The necessary C header files for compilation.
awk or gawk or mawk	An interpreter.
sed	A stream editor tool.

These packages might themselves have dependencies. The kernel-source package on Fedora currently requires gtk2-devel, which in turn needs a lot of graphical X-based development packages. Most of these packages are, with the exception of the first two, typically installed on a normal base system.

> The lack of the gmp development package is probably the most common problem people encounter when attempting to build Openswan. If your build process fails, double-check if you have the gmp-devel package installed. This is the #1 FAQ about compiling Openswan.

Rebuilding the Openswan Userland

To rebuild the Openswan userland from the source RPM, first download and install the RPM with:

```
# rpm -ihv openswan-2.4.1-3.src.rpm
```

This will install various files in /usr/src/redhat (or /usr/src/packages/ on SuSE). The Openswan archive itself will be placed in /usr/src/redhat/SOURCES, along with any potential patches that the distribution package maintainer feels are needed. Naturally, source RPMs from the Openswan project will not contain any patches. An instruction file on how to rebuild a binary package from these sources and possible patches, which includes distribution-specific issues such as start/stop scripts and custom locations of lock files, is placed in the /usr/src/redhat/SPECS directory.

To build a binary RPM for the machine that is running the build process, use:

```
# rpmbuild -bb /usr/src/redhat/SPECS/openswan.spec
```

This will build a binary package for the currently running kernel, and, on our example Pentium-III machine, place the package in /usr/src/redhat/RPMS/i386. You can then install the package just as we explained at the beginning of this chapter. If you wish to build a src.rpm file for use on another machine, use:

```
# rpmbuild -bs /usr/src/redhat/SPECS/openswan.spec
```

You can specify different builds, and builds for different or multiple CPUs, by supplying various flags to the rpmbuild command. See the RPM documentation for further details.

Building src.rpm from Scratch

Of course, if there is no src.rpm available for your system, you can't use rpmbuild to build a src.rpm. You will have to use the spec files from the source archive (openswan-version.tar.gz). These spec files are included in the package subdirectory. For example, to build an Openswan binary RPM from scratch on an Intel Itanium computer running SuSE Linux for which no src.rpm is available, we first build a source RPM:

```
# cd /usr/src/packages
# wget http://www.openswan.org/code/openswan-2.3.tar.gz
# tar zxvf openswan-2.3.tar.gz
# rpmbuild -bs openswan-2.3/packaging/suse/openswan.26spec
```

Now that we have our source RPM, we can build and install the binary RPM for Openswan on this (or another) SuSE machine with the following commands:

```
# rpmbuild -bb SRPMS/openswan-2.3-0suse9.src.rpm
# rpm -ihv RPMS/ia64/openswan-3.1-0.ia64.rpm
```

Openswan Options

For almost everyone, the default options and features for Openswan should be fine. At present, all the binary and source RPM packages assume the build only needs to supply RPMs that use the standard options and features. This might not always be the case. Some of the options cannot be set from the spec file at this point, so to change options, you need to either write a patch against Makefile or Makefile.inc, or manually build and install Openswan outside the packaging system. Always check the spec file to see if options can be changed from there.

You can further change these compile-time options by changing the MODULE_DEF_INCLUDE variable to point to a file that differs from the supplied packaging/linus/config-all.h file.

Building the Openswan Userland from Source

Use of a package manager is not essential: Openswan can of course also be built without one. Though this method offers you greater control, there is less protection from unwise decisions. When building from source fails, it will be more difficult to figure out what went wrong and why.

This section covers the process of building Openswan from source for those who do chose this option, explaining some of the advanced options not previously discussed.

Downloading the Source Code

First, we download and verify the source:

```
# wget http://www.openswan.org/code/openswan-2.4.1.tar.gz
# wget http://www.openswan.org/code/openswan-2.4.1.tar.gz.asc
# gpg --verify openswan-2.4.1.tar.gz.asc
    gpg: WARNING: using insecure memory!
    gpg: please see http://www.gnupg.org/faq.html for more information
    gpg: Signature made Fri 13 Aug 2004 12:34:30 AM CEST using RSA key ID B7E82DF8
    gpg: Good signature from "Openswan Master Signing Key <build@openswan.org>"
    gpg: checking the trustdb
    gpg: no ultimately trusted keys found
    gpg: WARNING: This key is not certified with a trusted signature!
    gpg:          There is no indication that the signature belongs to the owner.
    Primary key fingerprint: D450 193B D905 43FE D929 C9C5 0D58 2984 B7E8 2DF8
```

You should of course check the Openswan website to confirm the currently recommended version. Normally there are full releases, test releases meant only for developers ('dr'), and release candidates ('rc'), which can be tried by both developers and users.

Configuring the Userland Tools

If you build Openswan from source, the default installation directory will be inside /usr/local. This is to distinguish a custom compile from the distribution software, which is typically installed in /usr. It is therefore important to remove any possible *swan package that is installed as part of the distribution. If you do not, older versions might get (partially) used because they appear in the $PATH before /usr/local/sbin. If using the default locations, the ipsec command is installed in

/usr/local/sbin, and the sub-commands are installed in /usr/local/libexec/ipsec/*. Some helper applications are installed in /usr/local/lib/ipsec/. Finally, depending on the distribution, the daemon start-stop script (also called ipsec) is installed in /etc/init.d/.

Openswan does not use a GNU-style configure script. Instead, everything is controlled directly by the top level Makefile. Most of the user-configurable options are located in the file Makefile.inc: Makefile itself should not be changed, only Makefile.inc. Unfortunately, Makefile.inc does not just contain those options you can set, but lots of others too. In general, however, the options that are meant to be configurable use the following syntax:

    VARIABLE?=value

This is make syntax. The ?= means that if the environment $VARIABLE has not been set, then create one with the specified value, otherwise leave the existing value untouched. This makes it easy to configure the build process without even editing Makefile.inc, as you only need to specify the right shell variables before you run make.

If you are building Openswan on the machine that needs to run it, and it is a full-blown Linux distribution, then you very likely do not need to set or change any of these options anyway.

Optional Features

The following options are supported in Makefile.inc or as shell environment variables:

Option name	Description
USE_LWRES (true or false)	Use the ISC BIND version 9 resolv library. This is necessary for various DNSSEC functions, but is not yet available for all Linux distributions. Enable this if your distribution has a version 9 BIND package.
USE_IPROUTE2 (true or false)	Use the iproute2 package (and the kernel's advanced routing features). This should only be false for Linux 2.0 and early 2.2 kernels.
IPSEC_FIREWALLTYPE (iptables, ipchains, or ipfwadm)	This should be set to the type of firewall commands that are to be used. On modern distributions this is iptables. On older kernels or distributions, this can be ipchains or ipfwadm.
USE_IKEPING (true or false)	This option compiles a small test program called ikeping. This should only be disabled for small embedded devices.
USE_KEYRR (true or false)	This option adds support for the DNS KEY record. See Chapter 6.
USE_KERNEL26 (true or false)	Enables support for the 2.6 kernel. This should only be disabled on small embedded systems running a 2.4 (or older) kernel.
USE_VENDORID (true or false)	This enables sending a vendor ID identifying the software as "Openswan". This is disabled by default for security reasons.

Option name	Description
USE_XAUTH (true or false)	Builds the userland with XAUTH support. See Chapter 9.
USE_XAUTHPAM (true or false)	Add PAM support to XAUTH. With this you can use your system's user and password information for XAUTH.
USE_NAT_TRAVERSAL (true or false)	Support NAT traversal. Strongly recommended in today's imperfect world.
USE_NAT_TRAVERSAL_TRANSPORT_MODE (true or false)	Support NAT-T in Transport mode. This is a security problem and should be disabled. However, it is necessary if you wish to be compatible with Microsoft clients using L2TP over IPsec. See Chapter 8.
USE_LDAP (true or false)	Support fetching Certificate Revocation Lists over LDAP. See Chapter 5.
USE_LIBCURL (true or false)	Use libcurl instead of native code for fetching over LDAP.
USE_SMARTCARD (true or false)	Add smartcard support. This requires openct and opensc.
USE_OE (true or false)	Enable Opportunistic Encryption per default. See Chapter 6.
HAVE_THREADS (true or false)	Include support for POSIX threads. This is necessary for XAUTHPAM and LDAP. It is recommended to disable this if you don't include support for PAM or LDAP.

Compile Flags

The following are compile options:

Option name	Description
KERNELSRC (for example: /usr/src/linux)	The location of the Linux kernel source you wish to use. If not set, it will first try /usr/src/linux-2.6, then /usr/src/linux-2.4, then /usr/src/linux.
RH_KERNELSRC (for example: /usr/src/linux-2.6.8-1.520)	The location of the Red Hat modified Linux kernel source tree. This option is only used for the make rpm target. See packaging/redhat/openswan.spec.
RH_KERNELSRC_POOL (for example: /vol/bigstorage/)	The location of the Red Hat kernel source pool. This is used for automating the compilation of a large number of binary RPM packages for our official binary Red Hat releases. See packaging/redhat/openswan.spec for details.

Option name	Description
USERCOMPILE (for example: -O3 or -g)	The compiler flags for building the Openswan userland.
KLIPSCOMPILE (for example: -O3 or -g)	The compiler flags for building the KLIPS kernel module.

Do not put -L, -I, or other cross-compile options in these compile flag variables. The above options are only meant for generic options such as -O3 for optimizing, or -g, which adds debug information into the binary object code.

File Path Options

The following options affect the paths used within the scripts and binaries:

Option name	Description
DESTDIR (for example: /vol/bigspace/arm-port)	This is the exact location where the files will be installed. If unset, it is ignored.
INC_USRLOCAL (for example: /usr/local or /usr)	This is the exact location where the files consider themselves installed for the running system. Various scripts will have this path hard coded in them.
PUBDIR	The location of the ipsec command. This should be within the $PATH of the root user. Note that some systems, such as Red Hat and Fedora, call the startup script ipsec as well. These are entirely different commands though!
FINALCONFFILE	The location of ipsec.conf. Normally this is /etc/ipsec.conf, but Gentoo for instance uses /etc/ipsec/ipsec.conf.
INC_RCDIRS	This contains a list of directories in decreasing preference for the daemon start-stop script. The first directory found on the system in this list is used. This option is mainly to recognize new distributions automatically. It is unlikely you'll need to change this.

There are a few more settings that fine-tune the paths where files are installed. See the comments in Makefile.inc for details. Usually, if compiling Openswan for the host system itself, these do not need to be changed.

Obscure Pluto Options

There are three more options hidden in Pluto's Makefile at programs/pluto/Makefile. It is very unlikely that you need to change these. These options haven't made it into Makefile.inc yet, but will probably move there in the future.

Option name	Description
`LDAP_VERSION`	Which version of LDAP libraries to link against. Defaults to 3, but 2 is also supported. Note that these numbers do not correspond with the number in the openldap version. `openldap-2.2` supports LDAP version 3.
`#-DUSE_1DES`	The # character should be removed to enable 1DES encryption in Pluto. As of openswan-2.4 and up, this option is controlled in `Makefile.inc`'s `USE_WEAKSTUFF` and `USE_BROKEN` variables
`-DLEAK_DETECTIVE`	This define helps to find memory leaks. If Pluto is taking up all of your memory, and you suspect a memory leak, then define this option. Start Openswan and when it has consumed a large amount of memory, but before you run out of it, gracefully shut down Openswan. Memory debug information will then be logged through `syslog`.

Compiling and Installing

Building the userland tools now simply requires two commands:

```
# make programs
# make install
```

If you are building the userland for the host system itself, it is now ready to be used. If you are building Openswan for another machine, your installation can be found in `$DESTDIR`.

If you are going to use NETKEY, and you were compiling Openswan for the host system itself, you can skip the rest of this chapter and go to the next chapter where we configure Openswan.

If the compilation failed, verify that you are using the latest stable release of Openswan. Double check your options in `Makefile.inc`. Chapter 12 and Appendix C lists some common problems and resources where you may find additional information that might be useful.

Binary Installation of KLIPS

If you want to install KLIPS using a binary package, you must be running a kernel for which a binary package of KLIPS has been built. If you are running your own compiled kernel, you cannot install a binary package of KLIPS. The Openswan project precompiles binary KLIPS packages for a number of known binary kernels as shipped by the major distributions. Note that these packages are also different depending on the CPU you are using; or rather the CPU model of the kernel of the kernel package you are currently using.

You can determine which kernel packages are installed on your system using the package manager.

```
# rpm -q kernel kernel-smp
```

> kernel-2.6.7-1.478

> kernel-2.6.8-1.520

Here, two kernel packages have been installed. Most packages don't allow multiple versions to be installed simultaneously, but the kernel is an exception; you might need to fall back to the older kernel if the new one doesn't boot your system. The bootloader (`grub` or `lilo`) then lets you choose between the two. To see which is currently running, use the `uname` command:

```
# uname -a
```

Linux bofh.xtdnet.nl 2.6.8-1.520 #1 Sat Aug 14 05:57:37 EDT 2004 i686 i686 i386 GNU/Linux

So, if KLIPS is available as a binary package for your (Pentium-III) kernel from the Fedora Core 2 distribution listed in the above uname command, then the package would be available at:

```
ftp://ftp.openswan.org/openswan/binaries/Fedora/FC2/RPMS/2.6.8-1.520/openswan-
klips-2.2.0_2.6.8.520-0.i686.rpm
```

If there are no binary packages available, you will have to compile your own. But don't worry, we might be able to use rpm for that too.

Building KLIPS from Source

Before applying any kernel patches, it is important to confirm that your current Linux distribution is capable of compiling a standard kernel. Often people report errors on the Openswan mailing lists that are really errors of their Linux system. Common problems include having a gcc compiler that cannot build any kernel. Or having updated the gcc compiler after building the kernel, so that the kernel and the modules are built with a different compiler. Or certain packages needed for building are not installed. Or because people are trying to compile linux-2.6.79-pre4-ac8 that was released five minutes ago.

However, the most common compile failure is due to missing header files for the GNU Math Precision library (gmp.h). These are often located in a package named gmp-dev or gmp-devel, and not installed by default on most distributions.

Therefore, if you are going to compile your own kernel with KLIPS, it is recommended to first build a regular custom kernel. When this build has been successful, KLIPS or NAT-T can be patched into the kernel, and the kernel can then be rebuilt. Very few people seem to be willing to wait for two kernel compiles, but I would like to stress the following advice:

> If your KLIPS compile failed, first try to build a unpatched kernel before asking for support on the mailing lists or on the IRC channel!

Kernel Prerequisites

For Openswan to work properly, some functionality in the Linux kernel needs to be present. Most of the functionality, like basic TCP/IP networking, will surely be part of any distribution kernel. Some other features may be left out, especially if the kernel is designed for a small embedded system, where every byte counts. For example, Red Hat makes an effort to try to compile support for everything into the kernel, and tries to make most of that a kernel module, so that it is only loaded into the kernel when needed, such as for some specific piece of hardware. An example of the other extreme is Openwrt, a mini-Linux distribution that is an alternative firmware for Linksys Access Points. Since some of these APs only have 8 MB of flash memory, the kernel has been stripped clean, and only functionality that is absolutely essential is included. But not all these vendors have IPsec in mind, so what they might consider a waste of precious flash space, might be a necessity for a kernel that needs to support IPsec.

Identifying your Kernel's Abilities

By far the easiest way to find out what your kernel supports is by looking at the kernel configuration file on the build system. Since the Linux kernel has a GPL license, that build environment should always be available, no matter what vendor made the hardware. If it runs Linux, you should have access to the Linux kernel source code.

The kernel source is not always installed on the default system. For Red Hat or Debian, you will need to install the `kernel-source` package. The kernel build tree is normally installed in `/usr/src/`. The standard configuration file is created in the top level of the Linux kernel directory, and is called .config. If that file does not exist, the easiest way to create it is using the command:

```
# make oldconfig
```

Some distributions have the .config file in the module directory:

```
# more /lib/modules/`uname -r`/build/.config
```

As of Linux 2.6, there is also a way to bundle the .config file within the kernel image itself. The configuration file of your kernel is then available in the /proc/ filesystem:

```
# zmore /proc/config.gz
```

Most distributions store a copy of the used .config file in /boot. For embedded systems, it is unlikely that this will have been added to the kernel, due to the space constraints previously mentioned.

Using Both KLIPS and NETKEY

If you want to test both stacks before making a final decision, you will have to compile both stacks as modules. By default, Openswan uses the stack that is already loaded when it starts. If it doesn't find any stack, it will first try to load NETKEY, and if that fails it will try to load KLIPS. In the future, there will probably be a configuration option in /etc/ipsec.conf to choose your stack.

Unfortunately, modules cannot easily detect other modules. Therefore, a module cannot detect whether its competitor is already loaded in the kernel. This means that you can actually manually load both stacks in the kernel. The results of this are completely unpredictable, and your kernel will likely blow up in your face. The Openswan userland will refuse to start when it detects that both modules are loaded.

The Kernel Build Options

Listed overleaf, are the required and recommended options. Note that regular options, like CPU or network card, are not listed, but only those options that a *sane* kernel might not have set, but which is required or desired by Openswan.

Required Kernel Options

The following options must be enabled for a kernel that is to run Openswan:

Option name	Description
CONFIG_UNIX	Unix domain sockets. Openswan userland (Pluto) uses these.
CONFIG_PROC_FS	The /proc filesystem (needed by both KLIPS and NETKEY).
CONFIG_CRYPTO	CryptoAPI, pluggable crypto modules. Necessary for NETKEY; optional for KLIPS.
CONFIG_CRYPTO_*	Various crypto modules. HMAC, MD5, 3DES, AES, SHA1 are necessary for NETKEY; optional for KLIPS. Most of the other crypto modules should be treated with severe skepticism and probably not used at all.

Desired Options

The following kernel compile options are strongly recommended:

Option name	Description
CONFIG_IP_ADVANCED_ROUTER	This gives far better routing control and is needed for some script features, such as _updown.
CONFIG_PACKET	Necessary for tcpdump, a debugging tool, as well as KLIPS and NETKEY
CONFIG_NETFILTER	TCP/IP packet filter. You need this to make a firewall, or to support NAT.
CONFIG_IPSEC_NAT_TRAVERSAL *This option only appears after the kernel has been patched with the NAT-T patch*	This adds support for NAT traversal by encapsulating ESP packets in UDP packets. This is needed if you wish to connect from behind a NATed network to your Openswan server. Older versions of this code call this option CONFIG_ESPINUDP. These versions are broken and should not be used.

NETKEY Stack Options

The following options are part of the NETKEY stack. These must be built as modules if you wish to be able to switch between the NETKEY stack and the KLIPS stack. If not, these features can be built into the kernel itself.

Option name	Description
CONFIG_NET_KEY	PF_KEYv2 (IPsec) sockets.

Option name	Description
CONFIG_XFRM_USER	IPsec user configuration interface (Openswan userland uses this).
CONFIG_INET_AH	Authentication Header (AH) for IPv4. You probably don't need this.
CONFIG_INET_ESP	Encapsulating Security Payload (ESP) for IPv4.
CONFIG_INET_IPCOMP	Payload compression support.
CONFIG_INET_TUNNEL	Generic IP tunnel transformation, needed by ipcomp.
CONFIG_INET6_AH	Authentication Header (AH) for IPv6. You probably don't need this.
CONFIG_INET6_ESP	Encapsulating Security Payload (ESP) for IPv6.
CONFIG_INET6_IPCOMP	Compression mode for IPv6.

KLIPS Stack Options

The following options are part of the KLIPS stack. These must be built as modules if you want to alternate between NETKEY and KLIPS, otherwise these features can be built into the kernel itself. Older versions of Openswan, and all versions of FreeS/WAN, call these options CONFIG_IPSEC_* instead of CONFIG_KLIPS_*.

The following table lists the KLIPS options that are available:

Configuration Option	Description
CONFIG_KLIPS	Enables KLIPS as either a module or as part of the kernel.
CONFIG_KLIPS_IPIP	This enables tunnel mode. You will always want to support this, with the exception of building a dedicated Windows L2TP VPN server. But even then it makes sense to add support for this, unless space restrictions are an issue.
CONFIG_KLIPS_AH	AH mode is disabled by default, since it only authenticates, but does not encrypt packets and also cannot pass through a NAT. It is very unlikely that you will need this.
CONFIG_KLIPS_ESP	ESP mode, aka VPN. This enables authentication plus encryption. You must enable this option.
CONFIG_KLIPS_ENC_3DES	3DES cipher support. (1DES can come in through CryptoAPI only.)
CONFIG_KLIPS_ENC_AES	AES cipher support.
CONFIG_KLIPS_AUTH_HMAC_MD5	HMAC-MD5 algorithm support.

Configuration Option	Description
CONFIG_KLIPS_AUTH_HMAC_SHA1	HMAC-SHA1 algorithm support.
CONFIG_KLIPS_ALG	IPsec Modular Extensions. Support for using ciphers and algorithms from the Linux CryptoAPI. This has the advantage that you can add other less standard ciphers (such as blowfish), but it is also often used to attach to hardware accelerator device drivers.
CONFIG_KLIPS_IPCOMP	Compression for IPsec. There have been some reports that compression isn't always working, though this is often because of misconfigured Racoon configurations. If you experience problems, you can try turning compression off. Note that the ipsec.conf option compress=no only changes whether Openswan advertises the ability. If the other end requests compression, it is still used if compression support was added to KLIPS even when compress=no is used.
CONFIG_KLIPS_DEBUG	IPsec Debugging. You should enable this unless you are severely limited in memory and disk space, as on an embedded device.
IPSEC_CONFIG_REGRESS	Regression testing support. This is additional support for the nightly regression testing system using UserModeLinux (UML) that Openswan uses. You probably want to disable this.

L2TP Options

If you are going to use Microsoft's L2TP, then you also need the following options:

Option name	Description
CONFIG_UNIX98_PTYS	Unix PTYs.
CONFIG_PPP	PPP support.
CONFIG_PPP_SYNC_TTY	Synchronous PPP support.
CONFIG_PPP_DEFLATE	Deflate support.
CONFIG_PPP_BSDCOMP	BSD (de)compression support for IP headers.

And on 2.6 you have one further option:

Option name	Description
CONFIG_LEGACY_PTYS	Legacy PTYs (only needed when using certain older L2TP daemons). Note: This is disabled in the stock kernels for Fedora Core 2 and up.

Patching the Kernel

Kernel patching is only necessary if you wish either to add NAT-Traversal support to a 2.4 kernel, or to add KLIPS support to a 2.4 or 2.6 kernel image without using kernel modules. You can build KLIPS as a module without manual patching.

NAT-Traversal Patch

If you are going to use KLIPS on either a 2.4 or a 2.6 kernel, it is strongly recommended to apply the NAT traversal patch to the kernel, which can be generated from the Openswan source code. It modifies some internal structures of the UDP packet format in the kernel. Note that this is not a change to a kernel module, but a change to the kernel core itself.

> If you apply the NAT-T patch, you MUST rebuild both the kernel image (bzImage) and all the kernel modules.

We first generate the patch file, and then apply it to our kernel:

```
# KERNELSRC=/usr/src/linux-2.6.11
# cd openswan-2
# make nattpatch > /usr/src/openswan-ipsec-natt.patch
# cd /usr/src/linux-2.6.11
# cat /usr/src/openswan-ipsec-natt.patch | patch -p1 -s
# make clean
# make oldconfig
```

When running the last command, the configuration options that have already been configured will fly by, but the program will pause when it encounters a new option, such as in our case the option to enable NAT-Traversal:

    IPSEC NAT-Traversal (CONFIG_IPSEC_NAT_TRAVERSAL) [N/y/?](NEW)

After answering Y to this option, the process will continue and end with a new kernel configuration. Remember that since this is a patch against some core functions of the kernel image itself, and is not a separate kernel module, you **must** build a new kernel image and you **must** rebuild all the modules for that kernel. For Linux 2.4 or earlier, you must build the dependencies first:

```
# make dep
```

The command to build the kernel and modules is:

```
# make bzImage modules modules_install
```

KLIPS Compile Shortcut

If you do not need to apply the NAT-T patch, because you do not need it or because your kernel already has the NAT-T patch applied, you can use a shortcut, which avoids the need to recompile the entire kernel. Obviously, this only works if you are happy with KLIPS as a kernel module:

```
# cd /usr/src/openswan-2.4.1
# export KERNELSRC=/usr/src/linux-2.6.11
# make module
# make minstall
# depmod -a
```

Note that the make target is called module, in the singular, and not the plural as is the case for the Linux kernel itself which uses the target modules. If you want use this shortcut, you can customize the KLIPS compile-time options from the file openswan-2/linux/net/ipsec/defconfig.

Activating KLIPS

If you compiled KLIPS statically as part of the kernel image or if you applied the NAT-T patch, you will now need to install your new kernel by copying it to the right place (usually /boot), updating your bootloader, and rebooting into your new kernel. Check the documentation for your distribution if you are not familiar with this process.

If you compiled KLIPS as a module, the result of make minstall or make modules_install will be a single module called ipsec.ko (ipsec.o on 2.4) that will be installed in the appropriate directory under /lib/modules/. If you built the module for the currently running kernel, you do not need to reboot.

Before you load KLIPS, ensure that NETKEY is not loaded with the following command:

```
# rmmod xfrmuser af_key esp4 ah4 ipcomp xfrm4_tunnel
```

Then you are ready to load KLIPS thus:

```
# modprobe ipsec
```

In older versions, some algorithms and ciphers came in their own separate module (such as ipsec_aes.o). This is currently no longer the case.

Determining the Stack in Use

You can test which stack is loaded by checking to see if the files listed in the following table can be found in the /proc filesystem:

Stack	File to detect this stack
KLIPS IPsec stack	/proc/net/ipsec_version or /proc/net/pf_key
NETKEY IPsec stack	/proc/net/pfkey *note the lack of underscore in the filename*
KLIPS NAT-Traversal support (openswan-2.4.0 and up)	/proc/net/ipsec_natt

If you have also installed the userland, you can use the --version command. The stack in use appears between brackets right after the version number:

```
# ipsec --version
```
    Linux Openswan 2.4.1/K2.6.8-1.520 (netkey)

    See 'ipsec --copyright' for copyright information.

```
# ipsec --version
```
    Linux Openswan 2.4.1 (klips)

    See 'ipsec --copyright' for copyright information.

Building KLIPS into the Linux Kernel Source Tree

Sometimes it is more desirable to manually build KLIPS. This involves patching the kernel directory itself, but the resulting source could be used on multiple systems. You may want to change some of the default options in KLIPS. Perhaps you do not want to use modules but want KLIPS as part of your kernel, for instance because you are building a firewall and do not want the security risk of loadable modules for your kernel.

Manually building KLIPS, either as a kernel module or as part of the kernel, can be a little bit more difficult. You will also need to maintain this part if you (or your distribution) upgrade the system's kernel.

Building a Standard Kernel

The kernel source as shipped with most distributions has not been configured, so you will always need to configure the kernel source first.

At some point Red Hat kernel source trees needed some cleanup before you could configure them:

```
# make distclean
```

> Running `make distclean` will delete your `.config` file. If you are using your own `.config` file, copy it somewhere outside the kernel tree before running this command, then copy it back in.

If you want to build the kernel according to the default settings provided by the vendor, either from your distribution or the defaults from Linus himself, you can simply run:

```
# make oldconfig
```

And if you are using a 2.4 or older kernel, you will also need to run:

```
# make dep
```

Of course, if you do not wish to use those defaults, you can run any of the kernel configure commands to reconfigure the kernel to suit your needs. You can use any of these commands:

Method	Description
make config	This uses a simple command line.
make menuconfig	This uses an 'ncurses'-based menu system.
make xconfig	This uses a full graphical menu system using 'qt'.

If you change your kernel configuration, we strongly recommend building the entire kernel at this stage, so that if you encounter problems when compiling KLIPS later on, you know that it is not a general kernel problem. Too often, the Openswan developers find people blaming KLIPS for their compile errors, while in fact the kernel itself or the build system itself was broken. Also do not forget to apply the NAT-T patch as described above.

To make a kernel on an Intel-based computer, run:

```
# make bzImage
```

And if you are also using kernel modules:

```
# make modules modules_install
```

If these compilations work, you have confirmed that your current-build system and kernel directory are good. You can then proceed to compile KLIPS.

NAT Traversal

Remember that you should also apply the NAT-Traversal patch if you wish to support IPsec connections from behind NAT.

Patching KLIPS into the Linux Kernel

First we set the KERNELSRC shell variable to point to our Linux kernel source directory, so we do not accidentally compile against a different kernel than the one we're expecting.

Patching KLIPS into the kernel directory then becomes pretty straightforward:

```
# KERNELSRC=/usr/src/linux-2.6.11
# cd openswan-2
# make applypatch
```

You cannot start the kernel compile yet, because some new features (KLIPS) have been added to the kernel configuration file. The kernel configuration needs to be re-run.

```
# cd $KERNELSRC
# make oldconfig
```

You will be prompted for all the new kernel options related to KLIPS as described earlier. For each option, help information is also available. Of course, you can also use make menuconfig or make xconfig at this point. If using a 2.4 kernel, you should run make dep at this point.

The following figure shows how to enable NAT-T in a kernel using `make xconfig`:

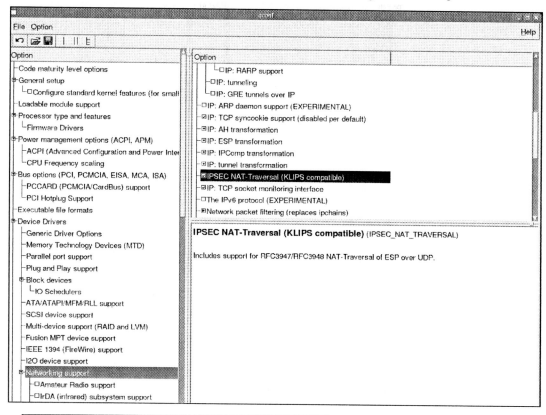

Be aware that you must not configure both NETKEY and KLIPS to be part of the kernel itself. Such a kernel will act completely unpredictably, and very likely will either fail to build, or crash.

In general, all the ciphers and algorithms can be enabled, since they can be disabled at run time if necessary using the `ike=` and `esp=` options. For detailed information about these ciphers and algorithms, see Chapter 2.

One exception is if you want to disable the KLIPS ciphers and algorithms in favor of the Linux CryptoAPI, which provides these ciphers as well. 3DES will always come from the KLIPS code if present. If you really wish to use the CryptoAPI version, disable 3DES in KLIPS. In the future this will change, when proper synchronous and asynchronous CryptoAPI support is added to KLIPS, and KLIPS is able to pick either its own 3DES or the CryptoAPI 3DES routines.

Once you have configured your kernel, and run `make dep` if using a 2.4 kernel, you are ready to build your new kernel using the same commands as described earlier in this chapter. Depending on whether you build KLIPS as module or not, and whether you applied the NAT-T patch, you need to execute one or both of:

```
# make bzImage
# make modules modules_install
```

Verifying the Installation

You can see if Openswan is properly installed by issuing the following command:

```
# ipsec --version
     Linux Openswan 2.4.1 (klips)
     See `ipsec --copyright' for copyright information.
```

If you did not install KLIPS, but plan to use NETKEY, the output will look slightly different:

```
     Linux Openswan U2.4.1dr1/K2.6.11-1.27_FC3 (netkey)
     See `ipsec --copyright' for copyright information.
```

If you just installed Openswan, you might not have an IPsec stack loaded yet, in which you will see the following:

```
     Linux Openswan U2.4.1/K(no kernel code presently loaded)
     See `ipsec --copyright' for copyright information.
```

You should further have a skeleton configuration file in /etc/ipsec.conf, and for most distributions there will also be a freshly generated /etc/ipsec.secrets. Some additional directories and configuration files can be found in /etc/ipsec.d. The programs, apart from the

ipsec command that will be installed in /usr/sbin or /usr/local/sbin, are all installed in /usr/lib/ipsec and /usr/libexec/ipsec, or their equivalents in /usr/local. The startup script, which is also called ipsec, is installed in the appropriate location within /etc, which depending upon your Linux distribution will be somewhere in /etc/init.d or /etc.rc.d.

Summary

In this chapter, we have looked at the features of each distribution and each IPsec stack, and we can now make the decision of which distribution to use. We can choose our IPsec stack, and we should be able to set up our build, compile, and install the Openswan userland, and if needed a new kernel with the features our system will need.

We are now ready to configure Openswan.

4
Configuring IPsec

This chapter will explain how to configure various kinds of IPsec tunnels. It will discuss:

- Automatic versus manual keying
- PSK versus RSA
- Basic IPsec tunnels
- Syntax and options in `ipsec.conf`
- Syntax and options in `ipsec.secrets`
- Basic `ipsec` commands
- Testing IPsec connections

The chapter addresses Openswan configuration for the most common types of VPN networks.

Manual versus Automatic

Often, the first kind of setup that is discussed is the so-called manual keying setup, since from a technological point of view, it is the easiest way to set up an IPsec tunnel. However, with Openswan, contrary to most other VPN software, automatic tunnels are actually easier to set up than manual tunnels. Manual keying—where one manually configures the encryption keys and the SPDs and SPIs used—is quite difficult to configure. With Openswan, it is much easier to configure automatic keying using the IKE protocol.

To understand the difference between manual and automatic keying, think of the gears of a car. No one can deny that using an automatic, where the car itself shifts the gears on your behalf, is easier to master than manually shifting the gears at the right time. You are busy enough as it is looking in the mirrors, steering the car to keep it on the road, checking the speedometer and keeping an eye on traffic. Of course, those who learned driving cars using manual gears will swear by it. They claim it will give them more control and that they can shift better than the machine. It's hard to let the control go.

Automatic keying is much easier and safer to set up than manual keying.

PSK versus RSA

A similar discussion can be held regarding the type of authentication. Though using a Pre-Shared Key (PSK) might seem easier than using a full blown public/private key algorithm like RSA, it often causes more headaches than RSA. But regardless of which is the easier to set up, there is a much more important issue at hand here.

People believe a PSK is like a passphrase on their PGP key, but this is wrong. A PSK is not a password or passphrase. A pre-shared secret is used as the **key**! A short PSK means that the VPN tunnel becomes susceptible to a simple brute force attack.

Using a PSK like 'test' or even a line of random characters is just not good enough. It can be easily cracked on modern CPUs. Do not use PSK unless you have to, which usually only happens when you're stuck with some low-cost hardware appliance that has not implemented all parts of the IPsec specification.

Therefore, we will start our basic configuration with an example that uses both automatic keying and RSA authentication.

Pitfalls of Debugging IPsec

Before we start our first configuration, you need to understand the security provided with a properly (and even improperly!) configured IPsec tunnel. To protect against various types of attacks, such as spoofing attacks, an IPsec peer that has been configured to talk to a remote host using IPsec will *not* talk to that peer without encryption, except for those packets needed to set up the IPsec tunnel, such as IKE packets.

If you are configuring IPsec, you are normally working locally on one endpoint, and have one remote endpoint. A secure login, usually using SSH, is used to configure the remote endpoint from the local one. Once both ends are configured, the IPsec subsystem can be started on both sides.

So imagine what happens if you made a mistake on the remote endpoint. The IPsec tunnel will fail to establish. It will refuse all cleartext packets from the local endpoint except IKE. This means you can no longer log in to the remote endpoint using SSH to fix its configuration!

> Always have an independent, non-IPsec, third machine from which you can log in to both IPsec endpoints. This machine should NOT appear in the IPsec configuration of either endpoint and should be able to use SSH to log in to both IPsec endpoints.

Even the most experienced IPsec guru has been bitten by this, current authors not excluded.

Here we are using the client at Sunset and use SSH to configure both, West and East to configure an IPsec tunnel between East and West. If we make an error, we can SSH from Sunset to South and from South to East to repair our configuration.

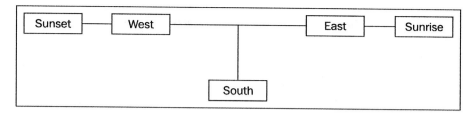

The previous figure is of a typical LAN-to-LAN setup. The networks Sunset and Sunrise are connected by the IPsec servers East and West. South is an independent hop that involved with IPsec that can be used to SSH from East to West when its IPsec configuration has been incorrectly configured.

Pre-Flight Check

Now, before we configure our first tunnel, we have two tests that we can run to confirm that our setup should work if we configure it correctly. First we start Openswan, which is unfortunately rather distribution specific. See the following table:

Distribution	Start command
RedHat (and Mandrake)	service ipsec start
SuSE	/sbin/rcipsec start
Debian	/etc/init.d/ipsec start
Gentoo	ipsec setup start

The ipsec verify Command

We can now run our first pre-flight check command: ipsec verify. This command will check a few basic settings of the Linux kernel and its network configuration.

```
# ipsec verify
    Checking your system to see if IPsec got installed and started correctly:
    Version check and ipsec on-path                                    [OK]
    Linux Openswan 2.2.0dr4 (klips)
    Checking for IPsec support in kernel                               [OK]
    Checking for RSA private key (/etc/ipsec.secrets)                 [OK]
    Checking that pluto is running                                     [OK]
    Two or more interfaces found, checking IP forwarding              [OK]
    Checking NAT and MASQUERADEing                                    [N/A]
    Checking for 'ip' command                                         [OK]
    Checking for 'iptables' command                                   [OK]

    Opportunistic Encryption DNS checks:
        Looking for TXT in forward dns zone: west.testlab.xelerance.net   [OK]
        Does the machine have at least one non-private address?           [OK]
        Looking for TXT in reverse dns zone: 30.157.110.193.in-addr.arpa. [MISSING]
        Looking for TXT in reverse dns zone: 84.230.126.80.in-addr.arpa.  [MISSING]
```

The ipsec verify command tells us that our software has been correctly set up. Our kernel supports IPsec, in this case using the KLIPS stack. The ipsec command is properly installed somewhere in the path for scripts that call it. There is at least one RSA key generated for this host, generated when the IPsec service is started.

The Gentoo startup services scheme is not yet supported by Openswan, so generating an RSA hostkey must be done manually:

```
# ipsec newhostkey --output /etc/ipsec.secrets
```

Some Gentoo distributions might expect this file to be in a subdirectory called /etc/ipsec/.

The verify command further tells us that Pluto, the Openswan IKE daemon, is running. It finds two network interfaces, which in general means that someone is trying to set up a LAN-to-LAN tunnel. For this to properly work, the kernel must be configured to use IP forwarding. If this test fails you can manually enable IP forwarding with the command:

```
# echo "1" > /proc/sys/net/ipv4/ip_forward
```

On most distributions, you can edit the /etc/sysctl.conf file and change the setting net.ipv4.ip_forward to 1. This will cause IP forwarding to be automatically enabled during the boot process.

While you are editing /etc/sysctl.conf, it is also a good idea to disable net.ipv4.conf.default.rp_filter by setting it to 0. The rp_filter setting controls the built-in spoof protection of the Linux kernel. It is a very simplistic protection that discards packets that appear to have arrived at the machine from the wrong network device, as is the case in some IP spoofing attacks. However, when using KLIPS, the packets *suddenly* appear from ipsec0, while rp_filter deems they should have come in on the external physical interface (for instance eth0) and concludes these packets are spoofed and the Linux kernel will thus drop them. Openswan used to warn about rp_filter when running the ipsec verify command, but this test has been removed in more recent versions because Openswan will just detect and disable rp_filter automatically.

NAT and Masquerading

The next test that the ipsec verify command performs tries to determine whether any iptables rules are present that rewrite packets. If so, it tries to determinate whether these rewriting rules would actually rewrite IPsec packets. IPsec packets may *never* be rewritten or mangled, as this invalidates the cryptographic signature on these packets and breaks the encrypted payload.

For instance, if we added the following (unwise!) iptables rule on West to enable NAT for its LAN network 192.0.1.0/24:

```
# iptables -t nat -I POSTROUTING -s 192.0.1.0/24 -j SNAT --to 193.111.228.1 -o eth0
```

then verify would correctly warn us that this would break the IPsec tunnel between Sunset and Sunrise:

```
. . .
Checking NAT and MASQUERADEing
Checking tun0x1070@193.111.228.1 from 205.150.200.209/32 to 193.111.228.1/32 [FAILED]
SNAT from 192.0.1.0/24 to 0.0.0.0/0 kills tunnel 192.0.1.0/24 -> 193.111.228.1/32
. . .
```

Checking External Commands

Next, ipsec verify checks whether the necessary external commands it relies on are available. Currently, it checks for ip, ipchains, and iptables, and when using NETKEY, it also checks if the setkey command is available.

If you see a warning in this section you must fix it by installing the appropriate package. The ip command comes from the iproute package, which is sometimes called iproute2. The iptables command comes from the iptables package, and the setkey command is part of the ipsec-tools package. Openswan versions 2.3.0 or later no longer depend on the setkey command for NETKEY, but use the ip xfrm command instead. The XFRM framework for the ip command should be available on all modern versions of the iproute package.

> The iproute package is sometimes called iproute2.

Opportunistic Encryption

The last check that ipsec verify performs is whether it can successfully retrieve Opportunistic Encryption records for itself from DNS. Failures in this section can normally be ignored, unless of course you are attempting to run Opportunistic Encryption. Using Opportunistic Encryption is further explained in chapter 5.

The ipsec livetest Command

The second pre-flight check we can perform is ipsec livetest. This command, available in Openswan 2.5 and later, will perform various tests to a specific test server, livetest.xelerance.net, to determine whether your ISP is filtering any packets, or is incorrectly mangling packets, for instance because of broken path-MTU discovery.

> If you are uncomfortable with having your IPsec machine send packets to a public test server, you should not use the ipsec livetest command.

```
# ipsec livetest
      Checking that Openswan has not been started              [OK]
      Checking for livetest.xelerance.net connectivity using ping   [OK]
      Checking for free path on UDP port  500 (IKE)            [OK]
      Checking for free path on UDP port 4500 (IKE NAT-T)      [OK]
      Starting barebone Openswan                               [OK]
      Fetching connection information from livetest.xelerance.com  [OK]
      Loading IPsec conn livetest                              [OK]
      Starting IPsec conn livetest                             [OK]
      Sending packets over IPsec conn livetest                 [OK]
      Sending large packets over IPsec conn livetest           [OK]
      Tearing down IPsec conn livetest                         [OK]

      NAT Traversal detected in (/etc/ipsec.conf), testing NAT-T
      Loading IPsec conn livetest-natt                         [OK]
```

Triggering conn livetest-natt	[OK]
Sending packets over IPsec conn livetest-natt	[OK]
Sending large packets over IPsec conn livetest-natt	[OK]
Tearing down IPsec conn livetest-natt	[OK]
Testing for OE record in FQDN (west.xelerance.net)	[OK]
Loading iOE conn livetest-ioe	[OK]
Starting iOE conn to oe.livetest.xelerance.net	[OK]
Stopping iOE conn to oe.livetest.xelerance.net	[OK]

Testing for OE record in reverse dns zone: 81.157.110.192.in-addr.arpa. [OK]
Triggering responder OE   [OK]

If livetest passes all checks, your end of the network is healthy. Of course, it could still mean the other end has problems. Worse, the connection between the two endpoints could pass through some router that breaks things. Passing the livetest command is no guarantee for success, but it does eliminate the possibility that your immediate upstream ISP is blocking IPsec traffic. For more detailed information, you can also use ipsec livetest verbose.

> ipsec livetest is still under heavy development. The output in the book might be different to that of the current version of Openswan.

Configuration of Openswan

We have done all we can to prepare our machines and test our network to see that it is possible to run IPsec. Now it is time to actually configure our first IPsec tunnel. Openswan is mainly configured from two configuration files.

Openswan configuration file	Description
ipsec.secrets (usually in /etc, sometimes in /etc/ipsec/)	Contains private RSA keys and preshared secrets (PSKs)
ipsec.conf (usually in /etc, sometimes in /etc/ipsec)	Contains everything else (settings, options, defaults, connections)

Both of these files have very elaborate man pages explaining all the options and their syntax. For some advanced features, such as X.509, XAUTH, and Opportunistic Encryption-related IPsec connections, some additional directories are used:

Directory or file	Description
/etc/ipsec.d/cacerts	X.509 Certificate Authority certificates ("root certificates")
/etc/ipsec.d/certs	X.509 client Certificates
/etc/ipsec.d/private	X.509 Certificate private keys

Directory or file	Description
/etc/ipsec.d/crls	X.509 Certificate Revocation Lists
/etc/ipsec.d/ocspcerts	X.500 Online Certificate Status Protocol certificates
/etc/ipsec.d/passwd	XAUTH password file
/etc/ipsec.d/policies	The Opportunistic Encryption policy groups

These directories are explained in their respective chapters.

The ipsec.conf File

To distinguish modern Openswan 2 configuration files from older, incompatible configuration files, the first non-empty, non-comment line needs to contain:

```
version 2
```

Old versions, such as FreeS/WAN 1.x, Super FreeS/WAN, and Openswan 1, do not support version 2 configuration files.

> If you are upgrading from these old *swans to Openswan 2, you most likely can get away with adding the version 2 line at the top of your old configuration file, and removing the plutoload= and plutostart= directives.

After the version line, there are usually three sections of the configuration file, as described in the following table:

Section	Description
config setup	Global parameters and options
conn %default	Optionally, a default section for connection parameters for conns that don't specify certain options themselves
conns	The connection definitions themselves

These sections need to be separated with a blank line. Unfortunately, there are some other peculiarities with how the ipsec.conf file is parsed. The worst part is that it is currently dependent on whitespace (such as spaces or tabs) at various places. Make sure that every conn starts at the beginning of a new line, and ensure it is separated from other sections or conns by an empty line. Ensure that all options are indented with at least one tab, and that no conn contains an empty line.

These limitations might vanish when the scripts are replaced by the starter binary. This is, however, still a work in progress.

To make it easier to maintain, you can use include statements in the configuration files, which may contain wildcards. This can help you organize your VPN connections, for instance by grouping them in directories per region:

```
include /etc/ipsec.d/canada/*.conf
include /etc/ipsec.d/netherlands/*.conf
include /etc/ipsec.d/ussa/*.conf
```

Host-to-Host Tunnel

Now let us make an example ipsec.conf configuration for a VPN tunnel from East to West. This ipsec.conf configuration file needs to be created on both ends.

```
version 2

config setup
    interfaces=%defaultroute
    # klipsdebug=all
    # plutodebug=control

conn %default
    authby=rsasig

conn west-east
    left=193.110.157.131
    right=205.150.200.209
    type=tunnel
    leftrsasigkey=0sAQOkF1Ggd4iFfI2nQxJYbN9HGD...
    rightrsasigkey=0sAQPEA1+N52EIRrIAA5cx18U...
    auto=start
```

And that is all you need to define an IPsec tunnel with Openswan. It can't be easier! Though most options should be self explanatory, let's review all of them so we will fully understand their usage.

Left and Right

Most network administrators are used to the concepts of *source* and *destination* addresses, and they expect an IPsec configuration to have a source and a destination. But this doesn't really apply to IPsec, bearing in mind that an IPsec connection actually contains two halves, one for incoming and one for outgoing packets. It would be confusing, and not to mention extremely annoying, if after transferring a file to the other IPsec endpoint you had to then swap source and destination parameters. And the terms client and server won't help either, since IPsec really is a peer-to-peer protocol. Not all IPsec peers are either clearly the client or the server. They could even be considered a client for one tunnel, and a server for another.

For these reasons, the concepts of **left** and **right** are used. These terms are dependent on your point of view (look in a mirror, or teach in front of a group of people to see how left and right can become exchanged). So the choice of which end to call left or right is completely up to you. You might look at your draft network sketch and call the one you drew on the left "left".

The good thing is that when Openswan loads a new connection, it will look at both left and right entries, and it will try to figure out which end it is. It does so by comparing the specified IP address (or resolved hostnames) to the list of currently active IP addresses on the host. In our example, West will figure out it is left because it can see that its network configuration has the IP address 193.110.157.89, which matches the `left=` option. East will figure out it is right, because the `right=` option matches one of its IP addresses. If Openswan cannot determine whether it is left or right, the connection will fail to load, and a warning will be logged.

> Because of Openswan's automatic left/right detection, simple connection definitions can be used on both IPsec endpoints without editing them. The exception is when you are using roadwarrior connections.

The type Options

The `type=` option sets the IPsec mode to use. When left out, it defaults to **tunnel mode**, which should be correct for most cases, with the exception of Microsoft L2TP connections.

IPsec mode	Description
type=tunnel (default)	Use tunnel modes
type=transport	Use transport modes
type=passthrough	Do not process packets, just pass them through to the kernel

The auto Option

The `auto=start` option tells Openswan to immediately start this connection on startup. The `auto` option can have the following values:

Start-up option	Description
auto=start	Load, route, and initiate the connection
auto=add	Load the connection and respond to an incoming request
auto=ignore (default)	Ignore this connection completely
auto=manual	This connection will be keyed manually (not recommended)
auto=route	Load and route the connection (used for special routing cases)

The first two are the most common. `auto=start` is used for static IPsec tunnels, whereas `auto=add` is used mostly when the connection defined cannot initiate, but only respond. This is for instance the case with roadwarriors, where the server end does not know where or when the roadwarrior will appear, because it is a roaming user that pops in at various dynamic ISP-dependent IP addresses assigned through DHCP.

The rsasigkey Options

The last remaining question in our example is that of where the RSA key entries come from. These entries correspond to the public RSA keys of the RSA key-pairs that were generated when we first started Openswan. It is unique for every host.

Both these private and public RSA keys are stored in ipsec.secrets; you could cut and paste the public key from there, but it is usually easier to use the following command, which will do the formatting for you. For example, to create a leftrsasig= statement on West, we simply run the following command on West:

```
# ipsec showhostkey --left
    # RSA 2192 bits   west.testbed.xelerance.net   Sun Jan  5 16:21:41 2005

    leftrsasigkey=0sAQPEAl+N52EIRrIAA5cxl8UanVSr2mCVPWmzgLK62G1jeKrZ6OxM9kdY1jm
    9Fv/7HOmLWzYJZSYdPnh9DIHY15ipfZkXDapewaFvSH0yX3V7GUrVF9N8dZSAkPg/nOc+A
    VjJfWHHxT4/e4AA6syOYFGQCyRt4BXZ5xY0U/10QRL/Ra2xtF4aV1GdNCfcFT4/VeUbrfMB0e
    RI++hTUx4MriX2zO5VwRxRSoMpMcSqv7QbICiKw+gRu/63HroR0n1Wmp8VQzWd3SMpUCw
    QhoBSkeP5lb8jXg+sNrb7LDC7fSNHbAzgg8vGSwcotBisUiES/8JXkI9PQAPrRaxrY2fP8sWky0
    tsySlJytweSWLdfjPwcoOZ
```

The first # line is a comment, which you can also keep in your connection definition if you like. Be careful when copying and pasting such a line from one window to another. It is one big line and some desktop environments, or email programs, may automatically *wrap* this line for you. You must not break up the line!

Note that in the rest of this chapter, to save space and improve clarity, we won't show these long rsasigkey= lines in full, and they will instead appear thus:

```
    leftrsasigkey=0sAQPEAl+N52EIRrIAA5cxl8UanV.....
```

When you see such a line, be aware that you should put in *your* key, which might be several lines long.

Bringing Up the IPsec Tunnels

Once we have copied our ipsec.conf file from West to East, and restarted Openswan on both ends, we will see something in the logs that looks like this:

```
    Sep 15 20:05:05 west pluto[20362]: "west-east" #365: initiating Main Mode
    Sep 15 20:05:05 west pluto[20362]: "west-east" #365: transition from state
      STATE_MAIN_I1 to state STATE_MAIN_I2
    Sep 15 20:05:05 west pluto[20362]: "west-east" #365: I did not send a
      certificate because I do not have one.
    Sep 15 20:05:06 west pluto[20362]: "west-east" #365: transition from state
      STATE_MAIN_I2 to state STATE_MAIN_I3
    Sep 15 20:05:06 west pluto[20362]: "west-east" #365: Peer ID is ID_IPV4_ADDR:
      '205.150.200.209'
    Sep 15 20:05:06 west pluto[20362]: "west-east" #365: transition from state
      STATE_MAIN_I3 to state STATE_MAIN_I4
    Sep 15 20:05:06 west pluto[20362]: "west-east" #365: ISAKMP SA established
    Sep 15 20:05:06 west pluto[20362]: "west-east" #366: initiating Quick Mode
      RSASIG+ENCRYPT+TUNNEL+PFS+UP {using isakmp#365}
    Sep 15 20:05:06 west pluto[20362]: "west-east" #366: transition from state
      STATE_QUICK_I1 to state STATE_QUICK_I2
    Sep 15 20:05:06 west pluto[20362]: "west-east" #366: sent QI2, IPsec SA
      established {ESP=>0xe5f72aaa <0xc51033f4}
```

In the last line, you'll note the message *IPsec SA established*, meaning we've successfully set up an IPsec VPN tunnel between West and East. The *ESP* in curly braces tells us that we are using Encapsulated Secure Payload, which means tunnel mode with full encryption, commonly called VPN.

The log file locations differ from distribution to distribution. Red Hat and Fedora Core log this information in /var/log/secure, while Debian logs it in /var/log/auth.log. If in doubt, check /etc/syslog.conf and look where the authpriv.* priority is logged to.

Listing IPsec Connections

The **eroutes** are the kernel's internal *encrypted routes* and reflect the internal **SPD policies**. It is easy to think of eroutes as encryption routes—all active IPsec connections correspond with one eroute entry. Since the eroutes are displayed as one line per IPsec connection, they provide a condensed and clear view of the IPsec connections for a machine.

```
# ipsec eroute
    5   193.110.157.131/32  ->  205.150.200.209/32  => tun0x109a@205.150.200.209
```

The eroute output tells us that five packets have been sent or received over the IPsec tunnel between our local machine (West, 193.110.157.131) and the remote endpoint (East, 205.150.200.209), and that the tunnel policy says that only packets between 193.110.157.131 and 205.150.200.209 are allowed to be sent through this tunnel.

If you need more details on the connections, use the following command:

```
# ipsec auto --status
```

This will produce an enormous amount of output, but it will contain all the details you might want to know. When using NETKEY, you can also use setkey -D and setkey -P -D directly, which also give a few screens of information.

Testing the IPsec Tunnel

To actually confirm your VPN connection works, you can run a traceroute. Running one on West to East will show us:

```
# traceroute 205.150.200.209
    traceroute to east.testbed.xelerance.net (205.150.200.209) from 193.110.157.131, 30 hops
    max, 38 byte packets
    1 east.testbed.xelerance.net (205.150.200.209)  136.378 ms  137.755 ms  136.478 ms
```

West is in Canada, and East is in Amsterdam, but instead of the many hops across the Atlantic such a packet would travel without IPsec, we now see it travels only one hop, since the packet is traveling through the tunnel. Note that the hop takes about 136ms, which is roughly the time it takes to cross the Atlantic.

You can run tcpdump to check that traffic actually got encrypted. First, let us show an example using KLIPS, which is the easiest to read because it separates traffic on the physical and virtual interfaces:

```
# tcpdump -n -i eth0
    20:20:50.322743 193.110.157.131 > 205.150.200.209: ESP(spi=0xe5f72aaa,seq=0x19)
    20:20:50.370512 205.150.200.209 > 193.110.157.131: ESP(spi=0xc51033f4,seq=0x19)
```

```
20:20:50.372185 193.110.157.131 > 205.150.200.209: ESP(spi=0xe5f72aaa,seq=0x1a)
20:20:50.402157 205.150.200.209 > 193.110.157.131: ESP(spi=0xc51033f4,seq=0x1a)
20:20:50.402623 193.110.157.131 > 205.150.200.209: ESP(spi=0xe5f72aaa,seq=0x1b)
20:20:50.413297 205.150.200.209 > 193.110.157.131: ESP(spi=0xc51033f4,seq=0x1b)
```

The packets are no longer visible as traceroute packets. All we see are IPsec packets using the ESP protocol. We can still see the plaintext packets, if we run tcpdump on the virtual interface:

```
# tcpdump -n -i ipsec0
    18:00:44.130014 IP 193.110.157.17 > 205.150.200.209: icmp 64: echo request seq 0
    20:20:44.144720 IP 205.150.200.209 > 193.110.157.17: icmp 64: echo reply seq 0
    20:20:45.131177 IP 193.110.157.17 > 205.150.200.209: icmp 64: echo request seq 1
    20:20:45.146790 IP 205.150.200.209 > 193.110.157.17: icmp 64: echo reply seq 1
    20:20:46.132104 IP 193.110.157.17 > 205.150.200.209: icmp 64: echo request seq 2
    20:20:46.147400 IP 205.150.200.209 > 193.110.157.17: icmp 64: echo reply seq 2
```

With NETKEY, things look a bit different:

```
# tcpdump -n -i eth0
    00:08:15.311865 IP 193.110.157.131 > 205.150.200.209: ESP(spi=0xc7fb9fab,seq=0xb)
    00:08:16.227426 IP 205.150.200.209 > 193.110.157.131: ESP(spi=0x55b8f8aa,seq=0x6)
    00:08:16.227426 IP 205.150.200.209 > 193.110.157.131: icmp 64: echo reply seq 6
    00:08:16.311724 IP 193.110.157.131 > 205.150.200.209: ESP(spi=0xc7fb9fab,seq=0xc)
    00:08:17.275456 IP 205.150.200.209 > 193.110.157.131: ESP(spi=0x55b8f8aa,seq=0x7)
    00:08:17.275456 IP 205.150.200.209 > 193.110.157.131: icmp 64: echo reply seq 7
    00:08:17.311578 IP 193.110.157.131 > 205.150.200.209: ESP(spi=0xc7fb9fab,seq=0xd)
```

The unencrypted packet is caught and encrypted before it hits the Ethernet, so tcpdump only sees the encrypted packet going out. For the incoming packet, tcpdump first sees the encrypted packet coming in, and then it sees the same packet again, but in unencrypted form. This is because the NETKEY stack grabs the packet after it has been received (and seen by tcpdump), decrypts it, and then puts it back in the incoming packet stream, so tcpdump sees this packet too. If you used tcpdump on a machine further down the line, you would only see encrypted packets.

When using NETKEY, running tcpdump on the endpoint will give confusing results. To resolve this, run tcpdump on a router between the two IPsec endpoints, or hook up the endpoint to a hub, and attach another machine to the same hub and run tcpdump on that second machine.

Connecting Subnets Through an IPsec Connection

Now that we have our first host-to-host tunnel running, we can attempt to set up a subnet-to-subnet tunnel, which you'll find to be just as easy. The following example connection, when installed and activated on both West and East, will create a VPN tunnel between the networks Sunrise and Sunset:

```
conn sunset-sunrise
    left=193.110.157.131
    leftsubnet=193.111.228.0/24
    right=205.150.200.209
```

```
rightsubnet=192.0.2.0/24
leftrsasigkey=0sAQ43A1....
rightrsasigkey=0sAQfP63....
auto=start
```

Remember that we are now abbreviating the key entries; in your file they will be the same as before, covering four lines. Also remember that to set up this new connection, you can edit the config file while Openswan is still running, and run the following command to activate it:

 # ipsec auto --add sunset-sunrise

The `eroute` command will now show two tunnels:

```
# ipsec eroute
  5  193.110.157.131/32  ->  205.150.200.209/32  => tun0x109a@205.150.200.209
  0  193.111.228.0/24 ->  192.0.2.0/24    => tun0x109b@205.150.200.209
```

One is our host-to-host tunnel from West to East, and the other is our new subnet-to-subnet tunnel from Sunrise to Sunset.

Testing Subnet Connections

Testing a subnet-to-subnet connection is a little bit trickier than testing a host-to-host connection. West has two IP addresses. On its external network interface it has the IP address 193.110.157.131, which is part of our host-to-host tunnel. On its internal network interface it has the IP address 193.111.228.1.

The question you have to ask is, "If I try to ping 192.0.2.13 from West, which IP address is it going to use?" Because if it is going to come from 193.110.157.131, the ping will fail, as there is no IPsec tunnel from 193.110.157.131 to 192.0.2.0/24. If it picked our internal address of 193.111.228.1, it would work, since that is covered by the policies of our subnet-to-subnet tunnel.

Unfortunately for us in this case, the ping will fail. The Linux kernel will automatically pick the closest IP address and use that as its source for the outgoing packet. On NETKEY, such packets will be dropped by the SPD's firewall in the IPsec stack. KLIPS, on the other hand, does not play firewall. It will allow this packet through, since it doesn't match any of its IPsec policies. The unencrypted packet would be sent onwards, and would likely be dropped by the next machine, which does not have a route for 192.0.2.0/24.

Testing Properly

If you can, the easiest method to test the subnet-to-subnet tunnel is to just walk over to a host in the Sunset LAN, for example 193.111.228.13, and ping a machine in the Sunrise LAN, for example 192.0.2.13. But in practice, a lot of this work is done remotely, and one cannot easily walk over to a machine in the other LAN.

The alternative is to specify which source address to use on our outgoing test packets. After all, the internal IP address of our gateway is part of the subnet range we just connected through an IPsec connection. Whether you can do this depends on the application, but `ping`, `mtr`, and `traceroute` all allow this. For example, on West we can ping a host in the Sunrise LAN, using West's own IP address from the Sunset LAN:

```
# ping -I 193.111.228.1 192.0.2.13
```
PING sunrise-13.testbed.xelerance.net (192.0.2.13) from 193.111.228.1 : 56(84) bytes of data.
64 bytes from sunrise-13.testbed.xelerance.net (192.0.2.13): icmp_seq=1 ttl=64 time=136.9 ms

This time we have created a packet on West with source address 193.111.228.1 and destination address 192.0.2.13. This packet now falls under the definition of our Sunset-Sunrise IPsec tunnel, so the packets sent and received will properly travel back and forth through the IPsec tunnel.

Encrypting the Host and the Network Behind It

Usually, when you connect two LANs, you also want the two gateways to talk to each other. Since the gateways have an IP address in the LAN, you would also expect that defining a single subnet-to-subnet IPsec tunnel would be enough. As we have seen though, since the gateways use their external IP address to communicate to the outside, these gateways cannot easily initiate connections across the VPN. Responding usually is not a problem, as in that case the gateway's internal IP address is specifically targeted, and thus part of the IPsec tunnel. There are two ways to address this issue.

Employing Advanced Routing

The first approach is to trick the Linux kernel to always use the internal IP address, even when talking to the other end's remote IP address (unless it is an IPsec packet). This can be accomplished with advanced routing on West:

```
# ip route add 205.150.200.209 via 193.110.157.82 src 193.111.228.1
```

This tells West's kernel that if a packet for 205.150.200.209 is created on West, do not use the *closest IP address*, but use 193.111.228.1 instead. Of course, you will need a similar rule on East for 193.110.157.131. The above ip route command is automatically executed for you if you use the leftsourceip= or rightsourceip= option, as in this example:

```
conn sunset-sunrise
    left=193.110.157.131
    leftsubnet=193.111.228.0/24
    leftsourceip=193.111.228.1
    right=205.150.200.209
    rightsubnet=192.0.2.0/24
    rightsourceip=192.0.2.1
    leftrsasigkey=0sAQ43A1....
    rightrsasigkey=0sAQfP63....
    auto=start
```

Creating More Tunnels

The second approach might be easier: just create another two IPsec tunnels. One goes from West to Sunrise, and the other from East to Sunset. It might not seem very elegant to have a total of four IPsec tunnels to encrypt all traffic between two subnets and their gateways, but it is the easiest to configure. For instance, the West-Sunrise IPsec tunnel would look like this:

```
conn west-sunrise
    left=193.110.157.131
    # leftsubnet=193.111.228.0/24 is not used now
    right=205.150.200.209
    rightsubnet=192.0.2.0/24
    leftrsasigkey=0sAQ43A1....
    rightrsasigkey=0sAQfP63....
    auto=start
```

Avoiding Duplication

As a general rule, you should avoid duplicating information on different computers, if only to make it easier to change information when necessary. The host-to-host connection between West and East and the subnet-to-subnet connection between Sunset and Sunrise are almost identical. The only differences are the subnet= lines. There is a way to avoid this duplication.

The Also Keyword

We can write two similar connections to avoid repeating information with the also= keyword:

```
conn sunset-sunrise
    leftsubnet=193.111.228.0/24
    rightsubnet=192.0.2.0/24
    also=west-east

conn west-east
    left=193.110.157.131
    right=205.150.200.209
    leftrsasigkey=0sAQ....
    rightrsasigkey=0sAQ....
    auto=start
```

Unfortunately, due to how the parser works, you have to put all the sections referenced by an also= statement *below* the connections that include such an also= statement, even though it might seem more logical to place them in the reverse order.

KLIPS and the ipsecX Interfaces

If you are using KLIPS, you are likely using it because you prefer to have the virtual interfaces. These ipsecx interfaces are configured in the setup section with the interfaces= line. This line is ignored when using NETKEY. If the interfaces line is missing, it will have the same effect as:

```
interfaces=%defaultroute
```

This means that one virtual interface (ipsec0) will be created, and it will be bound to the interface that currently has defaultroute pointing to it. After all, it is most likely that IPsec is to be used to communicate with the outside world. If this is not the case, of if you want to use IPsec on multiple physical interfaces, this should be specified explicitly:

```
interfaces="ipsec0=eth0 ipsec1=ppp0 ipsec2=eth1 ipsec3=eth0:1"
```

This line creates four ipsecN interfaces, which are attached to eth0, ppp0, eth1, and eth0:1. This last entry is an **IP alias**, and is treated as a physical interface.

> Often people first try out KLIPS in a test environment that has no internet connectivity, and thus often no default route. In such a case, the interfaces= line should also be set explicitly.

Pre-Shared Keys (PSKs)

Sometimes you will need to connect Openswan to a device that cannot deal with RSA keys. When a VPN connection to such a device needs to be made, Openswan can use the PSK method. Imagine East is such a device. First, we would add the PSK to `ipsec.secrets`:

```
193.110.157.131 205.150.200.209 : PSK "secret shared by two hosts"
```

Then we set our West-East connection to use the PSK:

```
conn west-east
    left=193.110.157.131
    right=205.150.200.209
    authby=secret
    auto=start
```

Note that to use many PSK connections, for example if you have a lot of PSK-only network devices out in the field, you could put the `authby=secret` line in the conn `%default` section, and remove it from all the separate conn definitions.

Proper Secrets

Of course, using secret or any other human-readable word or phrase as a PSK is extremely insecure. Instead, the PSK should be generated from purely random characters. Since most vendors allow no more than 48 characters in base64 format, the following command would create a key as long as possible yet still compatible with all IP devices:

```
# openssl rand -base64 48
```

If the `openssl` command is not available, for instance if you are using some tiny Linux distribution on an embedded device, you can use the following, slightly less secure method:

```
# dd if=/dev/random count=256 bs=1 | md5sum
```

Note that this is not the same as using a 32-bit random string, since the output of `md5sum` is limited to hexadecimal characters, but it is far better than using an English word or phrase. If the `md5sum` command is also not available on your machine, then you might want to generate the random key elsewhere, and copy and paste the key onto the device.

> If you absolutely have to use PSK, please remember to regularly change the PSK for your VPN tunnels!

Dynamic IP Addresses

In our examples so far, we have assumed that the IP addresses of the IPsec endpoints are known and do not change. This is not always the case, though often the VPN server at the office will be static, and only the connecting clients will use various unknown IP addresses.

Hostnames

First, you could use a fully qualified domain name (FQDN) instead of an IP address. This way, if one endpoint changes IP address, as long as the DNS is changed, changes on all the connecting peers will not be necessary. Even though DNS is not secure, and anyone can spoof DNS answers, it will suffice for our use here, because all our peers have already exchanged their public RSA key or PSK. Even if some attacker spoofs the DNS, no information could leak, because the IPsec tunnel to the rogue endpoint would never get established. It is missing vital credentials—either the private RSA key or the PSK. So we can safely use:

```
left=west.testbed.xelerance.net
right=east.testbed.xelerance.net
```

Openswan would automatically resolve these DNS names to IP addresses when a connection is started. This method can be used with free DNS services, such as DynDNS.org.

Roadwarriors

While FQDNs are appropriate for infrequently changing IP addresses, it does not really address the problem of frequent IP address changes, such as in the case of a traveling laptop. We do not want to change some DNS entry every time we turn on our laptop. The issue we need to solve here is how to properly recognize an incoming, unknown IP address as our roadwarrior. This can be done by explicitly setting the ID for a connection. So far, we have not used the `leftid=` and `rightid=` option, and Openswan has automatically set our unused ID to the IP address. We can, however, choose to set it to something else. And remember, we only need to *tell* the other end who we are, not *prove* it. The security of the connection still depends on both ends having inside information about the other party, in the form of a public RSA key or a PSK.

On West, we would use:

```
left=west.testbed.xelerance.net
right=%any
rightid=@east
```

On East, we would use:

```
right=west.testbe.xelerance.net
left=%defaultroute
leftid=@east
```

When East, coming from an unknown IP address, initiates a connection to West, the two will first go through Phase 1 of the IKE negotiation. This gives them privacy. Then East will send its ID @east to West, which can then select the proper credentials (such as RSA key) for communicating to East, and finish Phase 2. Only the real East could read (and write) the required encryption.

> The `%any` keyword is used to denote an unknown incoming IP address. The `%defaultroute` keyword is used to denote the current IP address we have as our outgoing IP address.

Due to the difference with `%any` and `%defaultroute`, you can't just copy such a connection definition from one end to the other. You will have to change `%any` to `%defaultroute`. It is also recommended to use left parameters for the local side of roadwarriors.

For clarity, one could also switch West to use a `leftid=` when `rightid=` is used, though this is technically not necessary.

The @ symbol prevents Openswan from doing a DNS lookup on the string. This is to differentiate the string "west.testbed.xelerance.net" from the hostname west.testbed.xelerance.net. A hostname would be resolved to an IP address, which would then be used to determine the proper connection, which is not what we intend to happen here in our roadwarrior example.

Although this mechanism would allow both ends to be on dynamic IP, in practice there is the fundamental problem that neither party would know where to find the other.

> The `right=%any` and `left=%defaultroute` settings cannot be used in the same connection definition. Openswan would be unable to orient this connection and would not be able to determine whether it is supposed to be left or right, even though it could possibly deduce this from the known RSA keys.

Multiple Roadwarrior Connections

This mechanism also allows for multiple connections. For instance, if we want a connection from North (also on dynamic IP) to West, we could set up the following connections:

```
conn west-east
    left=west.testbed.xelerance.net
    right=%any
    rightid=@east
    leftrsasigkey=0sAQQED1....
    rightrsasigkey=0sAQV7yV....
    auto=add

conn west-north
    left=west.testbed.xelerance.net
    right=%any
    rightid=@north
    leftrsasigkey=0sAQQED1....
    rightrsasigkey=0sAQ5GP....
    auto=add
```

Note that the `rightrsasigkey=` settings for these two entries are different. The first would contain East's public RSA key, and the second connection would contain North's public RSA key.

Dynamic IP and PSKs

There is an additional problem with PSKs that constitutes another reason not to use them. Our examples stored the PSKs based on the IP addresses of both endpoints. We can use hostnames instead of IP addresses, but how do we handle secrets and dynamic IP addresses for roadwarriors? Well, we can use the %any keyword to specify the PSK in `ipsec.secrets`:

```
193.110.158.81 %any : PSK "the passphrase"
```

While this works, we cannot use multiple secret entries with %any. We cannot try a bunch of PSKs one after the other for each packet, and we cannot use the `rightid=` to distinguish connections and pick a different PSK either. The server (West) needs to look up the secret before it can decode the client's payload containing that ID, a limitation of the current Main Mode protocol. The only way out of this dilemma is a bad one—give all the roadwarriors the same secret.

We strongly discourage the use of one secret for a group of connections, and recommend not using PSKs with roadwarriors wherever possible. Windows and Mac OS X roadwarriors can use X.509, although if you need to support Apple roadwarriors, PSK is often the only way.

PSK and NAT

One question that is often asked is how to use PSK with dynamic IP addresses when NAT is also involved, sometimes even with port forwarding or IPsec passthrough. While you might get it to work, it will be a long painful experience. PSKs without IDs or public keys are identified based on the IP address. If the address is in any kind of way dynamic or rewritten, or port forwarded, you are asking for a lot of trouble. One thing to be aware of, if trying this type of solution in spite of the warnings, is that the file `ipsec.secrets` has no left-and-right-style mirroring like `ipsec.conf` because it is just too dangerous to mix up the PSKs of various connections.

Mixing PSK and RSA

In the past, there have been problems with Openswan correctly identifying different PSK- and RSA-based connections using the %any keyword. This was due to Openswan finding out too late what kind of connection was being requested. The result was that you could only have one connection with %any, not two or more.

This problem has been partially fixed in Openswan 2.3.1. You can now have multiple RSA connections with %any, but still only one PSK connection with %any.

Connection Management

For small VPN systems, restarting the entire Openswan subsystem is not a problem. For larger systems with production tunnels though, it's obviously not an option. Openswan allows you to change connection definitions, remove them, or add new ones just by editing `ipsec.conf` or its include files. You can then use the `ipsec auto` command to activate your changes without the need to completely restart Openswan.

Command	Description
`ipsec auto --add newconnection`	Load a new connection into Openswan.
`ipsec auto --delete connection`	Remove a connection from Openswan. If active it will first close the connection.
`ipsec auto --up connection`	Initiate a loaded connection.
`ipsec auto --down connection`	Tear the current IPsec tunnel down.
`ipsec auto --replace connection`	The equivalent to sequentially run down, delete, and add.
`ipsec auto -status`	Show a status report about connections.

To first delete, and then add a connection, you can use --replace. If a connection is active, delete will bring it down before deletion, thereby notifying the other end.

The auto= option is ignored when using these commands explicitly, otherwise one could never change a connection from its default state. This means one can bring up a connection that has auto=ignore. It also means that to load and activate a connection, you have to use both add and up, even if auto=start is defined for the connection.

> Be sure to delete a connection before removing it from ipsec.conf, otherwise you will not be able to get rid of the tunnel without a full restart, since the --delete command will no longer be able to find the removed connection section.

If you want to see only active tunnels, ipsec eroute might be a more convenient command than the status command. The status command will provide a lot more information, however. Another command that can be used is ipsec look.

If you change ipsec.secrets, you must tell Openswan to re-read the secrets using:

```
# ipsec auto --rereadsecrets
```

or you can play safe and issue:

```
# ipsec auto --rereadall
```

Subnet Extrusion

With IPsec tunnels, we can do more than just connect two existing subnets with each other. We can also *move* a subnet, or a part of a subnet, through an IPsec tunnel to another location. This is called **subnet extrusion**, as shown in the diagram below:

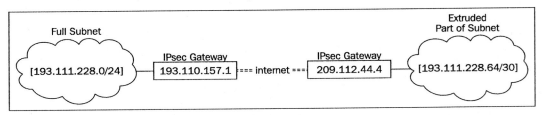

In this figure, packets for 193.111.228.64/30 that end up on 193.110.157.1 will now be sent further via IPsec to 209.112.44.4. Response packets travel back the same way and once they reach 193.110.157.1 will be sent plaintext onto the subnet.

Imagine we want to move a small part of Sunset, the first 64 addresses, to appear at East. We would use the following conn definition:

```
conn sunset-extrude
    left=193.110.157.131
    leftsubnet=0.0.0.0/0
    leftrsasigkey=0sAQ1234....
    right=205.150.200.209
    rightsubnet=193.111.228.0/26
    rightrsasigkey=0sAQ5678....
    auto=start
```

The example uses RSA, but you can also use PSK if you want to. The important option is to define the leftsubnet= as the entire Internet. This will cause all packets on East with a source address in the righsubnet= range, and destination anywhere on the net, to be sent over the tunnel to West, where they are sent on into the real world. Packets from elsewhere to the sunset-extrude subnet would be sent through regular routing to West, which will then send the packets over the IPsec tunnel to East.

With KLIPS, these packets are caught by a special route entry into the ipsecN device. In this case, a route entry for 193.111.228.0/26 into an ipsec device would be added on West. For East it is a little bit more complex, as we need to catch all packets. For this we cannot use a route of 0.0.0.0/0 into the ipsec0 device, because such a route already exists for the regular physical device (for example eth0). The trick Openswan uses is to split the *whole* Internet into two parts, 0.0.0.0/1 and 128.0.0.0/1, and route those two subnets, which together describe the entire internet, into the ipsec0 device. This trick works because these routes are more specific than the normal default route.

With NETKEY, you will not see any special routes.

Several people use this type of setup to get more public IP addresses on their home ADSL network. Of course, one should realize that all packets to and from such a subnet will first travel to West and then to East, so if West has limited uplink capacity, this might be a problem, even if East has enough bandwidth. Though one could theoretically send the packets from East outside the IPsec tunnel, straight onto the Internet, this might be blocked by some ISPs. Most ISPs block packets with a source address that is not their own. And some ISPs check the BGP routing table and could decide these are spoofed packets. Additionally, asymmetric links are always a bit more problematic than symmetrical links, so even if the packets make it, it might still be better to first send them back to West.

You can even combine this with NAT. If you use sunset-extrude's IP behind a NAT gateway with some single ADSL IP address on it, all the packets that you do not send back through the tunnel will get translated by the NAT gateway and hit the Internet from East. This can be useful for large transfers of public data from a fixed IP address for which you don't need the encryption per se, such as an internet radio station, or a big public file repository site. With KLIPS, you can just use a host route that is more specific to point to your default outgoing interface, for instance to exclude ftp.openswan.org from your ADSL (PPTP-based) link, you could use:

```
# route add -host ftp.openswan.org gw yourdefaultgw dev ppp0
```

Since this route is more specific than the route into the ipsecN device, these packets would not be sent through the VPN tunnel, and would be translated by the NAT rules as if no IPsec setup existed. On NETKEY you would have to define a special passthrough conn:

```
conn pass-ftp.openswan.org
    left=205.150.200.209
    leftsubnet=193.111.228.0/64
    right=ftp.openswan.org
    type=passthrough
    authby=never
```

One can also use right=%any with a rightsubnet= to exclude a range of IP addresses.

NAT Traversal

Before we enable NAT traversal, let us remind you of a few common problems with NAT traversal that cannot be prevented.

The most important issue is that if you are adding NAT traversal to a VPN connection for an office network that is on a private IP space, you cannot support remote clients on that same private IP space. So if you use 10.0.1.0/24 at the office, and your roadwarrior is behind ADSL on 10.0.1.2, the IPsec tunnel will fail. An IP address cannot be at both endpoints at once.

> IP ranges that are used as a subnet must be excluded from NAT-Traversal usage. It is very important to pick good and small ranges for both ends. For instance, 192.168.0.0/16 is often used by ADSL modems. 10.0.0.0/8 is also frequently used. These would be poor choices for a company network IP range. Much better choices would be 10.145.1.0/24 or something similarly random. If there is an IP conflict, it is possible to do some NAT on them (outside the VPN tunnel, not inside!) but it might turn out to be more costly and problematic than just renumbering one end, especially if this is an end user's home network.

Another implication of this is that you should make your office network reasonably small. Do not pick 10.0.0.0/8 because you will be causing a huge overlap with all the home networks that you want to connect to you. Of course, this already applies to office-to-office networks as well. If you have a few hundred offices, you should pick their network ranges wisely. For instance, if you have a four digit shop number that is used internally, number the networks according to those unique digits, for instance 10.ab.cd.0/24 where abcd is the branch office number.

```
config setup
    interfaces=%defaultroute
    # klipsdebug=none
    # plutodebug=control
    nat_traversal=yes
    virtual_private=%v4:10.0.0.0/8,%v4:192.168.0.0/16,%v4:!10.3.4.0/24
    # keep_alive=20

conn sunset-roadwarrior
    left=193.110.157.131
    leftsubnet=10.3.4.0/24
    leftrsasigkey=0sAQ....
    right=%any
    rightsubnet=vhost:%no,%priv
    rightrsasigkey=0sAQ....
    auto=start
```

So first we enable NAT-T support for Openswan with `nat_traversal=yes`. Remember that NAT-T requires kernel-level support. NETKEY supports NAT-T, but for KLIPS, you must apply the NAT-T patch.

Next, we specify which IP ranges may occur behind a NAT device. In the case above, we allow the 10.0.0.0/8 and 192.168.0.0/16 ranges. The last entry, which uses an ! symbol to mean *not*, excludes the range 10.3.4.0/24 from being a valid range, since that is the range used for Sunset's LAN in our example.

When a connection using NAT-T is detected, Openswan will send **keep alive** packets to prevent the NAT router from deleting the connection as unused. These packets are sent every 20 seconds, but this behavior can be changed using the keep_alive= option.

In this connection definition, a new line appears specifying rightsubnet=. This entry is going to match the internal IP address of the roadwarrior in a /32 subnet. The %priv contains the ranges we put in our global virtual_private range. The %no is there to signify the subnet might not be specified in all cases. This is to ensure our roadwarrior can still connect when it is not behind a NAT router. After all, when NAT-T is not triggered, no rightsubnet= would be received for that connection.

For roadwarriors to work from public IPs as well as from behind NAT, you must specify rightsubnet=vhost:%no,%priv

---

Most often, this type of connection will be used not for just one roadwarrior connection, but for many different ones. They will not all be using the same RSA key. Though you could make multiple connections of these types, differentiating each with its rightid= line, there is a better way to do this using X.509 Certificates. We will discuss these in the next chapter.

Deprecated Syntax

Openswan still supports an older format for specifying NAT-related options using the subnetwithin= syntax. This code was part of the X.509 patch and accomplishes the same as the vhost= syntax, but has less flexibility. It will likely be removed in the future, so we do not recommend using this syntax.

Confirming a Functional NAT-T

If you start Openswan and the kernel supports NAT-T, you will receive a message similar to:

```
Aug 30 23:15:08 nsavax pluto[22096]: Starting Pluto (Openswan Version 2.1.5 X.509-1.4.8-1
PLUTO_USES_KEYRR)
Aug 30 23:15:08 nsavax pluto[22096]: including NAT-Traversal patch (Version 0.6c)
```

If your kernel does not support NAT-Traversal, you will see:

```
Aug 30 23:17:01 nsavax pluto[5862]: NAT-Traversal: ESPINUDP(1) not supported by kernel --
NAT-T disabled
```

If the Openswan userland (pluto) supports NAT-T but it has not been enabled in /etc/ipsec.conf, you will see a message similar to:

```
Aug 30 22:53:19 nsavax pluto[4818]:   including NAT-Traversal patch (Version 0.6c) [disabled]
```

You can further confirm that NAT-Traversal is enabled and working by checking whether the host is listening on UDP ports 4500 (special NAT-T IKE). This can be done with the netstat command:

```
# netstat -uln
    Active Internet connections (only servers)
    Proto    Recv-Q  Send-Q  Local Address     Foreign Address  State
    udp 0        0          127.0.0.1:4500    0.0.0.0:*
```

udp 0	0	193.110.57.17:4500	0.0.0.0:*
udp 0	0	193.110.157.17:4500	0.0.0.0:*
udp 0	0	127.0.0.1:500	0.0.0.0:*
udp 0	0	193.110.57.17:500	0.0.0.0:*
udp 0	0	193.110.157.17:500	0.0.0.0:*
udp 0	0	::1:500	:::*

You can see both the regular IKE port (on UDP 500) and the NAT-T IKE port (on UDP 4500). The last entry shows an IPv6 localhost address.

Dead Peer Detection

Sometimes a VPN tunnel may die without detection, for example if one of the two peers crashes and reboots. If you add NAT and NAT-T into this picture, it becomes even more complex. If some IPsec tunnel has very low traffic, a NAT device in the middle might decide this connection has gone away, and drop its translation entry for it. Now both peers think the IPsec connection is up, but when one of them tries to send a packet, it finds the VPN has silently vanished.

With unencrypted connections, such connections would simply fail on their first packet, since the remote host would send an ICMP message about the (for the remote end) unknown connection.

With IPsec this becomes harder, as the peer that didn't get rebooted cannot just trust any unencrypted ICMP message from the other end.

With the uniqueid=yes option set, which is the default for Openswan, the rebooted end can establish a new tunnel, and since all tunnels are considered unique, the stable end of this connection will terminate the old connection when it establishes the new connection. Unfortunately, not all hardware vendors act in the same way. Some may plainly refuse to speak unencrypted to the rebooted peer to even allow it to establish a new connection until the current keylife has reached its end, and rekeying that connection has failed. Others might want to find out a tunnel is dead before any traffic is lost, such as an IPsec connection for a payment terminal. There is hardly any traffic, but once there is, you really want the tunnel to work and not find out at the most awkward time that the tunnel is indeed down. DPD makes this possible.

DPD also has the additional benefit of preventing NAT timeout, since the connection isn't idle for long periods due to the DPD testing packets.

Another use for DPD is to allow large-scale VPN servers to kill off VPN connections for which the other end has vanished. Common scenarios for this include a user accidentally pulling the phone line out of their laptop, a wireless network that just lost its connection, or a GPRS connection failure when hopping between GSM cells. There are many reasons why a connection can suddenly stop uncleanly without the other end knowing that you have dropped off the network. Especially for big VPN servers, you do not want to have too many of these dead connections hanging around.

This is of course a classic problem, and has been solved before. Just send a **keep alive** packet once in a while when there is no other traffic. If no response is received for a certain time, the remote peer is considered dead and the connection is torn down.

Though purists find this a bad protocol design and will call these packets **make deads** because in some scenarios these keep alive packets can kill a perfectly fine connection if the packets are lost somehow. One very common scenario is one where the uplink is congested, and some packet loss is bound to happen. If the packets dropped because of the congestion happen to be the keep alive packets, the entire connection will soon find itself terminated.

> Do not use Dead Peer Detection on congested links.

DPD Works Both Ways

It is important to realize that DPD is not the same as other **keep alive** packets. If both IPsec peers have announced their DPD capability, it does not mean that DPD is activated. The choice of whether a certain connection should have DPD protection enabled is made independently by both ends. The big VPN gateway for instance can decide it wants to know about these clients, but it does not need to know this every 5 minutes. It could decide to check client connections every 3 hours. While for our cash terminal, it might be decided the IPsec connection is so important that it warrants a DPD check every 30 seconds.

It can also be that one of the two ends doesn't care about whether the other end goes away (for instance a roadwarrior). Therefore, each end can decide if and how often it wants to send DPD packets. The only rule for all is that if you announce (through the VendorID) that you are capable of DPD, then you *must* answer all DPD packets from the other end, even if you yourself do not care about DPD and do not send any DPD probes.

Configuring DPD

Openswan always announces its DPD capability, and will always respond to DPD requests from remote peers. It does not enable sending DPD requests by default. If you are interested in sending DPD requests, the following parameters need to be added to the connection:

```
dpddelay=30
dpdtimeout=120
dpdaction=hold
```

The example lists the default values. For static tunnels, dpdaction= should be set to hold or restart. Hold will ensure no packets will flow in the clear until the tunnel comes back online. Restart will cause the connection to be restarted, as if you had typed ipsec auto -up connname. For roadwarriors, you want to use a dpdaction=clear on the server end to forget this entire connection, since roadwarriors might be gone for long periods of time and show up on a different IP address later.

You will see two extra messages in the log files confirming the other end supports DPD when the IPsec connection establishes:

```
Sep 22 11:59:02 roadwarrior pluto[15377]: "sunset-rw" #10: initiating Main
Mode
Sep 22 11:59:02 roadwarrior pluto[15377]: "sunset-rw" #10: received Vendor ID
payload [Dead Peer Detection]
Sep 22 11:59:02 roadwarrior pluto[15377]: "sunset-rw" #10: transition from
state STATE_MAIN_I1 to state STATE_MAIN_I2
Sep 22 11:59:02 roadwarrior pluto[15377]: "sunset-rw" #10: transition from
```

```
state STATE_MAIN_I2 to state STATE_MAIN_I3
Sep 22 11:59:02 roadwarrior pluto[15377]: "sunset-rw" #10: Peer ID is ID_FQDN:
'@roadwarrior'
Sep 22 11:59:02 roadwarrior pluto[15377]: "sunset-rw" #10: transition from
state STATE_MAIN_I3 to state STATE_MAIN_I4
Sep 22 11:59:02 roadwarrior pluto[15377]: "sunset-rw" #10: ISAKMP SA
established
Sep 22 11:59:02 roadwarrior pluto[15377]: "sunset-rw" #11: initiating Quick
Mode RSASIG+ENCRYPT+TUNNEL+PFS+UP {using isakmp#10}
Sep 22 11:59:03 roadwarrior pluto[15377]: "sunset-rw" #11: Dead Peer Detection
(RFC 3706) enabled
Sep 22 11:59:03 roadwarrior pluto[15377]: "sunset-rw" #11: transition from
state STATE_QUICK_I1 to state STATE_QUICK_I2
Sep 22 11:59:03 roadwarrior pluto[15377]: "sunset-rw" #11: sent QI2, IPsec SA
established {ESP=>0x2cc3429d <0xb2004c39}
```

And every 30 seconds, you will see DPD IKE packets:

```
12:36:32.636308 194.109.83.36.isakmp > 193.110.157.131.isakmp: isakmp: phase
2/others ? inf[E]: [|hash] (DF)
12:36:32.636721 193.110.157.131.isakmp > 194.109.83.36.isakmp: isakmp: phase
2/others ? inf[E]: [|hash] (DF)
12:37:02.633520 193.110.157.131.isakmp > 194.109.83.36.isakmp: isakmp: phase
2/others ? inf[E]: [|hash] (DF)
12:37:02.642014 194.109.83.36.isakmp > 193.110.157.131.isakmp: isakmp: phase
2/others ? inf[E]: [|hash] (DF)
12:37:02.642365 193.110.157.131.isakmp > 194.109.83.36.isakmp: isakmp: phase
2/others ? inf[E]: [|hash] (DF)
12:37:02.644539 194.109.83.36.isakmp > 193.110.157.131.isakmp: isakmp: phase
2/others ? inf[E]: [|hash] (DF)
12:37:32.649015 194.109.83.36.isakmp > 193.110.157.131.isakmp: isakmp: phase
2/others ? inf[E]: [|hash] (DF)
12:37:32.649370 193.110.157.131.isakmp > 194.109.83.36.isakmp: isakmp: phase
2/others ? inf[E]: [|hash] (DF)
```

Notice how the first exchange was initiated by the Roadwarrior, while the second exchange was initiated by West. This is the result of adding the DPD parameters to both sides of the connection, and using the same (default) parameters. To avoid this, you can pick a different dpddelay= setting, or you could decide not to configure DPD on the roadwarrior.

Buggy Cisco Routers

There is a known bug in some Cisco routers, which send incorrect DPD packets with a broken rcookie in the **R_U_THERE** packet. Normally, these packets are dropped by Openswan, and a message is logged:

```
Sep 22 13:43:05 dev pluto[1888]: "to-cisco" #23: R_U_THERE_ACK has invalid
rcookie
Sep 22 13:43:05 dev pluto[1888]: "to-cisco" #23: sending notification
INVALID_COOKIE to 1.2.3.4:500
```

And after the time specified in dpdtimeout=, the connection will be torn down:

```
Sep 22 13:43:07 dev pluto[1888]: "to-cisco" #23: DPD: No response from peer -
declaring peer dead
Sep 22 13:43:07 dev pluto[1888]: "to-cisco" #27: deleting state
(STATE_QUICK_I2)
Sep 22 13:43:07 dev pluto[1888]: "to-cisco" #26: deleting state
(STATE_QUICK_I1)
Sep 22 13:43:07 dev pluto[1888]: "to-cisco" #23: deleting state
(STATE_MAIN_I4)
```

Older versions of Openswan had a workaround for this that disabled the rcookie verification code, and blindly accepted all rcookies. This workaround was enabled by defining **APPLY_CRISCO** in programs/pluto/dpd.c before compiling Pluto. As of Openswan 2.3.1, this define is removed and the code is always enabled. It has been extended to work around a different, but similar, bug in the Clavister VPN client. Accepting these bad cookies is strangely enough also what the RFC dictates as the correct behavior towards these broken packets.

Ciphers and Algorithms

Normally Openswan proposes all the ciphers and algorithms it supports, using a hardcoded preference. You can force which ciphers and algorithms to propose, and in which order to propose them, per connection. This can be useful for various reasons. The remote could have a buggy cipher implementation that would be otherwise selected. The remote could be a low-CPU appliance, and you wish to reduce the crypto strength. Some remotes do not respond at all after the first proposal, and you need to send the exact proposal for the remote as the first suggestion. Depending on the ciphers and algorithms that your version of Openswan and kernel support, you can define them using ike= and esp= lines. Ciphers and algorithms can either come from the KLIPS code or from the Linux CryptoAPI code. If a cipher or algorithm is available from KLIPS, it will be used instead of the CryptoAPI version.

You can use the following command to see what ciphers and algorithms are supported and loaded:

```
# ipsec auto --status
```

Using ike= to Specify Phase 1 Parameters

The ike= option is used to tune the IKE negotiation. This is sometimes called **Phase 1 encryption** on other devices. The esp= option is used to tune the ESP parameters for the kernel. This is sometimes called **Phase 2 encryption** on other devices. For example:

```
ike="3des-sha1-96,aes-md5-96"
```

In this example, Openswan will first propose 3DES encryption with the SHA1 hashing algorithm of 96 bits. Then it will propose AES encryption with the MD5 hashing algorithm using 96 bits. No other proposals will be sent, or accepted. Sub-options can be specified using underscores, such as 3des_cbc.

> Older versions only accepted sha and not sha1. Since sha2 will become a standard in the near future, Openswan now uses sha1 everywhere, and any occurrence of sha is treated as sha1.

You can also force a Diffie-Hellman key size (dhgroup):

```
ike="aes128-sha1-modp1536"
```

Openswan does not support using DH group names such as dh2 or dh5. If you need to translate the DH group name to MODP syntax, use the following table, which shows DH groups according to RFC 3526:

DH group	MODP	remark
1	768	No longer supported in Openswan 2 unless compiled with USE_WEAKSTUFF=true
2	1024	
5	1536	
14	2048	Not yet supported by Openswan 2
16	4096	Not yet supported by Openswan 2
18	8192	Not yet supported by Openswan 2

If you are just interested in forcing the cipher, but not any of the algorithms, you can leave those out. For example to just allow AES, for instance because the device has limited CPU power, you can use:

```
ike="aes"
```

Any proposal with 3DES would no longer be accepted.

Not specifying an ike= line, as we have done throughout the book until now, is the same as allowing all combinations of acceptable ciphers, secure hashes and DH groups. Currently this means AES128 or 3DES as cipher, and MD5 or SHA1 as secure hash, and DH group 2 or 5.

> Older versions of Openswan supported the pfsgroup= option. This option is obsolete. Use the appropriate ike= and esp= options instead.

Using esp= to Specify Phase 2 Parameters

To tune the kernel ciphers, also called **Phase 2 encryption**, you can use the esp= option:

```
esp=aes256-sha1,aes128-sha1,3des-sha1
```

> Currently, you cannot specify MODP groups in Phase 2. The DH group from Phase 1 will be automatically used for Phase 2 as well.

Defaults and Strictness

Not defining an ike= or esp= line, as we have done up to know, means we offer and accept all supported ciphers and algorithms. Currently this means AES and 3DES in different modes, MD5 and SHA1, and DH groups 2 and 5.

As soon as you specify an ike= or esp= option, that option becomes an exclusive list, and no other options are proposed or accepted. Older versions used an exclamation mark (!) syntax at the end of the line to signify strictness. This is no longer necessary nor allowed.

Unsupported Ciphers and Algorithms

1DES (single DES) is **not** supported by default on Openswan, since this cipher is too weak to use in today's (or even yesterday's) world. Support for 1DES in Pluto needs to be enabled manually before compiling by enabling the -D 1DES option in programs/pluto/Makefile. You will need to change the USE_WEAKSTUFF= option to true in the file Makefile.inc. This will also enable support for the insecure Diffie Hellman dhgroup=1 (modp768). If you try to use a weak cipher or DH group without enabling USE_WEAKSTUFF, you will see an error similar to:

```
034 esp string error: found modp group id, but not supported, enc_alg="des",
auth_alg="sha1", modp="modp768"
```

> 1DES and DH group 1 (modp768) are too weak for today's processing power. 1DES can be broken in a matter of hours using special, but dirt cheap, hardware. 768 bit DH keys are also considered extremely insecure.

Sadly, there are still too many old Cisco routers out there that only allow for 1DES encryption, unless you buy some additional license. Those devices should really be replaced or upgraded. 1DES is simply not safe, and Openswan might remove 1DES support altogether in the near future. This is really an issue where you should insist **very strongly** to the remote party requesting 1DES that their solution is just unacceptable.

Aggressive Mode

Aggressive mode support, which was always part of Openswan 1, has now also been added to Openswan 2. However, the code is entirely different. One of the problems of aggressive mode is that to save that extra round of negotiation from Main Mode, you need to do a lot of expensive Diffie Hellman computing upon sending and receiving the first packet. However, that opens up the possibility of a trivial denial of service attack, by simply sending bogus aggressive mode packets.

Another side effect of aggressive mode is that you *must* get the IKE and ESP parameters right in your first proposal, since there is no additional room to negotiate. It has to be precisely right after the first packet exchange. The handling of the CPU-intensive tasks has been split off into a separate process called crypto_helper. Pluto can be told how many helper processes to start using the --nhelpers argument. You can also specify nhelpers= in the **config setup** section of the ipsec.conf file. A value of -1 disables the cryptographic helpers. If this option is not used, Pluto starts two helper processes per CPU. These helper processes get a lower priority than Pluto itself, so the effects of someone trying to flood the system with aggressive mode packets should be minimal. Yet there is another risk: aggressive mode is vulnerable to a brute force attack. Software such as ikecrack has implemented this attack.

> Avoid aggressive mode if at all possible.

You can enable aggressive mode per connection with the following option:

```
aggrmode=yes
```

> To ensure the correct parameters are sent in the first packet exchange, Openswan requires that you specify an appropriate ike= line whenever using aggressive mode.

XAUTH

XAUTH is a strange and difficult addition aimed at extending the IKE protocol to support other authorization schemes. It is usually needed for interoperability, but often systems using XAUTH also use other, often proprietary extensions to the IPsec protocol. Chances are high XAUTH will actually not help you reach a working solution. This is also the reason that XAUTH support has been added only very recently, and has not been tested very well: XAUTH support in Openswan is still very experimental.

An additional problem is that some features of XAUTH are actually dependent on other parts of the system, which can at times be incompatible. For instance encrypting and decrypting MD5 or DES passwords, for example from /etc/shadow, does not always seem to work among different systems, and using XAUTH to authenticate against the system's user database using PAM opens up another Pandora's box of problems.

XAUTH stands for Extended Authentication. It is important to realize that it is not an authentication scheme on its own, and is used in addition to another scheme, usually RSA keys or PSKs. XAUTH with PSKs is often called **group PSK**, since one PSK will be shared with many clients, who then use a user/password or, for example, a SecureID token as the extended authentication. In such a setup, the PSK is used only for Phase 1 authentication, and XAUTH is used to complete the Phase 2 authentication.

This immediately brings us to a very important problem. Since many clients are using the same group PSK for the server, if a single client is compromised, the entire group's PSK is also compromised. Though one might think this is not that important, since another layer of authentication is still needed, this is not entirely true. Anyone with the PSK can play *man in the middle* and act as the server. The client will happily supply its user/password or SecureID credentials and the rogue server will now be able to log in to the real server as a client. Openswan makes this matter slightly worse by only supporting one group PSK, forcing all clients to use a single shared secret.

Another problem with XAUTH is that it is often misconfigured in such a way that the connection will rekey. When rekeying happens, the user needs to supply the username and password (or SecureID number) again. Since Openswan has no way of querying the user for this, the connection will terminate. XAUTH connections should never require rekeying. Most Windows clients cache the username and password, either in memory or on disk.

One can combine XAUTH with RSA keys instead of PSKs, but since most software clients and hardware vendors do not support XAUTH with RSA, this would only work on an Openswan-to-Openswan interop, in which case one wouldn't need to support XAUTH at all, unless one believes in the additional security of an (easy to guess) user/password combination. Also, since most services behind the VPN, such as a network fileshare, email server access, or printer access, are probably already protected with a required username/password combination for when the user is connecting from the local LAN network, adding yet another user/password combination, which is likely to be the same one anyway, is not adding any security to the system as a whole.

Yet another problem with XAUTH is that it is often combined with Aggressive Mode, which is inherently dangerous.

XAUTH Gateway (Server Side)

To configure Openswan as an XAUTH server using a single group PSK for Phase 1, we need to add the PSK in the `ipsec.secrets` file and add XAUTH requirements to the connection. We will use East as XAUTH server and a roadwarrior as an XAUTH client (normally called **supplicant**).

First we configure East. In `ipsec.secrets` we add:

```
193.110.157.131 %any : PSK "secret"
```

Be aware that Pluto does not support automatic left and right swapping for `ipsec.secrets` as it does for `ipsec.conf`, as this would be extremely dangerous.

For XAUTH you do not use the IP address or %any. Instead you must use the **groupname**. A groupname is really just a PSK, but shared with others.

```
193.110.157.131 @groupname : PSK "secret"
```

Our `ipsec.conf` connection entry on the server becomes:

```
conn xauth-roadwarriors
    leftxauthserver=yes
    left=193.110.157.131
    right=%any
    rightid=@mygroupname
    rightxauthclient=yes
    auto=add
    authby=secret
```

XAUTH Client (Supplicant Side)

One important difference when using XAUTH on the client as compared to other types of connections is that it needs to be interactive: the user must type in their username and password. Therefore, these connections cannot be loaded using `auto=start`, and instead should just be added using `auto=add`, and manually started using `ipsec auto --up connectionname`.

This process can be automated using Pluto's `whack` command directly:

```
# ipsec whack --xauthname 'username' --xauthpass 'password' --name xauth-roadwarriors --initiate
```

Of course this is not recommended, since you will be storing the username and password for the XAUTH exchange unencrypted in some script. If such a laptop is stolen, the additional security from XAUTH over a plain PSK IPsec tunnel is moot.

A successful XAUTH exchange looks like this:

```
002 "xauth-roadwarriors" #1: initiating Main Mode
104 "xauth-roadwarriors" #1: STATE_MAIN_I1: initiate
003 "xauth-roadwarriors" #1: received Vendor ID payload [XAUTH]
002 "xauth-roadwarriors" #1: transition from state STATE_MAIN_I1 to state
STATE_MAIN_I2
```

```
106 "xauth-roadwarriors" #1: STATE_MAIN_I2: sent MI2, expecting MR2
002 "xauth-roadwarriors" #1: I did not send a certificate because I do not
have one.
002 "xauth-roadwarriors" #1: transition from state STATE_MAIN_I2 to state
STATE_MAIN_I3
108 "xauth-roadwarriors" #1: STATE_MAIN_I3: sent MI3, expecting MR3
002 "xauth-roadwarriors" #1: Main mode peer ID is ID_FQDN: '@groupname'
002 "xauth-roadwarriors" #1: transition from state STATE_MAIN_I3 to state
STATE_MAIN_I4
002 "xauth-roadwarriors" #1: ISAKMP SA established
004 "xauth-roadwarriors" #1: STATE_MAIN_I4: ISAKMP SA established
041 "xauth-roadwarriors" #1: xauth-roadwarriors prompt for Username:
040 "xauth-roadwarriors" #1: xauth-roadwarriors prompt for Password:
002 "xauth-roadwarriors" #1: XAUTH: Answering XAUTH challenge with
user='username'
002 "xauth-roadwarriors" #1: transition from state STATE_XAUTH_I0 to state
STATE_XAUTH_I1
002 "xauth-roadwarriors" #1: XAUTH client - awaiting CFG_set
004 "xauth-roadwarriors" #1: STATE_XAUTH_I1: XAUTH client - awaiting CFG_set
002 "xauth-roadwarriors" #1: XAUTH: Successfully Authenticated
002 "xauth-roadwarriors" #1: transition from state STATE_XAUTH_I0 to state
STATE_XAUTH_I1
002 "xauth-roadwarriors" #1: XAUTH client - awaiting CFG_set
004 "xauth-roadwarriors" #1: STATE_XAUTH_I1: XAUTH client - awaiting CFG_set
002 "xauth-roadwarriors" #2: initiating Quick Mode 002 "xauth-roadwarriors"
#2: transition from state STATE_QUICK_I1 to state STATE_QUICK_I2
002 "xauth-roadwarriors" #2: sent QI2, IPsec SA established
004 "xauth-roadwarriors" #2: STATE_QUICK_I2: sent QI2, IPsec SA established
```

Fine Tuning

Sometimes it can be necessary to slightly alter the kind of keys, algorithms, ciphers, or lifetimes used for various components of the cryptographic systems used. These are all tunable per connection through configuration options.

You can find their descriptions in the ipsec.conf man page, but we will provide a few examples here. For all these options, the default setting is the setting used when not specified in the connection at all.

Perfect Forward Secrecy

Perfect Forward Secrecy is not supported by all IPsec implementations. Normally this should be enabled (pfs=yes), which is the default, as this protects previous key exchanges even if the current one is compromised. You almost never need to set this to no. One such exception is the MS-L2TP client.

If you are unsure whether the other end wants to use PFS, you can safely set pfs=no. If Openswan receives a request with PFS, it will allow it despite its own setting to disable PFS, because there is absolutely no reason not to use PFS if it is available.

Rekeying

Rekeying is normally enabled (rekey=yes). It will ensure that new keys are negotiated when the current key is about to expire. If rekey is set to no, then when the keylife is reached, the connection will be torn down. Note that this does not prevent the other end from rekeying. If you get lingering roadwarrior connections that you want to get rid of, you could disable rekeying, and make that the roadwarriors' sole responsibility. It is also often used on servers with Opportunistic Encryption connections.

You can further tune rekeying with `rekeymargin`, `rekeyfuzz`, `keyingtries`, `keylife`, and `ikelifetime`. These are mostly used to work around interoperability issues with other IPsec implementations.

Key Rollover

All keys should be thrown away at some point and be replaced with fresh new keys. Though most keys are session keys, so they are thrown away rather quickly, the RSA keys in connections are not thrown out as often. And furthermore, you cannot just replace an RSA key, since this would break the tunnel until both ends have replaced the changed RSA key. To assist RSA key rollover, there is an option `leftrsasigkey2=` (or `rightrsasigkey2=`) that you can use to specify the new key. A connection can be established with both the old `rsasigkey` and the second new key. Once the other end is only using the new key, the old key and the `rsasigkey2` option can be removed.

Summary

We have now discussed the most common types of IPsec tunnels for host-to-host, LAN-to-LAN, roadwarriors, and XAUTH scenarios. You now know the basic commands to manage these tunnels and how to test the tunnels. You have learned how to connect hosts and subnets, and how to deal with NATed networks. Armed with this knowledge, we can have a look at how to get IPsec running in more complex scenarios.

5
X.509 Certificates

In this chapter we will describe how to set up Openswan to use X.509 Certificates. We will cover the concepts and properties of X.509, and study some examples of how to use the openssl command to generate, sign, and revoke X.509 Certificates. This chapter is focused on Linux; refer to later chapters for information on setting up X.509 on Microsoft Windows, Mac OS X, and other platforms.

In the previous chapter, we looked at how to set up a specific IPsec connection for a specific user or configuration. But of course setting up an IPsec connection for each individual user does not scale. We want to be able to set up just one tunnel endpoint on our VPN server, while easily handing out (and retracting!) different VPN credentials to our individual users. The most common way of doing this relies on X.509 Certificates.

X.509 Certificates Explained

A certificate is more than just an RSA key for authentication. Additionally, there is a unique serial number for easy referencing and an identity, which can be a person, computer, or group. The certificate binds the identity to the RSA key. Certificates also contain a time period for which this binding is considered valid. They can even contain information on where to verify the certificate. Finally, a purpose or group limitation can be included in the certificate.

A certificate is given out by an **issuer**. To prevent forgery, the entire certificate is protected by a cryptographic signature. Certificates enable us to:

- Hand out digitally signed identities for hosts and users
- Set a duration for the validity of the credentials (begin and end time)
- Revoke an identity
- Create a hierarchical structure for decision making (such as access restrictions)
- Manage large numbers of identities
- Delegate the management of these identities hierarchically
- Set up trust relationships between two parties who have never met

You can think of a certificate as a passport. Both are issued by a known and trusted party, they are resistant to forgery due to various protection measures, they are bound to a single person and are useless for anyone else, and they both have limited lifespans. Those who value a passport do so on the trust they put in the issuer of the passport, in much the same way as for certificates.

X.509 Objects

X.509 is a standard for writing these kinds of relationships. X.509 is based on designs that are older than the IP protocol itself, being created in the era of leased lines and the X.25 protocol. Those familiar with LDAP, NDIS, or SSL certificates will find all this very familiar, as those standards also go back to the days of X.25. These standards use a hierarchical system of categorizing objects, sometimes referred to as trees and forests.

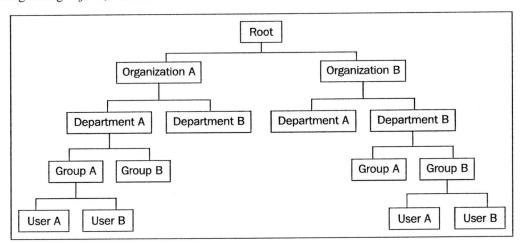

What we see is that the topmost node, the **Root**, is the same for everyone. In our example we have two organizations A and B, each having two departments A and B, and so forth. It is important to realize that in order to refer to one specific object, you need to do so in terms of the hierarchical relation, that is in terms of the object's parent, the parent's parent, and so forth.

For example, User A from Department B is not necessarily the same object as User A from Department A. These descriptions are called **Relative Distinguished Named (RDNs)**. A full description of an object fully from top to bottom is a **Distinguished Name (DN)**. A DN is written as a list of RDNs separated by commas (,) or slashes (/).

The following table lists the X.509 RDNs supported by Openswan:

Relative Distinguished Name	Meaning
DC	Domain Component
C	Country
ST	State or province

Relative Distinguished Name	Meaning
L	Locality or town
O	Organization
OU	Organizational Unit
CN	Common Name
ND	Name Distinguisher, used with CN
N	Name
G	Given name
S	Surname
I	Initials
T	Personal Title
E, Email, or emailAddress	Email address
SN or serialNumber	Serial Number
D	Description
UID	User ID
ID	X.500 Unique Identifier
TCGID [Siemens]	Trust Center Global ID

The most commonly used RDNs are C, ST, L, O, OU, CN, and E (or one of its alternatives).

An example DN is:

```
C=Ca, ST=Ontario, L=Toronto, O=Xelerance, OU=Support Staff, CN=Naomi Rae,
E=support@xelerance.com
```

Due to the various different implementations of X.509 and character sets and representations, you should avoid using any international characters or any character that commonly changes location between keyboards.

> We recommend use of only alphanumeric characters, spaces, and the minus character in Distinguished Names. A commonly chosen OU= value is 'R&D', which fails to work when trying to use Openswan with certain Windows IPsec clients.

X.509 Packing

X.509 Certificates are written in a specific machine-parsable way called **Abstract Syntax Notation One (ASN.1)**. This is then wrapped in a specific format such as the **Public-Key Cryptography Standards (PKCS)** of which there are various versions.

Because people wanted to be able to use more than just ASCII characters (and because some old network connections were not even 8-bit clean and could not even safely transport ASCII), these ASN.1 notations are packed in either the binary DER format, or in the base-64 PEM format. The DER format is used in OpenLDAP, but the PEM format is commonly used for SSL/HTTPS certificates for websites. Openswan detects the type of packing used, so you can use both formats interchangeably, though it is recommended to stick to PEM encoding. We will use PEM in all our examples.

Types of Certificates

Certificates with different purposes are also named differently. To make things more confusing, some vendors give these certificates or certificate containers different names. The most commonly known X.509 Certificates are those used in web servers and web browsers. Web servers obtain signed X.509 Certificates from a commonly *known* and *trusted* source. In practice this means from companies like Verisign / Thawte, but it could easily be your own **Certificates R Us**-generated certificate. Another example is the non-profit organization, CAcert.org. Browser manufacturers, such as Microsoft, Apple, or the Mozilla Foundation, supply their software with certificates for these organizations already built in, and the software will trust certificates signed by those authorities, also called Certificate Authorities (CAs).

Certificate Type	Description
Certificate Authority (CA)	The start of a trust chain. The CA is the only certificate that signs itself.
(Trusted) Root certificate	Another name for a CA certificate.
Intermediate Certificate Authorities	A CA that is not signed by itself but by another (parent) CA.
CSR Certificate	Certificate Signing Request. This is a certificate generated by a person, with an embedded request to sign. This request is then given to a CA to be signed.
Host (Local Computer) certificate	Certificate issued for a machine (usually signed by a CA).
User (Personal) certificate	Certificate issued for a person (usually signed by a CA).
Private Key	Private key file belonging to a public key of a .pem file. Can be pass-phrase protected.
PKCS#12 (.pl file)	Certificate plus private key issued and signed by a CA. Normally pass-phrase protected.
PKCS#15	Certificate standard for Cryptographic Tokens (for instance, USB crypto tokens). Usually PIN protected. Sometimes multilevel PINs differentiate user and admin access.
CRL	Certificate Revocation List, a list of revoked serial numbers of issued certificates.

The distinction between a host certificate and a user certificate is not as clear as it might seem. That is because normally IPsec requires administrative privileges, and therefore vendors tend to treat these user certificates as host certificates.

Passphrases, PIN Codes, and Interactivity

Often you want IPsec tunnels to establish without having to manually authenticate by PIN code or passphrase. It is possible to store such information in /etc/ipsec.secrets, but there is obviously some security impact. If a PIN or passphrase is necessary for Openswan to access certain data, it will try to prompt you for it. If there is no active login session (pty) this will automatically fail as if the wrong code was entered.

IKE and Certificates

When a connection is configured to use X.509 Certificates, instead of loading the RSA private key from /etc/ipsec.secrets, the private key is loaded from the certificate key file (.key), and the public key is loaded from the certificate file (.pem). These files are automatically loaded if they appear in the proper directories. Public certificates are read from the directory /etc/ipsec.d/certs, while private keys are read from the directory /etc/ipsec.d/private/. Private keys only load if they are not protected by a passphrase, or if the passphrase appears in /etc/ipsec.secrets.

They can also be specified with a relative or absolute path.

IPsec directory	X.509 related content
/etc/ipsec.d/cacerts	CA certificates
/etc/ipsec.d/certs	Certificates with public keys
/etc/ipsec.d/private	Private keys
/etc/ipsec.d/crls	Certificate Revocation Lists
/etc/ipsec.d/ocspcerts	OCSP

Using the Certificate DN as ID for Openswan

We will use the DN to match our ID in the rightid= or leftid= of an IPsec connection definition. Though this seems harder than making up strings such as '@PaulsLaptop', its advantage is that it allows wildcards to group a lot of people into a single connection. The following example should make this clear:

```
conn x509
    left=%defaultroute
    leftcert=vpnserver.pem
    leftid="C=Ca, ST=Ontario, L=Toronto, O=Xelerance, CN=VPN Server,
E=support@xelerance.com"
    rightid="C=Ca, ST=Ontario, L=Toronto, O=Xelerance, CN=* E=*"
    right=%any
```

This configuration will accept anyone with a certificate from the Xelerance organization in the Toronto locality, regardless of username, hostname, or email address.

There is sometimes confusion about `Email=` and `emailAddress=`. Openswan will match both of these to `E=`.

Generating Certificates with OpenSSL

X.509 Certificates can be generated and managed by various programs. Most people still use the command-line tool that comes with OpenSSL, but you can also look into managed web-based solutions, such as **TinyCA**. We will be using OpenSSL in our examples to create certificates.

Setting the Time

Since all certificates have time-limited validity, it is very important to have the correct time set on the hosts that are going to use certificates, as well as on the host that creates the certificates. You might think that a few seconds do not matter, but if you generate a certificate and transfer it to a machine that lives fifteen minutes in the past, you will have to wait 15 minutes before that certificate becomes valid. People regularly fall into this trap and waste a lot of time trying to get a connection to work properly, just because the time is set incorrectly. Another common mistake is using newly generated certificates on machines that have a different timezone or a clock that is, or is not, set to GMT. These types of errors are logged clearly though:

```
Feb19 22:21:02 west pluto[7946]: X.509 certificate is not valid until Mar 19
21:34:55 UTC 2005 (it is now=Feb 19 21:21:02 UTC 2005)
```

Some operating systems also confuse things by *automagically* changing the clock for winter time and summer time (Daylight Saving Time).

The easiest and most reliable way to get a consistent time set on all your machines is to use GMT in the hardware clock, and use the **Network Time Protocol** (**NTP**). Usually NTP comes as a system service called `ntp` or `ntpd`. You can also run a one-time time synchronization at boot using the `ntpdate` command. On modern Windows machines (2000/XP or newer), you can right-click the clock and configure the computer to use NTP.

Configuring OpenSSL

You should first make a decision whether or not to use the default `openssl.cnf` or to create your own configuration file just for use with Openswan. We recommend the latter, so you do not interfere with the existing SSL setup of your web server, and so that if your OpenSSL package is upgraded you do not run the risk of losing your changed configuration file. It will also allow you to change the default values to make creating a new certificate much easier. If you are going to be using crypto USB tokens, then you can also change the `LoadModule` options in this separate configuration file. To use your own `openssl.cnf` file, set the environment variable `OPENSSL_CONF`:

 # export OPENSSL_CONF=/etc/ipsec.d/openssl.cnf

Alternatively, use `-config /path/to/your/openssl.cnf` in all your OpenSSL commands.

Create this openssl.cnf file by copying the installed openssl.cnf. The exact location varies depending on the distribution, but it tends to live somewhere in /usr/lib/ssl/. You should change the dir option to point to the directory where you will store your X.509 Certificates, otherwise it will use the ./demoCA directory. You can also fill in the various RDNs you want by changing the *_default options, for example countryName_default=CA.

Be Consistent with All Certificates

Do not to edit the openssl.cnf file once you have started to generate certificates, because all certificates must be created with the same set of options. Adding or removing any RDN will result in all connections being refused because the number of RDNs has to match.

> Do not use . to fill in RDNs that you have filled in for other certificates such as for the CA. Using a . means that this RDN will not be included in the certificate. This is not want you want, since the number and type of RDNs in the CA and any certificate signed by it should be the same. If you use . anyway, your connection will never be allowed by Openswan, since it will not be able to find a matching DN, and you will see the much dreaded error message: no connection is authorized for <client DN>.

It is important that the CA never expires before any of the certificates' signatures it signs. It is recommended that you give your CA a very long lifetime, of the order of 10 years. You can then hand out certificates signed by that CA that are valid for a year for the next 9 years. You can use a shorter time period and re-sign the CA, but be aware that the validity of the CA should be longer than the lifetime of the signatures you make with it.

OpenSSL Commands for Common Certificate Actions

The table below lists the most common commands for generating and revoking certificates. Some of the options, such as -days, take their defaults from openssl.cnf.

X.509 Certificate operation	OpenSSL command line
Show certificate properties	openssl x509 -in file.pem -noout
Show certificate DN for use in left/rightid=	openssl x509 -in file.pem -noout -subject
Create CA	openssl req -x509 -days 3650 -newkey rsa:1024 -keyout caKey.pem -out caCert.pem [-passout pass:NewPassphrase]
Renew CA	openssl x509 -in caCert.pem -out caCert2.pem -signkey caKey.pem
Create host/user KEY and CSR	openssl req -newkey rsa:1024 -keyout file.key -out fileReq.pem (This can be done by a user who then gives fileReq.pem to the sysadmin.)

X.509 Certificate operation	OpenSSL command line
Create host/user KEY without CSR	`openssl genrsa -out file.key 1024`
Create host certificate from KEY	`openssl req -new -key file.key -x509 -out file.crt`
Sign host/CSR certificate	`openssl ca -in fileReq.pem -days 365 -out fileCert.pem -notext -cert caCert.pem -keyfile caKey.pem`
Package host cert for Windows (.p12)	`openssl pkcs12 -export -inkey fileKey.pem -in Filecert.pem -name YourName -certfile caCert.pem -caname "YourOrg CA" -out fileCert.p12 [ -passout pass:NewPassphrase ]`
Remove passphrase from a certificate	`openssl rsa -passin pass:CurrentPassphrase -in file.key -out file.key.unlocked`
Change passphrase for a certificate	`openssl rsa -passin pass:CurrentPassphrase -passout pass:NewPassphrase -in file.key -out file.key.unlocked`
Create empty CRL	`openssl ca -gencrl -crldays 30 -out /etc/ipsec.d/crls/crl.pem -keyfile caKey.pem -cert caCert.pem`
Revoke host certificate	`openssl ca -revoke fileCert.pem -keyfile caKey.pem -cert caCert.pem`
Update CRL (required after revoke)	`openssl ca -gencrl -crldays 30 -out crl.pem -keyfile caKey.pem -cert caCert.pem`
List CRL contents	`openssl crl -in crl.pem -noout -text`
Unwrap pkcs12	`openssl pkcs12 -nocerts -in file.p12 -out file.key` Use `-nodes` for no passphrase.

Configuring Apache for IPsec X.509 Files

You might want to re-use an IPsec X.509 host certificate within SSL for Apache too, so that your host only needs one X.509 Certificate to identify itself for both IPsec and HTTPS. The following entries should be added to your Apache's SSL configuration (sometimes called `ssl.conf`):

```
#   Some MIME-types for downloading Certificates and CRLs
#
AddType application/x-x509-ca-cert .cert
AddType application/x-pkcs7-crl    .crl
# use the same cert as IPsec for SSL/https
SSLCertificateFile /etc/ipsec.d/certs/gateway.cert
SSLCertificateKeyFile /etc/ipsec.d/private/gateway.key
```

If the private key is protected, starting the web server will cause a prompt, asking you for the passphrase. This is probably not what you want. See the above command list for how to remove a passphrase from a private key.

Creating X.509-based Connections

In this first example, we will use X.509 Certificates instead of raw RSA keys with `leftrsasigkey=` and `rightrisasigkey=` options. We are not using a CA yet, so we will sign the certificates with themselves, so-called self-signed certificates. In this case the trust comes from both ends having the public key of the other end preloaded. Only the real West and East have the private key corresponding to the public key obtained from the preloaded certificate.

> When explicitly loading a certificate, Openswan implicitly trusts it, even if it has expired!

For each host, generate a host keyfile containing the private key, and a host certificate file containing the public key and the DN. You should end up with four files: `west.key`, `west.cert`, `east.key`, and `east.cert`:

```
# openssl genrsa -out west.key 1024
# openssl req -new -key west.key -x509 -out west.cert
# openssl genrsa -out east.key 1024
# openssl req -new -key east.key -x509 -out east.cert
```

The second command will prompt you to fill in the RDNs to build a DN. It does not matter what you use for those DNs (such as country, name, or organization), since the DNs will be loaded from the two certificates, and will therefore always match. Each end will need its own private and public key, as well as the public key of the other end.

If you wish to use a passphrase to protect the key, you can add the option `-des3` to the OpenSSL command, or at any later time run the following:

```
# mv west.key west.key.old
# openssl rsa -des3 -in west.key.old -out west.key
# rm west.key.old
```

Next, define the proper connection definition on East and West. On West, this would look like:

```
conn west-east
    left=193.110.157.81
    leftcert=west.cert
    right=205.150.200.209
    rightcert=east.cert
    #sendcr=always
    #nocrsend=yes
    auto=add
```

The file `west.key` is placed in `/etc/ipsec.d/private/`. The file `east.key` should not be present on West, as this is East's private key. The certificate files `east.cert` and `west.cert` should be placed in `/etc/ipsec.d/certs/`. The private keys will be loaded when Openswan starts, or when you run `ipsec secrets`. If they are passphrase protected, you will either need to type in the passphrase when you bring the connection up, or you can put the passphrase in the file `/etc/ipsec.secrets`:

```
: RSA /etc/ipsec.d/private/west.key %prompt
```

or:

```
: RSA /etc/ipsec.d/private/west.key "YourPassphrase"
```

> It is best to avoid placing whitespace before the :, since older versions of Openswan are not able to parse such lines properly.

If you use prompt mode, then the private key will fail to load if Openswan is started from the system startup script, or if the service is restarted. To force Openswan to prompt for the passphrases, use the following command:

`# ipsec secrets`

If the passphrase is incorrect, Openswan will complain about this:

003 "/etc/ipsec.secrets" line 25: error loading RSA private key file

The logs would also show:

```
Feb 28 23:11:20 west pluto[24030]: forgetting secrets
Feb 28 23:11:20 west pluto[24030]: loading secrets from "/etc/ipsec.secrets"
Feb 28 23:11:20 west pluto[24030]:   loaded private key file
'/etc/ipsec.d/private/west.key' (1751 bytes)
Feb 28 23:11:20 west pluto[24030]:   invalid passphrase
Feb 28 23:11:20 west pluto[24030]: "/etc/ipsec.secrets" line 25: error loading
RSA private key file
```

If the certificates loaded correctly and the private key was successfully unlocked and loaded, you should see something like:

```
Feb 25 01:48:12 west pluto[9656]: Changing to directory '/etc/ipsec.d/cacerts'
Feb 25 01:48:12 west pluto[9656]: Changing to directory '/etc/ipsec.d/aacerts'
Feb 25 01:48:12 west pluto[9656]: Changing to directory
'/etc/ipsec.d/ocspcerts'
Feb 25 01:48:12 west pluto[9656]: Changing to directory '/etc/ipsec.d/crls'
Feb 25 01:48:12 west pluto[9656]:   loaded host cert file
'/etc/ipsec.d/certs/east.cert' (1610 bytes)
Feb 25 01:48:12 west pluto[9656]:   loaded host cert file
'/etc/ipsec.d/certs/west.cert' (1545 bytes)
Feb 25 01:48:12 west pluto[9656]: added connection description "west-east"
Feb 25 01:48:12 west pluto[9656]: loading secrets from "/etc/ipsec.secrets"
Feb 25 01:48:12 west pluto[9656]:   loaded private key file
'/etc/ipsec.d/private/west.key' (1751 bytes)
```

You can also use the `listall` command to show the status of the X.509 Certificates and keys:

```
# ipsec auto --listall
    000
    000 List of Public Keys:
    000
    000 Feb 28 22:20:44 2005, 1024 RSA Key AwEAAdJIV, until Mar 30 21:13:24 2005 ok
    000     ID_DER_ASN1_DN 'C=CA, ST=Ontario, L=Toronto, O=Xelerance, OU=Writers,
CN=west.xelerance.com, E=west@xelerance.com'
    000     Issuer 'C=CA, ST=Ontario, L=Toronto, O=Xelerance, OU=Writers,
CN=west.xelerance.com, E=west@xelerance.com'
    000 Feb 28 22:20:44 2005, 1024 RSA Key AwEAAdSGS, until Mar 30 21:13:59 2005 ok
    000     ID_DER_ASN1_DN 'C=CA, ST=Ontario, L=Toronto, O=Xelerance, OU=Writers,
CN=east.xelerance.com, E=east@xelerance.com'
    000     Issuer 'C=CA, ST=Ontario, L=Toronto, O=Xelerance, OU=Writers,
CN=east.xelerance.com, E=east@xelerance.com'
```

```
000
000 List of X.509 End Certificates:
000
000 Feb 28 22:20:44 2005, count: 1
000      subject: 'C=CA, ST=Ontario, L=Toronto, O=Xelerance, OU=Writers,
CN=west.xelerance.com, E=west@xelerance.com'
000      issuer:  'C=CA, ST=Ontario, L=Toronto, O=Xelerance, OU=Writers,
CN=west.xelerance.com, E=west@xelerance.com'
000      serial:  00
000      pubkey:   1024 RSA Key AwEAAdJIV
000      validity: not before Feb 28 20:13:24 2005 ok
000           not after  Mar 30 21:13:24 2005 warning (expires in 29 days)
000      subjkey:  38:66:c9:78:2a:81:74:dc:73:3b:21:d3:55:39:14:2c:0d:d7:be:f2
000      authkey:  38:66:c9:78:2a:81:74:dc:73:3b:21:d3:55:39:14:2c:0d:d7:be:f2
000      aserial:  00
000 Feb 28 22:20:44 2005, count: 1
000      subject: 'C=CA, ST=Ontario, L=Toronto, O=Xelerance, OU=Writers,
CN=east.xelerance.com, E=east@xelerance.com'
000      issuer:  'C=CA, ST=Ontario, L=Toronto, O=Xelerance, OU=Writers,
CN=east.xelerance.com, E=east@xelerance.com'
000      serial:  00
000      pubkey:   1024 RSA Key AwEAAdSGS, has private key
000      validity: not before Feb 28 20:13:59 2005 ok
000           not after  Mar 30 21:13:59 2005 warning (expires in 29 days)
000      subjkey:  93:23:8a:64:84:73:a1:17:99:a4:f3:9f:7b:b6:91:37:ba:dc:52:e8
000      authkey:  93:23:8a:64:84:73:a1:17:99:a4:f3:9f:7b:b6:91:37:ba:dc:52:e8
000      aserial:  00
```

Note that if the private key is not available on this host, either because it is the private key of the remote side, or because our local private key failed to load, you will be able to determine this by looking at the **pubkey:** line, which will be missing the text **"has private key"**. The above example shows we only have our own private key of East, and not the private key of West. On West, you should see the opposite situation. A good habit is to verify the **keyids** on the **pubkey** line to ensure you have transferred the proper key to the proper host.

Do not specify any `leftid=` or `rightid=`. Openswan will take the DN from the certificates and use that as the ID for IKE. In fact, either East or West can be a roadwarrior, while the other end can specify `right=%any` because the `rightid=` comes from the DN.

Now we can finally bring our connection up (or, if we use `auto=start`, it will come up automatically at startup unless the passphrase-prompting mode is enabled).

```
# ipsec auto --up west-east
```

If everything goes well, the log should show something like:

```
Feb 28 23:30:38 xsable pluto[24759]: "x509" #3: initiating Main Mode
Feb 28 23:30:38 xsable pluto[24759]: "x509" #3: transition from state
STATE_MAIN_I1 to state STATE_MAIN_I2
Feb 28 23:30:38 xsable pluto[24759]: "x509" #3: I am sending my cert
Feb 28 23:30:38 xsable pluto[24759]: "x509" #3: I am sending a certificate
request
Feb 28 23:30:38 xsable pluto[24759]: "x509" #3: transition from state
```

```
STATE_MAIN_I2 to state STATE_MAIN_I3
Feb 28 23:30:38 xsable pluto[24759]: "x509" #3: Peer ID is ID_DER_ASN1_DN:
'C=CA, ST=Ontario, L=Toronto, O=Xelerance, OU=Writers, CN=east.xelerance.com,
E=east@xelerance.com'
Feb 28 23:30:38 xsable pluto[24759]: "x509" #3: end certificate with identical
subject and issuer not accepted
Feb 28 23:30:38 xsable pluto[24759]: "x509" #3: X.509 certificate rejected
Feb 28 23:30:38 xsable pluto[24759]: "x509" #3: transition from state
STATE_MAIN_I3 to state STATE_MAIN_I4
Feb 28 23:30:38 xsable pluto[24759]: "x509" #3: ISAKMP SA established
Feb 28 23:30:38 xsable pluto[24759]: "x509" #4: initiating Quick Mode
RSASIG+ENCRYPT+TUNNEL+PFS+UP {using isakmp#3}
Feb 28 23:30:38 xsable pluto[24759]: "x509" #4: transition from state
STATE_QUICK_I1 to state STATE_QUICK_I2
Feb 28 23:30:38 xsable pluto[24759]: "x509" #4: sent QI2, IPsec SA established
{ESP=>0x7f55f371 <0xe26d3875}
```

> Openswan versions up to at least 2.3.0 give the error message you can see above about rejecting a certificate with identical subject and issuer when explicitly loading self-signed certificates without a CA, even though the connection works fine. This message actually comes from when a CA is used, and it is found that the CA's CN= is the same as the CN= which it signed for.
>
> The error message results from verification problems within the X.509 parser, which cannot clearly differentiate the CA and the host certificate when they have the same name, and the host certificate could be used to sign another host certificate. Therefore these certificates are rejected. Of course, self-signed certificates do have this property too, and that is why we see this error message. However, the message is misleading as our certificates, which are explicitly loaded, are in fact not rejected.

Using a Certificate Authority

When using a CA you can match many connections, usually roadwarriors, in a single connection. The trust now comes from the fact that we trust that the CA has only signed (and not revoked) valid client certificates. If an incoming connection presents a certificate with a public key that was signed by a CA that we trust, we allow the connection. We can limit the allowed connections based on the DN.

```
conn west-roadwarriors
    left=193.110.157.81
    leftcert=/etc/ipsec.d/certs/west.pem
    rightrsasigkey=%cert
    right=%any
    rightid="C=CA, O=Xelerance, OU=bofh, CN=*"
    auto=add
```

Using pattern matching on the DN in the rightid= you can implement access restrictions. You could use different conn definitions with a different leftsubnet= or even a leftprotoport= to give very specific access to groups or individuals. You can also make special connections using a leftsubnet= that points to a network printer. This might require careful planning of the RDNs in your certificates. You might want to add an extra OU for a certain access control, or use one of the less frequently used RDNs.

```
conn sales-printer
    leftcert=west.pem
    leftsubnet=10.0.2.2/32
    rightid="C=CA, O=Xelerance, OU=Sales, CN=*"
    also=base-conn
```

Some more examples of using the DN for access control:

```
# Match the entire organisation
rightid="C=CA, O=Xelerance, OU=*, CN=*"

# Match a single person
rightid="C=CA, O=Xelerance, OU=bofh, CN=Jane Jones"

# Match people from one office
rightid="C=CA, O=Xelerance, L=Ottawa, OU=*, CN=*"
```

Remember that you cannot leave out an RDN. If you do not care about the content of a certain RDN, match it with *.

> You need to have an equal number of RDNs (of the same types) in your DN for the match to succeed.

Using Multiple CAs

When organizations get bigger, the task of handing out signed certificates is usually broken up and handled by different branches or departments. You can use an intermediary CA to address this. The root CA creates and signs two or more intermediary CAs. They can be given to the different departments, who can then create and sign certificates. On the VPN server that serves the entire company, you can create different conns for different departments to restrict access to the department's network alone:

```
conn west-roadwarriors-all
    left=193.110.157.81
    leftsubnet=192.168.1.0/24
    leftcert=west.pem
    right=%any
    rightrsasigkey=%cert
    rightca="C=CA, O=Xelerance, CN=Root CA"
    auto=add

conn west-roadwarriors-development
    left=193.110.157.81
    leftsubnet=10.0.1.0/24
    right=%any
    rightrsasigkey=%cert
    rightca="C=CA, O=Xelerance, CN=Development CA"
    auto=add

conn west-roadwarriors-support
    left=193.110.157.81
    leftsubnet=10.0.2.0/24
    right=%any
    rightrsasigkey=%cert
    rightca="C=CA, O=Xelerance, CN=Support CA"
    auto=add
```

In this configuration, everyone can access the 192.168.1.0/24 network, for example the DMZ containing the email and web servers, but the support staff cannot get onto the developer network and vice versa. Of course you can further limit or grant access to groups or individuals by combining matching of rightca= and rightid=. The corresponding entry for the conn west-roadwarriors-all on the Openswan roadwarrior would look like this:

```
conn west-roadwarriors-all
    left=%defaultroute
    leftcert=east.pem
    right=193.110.157.81
    righttsubnet=192.168.1.0/24
    rightid=" C=CA, O=Xelerance, CN=Root CA, CN=west.xelerance.com,
E=west@xelerance.com"
    #rightca="C=CA, O=Xelerance, CN=Root CA"
    auto=add
```

Sending and Receiving Certificate Information

When no rightca= is specified, then all certificates signed by any of the loaded CAs from /etc/ipsec.d/cacerts/ will be allowed. Though it is possible to specify a leftca=, this is usually not needed since this value will be taken from the CA that signed the leftcert='s host certificate. Using rightca=%same only allows certificates that are signed by the same CA that signed the leftcert=, though usually in such situations, you will only have one CA in /etc/ipsec.d/cacerts/ listed anyway, so this option can usually be omitted as well.

Normally, the client (or rather, the initiator) sends its CA as part of the IKE exchange to indicate which trust chain applies to the current connection. From a security point of view, a server (responder) should not broadcast all the valid CAs it trusts to the (so far) unauthenticated client. This behavior can be fine-tuned using the leftsendcert= parameter:

leftsendcert parameter	Description
leftsendcert=ifasked	Sent certificate if asked
leftsendcert=no leftsendcert=never	Never sent certificate
leftsendcert=yes leftsendcert=always	Always sent certificate

Ideally, you should use the default ifasked option, but this breaks compatibility with some vendors, such as Cisco and Safenet. In those cases, you should set this option to always.

Creating your own CA using OpenSSL

The following command can be used to create your own Certificate Authority:

```
# openssl req -x509 -days 3650 -newkey rsa:1024 -keyout caKey.pem -out caCert.pem
Generating a 1024 bit RSA private key
..............
writing new private key to 'caKey.pem'
```

Enter PEM pass phrase: *****
Verifying - Enter PEM pass phrase: *****

You are about to be asked to enter information that will be incorporated into your certificate request.
What you are about to enter is what is called a Distinguished Name or a DN.
There are quite a few fields but you can leave some blank
For some fields there will be a default value,
If you enter '.', the field will be left blank.

Country Name (2 letter code) [CA]:
State or Province Name (full name) [Ontario]:
Locality Name (eg, city) [Toronto]:
Organization Name (eg, company) [Xelerance]:
Organizational Unit Name (eg, section) [Support Staff]:
Common Name (eg, your name or your server's hostname) []:Xelerance Root CA
Email Address []:ca@xelerance.com

Answers that appear in brackets are the defaults taken from the `openssl.cnf` configuration file. Run the following commands in the directory you specified for the `dir` option in the `CA_default` section of your `openssl.cnf` file:

```
# mkdir newcerts
# touch index.txt
# echo "01" > serial
```

> The Common Name (CN) of your Certificate Authority *must* be unique. It is strongly recommended to specify `Certificate Authority`, `CA`, or `Root CA` in the CN to prevent accidentally re-using this Common Name. For example: `CN=Xelerance Root CA`.

Creating Host Certificates with Your Own CA

Now that we have our own CA, we can start handing out X.509 Certificates for our users (or rather for the hosts our users are using, since these certificates are host-based and not user-based). The first certificate we need to generate is for the IPsec gateway itself. In our case we will re-use the machine West for this.

```
# openssl req -newkey rsa:1024 -keyout west.key -out westReq.pem
```

The output looks similar to the CA we generated above. Next, we need to sign the host certificate with our CA. Because some clients do not like the human readable part before the actual certificate, we use the -noout option to suppress it:

```
# openssl ca -in westReq.pem -days 365 -out westCert.pem -notext -cert caCert.pem
-keyfile caKey.pem
      Using configuration from /opt/vpn/ssl//openssl.cnf
      Enter pass phrase for caKey.pem:
      Check that the request matches the signature
      Signature ok
      Certificate Details:
            Serial Number: 1 (0x1)
```

```
Validity
    Not Before: Mar 14 11:33:19 2005 GMT
    Not After : Mar 14 11:33:19 2006 GMT
Subject:
    countryName          = CA
    stateOrProvinceName      = Ontario
    organizationName     = Xelerance
    organizationalUnitName   = Support Staff
    commonName               = west.xelerance.com
    emailAddress             = postmaster@xelerance.com
X509v3 extensions:
    X509v3 Basic Constraints:
    CA:FALSE
    X509v3 CRL Distribution Points:
    URI:http://certs.xelerance.com/revoked.crl
    URI:ldap://certs.xelerance.com/o=Xelerance,
c=CA?certificateRevocationList?base?(objectClass=certificationAuthority)

    Netscape Comment:
    OpenSSL Generated Certificate
    X509v3 Subject Key Identifier:
    E8:58:4F:EB:CD:9A:09:52:63:61:FE:7C:63:67:E9:AE:90:AC:FF:E9
    X509v3 Authority Key Identifier:
    keyid:FC:35:D9:23:FE:2B:5A:0E:AA:F6:A4:B8:AC:4A:AA:E0:DB:77:29:B0
    DirName:/C=CA/ST=Ontario/L=Toronto/O=Xelerance/OU=Support Staff/CN=Xelerance
Root CA/emailAddress=ca@xelerance.com
    serial:00

Certificate is to be certified until Mar 14 11:33:19 2006 GMT (365 days)
Sign the certificate? [y/n] y
1 out of 1 certificate requests certified, commit? [y/n] y
Write out database with 1 new entries
Data Base Updated
```

Do not forget to place all certificate-related files in their proper directories. In our case, we need to copy `cacert.pem` onto our VPN gateway in `/etc/ipsec.d/cacerts`. Our public certificate `westCert.pem` is placed in `/etc/ipsec.d/certs`, and `west.key`, which contains the private key for West, is placed in `/etc/ipsec.d/private`. No other files need to be copied onto West.

We can repeat this procedure to generate further certificates for other hosts that will be connecting to our gateway.

Host Certificates for Microsoft Windows (PKCS#12)

Most Microsoft operating systems, such as Windows 2000, XP, and 2003 require a slightly different key format, known as **PKCS#12**, which incorporates the CA certificate, the signed X.509 host certificate, and the private key corresponding to that X.509 host certificate in a single file. These can be generated after you have created a CA and a host certificate with the following command:

```
# openssl pkcs12 -export -inkey win.key -in winCert.pem -name UserName -certfile
caCert.pem -caname "YourOrg Root CA" -out winCert.p12
```

Since the .p12 file created by this command contains the private key, it should be protected by a passphrase. This is the **export password** you see in the output above. You can add -passout pass:NewPassphrase if you wish to automate this command in some script.

Certificate Revocation

When a certificate is lost or stolen, it should be revoked, so that it can no longer be used to set up an IPsec connection. Since the CA signed the now-lost certificate, we need a special exemption to deny such lost certificates even though they have been signed by our trusted CA. Revoked certificates are stored in the file crl.pem, which should be placed on the gateway in the directory /etc/ipsec.d/crls/.

An empty CRL file should be created if no certificates have been revoked yet, using:

```
# openssl ca -gencrl -crldays 15 -out crl.pem  -keyfile caKey.pem -cert caCert.pem
```

To revoke a certificate, the public certificate file is needed. You should always keep a copy of these on the signing machine. This machine should be well protected or perhaps not even be connected to the Internet at all. To revoke a certificate, use:

```
# openssl ca -revoke fileCert.pem -keyfile caKey.pem -cert caCert.pem
```

The crl.pem file will need to be updated after a new certificate has been added to the revocation list:

```
# openssl crl -in crl.pem -noout -text
```

This file should be copied onto the gateway machine, in the directory /etc/ipsec.d/crls. Openswan should then be notified to re-read the new CRL file:

```
# ipsec auto --rereadcrls
    Mar 19 23:54:16 peace pluto[16986]: Changing to directory '/etc/ipsec.d/crls'
    Mar 19 23:54:16 peace pluto[16986]:   loaded crl file 'crl.pem' (589 bytes)
```

> Revoking a certificate will not cause the Openswan server to drop any connections using that certificate. That IPsec connection will stay up until the next rekey, or the next (re)connect, when the now revoked certificate will be properly rejected.

An attempt by a revoked certificate to connect will be logged, and the connection will be rejected:

```
    Mar 19 23:58:57 peace pluto[16986]: "west-roadwarriors"[5] 193.110.157.17 #11:
    Peer ID is ID_DER_ASN1_DN: 'C=CA, ST=Ontario, O=Xelerance, OU=Support Staff,
    CN=revoked.xelerance.com, E=revoke@xelerance.com'
    Mar 19 23:58:57 peace pluto[16986]: "west-roadwarriors"[5] 193.110.157.17 #11:
    certificate was revoked on Mar 19 22:54:05 UTC 2005
    Mar 19 23:58:57 peace pluto[16986]: "west-roadwarriors"[5] 193.110.157.17 #11:
    invalid RSA public key deleted
    Mar 19 23:58:57 peace pluto[16986]: "west-roadwarriors"[5] 193.110.157.17 #11:
    X.509 certificate rejected
    Mar 19 23:58:57 peace pluto[16986]: "west-roadwarriors"[6] 193.110.157.17 #11:
    deleting connection "west-roadwarriors" instance with peer 193.110.157.17
    {isakmp=#0/ipsec=#0}
    Mar 19 23:58:57 peace pluto[16986]: "west-roadwarriors"[6] 193.110.157.17 #11:
    no RSA public key known for 'C=CA, ST=Ontario, O=Xelerance, OU=Support Staff,
    CN=revoked.xelerance.com, E=revoke@xelerance.com'
```

If the certificate was in use when the certificate was revoked, you will notice that after some time the connection will fail to rekey and expire:

```
Mar 20 00:09:46 peace pluto[17775]: "west-roadwarriors"[2] 193.110.157.17 #1:
ISAKMP SA expired (LATEST!)
```

Versions prior to 2.3.1 did not properly delete both Phase 1 (ISAKMP SA) and Phase 2 (IPsec SA). For version 2.3.1 and up you should also see the rejection of the IPsec SA after the ISAKMP SA expires:

```
Mar 20 00:44:47 peace pluto[18169]: "west-roadwarriors"[2] 193.110.157.17 #2:
IPsec SA expired (LATEST!)
```

Dynamic CRL Fetching

When deploying X.509 on a large scale, it is not convenient to have a single `crl.pem` file that needs constant updating and copying to the various IPsec gateways. Openswan supports a few dynamic methods where a server is periodically queried for CRL updates. These updates can come from a `crl.pem` file on a web server, but can also be obtained by other methods, such as LDAP. Another method is the Online Certificate Store Protocol (OCSP).

To use dynamic CRL fetching, you must ensure Openswan is compiled with support for **posix threads**, **cURL**, and optionally **LDAP**. These can be enabled in `Makefile.inc` by setting `HAVE_THREADS`, `USE_LIBCURL`, and `USE_LDAP` to true.

Your CA certificate and all signed host certificates need to be created with an additional CRL distribution section in your `openssl.cnf` file so that all certificates know about the type and location of the dynamic CRLs. Add the following line to the `[usr_cert]` section of `openssl.cnf`:

```
crlDistributionPoints= @crl_dp
```

And add a new `[crl_dp]` section listing the dynamic CRL methods and locations you wish to use:

```
[ crl_dp ]

URI.1="http://crl.yourorganisation.org/revoked.crl"
URI.2="ldap://ldap.yourorganisation.org/o=Xelerance,
c=CA?certificateRevocationList?base?(objectClass=certificationAuthority)"
```

Note that the values for `URI.1` and `URI.2` should each be given on a single line.

The first URI defines a dynamic revocation list on a web server. Openswan will use the `curl` command to fetch this from the web server. The second URI uses LDAP, which is also fetched using the `curl` command, which has LDAP support. Note that if you store CRL information in OpenLDAP, you need to use the DER format and not the PEM format. The OpenSSL command can create CRLs in either format. It will use PEM by default. If you need to use DER, add the option `-outform der` to the OpenSSL commands specified earlier in the chapter. You will need to add the appropriate scripts to update the CRL files or LDAP entry yourself, for instance by using the `scp` command from the secure signing machine to the web server if your CRL file is on a web server. You can also put this information in a special **CA connection** section:

```
ca XeleranceCA
    cacert=caCert.pem
    auto=add
    # the following lines are optional
    crluri=http://crl.xelerance.com/revoked.crl'
    crluri2="ldap:///O=Xelerance, C=CA?certificateRevocationList"
    ldaphost=ldap.xelerance.com
```

Using separate CA connection sections, you can specify different CRL servers for different intermediate CA certificates.

Configuring CRL

There are two important options that change the behavior of dynamic CRL fetching. These options should be placed in the `config setup` section of `ipsec.conf`:

```
config setup
    crlcheckinterval=600
    strictcrlpolicy=yes
```

The `crlcheckinterval=` period determines how often Openswan will try to fetch a new version of the CRL file. It will only try to fetch a new version if the CRL expires in a time shorter than twice the `crlcheckinterval=` time. Thus, if you make the CRL valid for a year, which you should never do, you will never see it try to fetch an updated version. A good CRL lifetime is something short. The shorter you make it, the quicker you can revoke someone's certificate. However, you should make sure that the CRL does not expire. CRLs are not stored between restarts of Openswan, but are fetched again from the specified distribution points.

Openswan uses a default of `strictcrlpolicy=no`, meaning that if no valid CRL is found, warnings are logged, but connections are not rejected. In this mode, an expired CRL is also treated as a valid CRL, meaning only entries in the expired CRL that have been revoked will actually be treated as revoked. To strictly enforce CRL settings, set `strictcrlpolicy=yes`. Be aware that if your CRL then expires, no new incoming connections will be accepted. If you access your dynamic CRL over an IPsec tunnel, this also means you are completely dead in the water when that tunnel needs to rekey. Another effect is that at startup, the first few connections might be rejected because a valid CRL has not yet been fetched and loaded.

To view the status of the CRL, issue the following command:

```
# ipsec auto --listcrls
    000
    000 List of X.509 CRLs:
    000
    000 Apr 04 17:27:47 2005, revoked certs: 2
    000      issuer:  'C=CA, ST=Ontario, L=Toronto, O=Xelerance, OU=Support Staff,
    CN=Xelerance Root CA, E=ca@xelerance.com'
    000      distPts: 'http://crl.xelerance.com/revoked.crl'
    000      updates:  this Mar 19 23:54:35 2005
    000      next Apr 04 00:54:35 2005 warning (expired)
```

In this case you can see that the CRL has expired, and if `crlstrictmode` had been enabled, no new IPsec connections would be allowed. This command would also show any pending CRL transfer attempts.

Online Certificate Status Protocol (OCSP)

Defined in RFC 2560, OCSP is an extension for dynamic CRL fetching. Instead of using a CRL, the gateway will now ask an OCSP server for information about a specific X.509 Certificate presented by a remote peer trying to initiate an IPsec connection. Based upon the answer of the OCSP server, Openswan will accept or reject the certificate. Like CRL responses, OCSP responses do not survive a reboot, and will be retrieved again from the OCSP server. OCSP is enabled in a separate CA section:

```
ca XeleranceCA
    cacert=caCert.pem
    ocspuri=http://ocsp.xelerance.com:81
    auto=add
```

The port number is arbitrary. You can manually load this CA connection using this command:

```
# ipsec auto --type ca --add XeleranceCA
```

You can also put options in the special ca %default section, which can also be used if there is only one CA certificate on the server. An example given is below:

```
ca %default
    ocspuri=http://ocsp.xelerance.com:81
```

You will need to run an OCSP server, in our example at ocsp.xelerance.com. The OpenSSL package contains an OCSP server. After creating a key and certificate for the OCSP server, just as they are generated for an IPsec host, the OCSP server can be started with the following commands:

```
# openssl ocsp -index index.txt -CA caCert.pem -port 81 -rkey ocspKey.pem -rsigner
ocspCert.pem -resp_no_certs -nmin 60 -text
```

You will also need to place a copy of the OCSP public certificate (ocspCert.pem) on the VPN gateway in the directory /etc/ipsec.d/ocspcerts/.

> It is strongly recommended not to run the OCSP server on the machine that has the CA private key used for signing certificates.

Additional commands for viewing and purging OCSP data	Description
ipsec auto --listocspcerts	List OCSP information
ipsec auto --purgeocsp	Purge the OCSP cache and fetching requests

The OCSP patches have not yet been fully integrated into Openswan. Please take a look at the website for the latest information on OCSP support in Openswan.

Summary

In this chapter, we have had a detailed look at X.509 Certificates: what they are, what they contain, and how to make them. We have also looked at how they may be used in Openswan and covered the configuration options you need, as well as other technologies related to them.

6
Opportunistic Encryption

This chapter will describe how Openswan can encrypt more than just a few prearranged tunnels. It will discuss:

- The concept of Opportunistic Encryption
- Storing IPsec information in DNS
- The different kinds of Opportunistic Encryption
- Subnet protection using Opportunistic Encryption
- Policy Groups for tuning Opportunistic Encryption

So far, we have used IPsec to secure communications between places and people we know. We have connected laptops, and branch offices, and secured some server-to-server and subnet-to-subnet connections. All these connections had one thing in common: we knew beforehand who we wanted to talk to, and we had some trusted method of communicating with the other side to set up our crypto arrangements. We exchanged a public key through email, used a phone call to verify the email was not tampered with, or used the PGP web of trust to verify the digital signature on the email. Or we were in control of both machines, and could transfer keys using other secure protocols such as SSH. We have seen that setting up IPsec is not that difficult, and now we are ready for an important question:

Why can't we talk IPsec to everyone by default?

The short answer is "We can." The long answer is this chapter.

In the old days of the Internet, when there was no spam, no copyright infringements, and no commercially-driven content, everyone shared everything. And when people got an IP packet, they went out of their way to assist and see if they could deliver it. This is no longer the case, with a few exceptions such as the big European Internet Exchanges. IP packets no longer go the shortest way, the fastest way, the reliable way, or the secure way. They go the cheapest way, and we all know that cheap and secure are mutually exclusive. In the old days, we also had a few trusted networks that interconnected. Now we have absolutely no idea if we can trust anyone with our packets. The result was that people scrambled to secure various protocols with additional layers, now mostly standardized using SSL/TLS for a very few sensitive websites, PGP or S/MIME for email, and IPsec for VPNs.

However, this does not protect all the other traffic. More wrappers have been added. Secure POP and IMAP, secure webmail, STARTTLS for SMTP servers, and right now security is being applied to the various Instant Messaging (IM) protocols. And people only started using them when faced with the reality that anyone anywhere could read, or even manipulate their packets, thanks to the success of wireless networks. GSM, UMTS, and GPRS were still too expensive for the average person to eavesdrop on; it requires serious money to obtain the right GSM equipment and it is usually illegal to operate without a license. But WiFi (802.11) finally killed the illusion of trusting the airwaves. The wireless industry's attempts at securing the WiFi protocols have failed again and again. WEP was hacked, WPA was hacked for most common keys, LEAP was broken. Tomorrow there will be another standard, but how long will that one last?

Instead of scrambling to secure all the different network protocols, there is another choice. Secure the IP layer. And why not use IPsec? After all, it is proven to be very secure and we already have all the software on our servers and clients to deploy it. We just need to find a way to set up an IPsec connection without prior arrangement. That method is called **Opportunistic Encryption**.

History of Opportunistic Encryption

Opportunistic Encryption (OE) was the primary motivation for the original FreeS/WAN project, all the way back in 1996. OE's goal was to use upcoming IPsec protocols to secure not just a few important links (aka VPNs), but each and every computer on the Internet. Unfortunately, the market was moving in different ways. There was money to be made on domain registrations, domain security, security software, and digital certificates for each and every user and application. Big corporations like Network Solutions and Verisign and Thawte provided the X.509 Certificate frameworks, and the big software vendors like IBM and Microsoft provided expensive groupware suites to authenticate these users, based on big corporate user hierarchies. Of course, this is not what the Internet is good at. The Internet's strength is not its few big players, but its decentralized way of handling everything. Even though the FreeS/WAN project pushed various technologies to the IETF, that process was very slow. The consequences of that slow process are still visible, as workarounds have had to be deployed to kickstart the entire acceptance and usability of OE. Most importantly, changes in the DNS have taken almost ten years to complete. Finally, there is now an official method for storing public IPsec keys in DNS. It is described in RFC 4025.

Trusting Third Parties

Let us move back to our original dilemma though. How do we encrypt communications between all hosts on the Internet? Securing two hosts is easy. A dozen is doable, but how are we going to secure millions of hosts? Of course, if we are talking about millions of hosts, we cannot use anything based on shared secrets, as the whole world would need to know this *secret* and it would not be a secret anymore. We have to use public key cryptography, such as RSA or DSA, and clearly we cannot call up all the system administrators and ask for their public keys. We need a place to store and retrieve these public keys dynamically.

This problem is not as new as it looks. It is very similar to the problem of finding a website, or sending email to a particular domain. These tasks are done with the largest distributed database ever designed, the Domain Name System (DNS). And the only information we need from the remote host is its public key. If we can retrieve the remote host's public key and the remote host can retrieve our public key, we could set up an IPsec tunnel.

The DNS would function as a trusted third party between the two hosts who want to communicate. And furthermore, we can have the DNS records point to other servers to delegate the IPsec tunneling to. So even if you have a server that does not support OE, you can add a DNS record for that server pointing to another (close by) server that will handle the IPsec tunnels on its behalf. This allows us to encrypt *most of the way* for servers that do not natively support OE.

Trusting the DNS?

Of course, there is one other problem with the DNS: it is not secure. Currently, anyone can spoof DNS answers or pollute DNS caches. Or someone can execute a man-in-the-middle attack and pretend to be the remote host you are trying to connect to, and you end up with a secure connection to the wrong host. Before discarding the DNS as a valid method of security, however, it is important to examine the two methods of breaching the security of communications between two hosts.

Firstly, an attacker could passively sniff network traffic and eavesdrop on the connection. Anyone can do this. If you are drinking your coffee in Starbucks right now, browsing the Internet on your laptop, the person next to you might be monitoring every site you visit. This is called a passive attack. Passive attacks are easy, but they generally are not targeted. People run sniffers and just wait until interesting information comes along. Passive attacks hardly cost any resources, and can (in theory) be undetectable.

The second method of attack is an active attack. An example of an active attack is a man-in-the-middle attack. Here, the attacker pretends to be someone else, or sends you malicious information to trick you into communicating with them instead of the host you were trying to reach. An active attack is targeted. It takes resources, it requires brains, it is hard to automate, and it can be discovered. There is an important legal difference between passive and active attacks. While a passive attack can be morally wrong, it is often still on the borders of legality. An active attack is almost always a criminal offense. Passive attacks are relatively easy to attempt, while active attacks are much more complex and therefore a rare occurrence. Unless of course, you are specifically targeted during, say, a business meeting.

Now if we go back to our goal of ensuring no one can eavesdrop on us, then we see that the most important type of attack to thwart is the passive attack. It would be nice to also be able to thwart the active attack, but we will get to that later. Preventing passive attacks is what is going to prevent the most attempts to eavesdrop on us. After that, we can focus on those few malicious hackers that are trying to specifically target us.

OE in a Nutshell

Opportunistic Encryption is a means of initiating IPsec tunnels to remote hosts by publishing and retrieving public keys from the DNS. We publish our own public key, and the remote server publishes its key, and then both servers can obtain the other's public key and set up an IPsec tunnel. No other pre-arrangement is necessary. This is a symmetrical process, and any host can initiate OE to another host. They are equal peers. However, for simplicity, we will sometimes talk about the server and the client. The intended meaning is that the client initiates, and the server responds.

If we use DNS to store our public keys, this will protect us against all passive attacks. If on the other hand DNSSEC is used, we are also protected against active attacks. The verification of DNSSEC records is not done by Openswan itself, but by the resolver library, which is called through a helper application, lwdnsq. Currently, BIND-9 is the only resolver that supports DNSSEC.

> To enable DNSSEC processing, one needs to install a DNSSEC-capable local resolver (such as BIND-9), and enable it in /etc/resolv.conf. Openswan needs to be compiled with support for lwdnsq, by enabling USE_LWRES in Makefile.inc.

The identity of a host is more or less coupled to the IP address of that host, though the initiating end can actually specify a fully qualified domain name (FQDN) within the IKE channel as well. This means that clients behind NAT have some problems running OE, since it is hard to distinguish between a benign NAT situation and a rogue man in the middle.

If a server supports OE, it will have published a special DNS record containing its public key. On a client that supports OE and which tries to connect to a new IP address, the initial packet is trapped and cached within the kernel (for KLIPS; NETKEY unfortunately still drops this packet) and Openswan is signaled with the IP address that some program was trying to connect to. Openswan will do a DNS lookup to determine if the remote host supports OE. If not, the cached packet(s) are released in the clear. No encryption will take place for this IP address. If the remote host does support OE, Openswan fetches the public key via this DNS record, and it will initiate an IPsec connection using a self-made instance of the **OE connection** that uses authby=rsasigkey. The remote end will respond to the IKE request and, after it has fetched our public key from DNS, will be able to set up its end of the IPsec tunnel.

An OE Security Gateway

OE can also be used through another machine. This way, even when the target machine itself does not support OE or IPsec in general, the machine right in front of it can encrypt most data on behalf of the target machine.

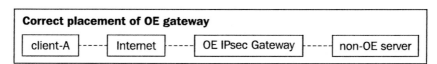

If client A is trying to talk to the non-OE server, they set up an IPsec tunnel to the OE IPsec Gateway, resulting in all but the last hop being encrypted. For this to properly work, the non-OE server should have the OE IPsec GW in its network path somehow. That is, it cannot be the machine *next* to it; it has to be a machine *in front* of it. Otherwise the non-OE server, which knows nothing about IPsec, would send client A packets back that would not pass through the OE IPsec GW, and would therefore not be encrypted (and worse, because there is an IPsec policy in place, would also get dropped at the client).

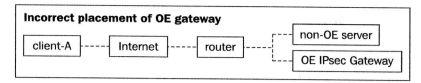

Using an OE security gateway, you can use a single IPsec-capable machine to enable OE communication to all servers on your network. This allows you to protect a whole cluster of Microsoft Windows machines that do not support OE. Only the LAN traffic between the OE security gateway and the Windows machines is unencrypted, but that should be part of your trusted (switched) network to begin with.

DNS Key Records

Back in 1996, there was no DNSSEC, which meant no specific DNS records for public keys were available. So the only record type that could be used to store the public key was the TXT record. When the first part of the DNSSEC specification was finished and implemented, it resulted in a new record, the KEY record. Although this record was originally meant for both DNSSEC and third-party applications that needed to publish public keys, and these KEY records could be subtyped, mixing DNSSEC and third-party key records came to be viewed as bad practice. RFC 3445 specified that the KEY record should only be used by DNSSEC, and other protocols should specify their own new records.

For IPsec, the IPSECKEY record was introduced. During all this time, the only reliable DNS record to use for OE had been the TXT record. Many DNS implementations never implemented the KEY record, and the IPSECKEY record is so new it hasn't yet even been implemented in the reference implementation of the IETF, the ISC Bind name server.

Together with the BGP protocol, the DNS protocol forms the core of the Internet. Without these two protocols, there would be no Internet. That is why the IETF was extremely reluctant to change anything in them, even though both protocols really needed security features. For the DNS protocol, the changes have finally been made, and the RFCs were published in the first few months of 2005. But most name servers on the Internet have not yet been updated to recognize all the new DNS record types. For the moment therefore, we recommend using both the new official IPSECKEY record and the old-style TXT record. In another year or two, the TXT records can probably be retired.

Forward and Reverse Zones

It is important to remember that there are two more or less different types of zones. These are commonly referred to as the **forward** and the **reverse** zones. The forward zone contains information indexed by name. For instance it contains an address (A) record showing that www.openswan.org has the IP address 193.110.157.129. The reverse zone does the opposite. It is indexed by IP address, and gives the host name for a certain IP address. To delegate this in a proper hierarchy, the reverse zone used is the IN-ADDR.ARPA. zone. The entry for 193.110.157.129 in the reverse zone is located at 129.157.110.193.IN-ADDR.ARPA., and contains a pointer (PTR) record to the name www.openswan.org. Both types of zones can contain additional information, such as MX (mail) records, free text (TXT) records, aliases (CNAME), or even SSH hostkey fingerprint (SSHFP) records.

The OE DNS Records

We will describe the three different records that we will be using. Currently, the TXT record is the most reliable, since all name server software supports this type of record. Support for the KEY record for OE will be discontinued now that the RFCs have reserved these records for DNSSEC keys. Instead, the IPSECKEY record is the new record for use with IPsec OE.

For example, the server at lists.openswan.org supports OE and has a DNS record to indicate this at 77.157.110.193.IN-ADDR.ARPA.:

```
# host lists.openswan.org
    lists.openswan.org has address 193.110.157.77
```

```
# host -t txt 77.157.110.193.in-addr.arpa.
    77.157.110.193.IN-ADDR.ARPA text "X-IPsec-Server(10)=193.110.157.77" "AQNxf6caK
    ULJkIYZycuo66Ko0U+iHaJUDr0QZHnG4MJ9IRNYi5H6kPxcwKIXkg+OGo+NeUyyWDEc+ox2
    7BFYViAHQNEyBRLZu0kyE681h+cHm7IfCSy0AOEBSCyZF3aGcL8GWxVhtimpJQ4tNxXZg7t
    LX5sfYw8mZnUBjkHvycclred/q3cNWbDlq2WU4TL+NBb5FnxXi9Hk/SRV7sMe56fvZuXkcJu4e
    2C7uocItzzF1b0BZx7yeXwHjzqAWn"
    "W/UA54fbSTvzgnrpSC+FMuhWTI1EdxcqGaOFIjGWWGV2nxg/QaPU9i8vpwFwrEEdCJTiqlb
    Y YNudblg4vYthnVNez0/RkfZHfhAaHdbJRSaQzOu88h"
```

First we need to put a marker in the TXT record to differentiate this from other TXT records that have nothing to do with IPsec, for example the anti-spam SPF records that also use the TXT record to store their data. This is why our TXT record starts with X-IPsec-Server.

The number in brackets shows the preference in a similar way to the mail (MX) record. You can have multiple OE gateways that lead to the host you are trying to reach. The lower the number, the higher the preference, as for MX records.

Next follows the IP address of the host's OE gateway, or its own IP address if it is capable of OE itself. This allows you to have one OE-capable gateway that will run OE for an entire subnet of machines behind it. If the gateway IP address is different from the host's IP address, an IPsec connection is made to the gateway, and it is assumed that the gateway can securely reach the host that is advertising the use of that gateway.

Finally, the raw key material of the public key follows.

Different Types of OE

Servers that are willing to respond to OE from initiating clients advertise this capability in a DNS record tied to their (static) IP address. Clients on a static IP address can do the same. Clients that are on dynamic IP, that is to say, they frequently change their IP address, can still publish their public key, but they will have to do that in a forward zone they control. When the client initiates the IPsec connection, after having read the server's DNS record confirming it can do OE, it will send a special leftid= option giving its own FQDN. So if the client on a dynamic IP is called laptop.xelerance.com, then its OE connection will use leftid=@laptop.xelerance.com. This ID is protected by the IKE protocol. When the server running OE sees this special ID, it will not try to look up the OE record based on the client's IP address, but instead will look for a DNS record in the forward zone at laptop.xelerance.com. As long as one of the two sides gets its authority from its IP address, and the corresponding record in the reverse, this process is safe.

Unfortunately, the parties cannot both have a key in the forward, since this would open up the entire process to a man-in-the-middle attack. Another important limitation is that when a client is using a key in the forward, it is not advertising its own OE capabilities to the world, since no one knows that the IP address it is using belongs to the hostname `laptop.xelerance.com`.

For servers, it can be quite an overhead to determine whether an incoming connection belongs to a client that can perform OE. In fact, it is probably very unlikely, because if the client could do OE, and the server is advertising its OE capability, the client would not be coming in using plaintext, but would first send an IKE packet for the OE initialization. Therefore, it makes sense to place servers in a responding-only mode known as **passive mode**.

The following table summarizes the four different kinds of OE peers.

Type	Resources needed	When to use	Limitations
Full OE	DNS entry in the reverse zone, a static IP	Whenever possible	Takes a lot of resources
Initiate-only OE (iOE)	DNS entry in any forward DNS zone	If no control of reverse, or when configured for DHCP	Does not advertise OE, will talk in the clear to other initiate-only peers
Passive OE	DNS entry in the reverse zone, a static IP	On very busy servers, or on responding-mostly servers (web servers, authoritative name servers)	All initiating connections from the host will be in the clear
NAT-OE / BTNS (currently not implemented)	None, keys exchanged inline (!)	Meant to be usable from behind NAT	Vulnerable to man-in-the-middle attacks

Policy Groups

Apart from these four classes of OE, there is a mechanism in place to fine-tune these modes even further. The policy files in `/etc/ipsec.d/policies/` are a few files that may contain IP addresses or subnets for explicit handling. 0.0.0.0/0 is used to denote the entire Internet.

Policy file	Purpose
`block`	Never talk to these hosts at all
`clear`	Always talk in the clear to these hosts
`clear-or-private`	Talk in the clear, but allow these hosts to initiate OE to us
`private`	Only talk encrypted to these hosts
`private-or-clear`	Attempt OE to these hosts, but talk in the clear if they do not support OE

> Any host configured to use OE by publishing OE DNS records must always run
> Openswan, as any OE-capable hosts will refuse to communicate with it in the clear.

Be aware that `private-or-clear` does not mean we will talk to those hosts in the clear if OE fails to initialize properly. Openswan refuses to talk in the clear to any host that advertises OE capabilities through DNS records.

For this reason, it is important to be aware that if you configure the DNS while experimenting with OE, and you later decide to no longer run OE on that host, you *must* remove the DNS records that advertise the OE capability. If this defense method was not in place, an attacker could easily cause a failure of OE by filtering IKE packets, and we would happily fall back to a cleartext connection without realizing what happened. By refusing to communicate, we will notice the connection fails to start, and we can investigate what is going on, and find out we are being attacked.

Internal States

We need to remember which IP addresses do not support OE, or else we would try those addresses indefinitely. Of course, they also have to be timed out, because otherwise we would end up with a very big list of IP addresses to remember. The following table lists the OE state information we have to keep for all these IP addresses or networks.

State	Description
trap	Packets going to these network ranges need to be trapped and checked for possible OE IPsec processing.
tun	Packets going to these network ranges already have an IPsec tunnel established.
pass	Packets going to these network ranges should be sent in the clear without attempting OE.
hold	Packets going to these network ranges need to wait. OE is being attempted currently, or OE has been misconfigured.

These states, with the exception of `trap`, are the same states used for regular IPsec tunnels. State information can be seen with the `ipsec eroute` command. `pass` eroutes are expired after a certain time, so an OE-capable machine does not end up with thousands of them.

Configuring OE

The goal of the Openswan project is to deploy IPsec as massively as possible. Therefore, the configuration needed for OE has been kept to a minimum. If you install Openswan from source, OE will be enabled by default. Everything should work automatically, and the end user does not need to be aware that some connections are encrypted. However, OE has seen some problems, and most distributions still focus on VPN connectivity, so they tend to play safe and disable OE. This can be done by including the following line in `/etc/ipsec.conf`, after the default section:

```
include "/etc/ipsec.d/examples/no_oe.conf"
```

Debian is the only distribution that asks you if you want to enable or disable OE when you install the Openswan package. Once OE sees a much wider audience and has proven to be stable on large scale deployments, we hope that more Linux distributions will start to ship Openswan with OE enabled.

Configuring Policies

The precise OE behavior can be fine-tuned using the entries in the policy files in /etc/ipsec.d/ policies. The default policy files only contain 0.0.0.0/0 in private-or-clear, which means OE will be attempted for all hosts, falling back to cleartext if the remote hosts do not support it. Especially if you are new to OE, it is recommended to add the name servers from /etc/resolv.conf in the clear-or-private policy. This will prevent the cascade failure in the first minute of trying to use OE for the name servers, and makes OE functional from the start of Openswan.

> To configure passive OE on a server, remove the 0.0.0.0/0 entry from the private-or-clear policy file and add it to the clear-or-private policy file.

Full OE or Initiate-Only

When Openswan starts, it tries to find out whether full OE is possible. It will regularly check for its own public key in the reverse DNS of its IP address.

If Openswan finds its own key based on the current IP address, it will run with full OE capabilities. If the section config section contains a myid= statement, that value is used as leftid= in the IKE protocol to enable initiate-only OE, if a valid DNS record is found for the host name specified in the myid= setting. If you specify a host name for myid=, do not forget to prepend the @ symbol to prevent it from being resolved to an IP address.

If the host is on a static IP address, and you control the reverse DNS for that IP address, you should set up TXT and IPSECKEY records in the reverse and enable full OE. If you do not control the reverse, you should create TXT and IPSECKEY records for the hostname in the forward zone. If your name server does not support the IPSECKEY record, you can use the KEY record instead, but remember that this should be avoided since RFC 3445 restricted the use of KEY records to DNSSEC only.

Generating Correct DNS Records

The ipsec showhostkey command is used to generate the proper public-key DNS records. For instance, if we wish to generate a TXT record for bofh.xelerance.com, which has a static IP address of 193.110.157.17, we use the following command on bofh.xelerance.com:

```
# ipsec showhostkey --txt 193.110.157.17
    ; RSA 2192 bits  bofh.xelerance.com    Thu Oct 17 12:32:33 2002
        IN    TXT    "X-IPsec-Server(10)=193.110.157.17" "AQOkF1Ggd4iFfl2
nQxJYbN9HGDhhIAKIXrG3+MCoAPX+z+fNI9j7rxxR9QhThlZZeOx+X9WB4hla8/8xAnELmcRhkD8
CxfznE4tCQ/Ws+9ibXUdD8Wee3JusSMrmLCuIScNUQuBtRe+l+nn16dzvw3/PGB67gid+AvGvJJJ
nxiFjibd/4ayVebJRj6Bu/FRexpXr3jEgg0TJwxu9y1xBR7i0tRYCdSQPKNCINrgmX7YZTp4bu6g
izhil63/sR6" "8eAqUz/DctDFDv7nrYsGDgGnfs03ncbY2m3lyPoiJyRJ34f4SILUBm+V44B5js
NDwFj7qx6wJ+dmXVkM7JGp5yLo93mfAhdKAcm5JkOpek2HszzO13"
```

You can use this data (called **RRdata**) to create a record both in the reverse DNS, in this case under 17.157.110.193.IN-ADDR.ARPA., and in the forward zone under bofh.xelerance.com. In our case, we add the following entry to our 157.110.193.IN-ADDR.ARPA. zone:

```
17.157.110.193.IN-ADDR.ARPA.  IN   TXT  "X-IPsec-Server(10)=193.110.157.17"
"AQN [...]"
```

In a similar way, we add the "IN TXT...." part in the zone for xelerance.com:

```
bofh.xelerance.com.           IN   TXT      "X-IPsec-Server(10)=193.110.157.17"
"AQ[...]"
```

Older versions of this command used to return a # instead of a ; for the first comment line, which breaks the zone, since # is not a valid comment character for the BIND name server. Make sure you do not paste in lines that mistakenly use # symbol as a comment character.

> You can also see that the key has been cut in two parts, each in double quotes, separated by a space. This was a workaround for an obscure BIND bug. Even if you do not use BIND yourself, it is safer to keep it in case some upstream ISP uses BIND. However, this syntax is not compatible with some other DNS implementations such as djbdns, in which case you cannot use it and should remove the inner quotes and spaces and turn this into a single continuous string.

Similarly, you can create the old KEY records. You cannot specify a gateway or preference with this record type:

```
# ipsec showhostkey --key
  ; RSA 2192 bits  bofh.xelerance.com   Thu Oct 17 12:32:33 2002
  bofh.xelerance.com. IN     KEY    0x4200 4 1 AQ[...]
```

You can change bofh.xelerance.com for 17.157.110.193.IN-ADDR.ARPA. and use this key record in the reverse as well.

And of course, you can use the command to generate the new IPSECKEY records. You need to specify a priority (1-255) and a gateway:

```
# ispec showhostkey --ipseckey 10 193.110.157.17
  ; RSA 2192 bits  bofh.xelerance.com   Thu Oct 17 12:32:33 2002
  bofh.xelerance.com. IN     IPSECKEY ( 10 5 193.110.157.17 AQ[...] )
```

The second argument within the brackets is the public key algorithm, 5 being RSA. If no gateway is specified, for instance because this entry is for initiate-only DNS in the forward zone, then . is inserted as the gateway.

Name Server Updates

Remember that after changing the DNS, it might take a while before the updated records appear, especially on secondary name servers. Be careful when triggering an OE connection to a remote host too soon, because if that remote host caches the negative DNS response "there is no key", it will only want to talk in the clear to your end, while your end is likely restarted and updated and will only talk encrypted to the remote host. This deadlock will remain until the remote clears its cache, when the TTL is reached.

As always, do not forget to increase the serial number of the zonefile, or else the secondary nameservers will never pick up your new OE record.

Verifying Your OE Setup

The ipsec verify command displays the relevant settings for OE. It is best to run this when Openswan has been shut down, so that packets sent or received by this verification process are not dropped because of OE policies. Alternatively, if you have a clear policy for your name server, you should be able to run ipsec verify when Openswan is already started.

```
# ipsec verify
...
    Opportunistic Encryption DNS checks:
        Looking for KEY in forward dns zone: bofh.xelerance.com
        [DEPRECATED]
        Looking for TXT in forward dns zone: bofh.xelerance.com
        [MISSING]
        Looking for IPSECKEY in forward dns zone: bofh.xelerance.com
        [MISSING]
        Does the machine have at least one non-private address?
        [OK]
        Looking for IPSECKEY in reverse dns zone: 17.157.110.193.in-addr.arpa.
        [MISSING]
        Looking for TXT in reverse dns zone: 17.157.110.193.in-addr.arpa.
        [OK]
        Looking for KEY in reverse dns zone: 17.157.110.193.in-addr.arpa
        [DEPRECATED]
```

We can see here that the old-style deprecated KEY records are still in the DNS for our bofh.xelerance.com host. A KEY record also appears in the reverse at 17.157.110.193.IN-ADDR.ARPA. And a TXT record for bofh.xelerance.com is missing from the forward zone, but it does have a TXT record in the reverse. This is not a problem because the machine is actually on a static IP address, and therefore able to use full OE. It does not need a TXT record in the forward, because the reverse record is always valid for this host. New-style IPSECKEY records have not been added for this host yet.

Furthermore, when you start Openswan, and OE is enabled, you should see the following entries in the log:

```
Nov  7 20:26:23 bofh pluto[1970]: loading group
"/etc/ipsec.d/policies/private"
Nov  7 20:26:23 bofh pluto[1970]: loading group
"/etc/ipsec.d/policies/private-or-clear"
Nov  7 20:26:23 bofh pluto[1970]: loading group "/etc/ipsec.d/policies/clear"
Nov  7 20:26:23 bofh pluto[1970]: loading group "/etc/ipsec.d/policies/clear-
or-private"
Nov  7 20:26:23 bofh pluto[1970]: loading group "/etc/ipsec.d/policies/block"
Nov  7 20:26:57 bofh pluto[1970]: using our IP (193.110.157.17:TXT) as
identity!
```

Note that if you do not have your name server in the clear policy and Openswan is running, than the last line might take a while, and some failures might show up while various DNS requests trigger more OE initiations and fail.

Testing Your OE Setup

Xelerance provides a few servers to test whether or not OE is properly running. If a functional OE setup is detected, ipsec livetest will run an OE test for you. But you can also manually trigger an OE connection. For example, www.openswan.org, lists.openswan.org, and www.xelerance.com all run full OE. The only thing you need to do is watch the logs and launch a ping to those sites. You should see something like this:

```
Nov  7 20:26:58 bofh pluto[1970]: "private-or-clear#0.0.0.0/0"[1]
...193.110.157.77===193.110.157.77/32 #1: initiating Main Mode
Nov  7 20:26:58 bofh pluto[1970]: "private-or-clear#0.0.0.0/0"[1]
...193.110.157.77===193.110.157.77/32 #1: received Vendor ID payload [Dead
Peer Detection]
Nov  7 20:26:58 bofh pluto[1970]: "private-or-clear#0.0.0.0/0"[1]
...193.110.157.77===193.110.157.77/32 #1: transition from state STATE_MAIN_I1
to state STATE_MAIN_I2
Nov  7 20:26:58 bofh pluto[1970]: "private-or-clear#0.0.0.0/0"[1]
...193.110.157.77===193.110.157.77/32 #1: I did not send a certificate because
I do not have one.
Nov  7 20:26:58 bofh pluto[1970]: "private-or-clear#0.0.0.0/0"[1]
...193.110.157.77===193.110.157.77/32 #1: transition from state STATE_MAIN_I2
to state STATE_MAIN_I3
Nov  7 20:26:59 bofh pluto[1970]: "private-or-clear#0.0.0.0/0"[1]
...193.110.157.77===193.110.157.77/32 #1: Peer ID is ID_IPV4_ADDR:
'193.110.157.77'
Nov  7 20:26:59 bofh pluto[1970]: "private-or-clear#0.0.0.0/0"[1]
...193.110.157.77===193.110.157.77/32 #1: transition from state STATE_MAIN_I3
to state STATE_MAIN_I4
Nov  7 20:26:59 bofh pluto[1970]: "private-or-clear#0.0.0.0/0"[1]
...193.110.157.77===193.110.157.77/32 #1: ISAKMP SA established
Nov  7 20:26:59 bofh pluto[1970]: "private-or-clear#0.0.0.0/0"[1]
...193.110.157.77===193.110.157.77/32 #2: initiating Quick Mode
RSASIG+ENCRYPT+TUNNEL+PFS+DONTREKEY+OPPORTUNISTIC+failurePASS {using isakmp#1}
Nov  7 20:26:59 bofh pluto[1970]: "private-or-clear#0.0.0.0/0"[1]
...193.110.157.77===193.110.157.77/32 #2: transition from state STATE_QUICK_I1
to state STATE_QUICK_I2
Nov  7 20:26:59 bofh pluto[1970]: "private-or-clear#0.0.0.0/0"[1]
...193.110.157.77===193.110.157.77/32 #2: sent QI2, IPsec SA established
{ESP=>0xa1ce4296 <0x738d2cd7}
```

For each OE connection, an instance of the private-or-clear connection is created. These OE connections also show up in the eroute table:

```
#ipsec eroute
   0   0.0.0.0/0            -> 0.0.0.0/0          => %trap
  10   193.110.157.17/32    -> 0.0.0.0/0          => %trap
  27   193.110.157.17/32    -> 193.110.157.2/32   => %pass
  13   193.110.157.17/32    -> 193.110.157.5/32   => %hold
   1   193.110.157.17/32    -> 12.110.110.204/32  => %pass
   3   193.110.157.17/32    -> 193.110.157.77/32  => tun0x1004@205.150.200.134
```

The eroute table shows us how many packets were sent through each eroute, the source and destination of the eroute, and the state of the eroute.

The trap eroute

In the eroute table given above, we see that all packets (0.0.0.0/0) are first trapped. This means that any packet with whatever source address to whatever destination address, for which we do not already have an eroute entry, will be cached while Openswan tries to determinate whether it can set up an OE-based IPsec tunnel for this destination.

The pass eroute

The eroute table also lists two pass eroutes. One of them is to 193.110.157.2. In our OE setup for bofh.xelerance.com, we had added 193.110.157.2 to our clear policy, since that is the IP address of the ns.xtdnet.nl name server, which is used by bofh.xelerance.com.

The hold eroute

The hold eroute in the table shows us there is a problem. It seems 193.110.157.5 is advertising OE, but an IPsec connection to it has failed to establish. Packets to this IP are being held, and if there are too many packets to hold, they will be dropped. The logs for this attempt also show us why:

```
Nov  7 20:28:41 bofh pluto[1970]: "private-or-clear#0.0.0.0/0"[2]
193.110.157.76===193.110.157.5/32 #4: initiating Main Mode
Nov  7 20:28:41 bofh pluto[1970]: "private-or-clear#0.0.0.0/0"[2]
...193.110.157.76===193.110.157.5/32 #4: ERROR: asynchronous network error
report on eth0 for message to 193.110.157.76 port 500, complainant
193.110.157.76: Connection refused [errno 111, origin ICMP type 3 code 3 (not
authenticated)]
```

To establish an OE connection to 193.110.157.5, we were apparently directed to the machine on the IP address 193.110.157.76. A DNS lookup confirms this:

```
# host -t txt 5.157.110.193.in-addr.arpa
    5.157.110.193.in-addr.arpa text "X-IPsec-Server(10)=193.110.157.76 AQOARC[...]
```

Indeed, 193.110.157.76 is the OE gateway for 193.110.157.5.

However, that machine was not running an IKE daemon on UDP port 500, as shown by the ICMP Connection Refused message. In other words, it is not running Openswan. Since the host is advertising its OE capability, but it is not working, we will not be able to communicate with that host unless Openswan is started on 193.110.157.76. A workaround would be to add 193.110.157.5/32 to the clear policy file.

Manipulating OE Connections Manually

Since OE uses instances of special connections, you cannot use ipsec auto --add or ipsec auto -delete on them as you would with static conns. But you can manually attempt to trigger an OE connecting using the following command:

```
# ipsec whack --oppowhere myipaddress --oppothere remotehost
```

Advanced OE Setups

A good system administrator usually uses separate IP addresses for separate services. When a service, such as a web server, mail server, or DNS server, is moved to another physical computer, the IP address moves along with it, and the transition happens smoothly without interruption. There are of course many other reasons why a server can have more than one IP address, but nevertheless many hosts on the Internet have multiple IP addresses.

Sometimes it can be desirable to exclude some IP addresses from OE, but to enable OE for the other IP addresses. For instance, a very busy DNS server may not have the resources to initiate OE for all incoming requests, but if that same server is an email server, you might wish to protect all outgoing SMTP connections using OE. This can be done, using the (old-style) IP aliases. The following is an example configuration for such a scenario:

```
config setup
    interfaces="ipsec0=eth0 ipsec1=eth0:2 ipsec2=eth0:3"
conn eth0_2-to-anyone
    # 193.110.157.5 is actually the IP address on eth0:2
    leftsubnet=193.110.157.5/32
    also=eth0-to-anyone
conn eth0_3-to-anyone
    # 193.110.157.7 is actually the IP address on eth0:3
    leftsubnet=193.110.157.7/32
    also=eth0-to-anyone
conn eth0-to-anyone
    left=193.110.157.76
    right=%opportunistic
    keylife=5m
    rekey=no
    # uncomment to enable incoming; change to auto=route for outgoing
    #auto=add

conn packetdefault
    auto=ignore
```

> Do not use the `ip` command to add IP address to a server if you want to exclude them with the above method.

Caveats

Of course there are a few tricks for solving some of the practical problems. First, OE has a **hole** for IKE packets, so they don't trigger the OE mechanism. Otherwise that would only result in both ends trying to set up tunnels simultaneously.

With KLIPS, packets triggering an OE connection are cached, but with NETKEY, these packets are lost and an obscure (and incorrect) `Resource temporarily unavailable` message is logged. We do not yet recommend using NETKEY with OE, but hopefully, NETKEY will add this functionality in the near future.

If you are behind NAT, you currently have to manually disable your OE settings.

As is to be expected, there are some problems with DNS. We do really want to protect DNS traffic with OE; such traffic is after all clearly worth protecting as part of your privacy. What if the name server supports OE? What if our resolver is behind OE? Well, we will have to live with some initial DNS problems. In practice, this means that for the first minute or so after starting Openswan with OE, a bunch of packets will be queued or lost, until we have established either a clear or encrypted connection to our name servers. Even if the name server supports OE, we will still have to reach it in plaintext before we query its records to use OE. This may all sound complex, but it's all rather harmless.

> When deploying OE for the first time, give it several minutes to start before declaring that it doesn't work.

Summary

This chapter has provided an in-depth examination of OE, a mechanism for the spontaneous setup of IPsec tunnels to hosts on the Internet without prior arrangement. We have shown how to configure it, how to add the proper DNS records, and how to protect subnets of hosts behind a single security gateway. If you wish to enhance the security of your DNS records, perhaps this is a good moment to configure and set up DNSSEC.

7
Dealing with Firewalls

This chapter explains the issues surrounding firewalls—devices that filter network traffic based on a set of policies. These devices can often interfere with the operation of your IPsec network, and careful consideration needs to be taken when setting them up. The following key topics will be covered:

- Where to place firewalls when using IPsec
- Configuring firewalls to permit IPsec traffic
- Firewalling on the IPsec device itself
- Managing Network Address Translation (NAT)

This chapter will not explain how firewalls work and a rudimentary knowledge of them is assumed.

Where to Firewall?

A firewall is in practice considered to be any network device, usually with two or more interfaces, that can filter network traffic. This includes everything from your home DSL/cable modem **router** (Linksys, D-Link, and Netgear being popular brands) up to enterprise-class commercial firewalls from vendors such as Checkpoint, Cisco, and Watchguard. Any machine running Linux, *BSD or Mac OS X also comes with firewall software, and many third-party firewall products are available for Microsoft Windows.

A firewall's primary purpose is to select which packets are allowed access to a certain host or network. Careful consideration must be taken when configuring your firewalls to permit IPsec traffic to pass within your networks. This chapter explains how to properly (and securely!) configure your firewalls to allow your VPN to function. Linux commands are given as examples for firewall rules, since many people want to combine the firewall and IPsec functionality onto a single machine, in this case a Linux machine with Openswan and the iptables command.

We will first discuss how to firewall IPsec traffic without NAT and then discuss tips and tricks for dealing with NAT devices. Dealing with devices that perform NAT is often the hardest part of setting up firewalls. These devices change all packets (including IPsec ones) as they are forwarded through the device, and can often complicate or mangle packets with the result that they fail the cryptographic and integrity tests performed by the receiving IPsec endpoint and are dropped.

There is much debate among security experts about how and where to firewall traffic. The old theory of putting a firewall on the perimeter and considering all internal traffic trusted has changed over the past few years. More often these days, software firewalls are also installed on hosts that need special protection. IPsec makes the old secure perimeter model even more difficult, since the outer firewall cannot decrypt the packets for further inspection. It has to make a decision without being able to read the content of the packets, meaning they can't always be trusted.

It is best to protect your IPsec gateway with some form of packet filtering. But since most packets the IPsec gateway receives will be encrypted, there is not much a firewall in front of it can do, since it cannot do any application-level firewalling as it cannot read the encrypted packets. At most, a firewall in front of the IPsec gateway can perform basic packet filtering. For simple packet filtering you do not need a fully fledged stateful application firewall—it can easily be done by the router in front of the IPsec gateway, since almost all modern routers can perform basic packet filtering.

More advanced packet filtering can be performed on the IPsec gateway itself, using host-based rules. With a Linux machine, you can combine `iptables` with Openswan to provide both packet filtering and IPsec capabilities. Such host-based firewalling is becoming more common, as most firewall vendors are now shipping IPsec stacks built into the firewall, so those IPsec devices have packet filtering available.

A further variation is to place a firewall on the inside of the network, between the IPsec gateway and the internal network. This allows the firewall to inspect traffic after it has been decrypted by the IPsec gateway, ensuring all policies are enforced.

We'll cover how to set up these types of configurations, and provide sample `iptables` rules for each.

Allowing IPsec Traffic

Chapter 2 explains in detail the IPsec protocols used to permit secure communication between hosts. From the firewall perspective, this comes down to:

Protocol	Port	Description
ESP (50)	N/A	ESP (Encrypted Secure Payload)
AH (51)	N/A	AH (Authentication Header)
UDP (17)	500	IKE
UDP (17)	4500 / high port	IKE, ESPinUDP encapsulation

Note that ESP is *protocol* 50, not *port* 50!

For IPsec to establish a full tunnel, you will need to permit both ESP and UDP port 500 traffic between peers. If you have IPsec peers behind NAT devices, you will also need to permit UDP port 4500, which is used by both IKE and ESPinUDP encapsulation to pass through the NAT device. Authentication Header (AH) is rarely used these days. It only provides authentication without encryption, and has come under recent attack by crypto experts as a possible vulnerability in the IPsec specification.

The rules that need to be added to the firewall rules to allow IPsec packets are shown below:

```
# Firewall Configuration to allow IPsec traffic to pass
# from a remote IPsec server (193.111.228.1) to our local
# IPsec server (12.110.110.204)
iptables -I FORWARD -s 193.111.228.1 -d 12.110.110.204 -p udp --dport 500 -j
ACCEPT
iptables -I FORWARD -s 12.110.110.204 -d 193.111.228.1 -p udp --dport 500 -j
ACCEPT
iptables -I FORWARD -s 193.111.228.1 -d 12.110.110.204 -p udp --dport 4500 -j
ACCEPT
iptables -I FORWARD -s 12.110.110.204 -d 193.111.228.1 -p udp --dport 4500 -j
ACCEPT
iptables -I FORWARD -s 193.111.228.1 -d 12.110.110.204 -p 50 -j ACCEPT
iptables -I FORWARD -s 12.110.110.204 -d 193.111.228.1 -p 50 -j ACCEPT
```

For a firewall that does not do NAT, this is all that is required to permit the two IPsec peers to establish any number of tunnels between them.

NAT and IPsec Passthrough

The IPsec protocols rely on traffic passing unchanged by intermediary devices, such as routers and firewalls. If a device changes the contents of packets (IP addresses, ports, checksums, and so on) as they pass between two IPsec peers, then the packet's cryptographic signature will no longer be correct and the packet will be rejected by the receiving peer.

This makes it difficult for NAT and IPsec to work properly together. The IETF IPsec Working Group identified this as a problem and wrote several drafts and RFCs to resolve the problem. The collection of drafts is known as NAT Traversal, or **NAT-T**, and they describe how two IPsec endpoints can determine if there is a NAT device between them, and how to deal with the situation.

During the IKE negotiation, if a peer can do NAT-T, it indicates this capability by adding VendorID information for each IETF NAT proposal it supports to the initiator. The responder also advertises its NAT-T capabilities via VendorID.

If both sites support a common proposal, the two sides send each other their real IP addresses, and then compare that with the header information in the IKE packets they have been receiving from the other end. If there is a mismatch, then whichever side detects the mismatch informs the other side that there is a NAT device in the path. The two sides then encapsulate outgoing ESP packets within UDP packets, using port 4500 (depending on the proposal), to complete the IKE negotiation.

IPsec passthrough (sometimes called VPN passthrough) was a kludge pre-dating the NAT Traversal proposals, and is performed by the NAT device itself without an understanding of the IPsec protocol at all. The NAT device tries to correlate IPsec traffic that is passed through it, and tweak the NAT accordingly. Usually these devices have a limit as to how many IPsec devices they can handle—many are limited to only a single host behind the NAT device. Unfortunately, IPsec passthrough breaks NAT Traversal.

> Vendors tend to promote 'IPsec Passthrough' as an important feature of their device. However, it really means that their device does not actually have an IPsec stack, and instead will mangle IPsec traffic that passes through the device, that should have been left untouched to properly work. If you can't disable this feature, avoid the device entirely!

You can not use IPsec passthrough and NAT-T between two peers at the same time. If you attempt this, you will see a message similar to the following in your log files:

```
Mar 18 18:29:42 gateway pluto[5096]: "nat_demo"[17] 192.168.89.10 #31:
Warning: peer is NATed but source port is still udp/500. Ipsec-passthrough NAT
device suspected -- NAT-T may not work.
Mar 18 18:30:47 gateway pluto[5096]: "nat_demo"[17] 192.168.89.10 #32:
Warning: peer is NATed but source port is still udp/500. Ipsec-passthrough NAT
device suspected -- NAT-T may not work.
```

If NAT-T is enabled on your IPsec peers, you must disable IPsec passthrough on any NAT device between them.

Configuring the Firewall on the Openswan Host

No matter which kernel stack is used, you still need to permit IPsec traffic in and out of the Openswan host. This portion of the firewall configuration is the same for KLIPS and NETKEY. Note that it is slightly different from the table listed earlier, and now uses the INPUT/OUTPUT tables instead of the FORWARD table:

```
# Firewall Configuration to allow IPsec traffic to be
# sent and received by this server.
iptables -I INPUT -s 193.111.228.1 -d 205.150.200.209 -p udp --dport 500 -j
ACCEPT
iptables -I OUTPUT -s 205.150.200.209 -d 193.111.228.1 -p udp --dport 500 -j
ACCEPT
iptables -I INPUT -s 193.111.228.1 -d 205.150.200.209 -p udp --dport 4500 -j
ACCEPT
iptables -I OUTPUT -s 205.150.200.209 -d 193.111.228.1 -p udp --dport 4500 -j
ACCEPT
iptables -I INPUT -s 193.111.228.1 -d 205.150.200.209 -p 50 -j ACCEPT
iptables -I OUTPUT -s 205.150.200.209 -d 193.111.228.1 -p 50 -j ACCEPT
```

These iptables commands are basic—you can further narrow down traffic by adding additional filtering commands, such as -i eth0, to specify that the packet must come in via your external interface eth0. The rules for ESP packets appear last, using an insert (-I) command. This causes them to appear at the top of the list, which is useful, since there will be many more ESP packets than IKE packets. They will be matched immediately, instead of traveling down the ruleset before getting accepted.

Although NATed IKE packets are sent out with a source port of 500 or 4500, these source ports might be changed by a NAT router in transit that needs to map many machines onto its own ports. Therefore you should not only allow port 500 to 500 and 4500 to 4500 packets, but all packets to and from port 500 and 4500, as in our example above.

One last reminder about firewall rules on your IPSec peer. If your peer is doing NAT itself (as is common in many Linux installations), you will need to exclude traffic for your IPsec tunnels from being NATed. We covered this in Chapter 4, but here it is again. This example assumes that your local network is 192.168.0.0/24, and that the remote side is 192.168.1.0/24—so you need to exclude the traffic destined for 192.168.1.0/24 from being NATed before it becomes encrypted:

```
iptables -t nat -I POSTROUTING -s 192.168.0.0/24 -d \! 192.168.1.0/24 -o eth0
-j MASQUERADE
```

Firewalling and KLIPS

When using KLIPS, there is an `ipsecx` device for each IPsec tunnel, which greatly simplifies the writing of firewall rulesets. When dealing with `ipsecx` devices, any traffic coming in from the virtual device has already been decrypted and checked by the KLIPS policies, so you can assume it is genuine traffic from the remote peer. Whether it is safe to forward to your network might also depend on the trust you have in that peer. Note that traffic flow with KLIPS is:

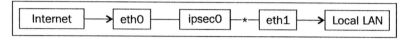

Where * denotes where the packet passes through the `iptables` FORWARD chain. So you can permit all traffic that comes in over the VPN with a single `iptables` rule:

```
iptables -I FORWARD -i ipsec0 -j ACCEPT
```

Another example shows how to only allow POP3 traffic (on TCP port 110) that comes in from a trusted VPN connection, but not from the Internet:

```
iptables -I FORWARD -i ipsec0 -p tcp --dport 110 -j ACCEPT
iptables -I FORWARD -i eth0 -p tcp --dport 110 -j DROP
```

If your default policy for `eth0` is to drop unmatched packets, you can even leave out the last rule.

Firewalling and NETKEY

IP firewalling when using NETKEY is quite different, as there are no `ipsecx` devices to easily identify IPsec traffic. Furthermore, this part of the networking code is under heavy development at the moment. At the time of writing (Linux 2.6.15), IPsec packets still appear to `iptables` in strange inconsistent ways. We see incoming encrypted packets and incoming plaintext packets, but there is no relationship between the two that we can observe. Some encrypted packets will cause plaintext packets to appear, others might not. And some plaintext packets might have arrived in plaintext to begin with.

Some packets might get killed by the built-in `rp_filter` anti-spoof protection if that is not disabled in `/etc/sysctl.conf`. You would expect a strict separation for encrypted packets to appear in the INPUT/OUTPUT tables, and the decrypted packets to go through the FORWARD table, but it is not that easy. There are patches by Patrick McHardy in the netfilter **patch-o-matic** to make the packets hit the `iptables` before *and* after encryption, but they have not been merged into the mainstream kernel yet. The patches can be found at `http://www.netfilter.org/patch-o-matic/pom-extra.html`. To accomplish the same as the **secure POP** rules above for KLIPS, you have to use the FWMARK facility of `iptables`. You can have the kernel *mark* IPsec packets.

This mark stays on the packet even after it has been decrypted. And since only the kernel, meaning you, can mark packets—it is not a state for packets on the network—you can distinguish plaintext traffic from decrypted traffic if you mark the encrypted traffic first:

```
iptables -t mangle -A PREROUTING -i eth0 -p esp -j MARK --set-mark 1
iptables -I INPUT -i eth0 -m mark --mark 1 -p tcp --dport 110 -j ACCEPT

iptables -I FORWARD -i eth0 -m mark --mark 1 -p tcp --dport 110 -j ACCEPT

iptables -A FORWARD -i eth0 -p tcp --dport 110 -j DROP
```

Alternatively you can split firewalling up for the two ethernet cards. On the external interface you drop port TCP 110, but accept IPsec traffic, and on the internal interface, you allow TCP port 110.

Packet Size

The MTU (Maximum Transmission Unit) size of packets can become a problem, as larger packets may be fragmented when being put into the IPsec tunnel. Also, a device somewhere between the IPsec peers might be silently fragmenting the packets, which, coupled with devices that cannot or will not reassemble the fragmented packets, leads to loss of communication.

Symptoms of this manifest themselves most commonly when loading a single web page is OK, but following any link on the website fails, or when you can log in via SSH, but issuing ls -al in a large directory seems to hang. Any situation where the initial connection works, but all subsequent data gets stuck, is usually an indicator of a packet size problem.

The issue is packet fragmentation—a device somewhere between the two peers is breaking the packets into two or more fragments. While a difficult problem to diagnose, it is not too hard to fix. If you are using KLIPS, simply add the following line to the config setup section of your ipsec.conf:

```
overridemtu=1419
```

This changes the MTU setting on the ipsecx interface. You can also do this manually by issuing the command:

```
ifconfig ipsec0 mtu 1419
```

We suggest starting with 1419, as IPsec encapsulated inside UDP using AES adds about 70-80 bytes of overhead to the packet, so by limiting packets to 1419 bytes, we stay inside the 1500 byte limit.

> Note: the MTU of the ipsecX interfaces defaults to 16260 bytes. This is so that the ipsecX device can accept packets from any phyiscal media (Ethernet, Token Ring, ATM, etc.) and fragment properly.

Using NETKEY, you must either adjust the MTU of the outer interface:

```
ifconfig eth0 mtu 1440
```

or add in specific routes and specify the MTU for the route:

```
ip route replace 192.112.90.50 via 193.111.228.1 dev eth0 mtu 1440
```

In the above example, 192.112.90.50 is the remote IPsec peer, and 193.111.228.1 is the next hop (usually default gateway) for the local IPsec peer.

In some situations, you might not want to adjust the MTU, as this is a global change and affects all traffic. For instance, if the MTU for one peer is only 500 bytes, and all the rest are 1500, all the remotes would be fragmenting each Ethernet packet into as many as three packets, which slows down network traffic. For such a case, you can try the following `iptables` rule as a workaround:

```
iptables -A FORWARD -p tcp --tcp-flags SYN,RST SYN -j TCPMSS --clamp-mss-to-
pmtu
```

This command enables TCP MSS clamping, which means that the device will adjust the parameters of the initial TCP connections on behalf of the peer, so that the packet size is kept within the MTU limits of this connection and will not be fragmented. The maximum segment size (MSS) is a parameter in the SYN packet sent during the initial connection setup. It specifies the maximum size of a single TCP packet that the sending peer will permit. Note that this only works for TCP connections, and not UDP.

If this does not solve the problem, then you can at least narrow down the packet size by sending ICMP packets of different sizes between the two IPsec peers:

```
ping -s 1400 ip.of.remote.host
```

Gradually increase the size until the ping fails. Once you know the largest successful size, you can enforce it with:

```
iptables -A FORWARD -p tcp --tcp-flags SYN,RST SYN -j TCPMSS --set-mss 1419
```

Here, 1419 is the largest packet that produced a successful ping in the above tests.

Summary

Armed with the knowledge from this chapter, you should now be able to securely configure firewalling on and/or around your IPsec peers. Remember to review your firewall rulesets often, and keep good documentation about when and why specific rules were added or modified.

8

Interoperating with Microsoft Windows and Apple Mac OS X

VPNs are still most often used for laptops. These computers represent the largest group of roadwarriors that need to connect to the central network. Though we have discussed how to use Openswan as client to an Openswan VPN server, Openswan only runs on Linux at this point, and Linux is a rare operating system for laptops, which normally run Microsoft Windows or Apple Mac OS X.

This chapter will explain how to set up these systems, and what changes are necessary on the Openswan side to ensure interoperability. This chapter also introduces Layer 2 Tunneling Protocol (L2TP), an extension to PPP/MPPE by Microsoft, and often used in combination with IPsec in transport mode.

Microsoft Windows

Even though it has been over ten years since Windows 95 was released, some people still use it, or one of its related successors, Windows 98 and ME. There is no native IPsec client for those platforms, but Microsoft does offer a locked-down version of what used to be the **SSH Sentinel** IPsec client as a free download for these platforms. This client is often called the **MSL2TP** client. It is no longer developed and lacks certain modern features, such as NAT-Traversal. We will not give an extensive tutorial on how to use these outdated systems, but if your configuration settings are similar to the modern Windows examples in this chapter, these clients will work to the best extent possible. Of course the standard answer to any Windows 9x problem is to upgrade the OS. There's a similar problem for old NT 3.5 and NT 4 systems, but even less people attempt to run IPsec on such systems. Again, upgrading those systems will save you a lot of time. In the remainder of this chapter, when we refer to Windows, we mean Microsoft Windows 2000, XP, and 2003. If something applies only to one specific version, we will mention this explicitly.

Mac OS X

Mac OS version 9 suffers from the same issues as Windows 9x: both simply predate large-scale deployment of IPsec. We will not discuss Mac OS 9 in this book. Mac OS X has seen three major releases so far, code named Jaguar, Panther, and Tiger, or version numbers 10.2, 10.3, and 10.4.

From a technical point of view, these Mac OS X versions have the same capabilities, since they all use KAME's Racoon under the hood. However, the Tiger GUI offers functionality not found in the earlier versions, for instance allowing user-friendly configuration of support for X.509 Certificates, VPN dial on demand, and whether to send the default route through the VPN or not. The GUI is geared towards L2TP, but if you manually configure Racoon with your own configuration files, you can also create IPsec tunnels without L2TP. Some third-party software, such as Securitas, is indeed just a GUI for creating Racoon configuration files avoiding Apple's VPN system altogether. Cisco ships its own IPsec client software for Mac OS X.

Always check for the latest updates on third party clients. Tiger especially broke much third-party software due to a massive kernel API change. Releases of Mac OS X before Tiger (10.4) do not implement NAT-Traversal, but all versions of Tiger (at least up to 10.4.3) implement NAT-T incorrectly. Due to an error in their IKE daemon, the kernel sends ESP instead of ESP-in-UDP packets.

Mac OS X Tiger Server contains another GUI utility called s2svpnadmin to set up site-to-site tunnels using PSK- or X.509-based L2TP/IPsec tunnels.

Layer 2 Tunneling Protocol (L2TP)

One of the limitations of IPsec that we have seen so far, from an end-user point of view, is the automatic configuration of an *internal* IP address. This is needed for two reasons. Mostly, LANs and WANs are secured against any unauthorized access from the Internet. Generally, firewalls ensure only LAN and WAN IP addresses may access the company's internal servers. The problem is that the IP address of the remote endpoint in an IPsec connection may be some ISP-determined address that would not be known beforehand.

When the firewall is not running on the VPN server, it is impossible to know whether such a connection is an authorized IPsec connection, or a rogue host on the Internet that has managed to get into the network somehow. The easiest solution is to have the VPN server give a connecting IPsec client another IP address, one from the company's IP address pool. Now the client can use that new IP for connections within the company network, and the company network can tell by the IP address that this is a teleworker connecting from home via the VPN server.

Another problem that makes IPsec connections with unknown ISP-assigned IP addresses difficult is NAT and NAT-Traversal. When NAT-Traversal is in use, an IPsec connection is actually established between the private IP address of the roadwarrior and the VPN gateway. The outer IP address of the roadwarrior is not used, except as the *envelope* around the inner packets. The problem arises when two teleworkers using the same internal IP addressing scheme try to connect to the VPN gateway. The chance of two teleworkers having the same internal IP address becomes pretty high since most ADSL and WiFi routers come with a default internal IP range (usually 192.168.0.0/24 or 10.0.0.0/24), and their DHCP services hand out IP addresses in that range (often 192.168.0.101 and 10.0.0101). The problem is aggravated when the same hardware is used by different teleworkers. Care needs to be taken to ensure everyone has a unique inner IP address.

Openswan 2.5 will support roadwarriors with identical IP addresses (it already does, but this code has not yet been released)

However, the teleworker's computer remains more or less inaccessible by the corporate network, as no one knows its internal IP address. L2TP solves this by handing out an IP address to those teleworker connections. Apart from assigning an IP, it is also often necessary to assign a DNS or WINS server from within the company network, so teleworkers are able to resolve the names of internal servers not published in the public DNS servers. The IKE protocol did not have any capability to relay this information. An extension was needed.

Assigning an IP for VPN Access

Microsoft and SSH worked on the **DHCP over IPsec** proposal. Though this proposal became an IETF standard, Microsoft never deployed it itself, and only the SSH-Sentinel client supported it. The SSH-Sentinel client was discontinued when it was bought by competitor Safenet. Therefore, DHCP over IPsec is not deployed anywhere, and we will not discuss how to set it up for Openswan.

ModeConfig with XAUTH was mostly a Cisco-driven extension to IKE to solve the IP address assignment issue. Nortel also supported this feature, but added its own proprietary extensions ensuring its client and server products could only interoperate with each other.

Microsoft's **Remote Access Service (RAS)** provides some of the infrastructure necessary for these features. RAS basically implements a PPP connection, with the typical Microsoft extensions. Microsoft then deployed its own encryption/VPN protocol, which was proven to be insecure on a few occasions. Microsoft ended up using a hybrid of the IPsec protocol and its own protocol called Layer 2 Tunneling Protocol (L2TP). This hybrid is confusingly also called L2TP. We will not delve into the political details of ModeConfig and XAUTH versus L2TP; both schemes are currently deployed on a large scale. Only L2TP, however, does not require one to buy or install a separate VPN client for Microsoft Windows. The same applies to Apple's Mac OS X.

L2TP Properties

L2TP uses IPsec transport mode with ESP. If NAT-Traversal is needed, another layer of ESPinUDP is added on top of that. But L2TP can also use its own encryption method, the one that has been proven insecure, within those packets. Inside the L2TP packets, PPP is used. In some configurations, when the inner Microsoft encryption is not used but the L2TP packets are still encrypted within the IPsec packet, Windows will complain because it is not aware of the outer-layer IPsec encryption. Some system administrators therefore enable this inner encryption layer as well, just to save the end user a bogus warning pop-up window, but not all L2TP daemons support this encryption.

Unlike PPP, which is a point-to-point protocol, L2TP is a routable protocol using UDP port 1701. IPsec connections established for an L2TP connection will request a special IPsec tunnel that limits the protocols and ports that are allowed over the IPsec tunnel to just those needed to *transport* L2TP packets. The L2TP packets contain the actual PPP packets, which contain the real IP packets with their source and destination addresses and ports. Openswan supports these protocol and port number restrictions using the `leftprotoport=` and `rightprotoport=` parameters.

Just like PPP, L2TP can automatically assign various network attributes, such as IP address, netmask, DNS, or WINS servers, just like the traditional PPP-over-RAS protocol can. It also offers better integration with proprietary Microsoft features, making it easier to integrate with the Windows login procedure. For the end user, L2TP is therefore very easy to configure and deploy.

When IPsec is used with L2TP, Microsoft currently only supports 3DES, not AES. PFS is also not supported by Windows clients in L2TP configuration. Openswan version 2.5 will support multiple L2TP clients behind the same NAT.

L2TP has another disadvantage: it adds even more encapsulations to a packet. This is likely to trigger more any **PMTU** or **packet fragmentation** issues.

Pure IPsec versus L2TP/IPsec

The question of what type of setup to use is difficult to answer. It depends on a few subjective choices. The easier you make it for VPN clients to connect, the harder your VPN server will be to set up. Ideally, you want to avoid the extra hassle of setting up and maintaining an L2TP infrastructure. And if possible, you want to avoid another layer of packet encapsulation, and even one layer of encryption, especially because these L2TP connections are userland processes on the Linux server. They do not run within the kernel, like IPsec does, and therefore require significantly more CPU power.

However, Windows and Mac OS X support L2TP out of the box. No separate VPN client needs to be installed. If you are installing a separate VPN client anyway, you might as well try to get a client that supports ModeConfig with XAUTH, and avoid the overhead of L2TP altogether. However, be aware that ModeConfig with XAUTH is a fairly recent addition to Openswan, which has not yet been widely tested with Windows clients.

If you are just connecting a handful of users to a single office subnet, then it is recommended that you skip L2TP and ModeConfig with XAUTH altogether. Instead, just ensure your users are set up to use unique LAN IP addresses at home to avoid collisions, and incorporate those ranges into your company firewall rules. Although you will then need to use a third-party VPN client for Windows or Mac OS X, such clients are freely available.

L2TP: PSK or X.509

L2TP's IPsec connection can use either PSK or X.509. We discussed the use of X.509 versus PSK in earlier chapters. In general, X.509 is much preferred over PSK because it is more secure. However, it is far easier to use PSK. Note that Windows 2000 only supports L2TP with X.509. It does not support L2TP with PSK. Mac OS X before Tiger did not support X.509, and with Tiger (10.4.4) it is still hard to configure properly.

In the following sections, we look at how to set up L2TP with either PSK or X.509, but we strongly advise everyone to switch to X.509 as soon as their platform supports it. Remember that PSK does not work too well when NAT-Traversal is involved. Finally, remember that anyone that gets hold of the PSK can pretend to be the VPN gateway and attempt to obtain user credentials. As the PSK needs to be identical for all clients, the larger the company, the larger this risk becomes.

Client and Server Configurations for L2TP/IPsec

Most of the information in this chapter regarding the installation and configuration of L2TP was originally collected by Jacco de Leeuw. He can be considered the definitive source on connecting Linux, Windows, and Mac OS X via L2TP to an Openswan VPN server. In fact, even Microsoft employees copy his information verbatim to their customers. Visit his site at http://www.jacco2.dds.nl/index.html for the latest information.

In our examples, the Openswan server is configured as a standard VPN gateway for home users to access a single office network, which uses 192.168.1.0/24. The office DHCP server hands out addresses in the range 192.168.1.100 to 192.168.1.127, while the L2TP server hands out virtual IP addresses in the range 192.168.1.128 to 192.168.1.254. One could imagine that the company servers have IP addresses in the range 192.168.1.1 to 192.168.1.99. The VPN server for our example company is called aivd.xelerance.com and has a public ISP-assigned IP address of 193.110.157.131 and an internal IP address of 192.168.1.98.

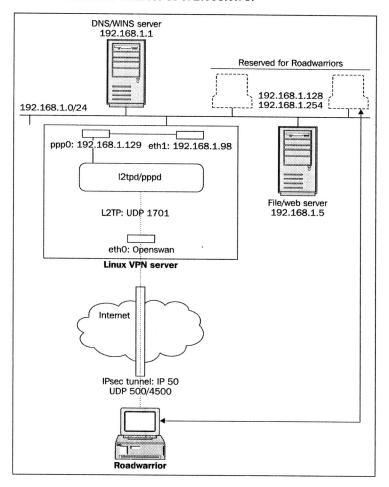

The L2TP Openswan Server

For Mac OS X and some PocketPC versions, only L2TP with PSK is currently working properly. However, it is possible to have both L2TP with PSK and L2TP with X.509 configurations on the Openswan VPN server, so clients that support X.509 can use it, while clients that do not support it can connect using PSK.

Configuring Openswan for L2TP/IPsec

We need to create a connection that is used solely for securely transporting L2TP packets from the client to the VPN server. Some people get confused here and try to configure a `leftsubnet=` on the Openswan server, because they want access to that subnet, but this is wrong. The `l2tpd` daemon and the pppd daemon handle the assignment of the virtual IP address to the client. This virtual IP is already part of the subnet at the server side. The only thing we are setting up is a host-to-host tunnel that will be used like a PPP connection. Your `ipsec.conf` would look like this:

```
version 2
config setup
    # klipsdebug=none
    # plutodebug="control parsing"
    nat_traversal=yes
    virtual_private=%v4:192.168.0.0/16,%v4:!192.168.1.0/24,%v4:10.0.0.0/8

include /etc/ipsec.d/examples/no_oe.conf

conn west-l2tp-psk
    left=193.110.157.131
    leftnexthop=193.110.157.158
    leftprotoport=17/1701
    rightprotoport=17/%any
    rightsubnet=vhost:%priv,%no
    right=%any
    auto=add
    authby=secret
    pfs=no
    # type=transport

conn west-l2tp-x509
    left=193.110.157.131
    leftnexthop=193.110.157.158
    leftprotoport=17/1701
    leftrsasigkey=%cert
    leftcert=aivd.xelerance.com.pem
    rightprotoport=17/%any
    rightsubnet=vhost:%priv,%no
    right=%any
    rightrsasigkey=%cert
    auto=add
    authby=rsasig
    pfs=no
    # type=transport
    # rightca=%same
```

Note that even though we are configuring a transport-mode tunnel, and so should specify `type=transport`, this currently does not work in combination with the `rightsubnet=` statement we need for NAT-Traversal. However, leaving out `type=transport` will work as a transport mode connection is still requested and granted to the incoming client connection. As of Openswan-2.4.5, when this bug was fixed, one should enable the proper option specifying transport mode, which is the reason we left it in our configuration file as a comment. Updated l2tpd configuration examples are located in `/etc/ipsec.d/examples/` as of openswan-2.4.5

Most clients do not support PFS, so this is disabled using pfs=no. However, Openswan will ignore this option if the incoming client suggests PFS anyway, since there is no reason to decline this added benefit. Using the option pfs=no therefore allows us to support all clients, irrespective of whether they support PFS.

Further note how we are using rightprotoport=17/%any. This will allow all UDP packets to be transported through the IPsec connection. Ideally, this could be limited to UDP port 1701. Unfortunately, unpatched Windows XP machines propose a rightproto=17/0 and some other implementations use a random high source port to connect to the L2TP daemon instead of port 1701. The configuration we used, though more liberal, will work for all clients. If you are using a dedicated VPN server, that runs no other UDP based services, this should not matter, as the IPsec transport mode connection is only allowed to connect to the VPN server itself, and not to other servers running UDP services. That is only allowed through the L2TP packets.

> There is currently a problem with having both an L2TP-PSK and a L2TP-X509 based connection at the same time. A workaround is described at http://bugs.xelerance.com/view.php?id=348 but it is not pretty. If you can avoid using PSK altogether that would be best. Another possible approach would be to use two different public IP addresses on the same server or to use two different VPN servers.

If using PSK, we need to add an entry for our PSK. If we are using X.509, we need an entry for our RSA private key, including password if it is still locked. In our examples we are using aivd.xelerance.com (193.110.157.131). This is configured in /etc/ipsec.secrets:

```
193.110.157.131 %any: PSK "TheSecretIsSquemischOssifrage"
              : RSA /etc/ipsec.d/private/aivd.xelerance.com.key "foobar"
```

You might have noticed another commented-out option: rightca=%same. This option should be enabled when you have clients that need to connect to multiple Openswan servers that have different CAs. The reason we do not add it by default is that some setups could involve intermediate CAs.

Linux Kernel Runtime Parameters for L2TP/IPsec

Since the Linux VPN server will be forwarding packets (between an ethx and a pppx interface), you must make sure **ip_forwarding** is enabled. You should also disable the inbuilt anti-spoof filters. Disabling various ICMP redirection packets is also recommended, especially on the 2.6 kernel, to prevent the kernel sending redirects for packets that come from and go to the same interface, something that usually happens when using NETKEY. These can be configured in /etc/sysctl.conf:

```
net.ipv4.ip_forward = 1
net.ipv4.conf.default.rp_filter = 0
net.ipv4.conf.all.accept_redirects = 0
net.ipv4.conf.all.send_redirects = 0
net.ipv4.icmp_ignore_bogus_error_responses = 1
net.ipv4.conf.all.log_martians = 0
```

Alternatively, you can use one of the rc scripts, such as rc.local, to set up these options by adding the following commands:

```
echo "1 " > /proc/sys/net/ipv4/ip_forward
echo "0 " > /proc/sys/net/ipv4/conf/default/rp_filter
echo "0" > /proc/sys/net/ipv4/conf/all/accept_redirects
echo "0" > /proc/sys/net/ipv4/conf/all/send_redirects = 0
echo "1" > /proc/sys/net/ipv4/icmp_ignore_bogus_error_responses
echo "0" > /proc/sys/net/ipv4/conf/all/log_martians
```

You do not need to configure any **proxyarp** setting, since the pppd daemon will that that for you.

Protecting the L2TP Daemon with IPsec using iptables

L2TP could in theory be used without IPsec. It is therefore recommended to make the L2TP server only available through an IPsec connection, to prevent L2TP connections being established without IPsec, and to add some additional security. Only clients who are able to establish an IPsec connection are then able to negotiate anything with the L2TP server. If there are any specific L2TP problems, either in the software or the protocol, they should be unreachable for any remote attacker that has no valid IPsec credentials. This can be accomplished on a single VPN server by binding IPsec to the external interface and binding L2TP to the internal interface, and then only forwarding packets that have arrived through an IPsec connection from the external IPsec interface to the internal L2TP interface.

First we need to limit the accessibility of the L2TP daemon from the outside for non-IPsec hosts. This can be done by ensuring the L2TP daemon listens only on the internal IP address using a listen-addr option, and using an iptables rule to NAT the traffic from the public IP address to the private IP address, if it has been determined that the packet came in through IPsec. Remember we cannot access the internal IP address until after we have a working L2TP connection that will give the client its internal IP address.

If KLIPS is being used, it is easy to distinguish those packets and use an iptables rule:

```
iptables -t nat --append PREROUTING -i ipsec0 -p udp --dport 1701 -j DNAT --
to-destination 192.168.1.98
iptables -i eth0 -p udp --dport 1701 -j DROP
```

With NETKEY, the rule is a bit more complex, but you can mark the IPsec packets before they are decapsulated. The mark actually survives this process, so any plaintext packet with a mark on it originally came in through an IPsec tunnel:

```
# iptables -t mangle -A PREROUTING -i eth0 -p esp -j MARK --set-mark 1
# iptables -A INPUT -i eth0 -m mark --mark 1 -j ACCEPT
# iptables -A INPUT -i eth0 -p udp --dport 1701 -j DROP
```

You could also dynamically add and remove these firewall rules in a custom _updown script, which can be configured for the Openswan L2TP connection using leftupdown=/path/to/your/script.

It might make more sense to first perform a standard setup, with the L2TP daemon listening on all interfaces, so you do not need complex firewall rules. Once the IPsec/L2TP combination works, you can secure the L2TP daemon as described above.

Remember that you will also need to allow IKE traffic on port UDP 500 and 4500, L2TP traffic on UDP port 1701, and ESP packets. The rules will be slightly different for KLIPS or NETKEY because the incoming interface is different, but should look roughly like:

```
iptables -A OUTPUT -p udp --sport 1701 -j ACCEPT #for KLIPS add -o ipsec0
iptables -A INPUT -p udp --dport 1701 -j ACCEPT #for KLIPS add -i ipsec0
iptables -A INPUT -p esp -j ACCEPT
iptables -A OUTPUT -p esp -j ACCEPT
iptables -A INPUT -p udp --dport 500 -j ACCEPT
iptables -A INPUT -p udp --dport 4500 -j ACCEPT
iptables -A OUTPUT -p udp --sport 4500 -j ACCEPT
```

Choosing an L2TP Daemon

There are a few different L2TP software packages available, and most of them are available in different patched versions.

The most commonly used daemon is still l2tpd, though the main website and source repository have vanished. A retirement page can be found at http://l2tpd.sourceforge.net/. RPMs for SuSE, Red Hat, Fedora, and Mandrake can be found on Jacco's L2TP pages. l2tpd is still included in Debian, though you might need to use the version in Debian **unstable** to get a modern enough version. The authors are maintaining l2tpd in Fedora Extras.

l2tpd is known to work with an IPsec/L2TP setup and has been used by many people.

> The old homepage for L2TP, www.l2tpd.org, has been squatted by a domain squatter. A malicious person could re-instate this domain with malicious code on it. We recommend downloading the source from the SourceForge page, or from Debian, Fedora Extra, or Jacco de Leeuw's website directly.

Another L2TP daemon is rp-l2tpd, though this project's activity seems to have stalled as well. There is not as much experience running rp-l2tpd with IPsec as there is with l2tpd, but it has been reported to work by various people. However, rp-l2tpd cannot assign virtual IP addresses by itself. You can either assign static virtual IP addresses per user, or let the PPP daemon (pppd) handle virtual IP address assignment either using a plug-in called ppp-dhcp, or using pppd 2.4.2 or newer, which supports RADIUS. However, this does require that you set up a RADIUS server that supports 'IP pools'.

> Be aware when testing different L2TP daemons that both l2tpd and rp-l2tpd use the same filename to install their daemon, /usr/sbin/l2tpd.

l2tpd can also use the PPP with RADIUS options mentioned for rp-l2tpd.

There are two more L2TP servers worth mentioning. One is being pushed by IBM, and is called OpenLTP. Another L2TP implementation, one that does not run as a daemon but as a kernel module, is confusingly called l2tp. You can find it under that name as a SourceForge.net project.

Some versions of the L2TP daemons used to require 'Legacy (BSD) PTY' support. Most modern Linux distributions no longer support this legacy feature, which has been replaced by Unix98

PTYs. Fedora Core and Mandrake are known to require a kernel recompile to add this feature. Both l2tpd and rp-l2tpd, no longer require Legacy PTYs. Debian and Fedora Extras contains a modern enough l2tpd implementation as well.

Configuring L2TPD

Configuration of the L2TPD program is fairly straightforward, especially when using Jacco's prepackaged version that is already set up for using L2TP with IPsec, and is also the basis for the Fedora Extras package. Most configuration options go into /etc/l2tpd/l2tpd.conf.

```
[global]
; if you run l2tpd on the internal interface only, enable the line below
; listen-addr = 192.168.1.98

[lns default]
ip range = 192.168.1.128- 192.168.1.254
local ip = 192.168.1.98
require chap = yes
refuse pap = yes
require authentication = yes
name = OpenswanVPNServer
ppp debug = yes
pppoptfile = /etc/ppp/options.l2tpd
length bit = yes
```

> Be careful not to create conflicting files in /etc/l2tpd.conf and /etc/l2tpd/l2tpd.conf.

In our example, we have reserved 192.168.1.128 to 192.168.1.254 for virtual IP addresses that can be assigned to incoming L2TP connections. Make sure the local DHCP server in the network does not assign these addresses as well. Our next step is to create the options for the pppd daemon that are specific to using pppd with L2TP. This is done in /etc/ppp/options.l2tp:

```
ipcp-accept-local
ipcp-accept-remote
ms-dns  192.168.1.1
ms-dns  192.168.1.3
ms-wins 192.168.1.1
ms-wins 192.168.1.3
noccp
auth
crtscts
idle 1800
mtu 1200
mru 1200
# change line below to defaultroute to make all traffic go through the VPN
nodefaultroute
debug
lock
proxyarp
connect-delay 5000
```

> It is important that no packet fragmentation occurs, because if multiple clients are trying to use L2TP behind the same NAT router, Openswan would not be able to distinguish the fragments. This is why the values of 1200 are chosen for the MTU and MRU in options.l2tp. It is also strongly recommended to set the public interface (in our example eth0) mtu to 1440 to prevemt fragmentation in the IPsec layer as well.

You can specify DNS and WINS servers inside the remote office network. Clients will then use those instead of the DNS/WINS servers assigned by their ISP's DHCP server. This is necessary to resolve machine names that are only available within the office network. If you use this L2TP connection to not only get a virtual IP and reach the office network, but also as the default connection for all packets, change the nodefaultroute option to defaultroute. This will also require you to make a similar configuration change in the client configuration to send all traffic over the VPN connection. The proxyarp parameter ensures that the virtual IP the remote client obtains appears to be located in the remote office LAN. The Linux server will answer ARP requests on the local Ethernet on behalf of all the L2TP-assigned virtual IP addresses.

Configuring User Authentication for pppd

pppd will need to authenticate users using their usernames and passwords. Do not confuse this with the PSK, which just authenticates a group of machines with IPsec for Phase 1. If you have a Windows Domain or some way to authenticate users on the office network, you'll want to hook pppd into this. Probably the easiest way is to use a recent version of pppd with RADIUS support. Configuring a RADIUS server falls outside the scope of this book. Take a look at FreeRADIUS for a good free RADIUS implementation.

For small setups, it is probably enough to use a simple /etc/ppp/chap-secrets file:

```
# Secrets for authentication using CHAP
# client    server   secret           IP addresses
paul         *       "mysecret"       192.168.1.128/25
*           paul     "mysecret"       192.168.1.128/25
ken          *       "anothersecret"  192.168.1.130
*           ken      "anothersecret"  192.168.1.130
```

In this example, the user paul has password mysecret. pppd will pick any available IP from the range 192.168.1.128/25 (which should fall within the subnet range specified in our L2TP configuration). The user ken has been given a static IP address of 192.168.1.130. Be careful not to overlap static addresses with address ranges or addresses might get handed out twice.

If you enable Use Windows logon on the Windows clients to enable them to log in to the office network over the VPN, then the client will authenticate itself as \\DOMAINNAME\username instead of just username, in which case you will need to use the full syntax for the username, such as \\XELERANCE\paul.

Microsoft Windows XP L2TP Configuration

Windows XP and 2003 can be configured to use either PSK or X.509 Certificates in combination with L2TP. Apart from the certificate import process, configuration of both versions is practically identical. First log in as a user that has administrative access to the local machine.

Start the New Connection Wizard. You will find it at Start | All Programs | Accessories | Communications | New Connection Wizard. Click Next when the wizard's splash screen appears. From the four options presented, choose Connect to the network at my workplace and click Next.

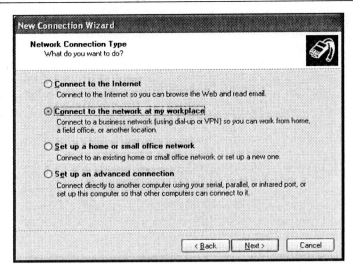

On the next screen, select Virtual Private Network connection, and click Next. Give the VPN connection a name and click Next. Then specify the gateway, in our example aivd.xelerance.com, and click Next, and then Finish.

Connect to the VPN and fill in the username and password that was previously set in the CHAP secrets file. Save the username and password if you wish by checking the box, and specify whether all users will be allowed to start the VPN or not.

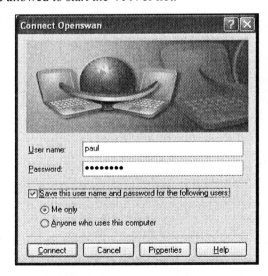

Don't start the connection yet. First, click the Properties button.

On the Options tab, check Include Windows logon domain if you wish to log in to a remote Windows domain.

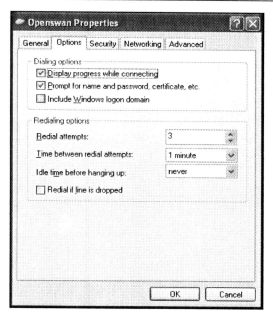

On the Security tab, choose Advanced (custom settings), and then click the Settings... button. On the Advanced Security Settings dialog, select Optional encryption in the Data encryption dropdown. This refers to the L2TP encryption. Since we are using L2TP/IPsec, we are already using IPsec for our encryption and there is no need to enforce encryption on the L2TP layer as well. Under Allow these protocols, make sure PAP is not selected and CHAP is selected. Select OK.

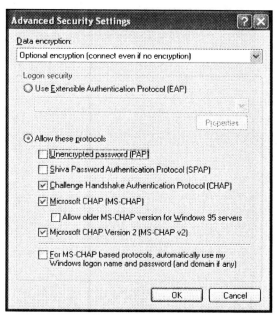

A pop-up will appear, warning you that encryption (for L2TP) may not occur. Since we are using IPsec, we don't really care so select Yes, and you'll be returned to the Security tab.

Click the IPSec Settings... button. On the dialog that appears, check Use pre-shared key if you want to use PSK, and type in the PSK that you put in /etc/ipsec.secrets on the Openswan server earlier.

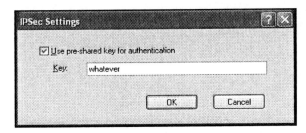

If you want to use X.509 Certificates, make sure this box is not checked and do not forget to import the appropriate certificates later. You can either use Xelerance's certimport.exe or follow the manual import procedure described at the end of this chapter. Click on OK, and open the Networking tab.

Change the Type of VPN to L2TP IPSec VPN. You can further configure the TCP/IP settings for the virtual IP that you will obtain by selecting Internet Protocol (TCP/IP) in the lower pane, and then clicking on Properties.

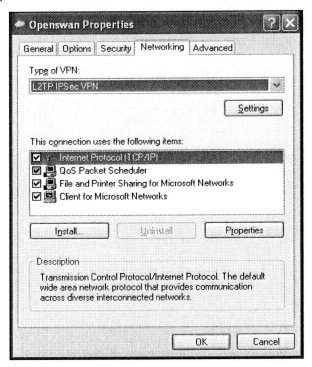

The settings in the Properties dialog include the WINS and DNS services, which allow host names that are only visible within the remote subnet to be resolved by the client. Also, if you do not want to tunnel all traffic through the VPN, you must uncheck the box labeled Use default gateway on remote network on the General tab.

When done, select OK and then Connect. This should bring the L2TP/IPsec connection up.

> If you are receive 789 errors, double-check the hostname. If that's not the problem, try using an IP address. If you still get error 789, make sure that the IPsec service is not disabled and stopped.

There is one other possible problem with Windows XP SP2. Some people put the L2TP/IPsec server behind their firewall and use NAT or packet forwarding between the VPN and the firewall. We have not covered how to set this up, as it is not a recommended scenario, and in fact Windows XP Service Pack 2 disabled this possibility for XP as the client. You can re-enable it by tweaking the Windows registry and setting the following DWORD entry to 2:

```
HKLM\System\CurrentControlSet\Services\IPSec\AssumeUDPEncapsulationContextOnSe
ndRule
```

Microsoft Windows 2000 L2TP Configuration

Windows 2000 can only be configured to use X.509 Certificates in combination with L2TP. The procedure is almost identical to the one described for Windows XP. Again, log in as a user that has administrative access to the local machine.

Open the Network Connection Wizard, found at Start | Programs | Accessories | Communications | Make New Connection. Click Next at the splash screen. Choose Connect to a private network through the Internet and click Next.

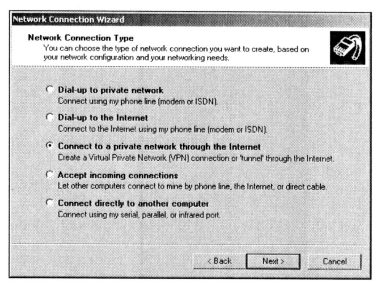

Specify the gateway on the Destination Address screen, aivd.xelerance.com in our example, and select Next. The next screen is Connection Availability. Choose either For all users or Only for myself, depending on whether you want all users on this machine to be able to access the VPN.

On the last screen, give the connection a name and create a desktop shortcut if you desire, and then click Finish.

Connect to the VPN and fill in the username and password that was previously set in the CHAP secrets file. Save the username and password if you wish by checking the box. Do not start the connection yet, but first click the Properties button.

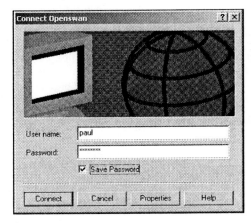

On the Options tab, tick Include Windows logon domain if you wish to log in to a remote Windows domain. Select the Security tab, and choose Advanced (custom settings), and click the Settings button.

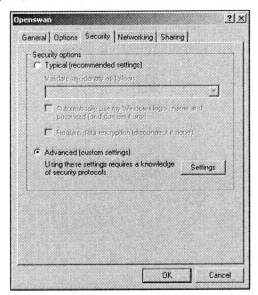

Select Optional encryption for the Data encryption dropdown. This refers to the L2TP encryption. As we are using L2TP/IPsec, we use IPsec for our encryption, and don't need to enforce encryption on the L2TP layer as well. Under Allow these protocols, make sure PAP is not selected and CHAP is selected and click OK.

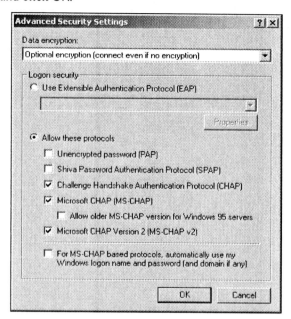

A popup will appear, warning you that encryption (for L2TP) may not occur. Since we use IPsec, this isn't a problem, so click Yes. Now we are back in the connection menu, select the Networking tab.

Change the Type of VPN server I am calling to Layer-2 Tunneling Protocol (L2TP).

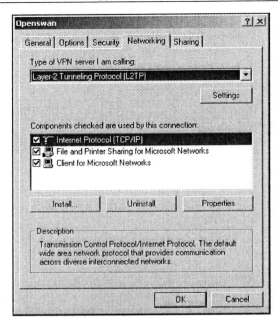

You can further configure the TCP/IP settings for the virtual IP that you will obtain by selecting Internet Protocol (TCP/IP) in the lower pane, and then clicking on Properties. Settings here include the WINS and DNS services, so that hostnames that are only visible within the remote subnet can be resolved by the client.

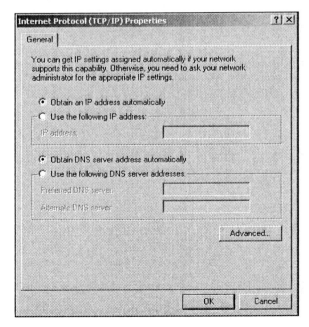

If you do not want to tunnel all traffic through the VPN, you must click the Advanced... button and uncheck the box for Use default gateway on remote network. Do not change any IPsec settings in the Options tab!

When done, click OK until you are back at the main connection window. You can now click Connect. This should bring the L2TP/IPsec connection up, provided you have imported the necessary X.509 Certificates.

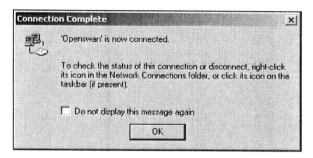

> If you receive 789 errors, double-check the hostname. If that is not the problem, try using an IP address. If that still gives an error 789, check that the IPsec service is not disabled and stopped.

Apple Mac OS X L2TP Configuration

Configuring L2TP using PSK on Mac OS X is very easy thanks to a nice simple user interface. With Mac OS X 10.4, codenamed Tiger, it should also be possible to use L2TP with X.509 Certificates, although it is not always as straightforward as we might like.

To make things worse, all versions of Mac OS X up to at least version 10.4.3, which is Tiger with all software updates at the point of writing, have a broken NAT-T implementation. Openswan 2.4.5 has a workaround to correctly interoperate with the broken NAT-T implementation of Tiger.

> All versions of Mac OS X up to 10.4.3 (Tiger) have a broken NAT-T implementation. Openswan 2.4.1 has a workaround for this problem, but this workaround doesn't always work yet. Hopefully the workaround will work in all cases in Openswan 2.4.2 or 2.4.3.

To configure a L2TP/IPsec VPN connection, open the Internet Connect application from the System Preferences menu, or from the wireless menu that appears when you click on the wave icon at the top.

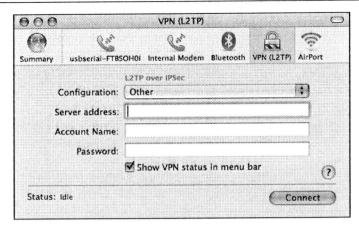

Change the Configuration dropdown from Other to Edit Configuration. A new window will open to configure your connection.

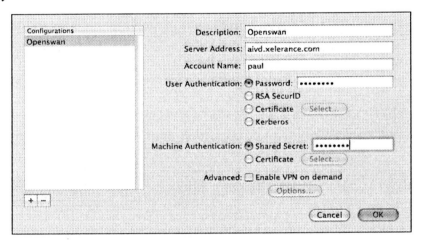

Fill in Description and Server Address. Fill in Account Name and for User Authentication select Password and fill in the password. At the Machine Authentication section, select Shared Secret and type in the PSK.

You can select Enable VPN on demand and then click the Options... button to add domains and host names. If you then cause a DNS lookup for any of these domains or host names, you will trigger the VPN connection.

One important option is not part of the VPN connection settings. If you don't want to use the VPN as default route to the Internet when you are using Tiger, you need to go to Internet Connect's main menu bar and select Connect and then Options. A new window will appear where you can remove the check from Send all traffic over VPN connection.

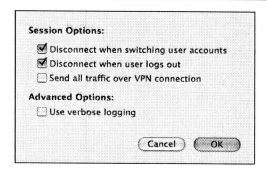

Unfortunately, older Mac OS X versions do not have this option. If you are running Panther, you will need to manually add and delete the default route. Here is an example script (taken from `http://guides.macrumors.com/`):

```
#! /bin/sh
dr=`netstat -nr | grep ' UHLW ' | awk '{print $1}'`
route delete default AAA.BBB.CCC.DDD
route add     default $dr
route add     AAA.BBB.0.0 AAA.BBB.CCC.DDD
```

Another method, which also comes from `http://guides.macrumors.com/`, is to replace pppd with a wrapper program. First move `/usr/sbin/pppd` to `/usr/sbin/pppd.original`. Then create the following file as pppd:

```
#!/usr/bin/perl
my @args = @ARGV;
s/^defaultroute/nodefaultroute/ for @args;
exec "/usr/sbin/pppd.original", @args;
```

When you have done this, select Connect in the VPN window, and the tunnel should come up automatically.

Server Configuration for X.509 IPsec without L2TP

All of the clients discussed below support both PSK and X.509. We will demonstrate configuration of X.509, since it is slightly more complex to set up. Remember that PSK and NAT-Traversal do not go together very well, so it is worth setting up the Windows clients using X.509. Again, we are using 192.168.1.0/24 as the remote office network that we wish our workers to connect to from home and the same VPN server, `aivd.xelerance.com`, with a public IP address assigned by its ISP of 193.110.157.131.

Openswan Configuration for X.509 without L2TP

The Openswan server configuration in `/etc/ipsec.conf` is fairly straightforward:

```
version 2
config setup
    # klipsdebug=none
    # plutodebug="control parsing"
    nat_traversal=yes
```

```
virtual_private=%v4:192.168.0.0/16,%v4:!192.168.1.0/24,%v4:10.0.0.0/8

include /etc/ipsec.d/examples/no_oe.conf

conn west-roadwarriors
    # left is local (aivd.xelerance.com)
    left=193.110.157.131
    leftcert=newwestCert.pem
    leftnexthop=193.110.157.158
    leftsubnet=192.168.1.0/24
    # right is roadwarrior/remote
    rightrsasigkey=%cert
    right=%any
    rightsubnet=vhost:%no,%pr
    auto=add
    #clients must initiate rekey
    rekey=no
```

As with the configuration of Openswan with L2TP, verify that the kernel has `ip_forwarding` enabled, and `rp_filter` disabled. See Chapter 5 for detailed instructions on how to set up the server and where to place the certificate, private key, and Root CA.

Client Configuration for X.509 IPsec without L2TP

Since Windows 2000, Microsoft actually ships with a built-in IPsec client. It consists of the kernel part which, much like KLIPS and NETKEY, holds the SPDs and SADs (the IPsec policies) and which also performs the actual packet encryption and decryption. There are also third-party clients that contain their own IPsec implementation and do not require or depend on Microsoft's IPsec.

Microsoft's IKE Daemon

The IKE daemon is a Windows Service, called the 'IPSEC Policy Agent' on Windows 2000 and 'IPsec Service' on XP. The actual service name to use with the `net start` or `net stop` command is `policyagent`. To talk to the IKE daemon, you need to have Microsoft's equivalent of the Openswan `whack` program. For Windows 2000, this is called `ipsecpol.exe`, and is part of the Windows 2000 Resource Kit. For Windows XP and newer, this command is called `ipseccmd.exe` and comes as part of the Windows XP Support Tools.

> When using Windows XP Service Pack 2, you will need to install an updated version of the Support Tools intended for use with Service Pack 2, otherwise `ipseccmd.exe` will not work properly.

These programs perform various tasks within the Windows Registry to glue together all IPsec-related tasks.

Microsoft's Certificate Store

The policy agent retrieves certificates from the Certificate Store that is located somewhere in the deep magic of the Windows Registry. You can use the **Microsoft Management Console (MMC)** to add or remove certificates. This is, however, a very tedious process, prone to errors.

> Do not be tempted to just double-click certificates on Windows, since it *will* load the certificates in the wrong place and your IPsec connection will not work.

Xelerance offers a small open-source tool called `certimport.exe` on its FTP server that can import these PKCS#12 certificates properly and without user interaction.

Clients using Microsoft Native IPsec Implementation

Unfortunately, we are still not really ready to use Microsoft's native IPsec. The command-line options for `ipsecpol.exe` or `ipseccmd.exe` are so complex that humans should not try to use them. Marcus Müller has written a wrapper around these two programs called `ipsec.exe`, which can be downloaded from `http://vpn.ebootis.de/`.

However, `ipsec.exe` still requires those additional programs mentioned previously. Alex Pankratov wrote **ipsec2k lib**, an API that handles all the Registry changes needed for Microsoft's IPsec without the need for `ipseccmd.exe` or `ipsecpol.exe`. The `ipsec2k` library has been used by various people to create Windows VPN clients that drive the Microsoft native IPsec implementation, such as the formidable **Isipsectool** client.

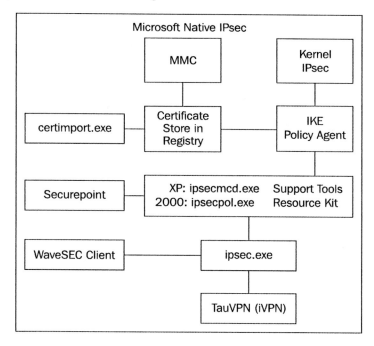

The ipsec.exe Wrapper

The advantage of the `ipsec.exe` wrapper is that configuration of the IPsec connection is performed through an Openswan-style `ipsec.conf` configuration file.

```
conn %default
    dial=MSN Internet

conn west-roadwarriors
    left=%any
    right=aivd.xelerance.com
    rightsubnet=192.168.1.0/24
    rightca="C=CA, S=Ontario, L=Toronto, O=Xelerance, OU=Support Staff,
CN=Xelerance Root CA"
    pfs=yes
    network=auto
    auto=start
    # mac=xx-xx-xx-xx-xx-xx
    # rekey=1800S/30000K
    # authmode=MD5
```

You can also use rightid= and leftid= options if necessary. The mac= option is used to select a network adapter if there is more than one adapter present. The network= option can be set to ras, lan, or auto. If you wish to tunnel all traffic over the VPN, and you are using leftsubnet=0.0.0.0/0 on the Openswan server, you need to use the syntax rightsubnet=* in the ipsec.conf file on Windows.

> The Windows ipsec.conf file uses rightca= to specify the DN of the Root CA that signed the certificates. It does not specify a rightid= and the DN of the remote certificate should *not* be used for the rightca= option. This is a very common mistake!

This screenshot shows `ipsec.exe` running in verbose mode with the -debug flag on Windows 2000. You can see the `ipsecpol.exe` commands used to load the IPsec policies into the Microsoft IKE PolicyAgent service. Windows will only start the IKE negotiation after it receives traffic that is destined for the tunnel. In our case, we would need to issue `ping 192.168.1.1` to trigger the IKE negotiation.

To bring the tunnel down, use `ipsec -off` or `ipsec -delete`.

IKE policies survive a reboot. If you uninstall `ipsec.exe` while you still have a loaded policy, you will need to use MMC to remove the policy.

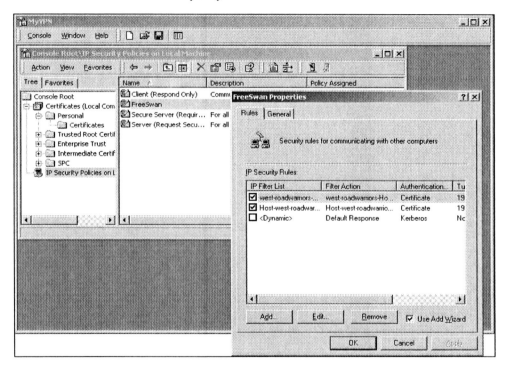

The `ipsec.exe` utility is not a fancy IPsec client. It has no tray icon, no point and click. At this point, it should only be used for testing, though even that can probably be done more easily with any of the new free wrapper clients that have come out more recently.

The Linsys IPsec Tool (lsipsectool)

http://sourceforge.net/projects/lsipsectool/

The Linsys IPsec Tool is a VPN client that uses the `ipsec2k` library to interface with Microsoft's native IPsec implementation and therefore it does not need `ipsecmcd.exe` or `ipsecpol.exe`. It has a very clear tray icon, which changes color depending on the state of the tunnel, being either red (down), green (up), or yellow (negotiating). It has the proper default proposals using 3DES and MODP-1024 with PFS.

It handles X.509 Certificate importing itself, and can import PKCS#12 formatted certificates, and it will automatically retrieve the DN of the CA it needs for the connection.

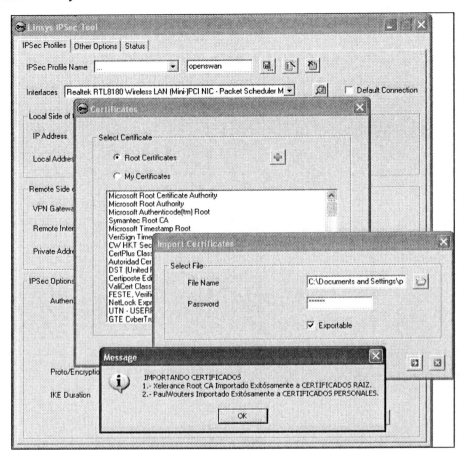

The Remote Internal IP address is used to trigger the connection, and monitor the state of the tunnel. It should be the private IP address of the gateway you are connecting to.

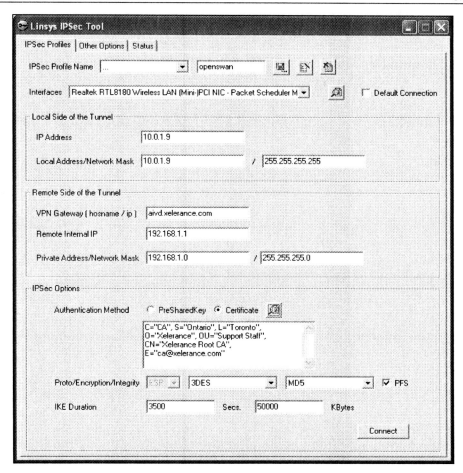

The only drawback is that it can only handle one IPsec connection at a time, but the author is currently working on extending the client to handle more tunnels. Since the client uses wxwidgets, a port to Linux is also fairly straightforward, and planned for the future. A few glitches in the internationalization support are still present, but they cause no problems.

Securepoint IPsec Client

http://www.securepoint.cc/

Securepoint is a vendor of VPN hardware machines. They seem to be based on FreeS/WAN. They also have a free client for Windows, called the **Securepoint Personal Firewall and IPSec VPN Client**. The license is "[...] *free to use,* [...] *but not free to distribute,* [...] *apart from code based on GNU Public License*". It is not clear what part is based on GPL, and what is not. There is currently no source available on sources.securepoint.cc indicating any GPL portion of the client. It might be based on ipsec2k-lib.

This client works on Microsoft Windows 2000, XP, and 2003. It is also a graphical wrapper around Microsoft's native IPsec implementation. The VPN client is bundled with a firewall, which may actually be a problem if you are already using another firewall. It is unclear whether switching the firewall on and off also affects the VPN. The phrasing is also a bit misleading, since starting the VPN connections shows Establish VPN tunnel and VPN tunnel(s) established, while all it has done up to that point is to load the IKE policies in Microsoft PolicyAgent. You then need to send some traffic that would be routed over the VPN connection to actually start the IKE negotiation. If you make an error, for example you forget to enable Perfect Forward Secrecy in the Security tab, your VPN tunnel will in fact *not* be established at all.

There are also some pop-up boxes that come up in German instead of in English. We also had occasional problems when starting and stopping tunnels frequently. This seems to be an interop issue between Openswan and Microsoft. A restart of the Microsoft PolicyAgent using `net stop policyagent` and `net start policyagent` fixed this problem. This is probably a bug in Microsoft Windows.

The client supports both PSK and X.509 Certificates. However, certificates need to be imported both in the Securepoint client and in the Windows IPsec subsystem. It is not at all clear this last step is needed, until you actually read the online manual. It instructs you, similar to the previous instructions for importing certificates for `ipsec.exe`, how to accomplish this. This means Xelerance's `certimport.exe` can be used in combination with Securepoint's client to make the import of certificates much easier.

Creating a new connection is straightforward, though it might look a bit strange to choose ANY as local network in combination with the netmask 255.255.255.255. Do not forget to enable Perfect Forward Secrecy in the Security tab.

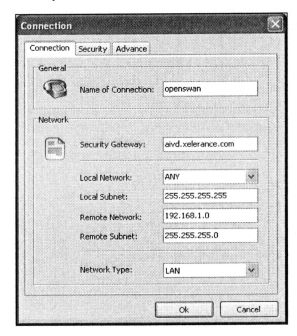

Because this client uses Microsoft's native IPsec, you can look at the loaded IPsec policies using MMC. You can also enable Microsoft's `oakley.log` debugging file without manually having to edit the Registry.

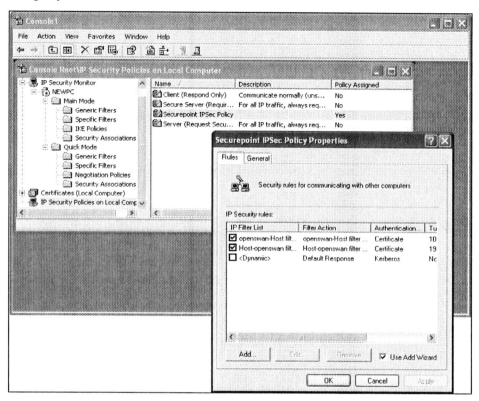

We ran successful interop tests for X.509-based IPsec tunnels, including NAT-Traversal. This client is probably the most mature wrapper for the Microsoft native IPsec implementation. It is free for personal use, but cannot be redistributed. It is not open source.

TauVPN (iVPN)

`http://sourceforge.net/projects/ivpn/`

This client was formerly known as iVPN. The TauVPN client is a GUI around the Windows `ipseccmd.exe` and `ipsecpol.exe` tools and therefore requires that the Windows XP Support Tools be installed. Be aware that the version on the XP CD is out of date, and a new version for use with Windows XP Service Pack 2 is available for download on the Microsoft website.

The advantage of this client is that it runs as a Windows service. It should therefore not need administrative privileges after it has been installed and the certificates have been imported. It can enable the `oakley.log` debug file for you, by setting the Windows Registry entry, and runs a `tail` command on the log file for viewing. TauVPN ships with Xelerance's `certimport.exe` tool for importing X.509 Certificates.

TauVPN also offers an option to enable or disable **PMTUD**. Disable this if you experience fragmentation problems, which usually result in subtle things like the `ping` command working, but freezes in SSH or FTP clients. A reboot might be required for these changes to take effect.

The user interface is very clumsy and you'll probably find yourself continually hovering the mouse cursor above icons waiting for the help text to pop up and explain their use. You have to manually type in the Root CA's DN when using X.509 Certificates, which can lead to errors. It does provide a tray icon. It also requires a Server local IP address, which is the private IP of the gateway. This is used with the `ping` command to actually trigger the connection with the Microsoft native IPsec.

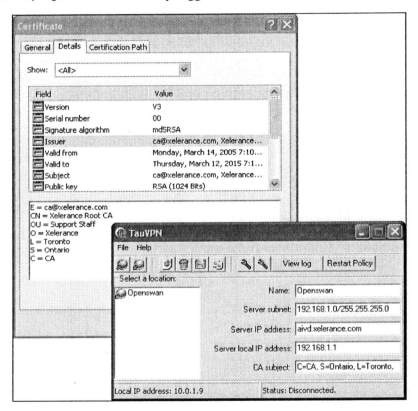

We could not get this client to work reliably on Windows XP SP2. We experienced crashes and failures to initiate the tunnel after it had loaded the Openswan IPsec policy into the PolicyAgent.

The WaveSEC Client

`ftp://ftp.openswan.org/openswan/windows/wavesec/`

Xelerance has written an NDIS-based installer around `ipsec.exe`, dubbed **WaveSEC**. This client combines `ipsec.exe` with the Microsoft binaries needed for 2000 or XP, together with `certimport.exe`, so that the Microsoft support CDs are not needed. This client was used in demonstrations for WaveSEC as a proof of concept, but should not be used for production systems.

However, the `certimport.exe` command-line tool is stable and is a great way to easily import certificates into Windows. It will warn you if doing so would replace an existing certificate, and you can specify a password using `-p`.

```
C:\WINNT\System32\cmd.exe - certimport -e -p foobar east.p12                    _ □ ×
C:\unzipped\certimport-v1.0\certimport\Release>
C:\unzipped\certimport-v1.0\certimport\Release>dir
 Volume in drive C has no label.
 Volume Serial Number is C467-6A55

 Directory of C:\unzipped\certimport-v1.0\certimport\Release

04/17/2005  11:19p    <DIR>          .
04/17/2005  11:19p    <DIR>          ..
04/05/2004  03:14p             7,133 BuildLog.htm
04/05/2004  03:14p           180,224 certimport.exe
04/05/2004  03:14p         1,166,336 certimport.pdb
04/17/2005  10:26p             3,276 east.p12
04/05/2004  03:14p           162,917 Main.obj
04/05/2004  03:14p           273,408 vc70.idb
04/05/2004  03:14p           167,936 vc70.pdb
               7 File(s)      1,961,230 bytes
               2 Dir(s)  11,057,991,680 bytes free

C:\unzipped\certimport-v1.0\certimport\Release>certimport -e -p foobar east.p12

Found a certificate in the PFX file: Xelerance Root CA
Attempting to import certificate into machine store...

An equivalent certificate already exists. Overwrite? (y/n)
```

Third-Party Replacement Clients for Windows

The following clients do not use the Microsoft native kernel IPsec driver, nor do they use the Microsoft IKE PolicyAgent, nor the Certificate Store in the Windows Registry. Therefore there is no `oakley.log` debugging file present and the PolicyAgent service should not be running. MMC is not needed to manage or import X.509 Certificates.

The GreenBow VPN Client

`http://www.thegreenbow.com/`

This is a commercial VPN client under active development that runs on all Windows platforms, ranging from Windows 98 to Windows XP. It has a 30-day evaluation period, with no further limitations during evaluation, so you can really test before committing an entire company to this client.

Certificates can be stored on a USB device to give some extra security. It supports XAUTH (untested with Openswan so far) and properly works with NAT-traversal. The GUI is quite comfortable to use, though it does assume that the end user has some knowledge of IPsec, such as knowing what a Phase 1 and a Phase 2 connection are. Of course, this is not an issue if an administrator is setting up the VPN for the end user.

In fact, the GreenBow client offers a recording mode if you run setup with the `-r` option that creates a configuration file called `setup.iss`. This way, the administrator can manually configure the client and ship a complete self-installable version for the end user that does not ask a single question, and does not even appear in the tray icon list, so the user cannot disable the VPN.

Configuration is fairly straightforward. First, a new Phase 1 is created by right-clicking the configuration tab and choosing **New Phase 1**. You then specify the Phase 1 parameters. The GreenBow client comes with good defaults, such as 3DES and Diffie-Hellman group 2 (MODP-1024) and PFS and Main Mode enabled. However, it does default to Pre-shared Key (PSK) instead of X.509 Certificates.

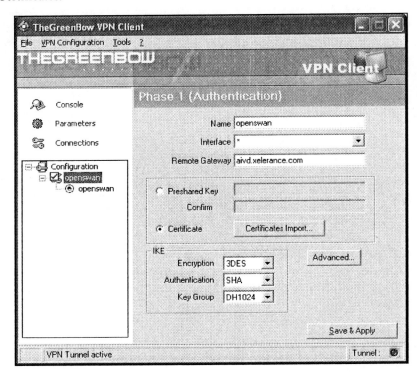

When choosing X.509 Certificates instead of Pre-Shared Key, an import window appears letting you import the Root CA, the certificate, and the private key.

Note that the private key needs to be unlocked. The client we tested did not support PKCS#12 (.p12) format files yet. Ensure that the root and user certificate filename extension is .pem, and that the private key file has the extension .key.

Once you have imported the certificates and key files, select the Advanced tab, where you can set a few more options. When using certificates with a Root CA, you should set both ID field types to DER ASN1 DN.

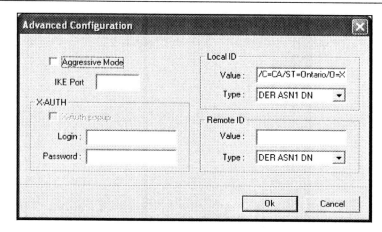

Here you can further fill in the XAUTH options, or enable Aggressive Mode if needed. This client even allows you to change the IKE port, so if your ISP blocks UDP port 500, you could change it on both the client and Openswan, though it will likely not work as expected for NAT-Traversal in such a case.

Unfortunately, the GreenBow client does not read the ID from the imported certificate, so you will have to type in the local ID yourself. You can use the openssl command on the Openswan server to get this:

```
# openssl x509 -in YourCert.pem -noout -subject
```

> The GreenBow VPN client does not support commas (,) as DER ASN1 DN separators and you must use slashes '/'. Note that the first character in the DN is a slash as well.

Once you are done with Phase 1, right-click the Phase1 to add as many Phase 2 items as needed. Again, sane defaults are used by the GreenBow client, such as 3DES, tunnel mode, and PFS. You should not fill in the VPN Client address, as it will be filled in automatically with your current IP address, which could be the local LAN address that will be NATed later on.

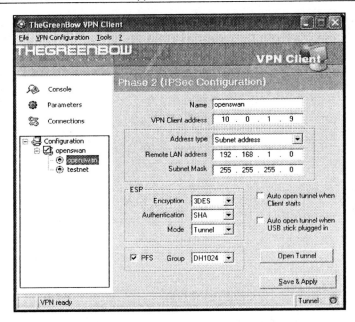

In our example we have created two Phase 2 items, which have as the only difference the 'Remote LAN' address. We have set up two tunnels between the same two machines, one for 192.168.1.0/24 and one for 192.168.2.0/24.

With Phase 2 configured, you can now Save and Apply the connection and start it with Open Tunnel, though this is not needed as the GreenBow client automatically brings up a tunnel if there is traffic for it defined in one of its Phase 2 connections.

The console log supports various kinds of logging. The screenshot below shows fairly minimal logging during setting up our VPN tunnel:

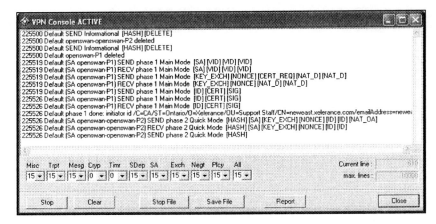

One minor criticism of this client is that it uses the color red in the tray icon to indicate that the IPsec tunnel is established, which can give the impression that something is seriously wrong.

As a final note, the GreenBow website contains a treasure trove of information. There is a FAQ, a number of problems listed with related Microsoft Knowledge Base articles, and an extensive list of VPN software that is known to work with the client. This often includes detailed descriptions with screenshots for those devices along with the specific options for the GreenBow client.

Astaro Secure Client

http://www.astaro.com/

The current Astaro Secure Client is based on the NCP IPsec client. It supports XAUTH, ModeConfig, PSK, and X.509. Configuration of the client is a bit cumbersome and confusing. The client throws many screens at you where only a single option needs to be specified, instead of trying to combine them all into a single page. After the initial installation, you get a New Profile Assistant, a straightforward wizard-type series of options, but when that has completed, you still need to configure some extra settings to make the connection work. On the screen, select Main Mode and DH-Group 2 or higher. Do not select IP compression, unless your bandwidth is really low, such as a GPRS or dialup connection.

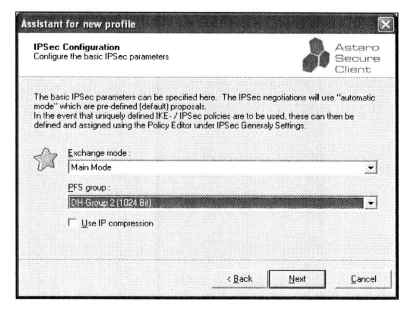

The next screen in the Assistant can be confusing. It is headed Pre-shared key, while we're actually configuring an X.509 connection. Leave the Shared secret field blank, and select ASN.1 Distinguished Name in the Type dropdown. You do not need to fill in the ID with the DN from your certificate—the client will do this for you automatically.

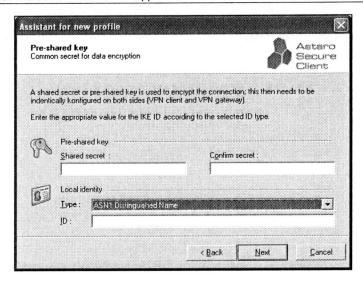

Once you have completed the Assistant, you then must address the extra settings. These settings are split over two separate configuration menus. One menu is called Configuration and is located on the main Configuration drop-down menu. The other menu appears when you select the newly created tunnel and then click the Configure button. In the window that opens, an entire menu of options appears on the left. Select Remote Networks from this menu and add the remote network and netmask.

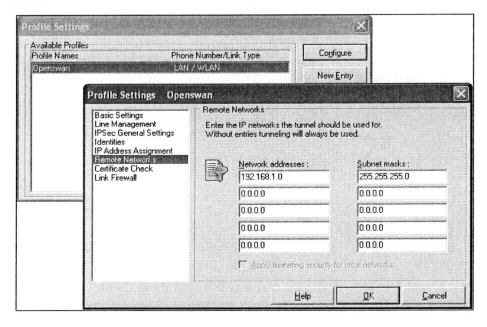

The next step is to import the X.509 Certificate. The certificate import process is separate and not attached to one specific tunnel. Select Configuration, then Certificates. On the User Certificate tab of the window that opens, select PKCS#12 and browse to the location of the cert.p12 file you have created for this client.

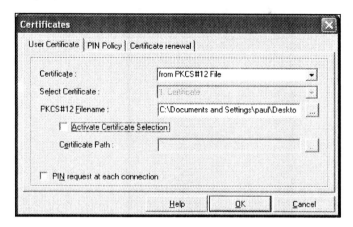

When you install the Astaro Secure Client, it stops the Microsoft IPsec Service and sets the startup type to manual. After uninstalling, the Microsoft IPsec Service is not re-enabled, so all clients relying on the native IPsec implementation, including L2TP connections, will fail to run with obscure errors. You can re-enable the IPsec Service through Control Panel | Administrative Tools | Services.

Finally, you are ready to hit the Connect button and start the IPsec connection.

Unfortunately, the Astaro VPN client does not store the certificate unencrypted, so every time you bring up the connection, you will be asked for the PIN on the certificate, which is the 'export password' used when creating the PKCS#12 file with openssl. It will then establish your connection, and the tray icon traffic light will go from red, to yellow (negotiating), to green (established).

Mac OS X IPSecuritas

http://www.lobotomo.com/products/IPSecuritas/

Mac OS X comes with the KAME IPsec stack and the Racoon IKE daemon. These can be manually configured, but this is a hell of a task and not at all suited for end users (or most developers for that matter).

IPSecuritas provides a GUI wrapper around Racoon that works reasonably well. The only problem at the time of writing was that all Mac OS X versions up to and including Tiger have a broken NAT-T implementation. Even though IKE will negotiate ESPinUDP encapsulation, Tiger will still send out ESP packets, which are then further broken by the NAT router, and will surely be dropped by Openswan. Hopefully Apple will fix this bug in the next Tiger update. A partial workaround for this problem was added in Openswan 2.4.1.

IPSecuritas uses its own Racoon configuration files generated on the fly, which are placed in /tmp. Therefore, it does not require certificates to be imported with Apple's KeyChain Access.app.

IPSecuritas has its own Import Certificate menu. It does not support PKCS#12 files, so you will have to copy the separate `cacert.pem`, `hostCert.pem`, and `hostCert.key` files. The IPSecuritas client supports both PSK and X.509 Certificates and comes with a manual that explains the features and limitations of the client quite well.

Select CA certificate, name it, and select Proceed. Then select Import Certificate again to import your own certificate. Point to your certificate and proceed. This will appear to have failed, but one word on the screen has changed. The word certificate changed for the word key, and you are in fact now importing your key file.

> The key file *must not* be password protected. IPSecuritas cannot import password-protected key files.

To remove a password from a key file, use the following command:

```
# openssl rsa -in macosx.key -out macosx.unlocked.key.pem
```

You can view the details of the certificate at Certificate Details. To start a new connection, select Edit connection. Name the connection. Choose Host To Network in the Mode of Operation dropdown. Type in the hostname of the VPN gateway, and the remote network with netmask. Select only Main for Exchange Mode.

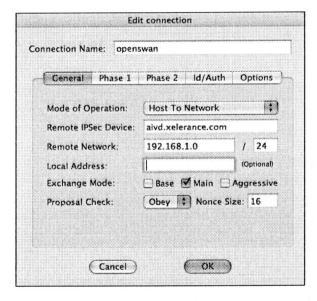

In the Phase 1 tab, make sure you use at least Mod1024 (2) and 3DES for encryption, and in the Phase 2 tab, select Mod1024 (2) for PFS Group, and 3DES or AES for Encryption.

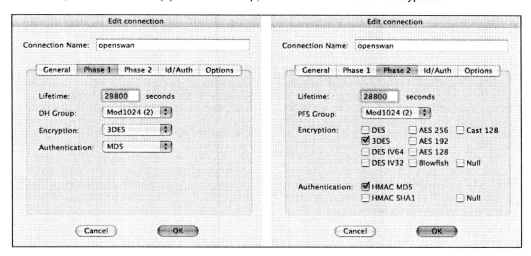

In the id/Auth tab, choose Certificate for Local and Remote identifier. You should not specify or type the DN information. Select Certificates for Authentication and select your imported certificates. Use the CA certificate you imported as Remote. This is a little counterintuitive, because the remote has another certificate itself (in our case with CN=west.xelerance.com).

You should not need to change anything in the Options tab. You can select the Preferences option of IPSecuritas to enable Verbose Debug information. The log and configuration files will all appear in /tmp. You can also use different DNS servers when the IPsec tunnel is active to assist in resolving host names that are only available in the internal DNS system of the remote network.

VPNtracker

VPNtracker is another popular VPN product for Mac OS X. It is straightforward in use, and supports PSK, X.509, and even SecureID cards. We will first show how to configure PSK and then how to configure VPNtracker for X.509. VPNtracker comes with default settings for a wide range of vendors. Click the New button to open the configuration screen.

Select Linux in the Vendor dropdown. Two entries will appear, Linux FreeS/WAN and Linux FreeS/WAN (X.509). For PSK, select the non-X.509 FreeS/WAN entry. Make sure to deselect Client Provisioning (Mode-Config), unless you are configuring for XAUTH.

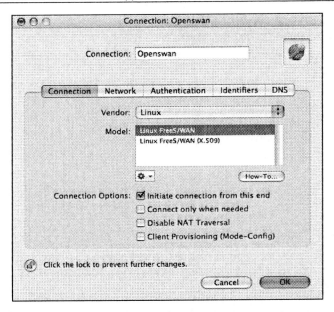

Double-click the Linux FreeS/WAN entry. Here you can edit the general Phase 1 options. The defaults should all be fine. Click Phase 1 Proposal.

By default, AES is not checked. You may want to enable this. In the Hash Algorithm box, you might want to change MD5 for SHA1, or at least add SHA1 to MD5. SHA1 is considered to be slightly more secure than MD5. You could also add Group 5 to the Diffie-Hellman Groups.

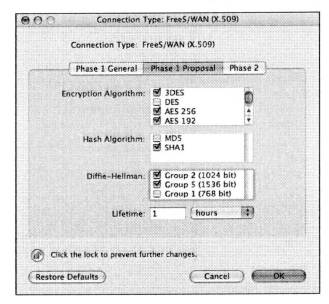

Click the **Phase 2** button. Here VPNtracker strangely only has DES selected. Unselect DES, and select 3DES and optionally the AES choices. You can change the PFS group to Group 5 if you wish to have some extra crypto strength. Select OK and then open the **Network** tab.

Select **Host to Network** in the **Topology** dropdown. Fill in the remote VPN gateway, the remote subnet, and the remote subnet's netmask.

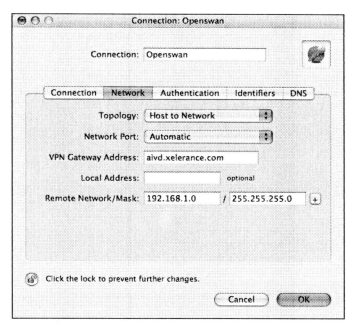

Select the **Authentication** tab. Click on **Edit...** next to the selected **Pre-shared Key** option. Fill in the PSK and click OK. Now we can move to the **Identifiers** tab.

If you are just using IP addresses, you can select the two endpoint **IP address** options. If you are using `leftid=` and `rightid=` in the connection on the Openswan side, then select the custom box where you can fill in the IDs. If you also want to set internal DNS servers, you can configure them in the **DNS** tab.

Click OK when done, and you can now click on **Start VPN** to bring up the tunnel.

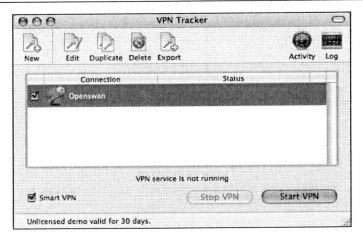

When using X.509 instead of PSK, things are a little more complicated because we need to import the certificates. The easiest way is to have three separate files, the X.509 certificate, the private key, and the CA certificate. Again, select New to create a new connection.

This time, double-click the Linux FreeS/WAN (X509) entry. Just as for the PSK-based connections, you can leave the Phase 1 General defaults, but make sure to unselect DES and select 3DES and optionally AES in the tabs for Phase 1 Proposal and Phase 2. Click OK and then select the Network tab.

These options are the same as for PSK. Select a topology of Host to Network, fill in the remote VPN gateway, the remote subnet, and the remote subnet's netmask. Select the Authentication tab.

Select Certificates, and click on the Edit... button. Since you have not imported anything yet, click on the Edit Certificates... button to start the Certificate Manager.

Click Import..., and use the Browse... buttons to point to your public certificate and private key files, then click Import.

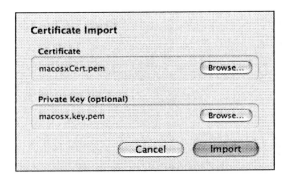

Select the CA tab, and repeat the import step, this time for the CA certificate. Close the Certificate Manager by closing the window.

Now you can select your newly imported certificate in the Own Certificate box. Set Remote Certificate to Verify with CAs.

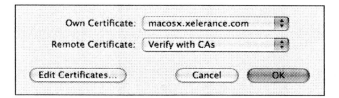

Click OK, and open the Identifiers tab. Choose Own certificate and Remote certificate for the Local and Remote Identifiers. Click OK, and now you are again ready to bring up the tunnel using Start VPN. There is also Log button, which provides a convenient way to access the log.

Manual Racoon Configuration

Since IPSecuritas nicely presents us with the configuration files, we include these here for those who wish to use Racoon manually in their own scripts. This is racoon.conf:

```
# IPSecuritas V1.0 racoon.conf
path pre_shared_key "/tmp/ipsecuritas_psk.txt";
path certificate "/tmp/ipsecuritas_certs";
padding
{
    maximum_length 20;      # maximum padding length.
    randomize off;          # enable randomize length.
    strict_check off;       # enable strict check.
    exclusive_tail off;     # extract last one octet.
}
# Specification of default various timer.
timer
{
    # These value can be changed per remote node.
    counter 5;              # maximum trying count to send.
    interval 20 sec;        # maximum interval to resend.
    persend 1;              # the number of packets per a send.
    # timer for waiting to complete each phase.
    phase1 30 sec;
    phase2 30 sec;
}

remote 193.110.157.131 {
    exchange_mode main;
    doi ipsec_doi;
    situation identity_only;
    certificate_type x509 "openswan.cert" "openswan.priv";
    verify_cert off;
    my_identifier asn1dn;
    peers_identifier asn1dn;
    verify_identifier off;
    lifetime time 28800 seconds;
    initial_contact on;
    passive off;
    proposal_check obey;
```

```
      support_mip6 on;
      generate_policy off;
      nonce_size 16;
      proposal {
        encryption_algorithm 3des;
        hash_algorithm md5;
        authentication_method rsasig;
        dh_group modp1024;
      }
    }
    sainfo address 10.0.1.2/32 any address 192.168.1.0/24 any {
      pfs_group modp1024;
      lifetime time 28800 seconds;
      encryption_algorithm 3des;
      authentication_algorithm hmac_md5;
      compression_algorithm deflate;
    }
    listen {
      isakmp 10.0.1.2;
    }
    log debug2;
```

And here is `setkey.conf` for the kernel policies:

```
    flush;
    spdflush;
    spdadd 192.168.1.0/24 10.0.1.2/32 any -P in ipsec esp/tunnel/193.110.157.131-
      10.0.1.2/require;
    spdadd 10.0.1.2/32 192.168.1.0/24 any -P out ipsec esp/tunnel/10.0.1.2-
      193.110.157.131/require;
```

This of course depends on your local IP address, in this case 10.0.1.2.

Importing X.509 Certificates into Windows

Unfortunately, Microsoft imports the X.509 Certificate (the .p12 file) into the wrong place in the Registry when you double-click it. Instead of the certificate becoming a 'local machine' certificate, it becomes a 'user certificate', and as a result, the Microsoft IPsec subsystem will not be able to find it. To make matters more complicated, adding a certificate to the 'local machine' certificate store unfortunately also requires administrative rights.

Do not double-click the certificate and use the Certificate Import wizard. Instead, use the Microsoft Management Console (MMC) by selecting Start | Run and typing mmc in the input box.

Select Console | Add/Remove Snap-in. When the Add/Remove Snap-in dialog opens, click the Add button to open the Add Standalone Snap-in dialog.

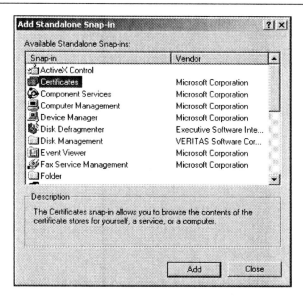

Choose Certificates from the list of snap-ins, and click Add again to confirm. When prompted, select Computer Account, not the default selection of User Account, which will not work. You will then be asked to select the computer that the snap-in is to manage. Choose Local Computer, and then Finish.

This gives us the starting point for the actual import. While we have MMC open, we might as well prepare everything, including the IPsec monitor. Click the Add button again, but now scroll down and select IPsec Security Policy Management. Choose Local Computer when prompted for the computer the snap-in will manage.

Close the Add Standalone Snap-in dialog and the Add/Remove Snap-in dialog. We now have all the MMC components that we need. Expand the Certificates node in the left-hand tree view, and right-click the Personal folder. Select All Tasks | Import... from the context menu.

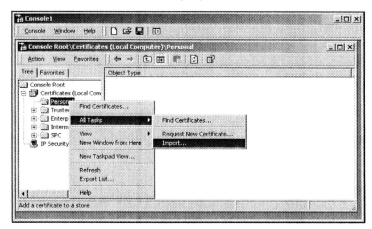

Browse to the .p12 file that you have created for this computer and click Next. If you have not removed the password from the file, you now need to type the password. Here you also have the possibility to make the key exportable, which will allow you to copy the key from the Registry to a file again. If you do not make it exportable, you will not be able to do this.

> Be aware that this is pseudo-security, at best. Windows hackers will still be able to get to the key. If the laptop is lost, always consider the key and certificate compromised and revoke them.

On the next screen, ensure that the import is set to Automatically select the certificate store based on the type of certificate. This ensures that your personal certificate will be imported under Personal, and the CA certificate will be imported under Trusted Root Certificates. You have now completed the import process. Click Finish, and if you expand the Trusted Root Certificates folder in the MMC tree view, you should now see your CA certificate.

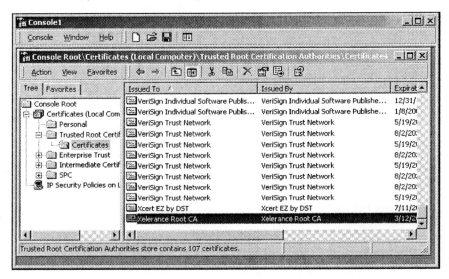

Similarly, you should be able to find your personal certificate in the Personal folder. If the import of the corresponding key went OK, then if you double-click your personal certificate, you should see You have a private key that corresponds to this certificate at the bottom. Furthermore, if you open the Certification Path tab of the certificate, you should see the Root CA listed as the parent certificate of the personal certificate. In the lower Certificate Status pane, it should say This certificate is OK.

Some extra information is shown in the Details tab of the certificate. If you added a dynamic CRL to your certificate, then you will see that displayed here.

If you can't find a certificate, which can easily happen if you have many, as is often the case in the Trusted Certificates store, you can use the Find Certificates option to locate it based on the (partial) content of the DN.

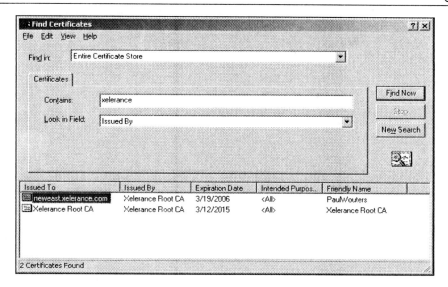

Do not forget that the Xelerance certimport.exe utility, discussed in the section on the WaveSEC client earlier in this chapter, will import certificates for you without a zillion mouse clicks, which is particularly useful if you are importing certificates on every computer in the company network.

Importing X.509 Certificates on Mac OS X (Tiger)

Mac OS X versions including Tiger do not make using X.509 Certificates for IPsec or L2TP/IPsec particularly straightforward.

Importing your own PKCS#12 certificate (.p12 file) that contains the CA certificate, your personal certificate, and your private key through the KeyChain Access.app will most likely fail, since such a root CA will not be trusted properly. This can be seen by a red warning sign when viewing the personal certificate details, and the text This certificate is not in the trusted root database.

This personal certificate will be listed as valid listed as valid but it won't be accepted as it is untrusted because the CA is itself untrusted.

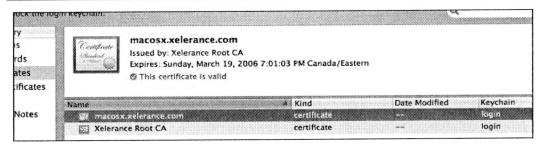

The following procedure has been put together with the help of Jacco de Leeuw, and should work in most instances. Your results may be completely different, however, and we welcome any feedback in this regard. Let us hope the next Mac OS X update will address these issues.

Firstly, the Openswan server side *must* have a FQDN or an IP address as its ID. This IP address or FQDN *must* match the value in the Server address input field on the L2TP configuration tab of Internet Connect. You can do this when creating the X.509 Certificate, if you add one or both of the following options to the openssl.cnf file before generating the certificate:

```
[usr_cert]
subjectAltName=DNS:TheFullyQuantifiedHostName
subjectAltName=IP:193.110.157.131
```

Log into your Mac OS X machine as an administrative user and start the KeyChain Access.app. You can find it using the Finder by selecting Application and then scrolling down to Utilities where you will find the KeyChain Access.app. Alternatively, start it with this command:

```
# sudo "/Applications/Utilities/Keychain Access.app/Contents/MacOS/Keychain Access"
```

Click on Show keychains and select System. Select Import from the menu and import the PKCS#12 file (.p12 file). You will notice three items will be added to your keychain. You need to move the imported CA certificate from the System keychain to the X509 Trusted Anchors keychain. Restart KeyChain Access.app and see if the imported certificates and private key now show up as valid.

Once you have done all of this, you can open Internet Connect and you should be able to select X.509 Certificate as the method for Machine Authentication. You need to specify the Openswan FQDN or IP address, as previously entered in Server address input field.

There have been some reports that this requires a restart of Internet Connect, or even a reboot, before the VPN will work properly.

An alternative approach is to use a third-party tool called **CertToolGui**. This presents a user interface that should help in importing the necessary files.

Choose Import Certificates, and select the cacert.pem file. It will ask you for your password to obtain access to the necessary keychains. Choose X509Anchors as the keychain to import the CA into.

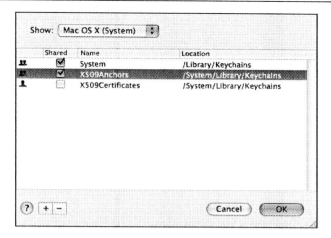

Change the extension of your personal certificate file from .pem to .crt and import it into the System keychain.

If you get errors about a certificate or key already existing in the keychain, then it is likely imported in another keychain. You first need to remove it from that other keychain.

A third method is to import the certificates from the command line. Open Terminal.app located in the Utilities folder. Copy the System's X509Anchors database to your local Keychains directory by executing the following command:

```
# cp /System/Library/Keychains/X509Anchors ~/Library/Keychains
```

Run certtool to import the cacert.pem file using:

```
# certtool i ~/caCert.pem k=X509Anchors
```

Move your local X509Anchors file back to the System's Keychains folder:

```
# sudo mv ~/Library/Keychains/X509Anchors /System/Library/Keychains/X509Anchors
```

Note that in theory, you should be able to do the following command as well:

```
# sudo certtool i ca.crt v k=/System/Library/Keychains/x509Anchors
```

In practice, the certificate will be imported, but it will not show up as valid.

Regardless of the method used, you should now start KeyChain Access.app and look at your certificate and your CA certificate. They should have a green check symbol in a circle, and say This certificate is valid.

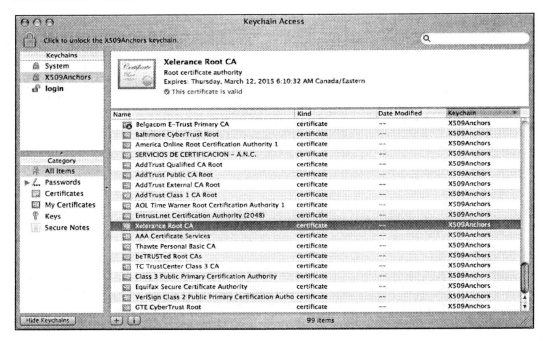

The CA certificate can be found in x509Anchors, and your personal certificate can be found in Certificates or System.

Summary

This chapter showed two ways of getting Microsoft Windows machines to connect to an Openswan server using a VPN, using either plain IPsec or L2TP/IPsec. It also walked through the process of how to connect to Openswan using Mac OS X, which unfortunately still has some way to go before it is really useful. You should now be able to configure both the Openswan server and Windows clients to connect safely using L2TP with PSK or X.509, or X.509 without L2TP using a third-party IPsec client. You should also be able to set up PSK-based L2TP connections with Mac OS X. You should always use Openswan-2.5.0 or never when using either Mac OS X or L2TP-based IPsec connections.

9
Interoperating with Other Vendors

So far, we have covered the ins and outs of interoperating Openswan with end-user computers running Linux, Microsoft Windows, and Apple Mac OS X. The choice of end-user platform is rather limited, which makes the interop procedure fairly simple and straightforward. Unfortunately, this is not true for connecting Openswan to various third-party IPsec appliances.

This chapter will describe a few examples and the issues involved with hardware interop, and will list a few appliances and the peculiarities involved in getting these to work with Openswan.

Openswan as a Client to an Appliance

Using Openswan on the server end is quite easy. You have all the logs of the incoming connection, and you know what your connection parameters for the clients are supposed to be. Using Openswan as a client on the other hand can be very hard. Often the server in such cases is a non-Openswan system and usually the VPN server logs are not available. People trying to use Openswan as a client to connect to these systems usually do not have the cooperation of the system administrator on the other end. The best source of tips and information in these cases is usually to have a look at the configuration of other clients using the same setup.

For Cisco's VPN client for example, you usually get a PCF file from the administrator of the Cisco Concentrator. In the Openswan `contrib` directory is a utility that will try to convert these files to `ipsec.conf` syntax.

Usually these VPN appliances are set up in a very strict way. They will want the first IKE packet to contain the exact proposal, instead of letting IKE negotiate this. This is of course always the case for Aggressive Mode, which does not support the negotiation of connection parameters. If your first packet fails to meet their requirements, they often silently drop the packet. In these cases you must specify `ike=` and `esp=` options to ensure the very first proposal that Openswan sends is the exact correct one.

> If you do not know the exact configuration for PFS, use `pfs=no`. If the other side uses PFS anyway, Openswan will still accept and use PFS.

Preparing the Interop

When you are trying to make two completely different systems work together, it is easy to immediately get lost in technicalities. People forget that there is usually a lot more going on when trying to make two completely different devices communicate correctly to each other. It is very likely that interop involves not only two different devices, but also two different IT departments. After all, people tend to stick to what they know works, and if it was all up to you, you would be working with two of the same devices to hook up together without a hitch. Keep in mind that you not only need to contend with technical issues, but also social issues. For instance, the other department might work different hours to you, or they might be a lot more or less formal than you. Remember to make an effort to interop with these human aspects as well.

The Human Factor

When attempting an interop between a *cheap, free,* and *unsupported* product, such as Openswan, and a *very expensive* commercial solution with the full support and backing of a large commercial vendor, there is another culture clash. One party will fully believe in the power of open source software, while the other is likely to believe in the expertise and reliability of the commercial vendor. Both parties will know exactly how their product works, and any failure to interop these two will obviously be the fault of the other party. Be careful not to raise the stakes and turn this into a political battle.

Do not make it impossible for the other party to admit fault, and do not be so cocky that you yourself will no longer be able to admit to a human error or bug. Such a charged atmosphere inevitably leads to situations where *"things just start working"* and *"no one changed a thing"*. If the humans do not interop, neither will the technology. If you can stay friendly and considerate with the other system administrator, chances are they will give you the same courtesy.

Terminology

The first technical hurdle to overcome is the difference in terminology. Those not familiar with Openswan will not understand what is meant by left and right. Most likely, they will be familiar with terms as Local and Remote. Subnets are sometimes called **Security Domain** or **Tunnel Policies**. Other rather misleading terms are **Medium Security** (for AH) and **High** or **Strong Security** (for ESP). The DH groups are often called **MODP groups**. Some appliances use **Tunnel** to refer to a Phase 1, and **Policy** to refer to a Phase 2 of an IPsec connection.

Preparation

If you have not yet purchased the appliance that you will deploy as the other end of your IPsec connection, then reading this chapter can assist you in deciding whether some appliance's price is worth the hassle associated with it. If you are looking at a product that we do not describe here, read the specifications for it very carefully. For many appliances, it is not enough to simply look at the box or the manual. A good look at the web configuration interface is often the best way to find out the limitations or additional features of the appliance. Probably the most important feature to be aware of is IPsec passthrough.

IPsec Passthrough

It seems vendors that do not implement IPsec at all like to advertise **IPsec passthrough**, or **VPN Passthrough** as a feature on their product packaging. IPsec passthrough is not IPsec. Ensure that the device actually supports IPsec. Even if it does support IPsec, the IPsec passthrough feature usually breaks the IPsec implementation.

> Avoid buying appliances that advertise IPsec passthrough.

IPsec passthrough predates the IPsec NAT-Traversal standards and is now obsolete. If it works at all, which is rarely, it will still never work for more than one user behind NAT. Usually IPsec passthrough cannot be disabled, so any such appliances behind a NAT router are about as useful as a brick.

Tunnel Limitations

Some devices come with a limitation on the number of IPsec tunnels you can set up. Sometimes this limit is artificial although sometimes the hardware in these appliances does not have the CPU power necessary for many concurrent tunnels.

You should be wary of deciding you do not need multiple tunnels prematurely, for instance by thinking you only need one tunnel from the appliance to the company network. If you need to connect to two different subnets at the company, for example 10.0.0.0/8 and 192.168.0.0/16, that means you need two tunnels, even though there is only one IKE connection (ISAKMP SA) and two ESP connections (IPsec SAs). Many appliances do not correctly implement such dual tunnels that share a Phase 1, and will tear down the first tunnel when the second tunnel is brought up.

Anticipate Known Problems

If you know the product or vendor that you are trying to connect to, it will help to first use a search engine to look up whether someone else has written some notes about this particular kind of interop. It is very unlikely you are the first to try an interop between Openswan and a particular third-party vendor. Do some homework and avoid reinventing the wheel.

Update the Firmware

If you are responsible for the hardware on the other end, check the vendor website for firmware updates. If necessary, flash the firmware to the latest version. Be aware that some appliances, especially small ADSL/ISDN combination routers, can have different versions of firmware for specific regions. This is usually due to the different phone standards used in different countries, or the appliance has limited firmware space and so has one version for analogue phone lines and another for ISDN. In the past, there were many export versions of firmware with inferior encryption strength. When checking or upgrading the firmware, check that the appliance supports at least 3DES. For example, the older Cisco VPN3000 products often come with only single DES, and will not interop with Openswan out of the box.

GUI Issues

Most often, the real problems for configuring appliances are the user interfaces. People who hate working from the command line might want to avoid certain models of Cisco routers, while others would avoid GUI tools. Most appliances these days come with a web interface, but the quality of these interfaces varies greatly. They are sometimes only tested with Microsoft Internet Explorer, and may fail with Mozilla/Firefox, Safari or other browsers. They might rely on Java or JavaScript in the browser, or worse, might not even work on the latest version of your browser. Sometimes they use pop-up windows that the modern browser blocks automatically. Too often, changing many fields at once will not actually update them all. We have also come across routers that offer combinations of options that are mutually exclusive, such as multiple IKE proposals when using Aggressive Mode. Other examples with a bad GUI include some types of Linksys devices, which auto-generate web SSL certificates, but the DN for these certificates is the same. As a result, if you try to configure two or more of these devices, your browser will detect "contradicting" certificates and refuse to let you configure the additional devices.

Keepalives

A lot of devices have ways of keeping the connection alive. This is almost never a properly implemented DPD or NAT-T keep-alive. Instead, vendors often use a simple ICMP ping packet. If you have an **always** on option, leave it disabled until you have a working configuration. Only then try to enable these features, since in some devices these keepalives actually cause more problems than they solve. Even if these features are properly implemented, if your bandwidth has peaks that reach the full utilization capacity, then these keepalives (whether pings or proper DPD packets) run the risk of getting dropped due to link congestion, which will cause the connection to get actively terminated by the end not receiving answers to the keepalives.

ISP Filtering

As with the Windows clients in the previous chapter, you might run into ISP filtering. Unfortunately some ISPs filter out UDP port 500 (IKE) to prevent people from starting VPN connections in an attempt to sell a 'business' subscription. If you think this might be the case for you, and you do not see any packet or log on the Openswan side, use the `ikeping` utility that ships with Openswan to test for these filters. Note that with `ikeping` you can only test for UDP port 500 filters, not ESP filters. For a full network test, see the `ipsec livetest` command.

Frequently used VPN Gateways

The remainder of this chapter will show and discuss a few commonly used appliances. Even if your appliance is not described here, it might be useful to read through for common problems that might apply to your appliance.

Webmin with Openswan

Webmin is a web-based administration program that supports many different operating systems and many software packages. It normally runs on `http://localhost:10000/` and is supported on all major Linux distributions. Webmin contains a module for the configuration of VPNs, although this module is unfortunately still somewhat focused on FreeS/WAN, and is therefore lagging a little behind current Openswan developments. This will not be a problem for fairly straightforward connections, such as Linux site-to-site connections, but if you need to use new options such as DPD or forced encapsulation, then you might find those missing from the GUI.

The interface is fairly straightforward and simple enough to control. It contains sane default values. One error is that it does appear to support NAT-Traversal, but does not support setting the virtual_private= parameter needed on the server side to make NAT-Traversal work. It is also not aware of NETKEY, which may cause problems. It does, however, fully support Opportunistic Encryption and changing the policy group files.

The following screenshot shows Webmin's IPsec VPN Configuration page.

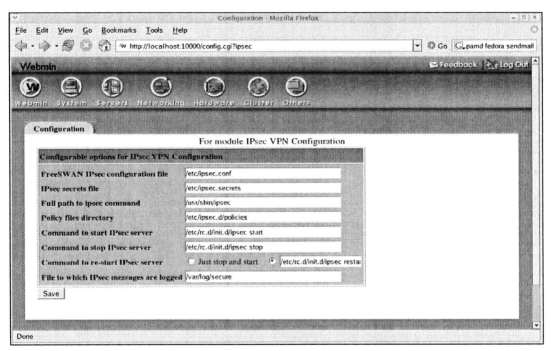

You should not need to edit any of these fields unless it has failed to detect the proper location of a file. This might happen on unsupported Linux distributions that use the /etc/ipsec/ directory to store ipsec.conf and ipsec.secrets.

The IPsec options page contains information about the OE policy groups, and whether to start IPsec at bootup. You can Add a new IPsec VPN connection, and it even supports the import of connection definitions from files. You can manage the public and secret keys, and go to the Global VPN server settings page, where you will probably need to change the Network interfaces for IPsec setting to Default route interface.

Most of the connection parameters for left and right are supported in Webmin. You can even choose to fetch the key from DNS.

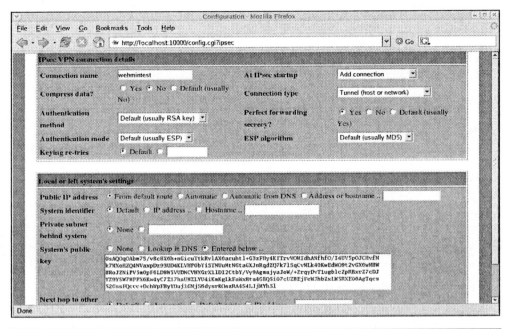

Cisco VPN 3000

The Cisco VPN 3000 is an old product that is still widely deployed. It required a special commercial license to support 3DES, and therefore many of the deployed units lack this. It was also decommissioned before AES made it as alternative algorithm. If you wish to use its 1-DES support, you will need to make sure Openswan is compiled with USE_WEAKSTUFF=true. On Openswan versions before 2.4.0, you also need to manually edit programs/pluto/Makefile.options and enable -DUSE_1DES. On Openswan 2.4.0 and higher, this requires setting the Makefile.inc variable USE_NOCRYPTO=true. You should be able to determine whether your CiscoVPN 3000 supports 3DES by using the show version command.

Usually, these deployments use the Cisco VPN client, and focus on using Aggressive Mode with ModeConfig and XAUTH. They do not support PFS. An example configuration that might work for you is the following:

```
conn cisco-3000
    aggrmode=yes
    authby=secret
    left=%defaultroute
    leftmodecfgclient=yes
    leftxauthclient=yes
    leftid=@xelerance
    ike=3des-md5-modp1024
    esp=3des-md5
    right=ip-of-cisco-3000
    rightsubnet=subnet-behind-cisco-3000
    rightxauthserver=yes
    rightmodecfgserver=yes
    modecfgpull=yes
    auto=add
    pfs=no
```

You cannot use auto=start, because XAUTH needs to prompt you for a username and password. It needs a controlling TTY to talk to the user. Instead, you must use auto=add, and then use ipsec auto --up cisco-3000 to get the username and password prompt. For more information on XAUTH and ModeConfig, see Chapter 2 and the documentation in openswan-2/doc/README.xauth*.

Cisco PIX Concentrator

The following is an example configuration for connecting using PSK to a Cisco PIX. This example uses 3DES: make sure that you have either 3DES or AES. If you are using an old Cisco, you might be stuck with 1-DES, in which case you should really just upgrade.

```
conn pix
    left=%defaultroute
    leftsubnet=10.0.1.0/24
    leftid=@openswan_to_pix
    right=CiscoIP
    rightid=CiscoIP
    rightsubnet=10.0.2.0/24
    authby=secret
    esp=3des-sha1-96
    compress=yes
    auto=route
```

And in /etc/ipsec.secrets:

```
@openswan_to_pix CiscoIP: PSK "presharedkey"
```

Here is the corresponding PIX configuration:

```
! normal pix configuration
nameif ethernet0 outside security0
nameif ethernet1 inside security100
enable password YourEnablePassword
passwd YourPassword
hostname pix domain-name pix.openswan.org
!
ip address outside CiscoIP 255.255.255.0
ip address inside 10.0.2.254 255.255.255.0
global (outside) 1 interface
!
access-list NO-NAT permit ip 10.0.2.0 255.255.255.0 10.0.1.0 255.255.255.0
access-list OPENSWAN-VPN permit ip 10.0.2.0 255.255.255.0 10.0.1.0
   255.255.255.0
! NAT everything except traffic on the NO-NAT access list, such as IPsec
traffic
nat (inside) 0 access-list NO-NAT
nat (inside) 1 10.0.2.0 255.255.255.0 0 0
! our default gateway
route outside 0.0.0.0 0.0.0.0 DefaultGatewayIP 1
! Permit IPSEC connections
sysopt connection permit-ipsec
! Create a transformation set called 'myset'
crypto ipsec transform-set myset esp-3des esp-sha-hmac
! Create a crypto map called 'mymap', to match the access list OPENSWAN-VPN.
! Peer it with public IP of the Openswan machine, and pick its IPSEC option
! set 'myset'
crypto map mymap 10 ipsec-isakmp
crypto map mymap 10 match address OPENSWAN-VPN
crypto map mymap 10 set peer OpenswanIP
crypto map mymap 10 set pfs group2
crypto map mymap 10 set transform-set myset
crypto map mymap interface outside
! Enable ISAKMP/IKE without XAUTH and ModeConfig
isakmp enable outside
isakmp key YourSecret address OpenswanIP netmask 255.255.255.255 no-xauth
   no-config-mode
isakmp identity address
isakmp nat-traversal 20
isakmp policy 5 authentication pre-share
isakmp policy 5 encryption 3des
isakmp policy 5 hash sha
isakmp policy 5 group 2
isakmp policy 5 lifetime 86400
```

The PIX 501 only has one interface. You can only have one crypto map per interface. If you need to set up multiple IPsec connections, you should add them as different priorities to the same crypto map.

Nortel Contivity

The Nortel Contivity is a popular VPN product for managing large numbers of end users on the MS Windows platform. It supports various authentication options, including X.509 Digital Certificates (for example, Entrust), as well as the XAUTH IKE extension (and the IETF Draft that has since expired). Openswan is known to work using X.509 Digital Certificates, but as this requires the Nortel Contivity administrator to purchase and set up an Entrust Certificate Authority, many Contivity administrators do not do this.

The Contivity supports XAUTH, but since Openswan has only recently included XAUTH support, this has not seen much testing yet. It is very likely that some proprietary extensions to the IKE protocol have been made by Nortel that would cause XAUTH interop to fail.

Most interoperability setups between the Nortel Contivity and Openswan therefore use pre-shared keys (aka PSK, or PSS). The ipsec.conf is straightforward. You can enable PFS with pfs=yes. Compression might give some problems, so the safe way is to disable it using compress=no. Since we are using pre-shared keys, we are using authby=secret. If you are using static public IPs, you can leave out any leftid= or rightid= and use IP addresses in the ipsec.secrets file.

> Nortel Contivity firmware older than 4.06_120 does not support DH group 2. Some versions also do not support 3DES. Verify your firmware supports these modes and upgrade the firmware otherwise.

Before you can define the remote subnet to connect to, you will need to add a definition for the local network.

In the Contivity's web interface, select Profiles | Networks, then enter a name for your local LAN, CorporateLAN for example:

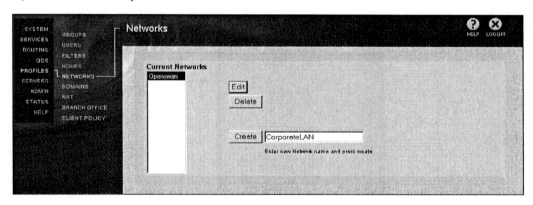

Fill in the network number (the lowest IP address in your range) and the netmask. Click Add and then Close. To configure the parameters for the remote end, we need to configure a **branch office**. Select Profiles | Branch Office | Edit Group.

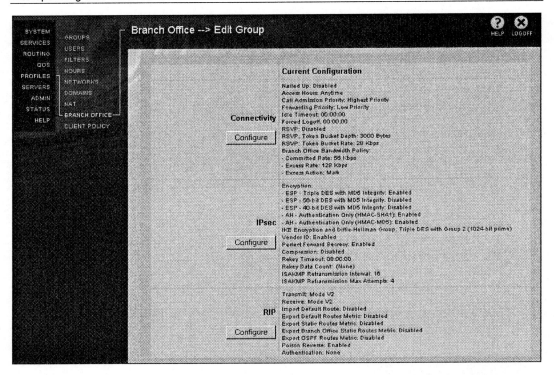

Disable the Nailed Up feature until you have a working configuration. Set the Idle Timeout to 00:00:00 to prevent the IPsec connection from getting closed. Disable 40 and 56 bit DES encryption and enable the 3DES option.

You can disable the AH options as well, if you are not using any L2TP with the Contivity. Make sure to enable Perfect Forward Secrecy, and to disable RIP, unless you already deploy RIP on your routers.

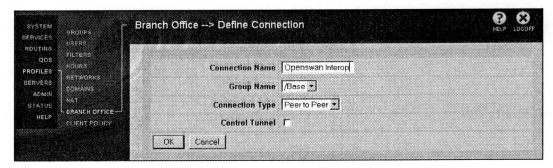

Go back to Profiles | Branch Office and select Define New Branch Office. Name the connection and select the Group Name and Peer-to-Peer for Connection Type. Click OK. Peer-to-peer here relates the direction allowed for the tunnel. Peer-to-peer means this side can both initiate and respond to IPsec connections.

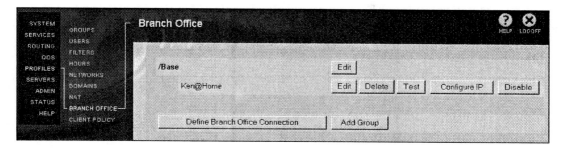

Click on Define Branch Office Connection. Fill out the Endpoint Addresses by selecting your external IP from the drop-down menu for Local. Enter the IP address of the Openswan Gateway for Remote. Enter your pre-shared key in the Text Pre-Shared Key box. Scroll down to the bottom of the page and click Continue.

Now pick the network you just defined from the drop-down menu for the Local Accessible Networks, and click Add under Remote.

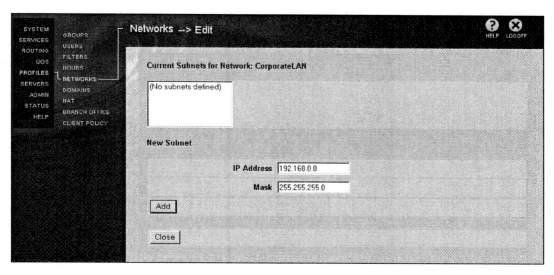

Fill in the IP address of your Openswan gateway and set the subnet mask to 255.255.255.255. Click on Ok and you will return to the previous page. Scroll down to the bottom, and click Ok again.

If everything is filled out correctly, you should be back at the Branch Office page and you should see the new connection. If you click Profiles | Branch Office, and then click on the Test button next to your tunnel, the Contivity will attempt to establish the tunnel.

If your connection fails, and the Openswan logs give no further hints, check the logs on the Contivity at Status | Event Log, where you will find the System Log and the Security Log.

Until very recently at least, the Nortel Contivity did not implement Path MTU Discovery for IPsec, instead using a hardcoded MTU of 1500. This can cause Openswan to send an ICMP error back to the Contivity when it tries to build packets that would have a size of 1500 plus the IPsec header. Setting the LAN or the Contivity's MTU to 1400 might avoid this issue.

Checkpoint

Checkpoint has a few VPN appliances in its portfolio. The best known is the VPN-1; other products are the NG VPN and the FP3.

Some checkpoint firewalls do not support PFS. You might need to add pfs=no to your connection.

One issue with a subnet-to-subnet tunnel between Checkpoint and Openswan is that Checkpoint seems to negotiate separate /32 tunnels for each machine in the local LAN. For instance if you have a subnet-to-subnet connection for 10.0.1.0/24 to 10.0.2.0/24, you will get messages like:

```
Cannot respond to IPsec SA request because no connection is known for
10.0.1.15/32===a.b.c.d[S-C]...e.f.g.h===10.0.2.101/32
```

Checkpoint also has a mode called **Hybrid Mode**, which is a precursor to what became XAUTH. It is supported by the Checkpoint SecureClient. This mode is used by default when PSK is used and when using SecureID cards. Openswan does not support Hybrid Mode.

Checkpoint has more issues stemming from its breaking of the RFCs by using ID_USER_FQDN without data, and by stripping the leading @ symbol of the user ID outside of XAUTH. Patches are floating around that send a null ID of type ID_USER_FQDN to mimic the SecureClient behavior, but as far as we know, no one has successfully interoperated Openswan in Hybrid Mode with Checkpoint.

The most problematic feature of Checkpoint is that it will claim to accept any IPsec SA if the authentication matches, even if the requested policies in Phase 2 are wrong. It will then silently drop the packets. This is rather confusing (and violate the IETF RFC standard) because the Openswan end will receive "IPsec SA Established", while, in fact, the Checkpoint appliance has not established the proper IPsec SA.

WatchGuard Firebox

The WatchGuard Firebox is a commonly used VPN gateway. We have seen problems where a WatchGuard appliance used an incorrect implementation of MD5 and would accept an IKE proposal with MD5 but would then send mangled packets that are dropped by Openswan. As a workaround you can tell Openswan to not allow MD5 by adding the following lines to the connection definition:

```
ike=3des-sha1
esp=3des-sha1
```

The WatchGuard Firebox SOHO 6tc and BF4S16E6 with a firmware release of 7.2 or earlier seem to have a typo in their code for handling NAT-Traversal. They incorrectly use a value of 61433 instead of 61443 as the code for the Encapsulation Mode Transform attribute signifying ESP over UDP encapsulation.

You can change this value to a matching setting in `openswan-2/include/ietf_constants.h`.

Symantec

Some Symantec VPN products contain a bug in the IKE negotiation. It sends packets with a length that does not match the length declared in the header length field. This manifests itself with the following error on the Openswan end:

```
Feb 12 14:58:52 CoffeeCompany pluto[12549]: packet from 193.110.157.17:500:
size differs from size specified in ISAKMP HDR (40)
```

Upgrade the firmware to 16Y or higher to resolve this issue.

Frequently used VPN Client Appliances

Many DSL routers and WiFi products now support IPsec. These devices should be able to connect to Openswan. Some of them might be limited to pre-shared key connections, but more and more devices now offer support for X.509 Certificates. We will discuss a few commonly used products.

ZyXEL

ZyXEL makes products ranging from end-user DSL routers with IPsec support to dedicated firewall/VPN products.

Some versions of the ZyXEL firmware seem to exhibit a bug at rekey or IPsec SA deletion. The problem is that the ZyXEL units seem to delete the Phase 2 sixty seconds after the deletion of Phase 1, even if one of them has not yet expired. The problem is that during these sixty seconds, Openswan still uses the Phase 2, since it did not get deleted, but the ZyXEL assumes that the Phase 2 is dead. No packets will flow during these sixty seconds.

To add to the problem, the longest lifetime (on both the Phase 1 and Phase 2, since they are treated the same) is 3600 seconds. So this bug happens for one minute every hour. DPD would solve this issue, but we have not heard any reports of DPD running successfully on the ZyXEL, and we are not sure if it is properly supported.

This bug is not necessarily fixed in newer versions of the firmware. We have seen reports of the Presteige 652R-11 with ZyNOS v3.40(FN.7) exhibiting this bug, but the same unit with ZyNOS v3.40(FN.6) worked fine. Firmware versions before May 2005 also exhibit problems with multiple tunnels.

If your version does support subnets properly, but you accidentally set the Local: Addr Type option to SINGLE instead of SUBNET, you will be able to tell by the following error on the Openswan side:

```
Nov 23 22:03:43 ikmisyella pluto[7517]: "zywall" #3: cannot respond to IPsec
SA request because no connection is known for
192.168.1.0/24===192.168.0.1[S=C]...192.168.0.254[S=C]===192.168.2.2/32
```

If your ZyXEL does not support subnets (we believe they all do), you can specify `192.168.2.2/32` instead of `192.168.2.0/24` as the `rightsubnet=` parameter on the Openswan side.

Other than these issues, configuration of the ZyXELs is pretty straightforward and all the options are pretty self explanatory. Below is an example using PSK with a ZyWALL. On the main VPN menu, you can edit and delete VPN connections.

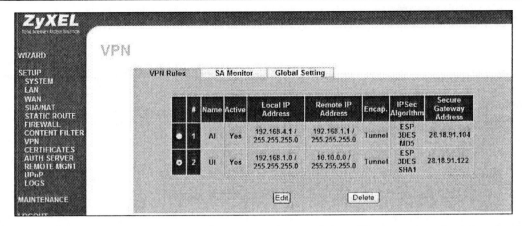

Below is the Edit menu. Be sure to set the Address Type to Subnet if you want a subnet-to-subnet connection. At the bottom of the screen, set the ESP encryption and authentication algorithms to 3DES and SHA1 respectively.

The Advanced menu is accessible by clicking the button at the bottom of the Edit screen. Set the Key Group and Perfect Forward Secrecy options to DH2.

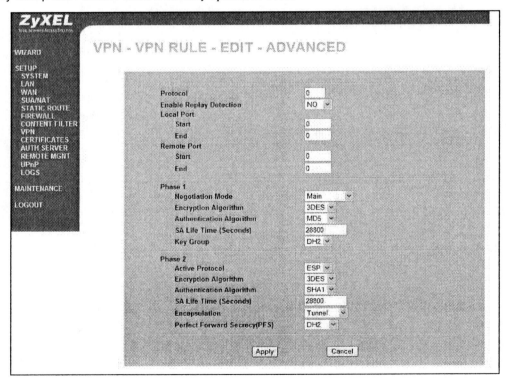

DrayTek Vigor

The DrayTek Vigors are fairly popular in Europe. They are cheap routers in a number of variants; some have an inbuilt ADSL modem, some also have wireless. The ADSL routers come in two versions. For ADSL with an analog line, the Annex A version should be used. For ADSL with an ISDN line, the Annex B version needs to be used.

Though the Vigors are cheap, they do have their own little issues, and it takes a little bit of time to get to know those issues. DrayTek sometimes fixes bugs in their firmware, so always check its website for firmware upgrades, but be very careful to flash the Vigors with the proper Annex version. DrayTek also responds well to email sent to its support staff, although we have had mixed results when reporting IPsec bugs in its implementation.

The Vigor Web Interface

The Vigors can be configured using a web interface. Though the username you give does not matter, with some browsers you have to fill in something or else they will not properly log in. In the default configuration, you can only configure the machine from the LAN, but the Vigor has a management menu where you can allow selective IP addresses or subnets on the Internet side to configure the Vigor remotely. Be aware though that when setting up an IPsec tunnel from the Vigor to your own subnet, you will break access to the management interface from the public IP. You will have to use the internal IP of the Vigor through the IPsec tunnel to reconfigure the Vigor. This can be slightly annoying when you are trying to configure the VPN, as depending on whether the VPN is up or not, you have to connect differently to the Vigor to manage it.

Another problem with the web interface is its pop-up boxes. Some pop-up boxes cause a looping JavaScript error in some browsers (such as Mozilla). Currently, we have only seen this behavior with the Call Schedule Setup, which is not all that important. We have also noticed that values do not always seem to be correctly filled in on a page where you have selected an Advanced option that causes a pop-up box to appear. Our advice is to always save the settings on each page, and update the pop-up boxes separately. Avoid changing both the page options and a pop-up in one go.

Below you can see the general setup screen accessible by going to Advanced Setup | VPN and Remote Access Setup | VPN IKE/IPsec General Setup. Here you can configure the PSK and deselect the Medium (AH) and DES options.

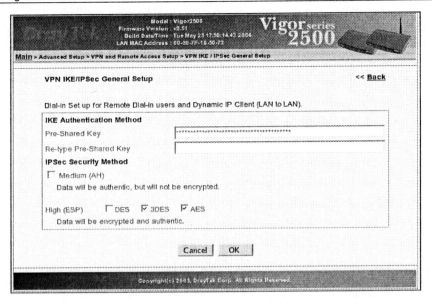

There are many places where you can fill in a PSK for IKE. There is one in the VPN General Setup screen (above), two in the profiles for the Lan-to-Lan connections, one for dial in and one for dial out which, depending on your call direction, might be grayed out. Always check if there are asterisks (****) in these boxes to confirm that you actually have a value set.

We have not actually tried different PSKs on different Lan-to-Lan settings, to see how this fits in with the global PSK setting. We assume the device is stuck with a single PSK for all connections.

Go to Advanced Setup | VPN and Remote Access Setup | LAN-to-LAN Profile Setup to configure a tunnel.

In the Common Settings section, you configure the name of the connection. Do not forget to select Enable this profile here.

The Call Direction section contains what is probably the weirdest Vigor issue, especially because Openswan has no such concept: the Vigor allows you to set a call direction. Dial-out means initiating, and Dial-in means responding to an IPsec IKE request. The problem starts when you want to have a 24/7 VPN tunnel. You can select Always on, but this really is a misleading name. It will just change the settings to Dial-out and dial immediately. In other words, if you set two Vigors to Always on, the IPsec connection will fail because neither end will allow Dial-in (responding). If you configure one end to Dial-in or Both it will work, but the Dial-in side will not be able to trigger the IPsec tunnel after a time out. And if you select the Enable PING to keep alive option, it *again* will change your call direction to Dial-out. So make sure you only select this ping option on the side that is set to Dial-out.

However, when a connection is Dial-out on the Vigor, you can still use ipsec auto –up to establish an IPsec SA, but it will not carry any traffic since the Vigor will attempt to delete it immediately. You will see confusing Delete Notify messages because the Vigor seems to set up its IPsec SA without confirming this to Openswan and it will then send a Delete Notify that Openswan cannot match.

Another important issue to keep in mind is that the rekey time can flip the direction of the call. If you use idle timeouts that are about the same, the dial-in site might decide to rekey just before the dial-out side starts its own rekey sequence. This will then be rejected by the dial direction policies defined. Currently, it seems you are best off using Both for call direction and an idle timeout of zero. (Do not use -1, as that will change the call direction too.) You can work with these limitations though. If you make a mistake but have enabled remote management for the dial out Vigor, you can use the web interface to set it to dial out towards you.

Finally, it seems that Openswan runs into rekeying issues when using a call direction of Both in the Vigor, which we hoped would actually circumvent all these problems. Using Dial-out with Always on seems to work better for rekeying. We think some of these problems might be due to lingering Phase 1 ISAKMPs.

The next section is the Dial-Out Settings. Select IPsec Tunnel for the Type of Server, and fill in the remote IP address or hostname. Unselect AH and change ESP to use 3DES with Authentication or AES with Authentication. Be careful with the Advanced button. You are better off saving these settings first and then coming back to click the Advanced button.

The lower half of the screen contains the Dial-In Settings and TCP/IP Network Settings.

Again set the Type to IPsec Tunnel, and tag Specify Remote VPN Gateway. Fill in the Peer VPN Server IP. Deselect AH and DES, and select 3DES and AES.

Again, be careful when selecting IKE Pre-Shared Key; it is better to finish and save this page first before handling pop-ups. Continue with the TCP/IP Network Settings.

Leave My WAN IP and Remote Gateway IP on 0.0.0.0/0 for now. Set the Remote Network IP (lowest IP in the subnet range) and the Remote Network Mask. Do not select More. Disable RIP and set For NAT operation, treat remote sub-net to Private IP.

Depending on how you configure the Openswan end, select or deselect Change the default route through this VPN tunnel. Select OK.

Windows Logon Issues

The VPN tunnel (lan-to-lan profile) seems to work best if you leave the WAN IP at 0.0.0.0. This allows the tunnel to work even if the Vigor's IP address on the outside changes. However, if pinging through the tunnel works, but the Windows logon fails with an obscure Active Directory DNS error, then you should try to change the WAN IP to the IP address you receive from your ISP's DHCP server. That solved the Windows Logon problem for us. Of course this type of setup requires that you use an ISP connection with a static IP, or you will have to fix your IPsec connection every time your ISP changes the IP address on you.

When you have completed this section, you can go through the pop-ups that you have skipped before, such as the Advanced pop-up, which is the only one you should need.

Here you can set Main mode or Aggressive mode, and enable or disable PFS. The Vigor's defaults have changed over time. For Openswan, choose Main mode and enable PFS. Leave the Local ID blank unless you need to specify one in ipsec.conf.

There is an IKE Phase 1 proposal pull-down menu, corresponding to Openswan's ike= setting. The only menu option that allows you to suggest a variety of options (both SHA1 and MD5, 3DES and AES, and DH group 1 and 2) will unfortunately also suggest 1DES. Worse, 1DES will be announced before 3DES, and DH group 1 before DH group 2, so you will always see an error on the Openswan end rejecting the first request for 1DES, and it will end up using a weaker DH group than necessary. We recommend setting this option specifically to 3DES_SHA1_G2.

Our findings were verified against the latest released firmware, dated June 1 2005. All bugs mentioned are still present in that version of the firmware.

Other Vigorisms

The Vigor calls AH **Medium Security** and ESP **High Security**. You will most likely want to disable all Medium Security options. The High Security modes come with 3DES, AES, and DES. You should always unselect DES as Openswan rejects the outdated (and insecure) DES mode by default. The Vigor also allows ESP without authentication, which is insecure and rejected by Openswan. Do not pick these options. Stick to 3DES or AES with authentication.

Another problem we have observed is that the Vigor can be very liberal in what it expects, so that the initial connection establishes without a problem, but that on a later rekey time, it will request something Openswan will refuse. We have seen this happen when disabling Perfect Forward Secrecy on the Vigor and enabling pfs=yes (the default) on Openswan. Of course, this is the mistake of the administrator, and not the device, but it could be quite a difficult problem to diagnose.

Unresolved Issues

As of version 2.55 (for the Vigor2500), there are still a few unresolved problems with the Vigor firmware, as detailed in this section. These might have been fixed by the time you're reading this. Check the Openswan interop pages for up-to-date information.

IPsec SA Limitation

The most important issue is that you cannot have two IPsec tunnels with the same two endpoints. Although we successfully established multiple tunnels with the same endpoints using a beta version of the firmware DrayTek gave us for testing the Vigor2600, this patch has not made it to the other models yet. With the buggy firmware, you will receive a Delete SA request for the first tunnel when you try to bring up the second tunnel. DrayTek considers this a *feature request* instead of a *bug report* and it has a low priority with its R&D department. If you need to set up multiple tunnels to the same VPN gateway, a common requirement for larger companies who have multiple locations with different subnets, then you should avoid Vigor units unless you can confirm that DrayTek has fixed this issue. This is irrespective of whether you define two separate lan-to-lan tunnels or use the More option to add the second tunnel. The second method has the additional problem that when you *dial* the VPN tunnel, only the first network is actually established with an IPsec SA. To bring up the second tunnel requires an initiation from the other (Openswan) end. According to DrayTek this is the normal behavior, and the Vigor would indeed send packets over the first tunnel with the second tunnel's IP address. This has not been verified by the Openswan team, because we simply can never work with such a solution, because Openswan would (as it should!) reject those packets, since they do not match any SPD/SAD entry.

Rekeying Issue

The Vigor sends a Delete SA request after its timeout has occurred. On Openswan 1 this informational message is ignored, and the result is a %trap eroute. The connection can't be triggered again within the Openswan's keylife, since it will ignore unencrypted IKE traffic sent by the Vigor as it believes it has a proper tunnel up. Upgrade to Openswan 2, which properly handles Delete SA requests.

Phase 1 Resets

If you change any Phase 1 (IKE) parameters, and you have already established a Phase 1 (ISAKMP) connection to the remote end, that ISAKMP will not be torn down. You must reboot the Vigor for your changes to take effect.

Monitor

The **VPN connections monitor** is not that great. It can only show the two states, established IPsec tunnel and not up. You only have a choice between dial and drop. It does not show whether Phase 1 is up, or what any error might be. So if you are stuck in Phase 1, you just see not up and you think you can still hit dial. Sometimes the monitor state is also just plain wrong. The IPsec tunnel is up, but the monitor does not know about it. We think this happens mostly (if not only) on the responding end. A ping is more reliable than the monitor. This also happens with Vigor-Vigor connections.

Logs

You cannot find IPsec logs on the device. The only way to get more logs is to enable syslog, which when enabled will send you a lot of syslog information. We do not recommend using the syslog feature over the Internet, since it generates a lot of syslog messages.

Spurious 1DES Requests

Sometimes we have seen 1DES/modp-768 requests even when 1DES was disabled, but these could be due to the web interface's inconsistency with advanced tabs as discussed earlier. Openswan will refuse these requests and both ends will decide on another acceptable proposal.

CIDR Writing Bug

Do not use CIDR notations that specify an IP address instead of the network address in the Remote Network ID setting, as this will not work with the Vigor. So you can use 10.0.2.0/24 but should not use 10.0.2.1/24.

UDP Fragmenting Option

The vigor has an option to allow UDP defragmentation, which can be found at Advanced Setup | IP Filter / Firewall Setup | General Setup. The option is called Accept Incoming Fragmented UDP Packets (for some games, ex. CS).

This option is disabled by default, and could influence IKE behavior when UDP fragmentation happens. This is not particularly likely, however, because the Vigors do not support X.509 Certificates with big RSA keys, which seems to be the main reason for IKE fragmentation. If at some point Vigor supports X.509 Certificates, this option might need to be enabled.

Enabling the IPsec VPN Service

The Vigor has an option to completely enable or disable the entire VPN system at Advanced Setup | VPN and Remote Access Setup | Remote Access Control Setup | IPsec VPN service.

You must enable this option, though you can disable the L2TP and PPTP VPN services in this menu if you do not use those.

NetScreen

(Thanks to Ghislaine Labouret of Hervé Schauer Consultants)

The NetScreen is a very popular router/firewall in North America. It has been acquired by Juniper Networks. There are various models available, usually small form factor, with two or more Ethernet ports on the device. It runs **ScreenOS**.

The VPN connection configuration menu is where you set whether to use Pre-Shared Key or Certificates, which IKE mode (Main or Aggressive) to use, and the IP address of the remote gateway.

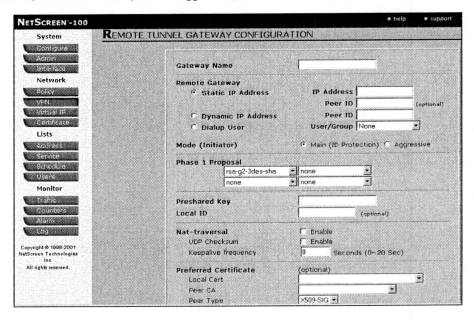

You can set the encapsulation mode (Tunnel or Transport), and the subnet you wish to connect in the Policy Configuration screen.

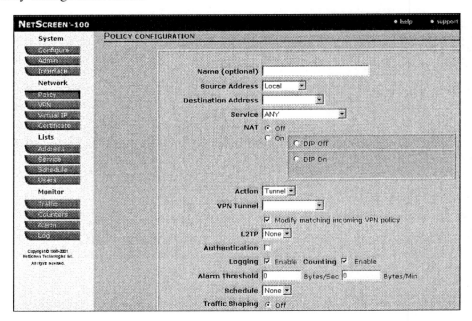

Known Issues

There have been numerous incompatibilities between ScreenOS and Openswan (and FreeS/WAN) over the years. Ensure you are running the latest version of ScreenOS on your NetScreen device. Also, check the NetScreen release notes, as they contain the latest information about known interoperability bugs. In general, people seem to have had more luck using Aggressive Mode than Main Mode, but we do recommend trying Main Mode first as it is much safer.

If you log in to the NetScreen device using SSH or Telnet, you can use the snoop command and set debug ike info or debug ike all.

Below is a configuration example for connecting Openswan to NetScreen. First we will show the Openswan side's ipsec.conf:

```
conn openswan-to-netscreen
     authby=secret
     aggrmode=yes
     ike=3des-sha1-modp1024
     left=%defaultroute
     leftid=@your.host.name
     right=YourPublicIP
     rightsubnet=172.16.20.0/24
     auto=start
```

And the corresponding ipsec.secrets entry:

```
YourPublicIP @your.host.name : PSK "netscreen"
```

The NetScreen side is using:

```
unset hardware wdt-reset
set clock timezone 0
set vrouter trust-vr sharable
unset vrouter "trust-vr" auto-route-export
set auth-server "Local" id 0
set auth-server "Local" server-name "Local"
set auth default auth server "Local"
set admin name "yyyyy"
set admin password "xxxxxx"
set admin manager-ip 192.168.0.0 255.255.0.0
set admin auth timeout 10set zone "Trust" tcp-rst
set zone "Untrust" block
unset zone "Untrust" tcp-rst
set zone "MGT" block
set zone "VLAN" block
set zone "VLAN" tcp-rst
set zone "Untrust" screen icmp-flood
set zone "Untrust" screen tear-drop
set zone "Untrust" screen syn-flood
set zone "Untrust" screen ping-death
set zone "Untrust" screen ip-filter-src
set zone "Untrust" screen land
set zone "V1-Untrust" screen tear-drop
set zone "V1-Untrust" screen syn-flood
set zone "V1-Untrust" screen ping-death
set zone "V1-Untrust" screen ip-filter-src
set zone "V1-Untrust" screen land
set interface "trust" zone "Trust"
set interface "untrust" zone "Untrust"
unset interface vlan1 ip
set interface trust ip 172.31.0.2/26
```

```
set interface trust natset interface untrust ip YourPublicIP/26
set interface untrust nat
unset interface vlan1 bypass-others-ipsec
unset interface vlan1 bypass-non-ip
set interface trust ip manageable
set interface untrust ip manageable
set interface untrust manage ping
set interface untrust manage ssh
set interface trust dhcp server service
set interface trust dhcp server auto
set interface trust dhcp server option gateway 192.168.1.1
set interface trust dhcp server option netmask 255.255.255.0
set interface trust dhcp server ip 192.168.1.100 to 192.168.1.199
set flow tcp-mss
set hostname ns5gt
set address "Trust" "inside net" 172.31.0.0 255.255.255.192
set user "user1" uid 1
set user "user1" ike-id fqdn "your.host.name" share-limit 10
set user "user1" type  ike
set user "user1" "enable"
set user-group "outsiders" id 1set ike gateway "outside_gw" dialup
  "outsiders"
Main outgoing-interface "untrust" seed-preshare
  "YourPreSharedSecret"
set ike gateway "outside_gw" cert peer-cert-type x509-sig
unset ike gateway "outside_gw" nat-traversal
set ike respond-bad-spi 1
set vpn "outside_vpn" gateway "outside_gw" no-replay tunnel idletime 0
proposal "g2-esp-3des-sha"
set pki authority default scep mode "auto"
set pki x509 default cert-path partial
set av scan-mgr pattern-update-url
  http://5gt-t.activeupdate.trendmicro.com:80/activeupdate/server.ini
  interval 0
set policy id 1 from "Trust" to "Untrust"  "inside net" "Any" "ANY"
nat src
permit
set policy id 2 from "Untrust" to "Trust"  "Dial-Up VPN" "inside net"
  "ANY"
tunnel vpn "outside_vpn" id 1
set global-pro policy-manager primary outgoing-interface untrust
set global-pro policy-manager secondary outgoing-interface untrust
set ssh version v2
set ssh enable
set config lock timeout 5
set modem speed 115200
set modem retry 3
set modem interval 10
set modem idle-time 10
set snmp community "public" Read-Write Trap-on  traffic version any
set snmp port listen 161
set snmp port trap 162
set user-group "outsiders" user "user1"
set admin auth server "Local"
set admin format dos
set zone "Trust" vrouter "trust-vr"
set zone "Untrust" vrouter "trust-vr"
set zone "VLAN" vrouter "trust-vr"
set vrouter "untrust-vr"
exit
set vrouter "trust-vr"
unset add-default-route
set route  0.0.0.0/0 interface untrust gateway YourPublicIP
set route  192.168.255.0/24 interface trust gateway 172.31.0.2
```

SonicWALL

SonicWALL has two versions of their OS called Standard and Enhanced. SonicWALL recommends using OS Enhanced for VPN usage. OS Standard has almost no debugging options, so while it can be made to work in a limited number of modes, it is very hard to diagnose problems. PSK-based connections work fine. We have seen configurations using X.509 certificates that failed to work. SonicWALL only supports sending the X.509 certificate inline, you cannot explicitly load an X.509 certificate. The documentation on the SonicWALL website is very outdated, and references FreeS/WAN 1.94. It therefore contains errors, such as, for example, stating that there is no support for Aggressive Mode, which is no longer true.

Do not forget to allow outgoing IKE packets on UDP port 500 and 4500 in the firewall configuration. When using PSKs, you might need to use the SonicWALL's Unique Firewall Identifier (UFI) as the `rightid=` for your IPsec connection. An example SonicWALL Pro-300 configuration file follows below:

```
Unique Firewall Identifier: YourUFIHere
Security Association: Openswan
IPsec Keying Mode: IKE using Preshared Secret
Name: Openswan
IPSec Gateway Address: 193.110.157.17
Phase 1 DH Group: Group 2
SA Lifetime (secs): 28800
Phase 1 Encryption/Authentication: 3DES & MD5
Phase 2 Encryption/Authentication: Strong Encrypt and Authenticate (ESP 3DES
HMAC MD5)
Shared Secret: YourPreSharedKey
Destination Networks:
192.168.1.0 255.255.255.0

Advanced Options:
Enable Perfect Forward Secrecy : Checked
Phase 2 DH Group: Group 2
```

In `ipsec.secrets`, we again use the Unique Firewall Identifier:

```
193.110.157.131 1.2.3.4 @YourUFIHere : PSK "ThePreSharedSecret"
```

You can set the UFI in the VPN General screen.

As of version 2.3.0, Openswan can now connect to a SonicWALL VPN Appliance as a roadwarrior. The example given here uses IKE with PSK as its keying mode. On the VPN Summary page of the SonicWALL administration interface, note the value of Unique Firewall Identifier for use in `ipsec.conf`. Make sure the SonicWALL Group VPN is set up as follows:

```
Phase 1 DH Group: Group 5
Phase 1 Encryption/Authentication: 3DES & MD5
Phase 2 Encryption/Authentication: Strong Encrypt and Authenticate (ESP 3DES
HMAC MD5)
```

And under Advanced Settings:

```
Enable XAUTH
Enable Perfect Forward Secrecy
Phase 2 DH Group: Group 5
```

The corresponding `ipsec.conf` is:

```
conn sonicwall
    left=%defaultroute
```

```
leftsubnet=your.subnet/mask
leftid=@home
leftxauthclient=yes
right=sonicwall.ip.address
rightsubnet=vpn.subnet/mask
rightxauthserver=yes
rightid=@sonicwall.unique.firewall.identifier
keyingtries=0
pfs=yes
aggrmode=yes
auto=add
auth=esp
esp=3des-md5-96
ike=3des-md5-96
authby=secret
```

And the ipsec.secrets file contains:

```
@home @sonicwall.unique.firewall.identifier : PSK
"your.shared.secret.goes.here"
```

BinTec

We have received a few reports on BinTec that suggest some models, for example the X8500, have some issues. One problem is failing to pick the correct IDs, especially when using X.509 Certificates. A workaround for this is to add a subjectAltname= specifying the IP address to the X.509 Certificate. Furthermore, it seems the failure messages for this ID issue (and possibly other failures in Phase 2), which happens after the ISAKMP SA has been established, are not sent encrypted, but in plaintext. Openswan ignores all those messages because at that point in the negotiation, it expects only encrypted IKE messages. The log will look like this:

```
Dec 17 15:06:29 Sunrae pluto[21106]: "toronto" #214: sent MR3, ISAKMP SA
established
Dec 17 15:06:29 Sunrae pluto[21106]: "toronto" #214: Informational Exchange
message must be encrypted
```

To see what is actually happening on the BinTec, you need to set the ipsecGlobMaxSysLogLevel to debug and then log in to the BinTec console, for example through its serial port, and run the debug ipsec command. From then on, you will see IPsec error messages appear on the console.

The BinTec routers apparently also come with the time unset, meaning the time on the unit starts at January 1, 1970. This will cause all certificates to be invalid, since this time is before the certificates' validity date.

LANCOM

The LANCOM DSL router comes with a web interface that is unfortunately completely inadequate. In fact, it is nothing more than a web interface to the device's SNMP MIBs. This may be handy for the programmers who made the device, but not for anyone who actually bought the device. LANCOM however does ship with Windows software and a user guide to configure the unit. The software at least offers a usable user interface, even though still a bit confusing, since it wants the user to create 'tunnels' and 'policies' and then requires the user to tie them together. Multiple tunnels between the same endpoints should be set up using the Extranet feature.

Older versions of the LANCOM devices require the same ID on both sides, but Openswan of course cannot use the same ID for leftid= and rightid=. It is also not RFC compliant.

Linksys

The Linksys BEFVP41 router's IPsec support is based on a very old version of FreeS/WAN. It is therefore not surprising that it is very compatible with Openswan, though the user interface is a limiting factor here.

Advanced Settings for Selected IPSec Tunnel

Tunnel 1

Phase 1:
Operation mode :   ⦿ Main mode   ⦿ Aggressive mode
Proposal 1:

Encryption :   3DES
Authentication : MD5
Group :   1024-bit
Key Lifetime : 3600   seconds
(Note: Following three additional proposals are also proposed in Main mode:
DES/MD5/768, 3DES/SHA/1024 and 3DES/MD5/1024.)

Phase 2:
Proposal :

Encryption :   3DES
Authentication : MD5
PFS :   ON
Group :   1024-bit
Key Lifetime : 3600   seconds

Other Options:
☐ NetBIOS broadcast
☐ Anti-replay
☐ Keep-Alive
☐ If IKE failed more than 5   times, block this unauthorized IP for 60   seconds

Apply   Cancel

It uses the term Local Secure Group for what Openswan calls the leftsubnet= and the term Remote Secure Group for the rightsubnet=. The Remote Security Gateway is what Openswan calls right=. It can be a host name or IP address.

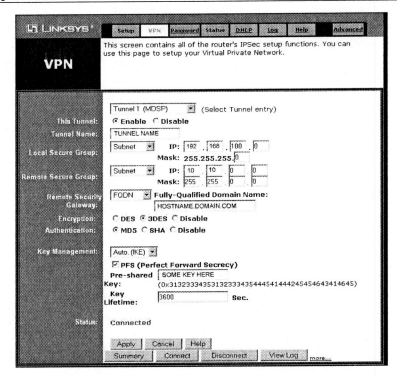

The BEFVP41 uses 1DES and modp-768 by default, which are not compiled into Openswan by default because they are too weak. You need to change the defaults to 3DES on the VPN page and the MODP group on the advanced page to 1024.

Lucent Brick

The Lucent VPN Firewall Brick is a two-tier system consisting of a managed firewall solution, which can span multiple firewalls, centrally managed by the Lucent Security Management Server (LSMS). On the Brick side, you need to configure the following parameters in your LSMS:

```
Preshared Key: whateversecretkeyis
```

Under the Policy tab:

```
ISAKMP Proposal:
D-H Group: Group 2 (Group 1 is not supported per default by Openswan)
Encryption Type: TRIPLE DES (1DES is not supported per default by Openswan)
Auth Type: HMAC MD5
SA Lifetime (sec): 28800 (OpenSWAN Maximum is 8 hours)
IPSec Proposal:
Protocol: ESP-50
Encryption Type: TRIPLE DES (1DES is not supported)
Auth Type: HMAC MD5
SA Lifetime (sec) 14400
SA Lifetime (Kbytes) 10000000
Check Enable Prefect Forward Secrecy
Uncheck Enable compression
```

NETGEAR

The configuration of NETGEAR devices, such as the FVS318, is straightforward. The terms are slightly different but speak for themselves. The following is a pre-shared key configuration example:

```
Connectionname                    YourConnName
Local IPsec Identifier            YourRightID
Remote IPsec Identifier           YourLeftID
Tunnel can be accessed from       any local address
    Local LAN start IP Address    YourNetworkAddress
    Local LAN finish IP Address   YourBroadcastAddress (may be empty)
    Local LAN IP Subnetmask       Your SubnetMask
Tunnel can access                 a subnet of remote address
    Remote LAN start IP Address   OpenswanNetworkAddress
    Remote LAN finish IP Address  OpenswanBroadcastAddress (may be empty)
    Remote LAN IP Subnetmask      Openswan SubnetMask
    Remote WAN IP or FQDN         Openswan hostname/ip address
Secure Association                Main Mode
Perfect Forward Secrecy           Enabled
Encryption Protocol               3DES
PreSharedKey                      YourPreSharedKey
KeyLife                           86600
IKE Life Time                     28800
NETBIOS enable                    <ticked>
```

KAME/Racoon

KAME has split off the IKE protocol from the SPD/SAD kernel entries. The IKE daemon is called Racoon and handles all the key management. The setkey binary is used to load the proper policies into the kernel. Unfortunately, Racoon does not call setkey for you, and you need to do all the work yourself. This makes automating KAME much harder. Another problem of Racoon is that you need to restart all its IKE connections when you make a change to its configuration, for example if you wish to just add one client.

Chapter 8 has an example of the Racoon configuration file with a setkey script. Mac OS X uses Racoon as well, but adds a GUI layer on top of it that can create Racoon configuration files. You can find instructions for Mac OS X in Chapter 8 as well.

Aftercare

If your interop has been successful, it is time to back up all your configurations as a precaution. This can be done using the device's backup mode, or if the device does not have such an option, by creating screenshots. If the remote end you hooked up to Openswan is a leaf node, it is worth powercycling the appliance to make sure it is able to come back up again without configuration changes. It also will confirm that the configuration running on that device is the same as the saved configuration.

Summary

We have discussed a few devices in great detail to give you an idea of the options available for IPsec appliances. We have discussed several common devices that people need to connect to and the common problems associated with those. It is always a good idea to Google for the latest information on these interop issues. With the information of this chapter, you are hopefully well-enough armed to handle any of the new devices that will undoubtedly hit the market in the next few years.

10

Encrypting the Local Network

We have now covered various methods for setting up a VPN connection between two hosts or two subnets over the Internet. However, in recent years a new problem has surfaced in the form of wireless internet connections such as 802.11 (WiFi) and Bluetooth. The need for encryption, even when two machines are next to each other in the same room, is stronger than ever. This chapter explains how to encrypt internal LAN connections using IPsec.

As with most emerging technologies, various vendors are implementing methods to protect the link layer against rogue intrusions, or methods for removing compromised hosts from the network. The IETF Dynamic Host Configuration working group (the same group that wrote the DHCP standard) is working on protecting the DHCP protocol with encryption, based on DNSSEC. Meanwhile, Microsoft has been adding a feature called Network Access Protection (NAP) into its latest beta releases of Windows, Longhorn, and Vista. These technologies are still being developed and tested, while IPsec technology has been around for a while and is supported on most platforms. Why not use IPsec to secure and encrypt LAN traffic?

Methods of Encryption

There are a few different ways to accomplish the task of securing the local network with IPsec encryption.

Host-to-Host Mesh

If you only have a handful of machines, you could set up a full mesh of IP connections. This solution is the easiest to set up, very ugly, and a nightmare to maintain. For three servers (A, B, and C), you need to configure three IPsec tunnels (AB, AC, and BC). For four servers you need six IPsec connections, for five servers ten connections. In general, you would need $(n-1) * n/2$ connections for n servers. These are straightforward host-to-host IPsec connections, containing:

```
conn ab
left=a.b.c.d
right=a.b.c.e
```

Sometimes host-to-host connections seem to fail in the LAN. If this happens to you, try adding type=%direct to the conn

Host-to-Gateway Setup

A slightly more advanced setup is where all machines have an IPsec connection to the default gateway, and they tunnel all traffic through this connection. However, this is not as simple as it may appear. Image you have:

```
conn ab
left=a.b.c.d
right=a.b.c.1
rightsubnet=0.0.0.0/0
```

Packets for a.b.c.e would still not be guaranteed to go through this tunnel. First of all, we have found inconsistent behavior on Windows in such a setup. Secondly, when using KLIPS, the problem is that it depends on the additional kernel routes into the ipsecx device, and since we are trying to connect to a machine in the same LAN, the routing is not used at all. The machine will simply send an ARP request to obtain the MAC address of the ethernet card of the other machine and then send the packet directly over the Ethernet (or over the real ether if this is a wireless connection). As a result, KLIPS never gets to see this packet and will not be able to send it over an IPsec connection. With NETKEY, however, this should not be a problem.

Single IP Extrusiautomation or L2TP

The next solution is to *extrude* an IP address onto machines in the LAN from the gateway using IPsec, and then use this IP address for all communication. The outer IP would be firewalled to only allow IPsec (or L2TP). Although such a setup would probably work, it has not been extensively tested. It requires two IP addresses per machine—each belonging to a different subnet. The first DHCP IP address can be anything from a large pool of IP addresses, such as 10.0.0.0/16. The second IP address is then taken from a pool that only hands out /32 addresses. That is, it does not come from a pool of /24 or /16. Since each address is a /32, it turns the link into the equivalent of a point-to-point link. All traffic from that IP is sent over the IPsec (or L2TP) tunnel.

However, administration of this type of setup is difficult. L2TP makes it easier, but requires Transport mode IPsec, and a RADIUS server to scale. It requires IP packets to be sent within IPsec packets, which means that packet sizes are decreased for the inner IP to prevent IP fragmentation. And it requires twice as many IP addresses. It is far from ideal.

Opportunistic Encryption in the LAN

If the LAN consists purely of Linux machines, our task would be easier. After all, Opportunistic Encryption, as explained in Chapter 5, allows each machine to find the key of any other machine and set up an IPsec tunnel based on the IPsec key information in the reverse zone of the local IP range used. Unfortunately, this still presents various problems.

The biggest problem at this point is that NETKEY currently does a very poor job when deployed as part of an Opportunistic Encryption setup because it lacks the packet-caching features needed for dynamically setting up tunnels. KLIPS, on the other hand, needs the routing hack that fails in the LAN, unless we copy the *split default route* trick as a *split the local LAN route* trick. We covered this route hack in Chapter 6.

Another problem with the OE solution is that some servers depend on other servers in the LAN. We have discussed the dependency on the name server and DHCP server in Chapter 5, but an additional problem could occur if the /usr partition is mounted from a Network File System (NFS) server. If Openswan is installed in the default /usr or /usr/local partition, you face a Catch 22 problem.

LAN machines also tend to use DHCP, so a mechanism for updating the IPsec DNS records needs to be in place. This issue has been resolved with the WaveSEC solution that we explain in this chapter, using DNS Dynamic Updates in combination with DHCP.

Non-OE-Capable Machines

Windows machines do not yet support OE, and X.509 connections would be needed instead. This leads to the question of how to distribute the certificates. This issue has been resolved with the WaveSEC for Windows solution that is also discussed in this chapter, by using an SSL web server to generate the X.509 Certificates. The drawback is that all traffic is sent through the gateway machine.

Designing a Solution for Encrypting the LAN

In most situations, especially in a well designed network, there is no need to encrypt traffic between machines in the same LAN. Even if using wireless, which is usually designed as a separate subnet with its own restrictions, the wireless clients will want to talk to either another subnet (for example the DMZ or server network), or they will want to talk to something else out there on the Internet. These clients mostly need to encrypt the wireless traffic to the first gateway; after that, the gateway's upstream is usually a trusted wired uplink. For situations where traffic destined for a second remote office network must be encrypted, you would configure a separate VPN tunnel.

Thus, the real issue is to ensure that anyone in a wireless network encrypts the first hop to the wireless AP, and trust the network beyond that. This is the security that WaveSEC and WaveSEC for Windows offer.

Design Goals

All modern WiFi cards support various methods for securing the wireless. There is WEP, WPA, WPA2, EAP, LEAP, PEAP, Dynamic WEP, and 802.1x. The fact that all these 'secure protocols' exist really only indicates that vendors of WiFi products have completely failed to devise a truly secure solution.

Most of these protocols have either been broken, or are so overly complex that they are bound to be broken. And that is if they are even implemented correctly to begin with. Since most of these protocols are implemented on the WiFi card or chip itself, these implementations have not received the scrutiny of many cryptanalysts.

Goldberg and Borisov, two Berkeley researchers, first broke WEP when they realized that most implementations were fairly weak. WPA was designated as WEP's successor but it was soon discovered that if WPA passphrases of less than twenty characters were used, the cryptographic strength of WPA was less than that of WEP. Next, Extended Authentication Protocol (EAP) saw the light.

EAP is very extendable, and therefore inherently complex. Cisco's LEAP got cracked to pieces, and it took Cisco nine months to develop PEAP, its successor, before it even admitted that LEAP was fundamentally broken. A whole nine months in which anyone could break into any LEAP-protected WiFi network.

Black-box (proprietary) encryption and the lack of structured protocol design such as through the IETF, coupled with the lack of source code review, reduces any WiFi chip encryption protocol to *untrustworthy* in our view.

> A truly secure WiFi solution should be based on public standards and (open source) auditable code.

Separation of WiFi and Crypto

Another problem is the WiFi chip itself. The processing strength of most WiFi chips is not sufficient to encrypt the maximum possible throughput that such a device could support. With the need for faster WiFi access, the WiFi protocol itself also keeps on changing rapidly, causing many interoperability problems. For every new WiFi protocol, the encryption layer must be adapted.

> Ideally, the encryption and WiFi operations should be separate.

Link Layer Protection

Some WiFi protection mechanisms are meant to keep unauthorized people out of the network. This requires some arrangement beforehand, such as handing over a WEP key or WPA authorization. EAP is based on other credentials, such as the SIM card, or a RADIUS back end. All these methods are meant to protect the link layer. But the link layer here is just a bunch of frequencies anyone can get on to—if there are no cryptographically signed beacons in the WiFi protocols, such protection is a farce, since we have no way of distinguishing between an official and a rogue Access Point. A rogue AP can, for instance, attack the wireless network by continuously sending 'disassociate' commands on the network, so all clients will leave this wireless segment in search of another one. Those clients then find the, usually weaker, WiFi network that is under the control of the attacker. In that network the attacker plays a man-in-the-middle attack on all IP addresses the clients are trying to communicate with, in an attempt to obtain their credentials.

On top of that, neither the DHCP nor the ARP protocol offers any cryptographic security, so a client cannot detect the difference between an official and a rogue DHCP server, or the difference between a real or forged ARP reply. The ARP case is further complicated by proxy-ARP scenarios, which are quite common and involve a gateway machine sending out ARP replies on behalf of another (usually dial-up or VPN) machine.

> Do not attempt to protect the link layer at this point in time, but instead implement authentication and encryption in the TCP/IP layer. Once the link layer protocols are protected by cryptography, such protection can and should be used to protect the link layer as well.

Furthermore, we are not only interested in protecting machines within our wireless segment, we are also interested in protecting the privacy of roaming users. That is, users we have had no previous contact or arrangement with. One can think here of WiFi hotspots. The customer associates with the network, passes some credentials or monetary verification, and is then allowed to use the network for a certain amount of time. It is important to offer encryption and privacy to clients we have no pre-existing agreement with.

The Logical Choice: IPsec

So far, we have concluded that we need a security protocol on the TCP/IP layer. This means we can look at solutions from before the time that there was even such a thing as wireless networking. One popular solution is VPNs based on SSL, but the problem with SSL of course is that it uses a TCP connection. An attacker can send a single spoofed TCP-RST packet to kill an SSL-based VPN tunnel. Another popular solution is OpenVPN, which provides a relatively easy to set up and use UDP-based VPN. However, OpenVPN clients are only available for a limited number of operating systems. It also needs pre-arrangement; you need to know each others' SSL credentials. OpenVPN has also been exposed to much less scrutiny from the crypto research community. Other alternatives used are **stunnel** (SSL wrapping) or **CIPE**. The CIPE protocol has turned out to be fundamentally flawed, and should not be used at all. Stunnel solutions suffer from the TCP-RST flag issue already mentioned.

The problem of all of these solutions is that they are created by individuals to solve a problem. But the problem has already been solved, and by a much larger group of very knowledgeable people needing military-grade encryption. The solution is called IPsec. IPsec uses well known, much researched algorithms and protocols, and open-source implementations have successfully been through software audits by universities or other specialists. IPsec is also not vulnerable to forged TCP-RST packets, since it does not use TCP at all.

Furthermore, IPsec has been deployed for years and is supported by many vendors, including all end-user operating systems. It is also not encumbered by any software patents or licensing issues.

Hotspot

We want to support a hotspot-style network where anyone on the wireless network is protected, after presenting some form of valid credentials (credit card, scratch card, or username and password). The first thing we need to do is to open the link layer, and allow clients to associate and get an IP address and DNS server through DHCP.

Note that we cannot protect the user from associating with a forged AP pretending to be our hotspot AP. AP beacons need to be cryptographically signed. Some OpenBSD people are working on an AP driver that supports this.

When the user starts a web browser, and requests a hostname through the DNS server, the hotspot redirects this request to itself. The client is then presented with an SSL-protected login page for the AP. After passing the credentials, the hotspot stops redirecting packets for this user. We then also want to start encrypting all traffic from this user's laptop to the AP, where we then decrypt it and send it further on. When the user runs out of time (or money), we enable the redirect again, and start from scratch.

> It is important that any DNS server used is rate limited, to prevent clever hackers from not paying and setting up a TCP-OVER-DNS network with software such as NSTX.

Now we need to combine all these design goals and choices into a functional design.

WaveSEC

Now that we know the goals we want to accomplish, we can look at the design and see how to implement our goals.

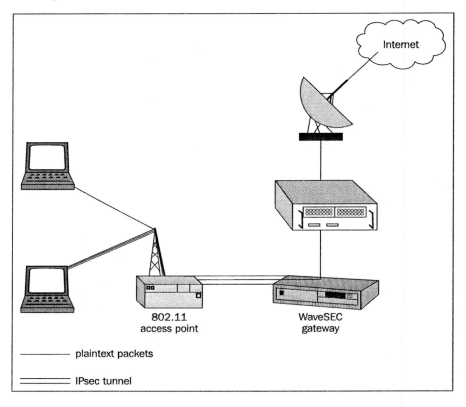

This diagram shows the result of an established WaveSEC connection. The client machine has an IPsec connection with the WaveSEC server. This WaveSEC server is located behind the wireless segment, on a trusted wired segment. The client encrypts its traffic and sends it over the wireless to the WaveSEC server where the traffic is decrypted, and sent it on further.

Note that the WaveSEC server here is in the direct path of all the packets. It has become a critical part of the infrastructure. This mode is the easiest to set up, and is called **inline mode**. This is usually the setup employed when the wireless network is on private IP space that needs to be NATed.

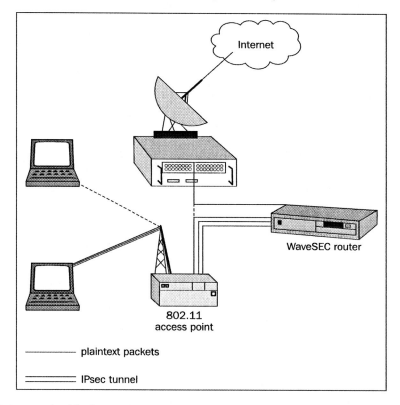

The WaveSEC setup in this figure shows **appendix mode**. It works the same as inline mode, except that the WaveSEC server is now a purely optional network component. Appendix mode has the advantage that WaveSEC does not become a part of the critical infrastructure. If the WaveSEC server dies in appendix mode, people can still use the network, though of course without the added security provided by WaveSEC. We have successfully run WaveSEC in appendix mode at various IETF conferences.

Appendix mode however, is slightly harder to set up and get working properly, especially when the wireless is on routable public IP addresses and no NAT is present in the network. In such a case, packets from the client to the Internet will be properly tunneled, but packets on the way back from the Internet to the client will not realize they are *supposed* to be encrypted. The routing will not properly route the packets through the WaveSEC server. Only traffic that is destined outside the LAN will be encrypted. If you want to make things easy, you can put all the functionality of the WaveSEC server on a single machine that also acts as the default gateway of the network, using inline mode.

WaveSEC needs support on both the client and server side. Since not all clients can easily support WaveSEC, we have created a somewhat different approach for those operating systems that cannot support WaveSEC natively. When clients have full support, we call it **Full WaveSEC**. Clients that do not support WaveSEC can run something we dubbed **WaveSEC for Windows**.

Full WaveSEC

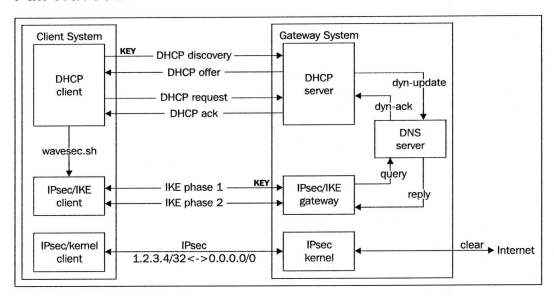

First, when a new client appears in the network, it performs a normal DHCP discovery on the network. The DHCP server sends back a DHCP offer that, apart from the IP address it is offering, contains a special x-waveSEC-server= option to inform the DHCP client that this network supports WaveSEC, and on which IP address the WaveSEC server can be found. The DHCP server then waits for the DHCP client to confirm the offer with a request for the offered IP address. The DHCP client then sends this request for the offered IP address, and it if supports WaveSEC, it will include its own public key as part of that request. The DHCP server then confirms the offer.

In a standard DHCP exchange, this is the end of the DHCP protocol, but when WaveSEC is supported by the DHCP server, it performs one extra task. It sends a **dynamic DNS update** for a TXT record of the reverse zone of the IP address it just assigned to the client to the DNS server. The TXT record contains the public key that the DHCP client has sent to the DHCP server. The DNS server acknowledges the update to the DHCP server.

Those who remember how Opportunistic Encryption works (see Chapter 5) know that the client is now fully set up to use OE. Of course, the default gateway already has its public key in the reverse DNS zone for its own IP address. The client then initiates an OE connection that is the equivalent of:

```
conn wavesec
left=IP.obtained.from.DHCP.server
right=IP.of.WaveSEC.server
rightsubnet=0.0.0.0/0
leftrsasigkey=YOUR-PUBLIC-KEY
rightrsasigkey=%dnsondemand
auto=start
```

When this connection is started, the client will perform a DNS lookup for the IP address of the WaveSEC server's reverse zone to see if it can obtain a public key from an IPSECKEY, TXT, or KEY record. The WaveSEC server, which is configured for full OE, will receive an incoming connection request, and perform a similar DNS lookup for the client's IP address. The result at this point is that both client and server have each other's public key, and they both can proceed to set up an IPsec connection throught which to tunnel all the client's traffic.

Catch 22 Traffic

There is one catch though. We left out a little detail. If the WaveSEC tunnel is up, then all the client's traffic will go through the tunnel. This unfortunately includes DHCP requests. When the client's DHCP lease expires, it will ask for an extension of the lease. These DHCP packets either need to be exempted from the tunnel, or they need to be relayed to the DHCP server and back. The first method is the easiest to implement, since it only requires a small script that uses the iptables fwmark option, and the ip command.

To make things a little easier, we will also exempt DNS traffic to prevent bootstrap problems. We have also found that it is very useful to exempt ICMP echo requests and replies, so that people can tell the difference between the wireless failing, and WaveSEC failing.

Building a WaveSEC Server

The components that are needed on the WaveSEC server are the DHCP service, the DNS service, and the IPsec service. We have used the Internet Software Consortium's DHCP server (and DHCP client), and their BIND-9 name server software. For the IPsec service, we naturally use Openswan. We also need to set up some iptables rules on the WaveSEC server.

DHCP Server Setup

You will need a patched ISC DHCP 3.0.1rc9 server. You can either download the patch, or the patched sources from the WaveSEC website at http://www.wavesec.org/.

You need to configure DHCP to use **dynamic DNS**. An example configuration for /etc/dhcpd.conf is listed below:

```
ddns-update-style interim;
# option definitions common to all supported networks...
option domain-name "wavesec.openswan.org";
option domain-name-servers ns.wavesec.openswan.org;
default-lease-time 2400;
max-lease-time 7200;
```

```
key update.1.168.192.in-addr.arpa. {
 algorithm hmac-md5;
 secret "TheSecretIswithXenu"
}

zone 1.168.192.in-addr.arpa. {
 key update.1.168.192.in-addr.arpa.;
 primary 192.168.1.1;
}

subnet 192.168.1.0 netmask 255.255.255.0 {
  authoritative;
  range 192.168.1.50 192.168.1.199;
  option broadcast-address 192.168.1.255;
  option routers 192.168.1.1;
  option domain-name-servers 192.168.1.1;
}

option oe-key      code 159 = string;
option oe-gateway code 160 = ip-address;

on commit {
  if (not static and
     ((config-option server.ddns-updates = null) or
      (config-option server.ddns-updates != 0))) {

    if exists oe-key {
      set ddns-rev-name =
        concat (binary-to-ascii (10, 8, ".",
                                 reverse (1, leased-address)), ".",
                pick (config-option server.ddns-rev-domainname,
                      "in-addr.arpa."));

      set full-oe-key = option oe-key;

      switch (ns-update (delete (IN, 25, ddns-rev-name, null),
                         add (IN, 25, ddns-rev-name, full-oe-key,
                              lease-time / 2)))
      {
      default:
        unset ddns-rev-name;
        break;
      case NOERROR:
        on release or expiry {
          switch (ns-update (delete (IN, 25, ddns-rev-name, null))) {
          case NOERROR:
            unset ddns-rev-name;
            break;
          }
        }
      }
    }
  }
}
```

You can download this configuration file from www.wavesec.org.

If you were not already running a DHCP service on the WaveSEC machine, you will need to create an empty DHCP lease file. The exact location depends on your distribution, but is usually /var/lib/dhcp/dhcpd.leases or /var/state/dhcp/dhcpd.leases. If you do not know where your distribution expects this file, just start dhcpd and check the error log. If you switched from a distribution dhcpd to a compiled dhcpd, you might want to move the lease file from one location to the other, or symlink them.

DNS Server Setup

The name server should be configured as a recursive name server. It should also be the primary name server for the IP range used on your WiFi network, which in our example is 192.168.1.0/24. Add the following section to your named.conf to allow the DHCP server to send dynamic DNS updates for the local network:

```
key update.1.168.192.in-addr.arpa. {
    algorithm hmac-md5;
    secret "TheSecretIswithXenu"
};
```

Also change or add the local zone so it will allow dynamic updates. The location of the BIND data files depends on the distribution, and could also be stored in /var/named. Our example uses /etc/bind/:

```
zone "1.168.192.in-addr.arpa" {
    type master;
    file "/etc/bind/db.1.168.192.in-addr.arpa";
    allow-update { key update.1.168.192.in-addr.arpa; };
};
```

You will also need to create the /etc/bind/db.1.168.192.in-addr.arpa file that contains the DNS information of your LAN's reverse zone:

```
$ORIGIN .
$TTL 604800; 1 week
1.168.192.in-addr.arpa IN SOA 1.168.192.in-addr.arpa.
root\@wavesec.openswan.org. (
                2005081613       ; serial
                604800       ; refresh (1 week)
                86400        ; retry (1 day)
                2419200      ; expire (4 weeks)
                604800       ; minimum (1 week)
                )
        NS  ns.wavesec.openswan.org.
$ORIGIN 1.168.192.in-addr.arpa.
$TTL 1200    ; 20 minutes
127         PTR localhost.wavesec.openswan.org.
$TTL 604800; 1 week
1           PTR wavesec.openswan.org.
            KEY 16896 4 1 (
                AQNzGEFs18VKTO0sA+4p+GUKn9C55PYuPQca6C+9Qhj0
                jfMdQnTRTDLeI+1p9TnidHH7fVpq+PkfiF2LH1ZtDwMu
                rLlwzbNOghlEYKfQ08OWlOTTUAmOLhAzH28MF7Oq3hzq
                Om5fCaVZWtxcV+LfHWdxceCkjBUSaTFtR2W12urFCBz+
                SB3+OM33aeIbfHxmck2yzhJ8xyMods5kF3ek/RZlFvgN
                8VqBdcFVrZwThOmxDCGN12HNFixL6FzQ1jQKerKBbjbO
                m/IPqugvpVPWVIUajUpLMEmi1FAXc1mFZE9x1SFuSrON
                zYIu2ZaHfvsAZY5oN+I+R2oC67fUCjgxY+t7
                ) ; key id = 25579
```

The key record listed here is the key record of the WaveSEC server itself. It needs to be in the DNS so that WaveSEC clients can look it up. All the clients' KEY records, or IPSECKEY/TXT records if that is what you are using, will appear dynamically when the clients register these through the DHCP protocol. BIND stores these dynamic DNS records in a separate journal file, /etc/bind/db.1.168.192.in-addr.arpa.jnl.

Do not edit or remove the journal file while the BIND name server is running.

Openswan Server Setup

We need to set up the WaveSEC conn on the server end. Unfortunately, we cannot bundle all the connections into one definition. We will need a separate conn for each local IP address that we wish to support WaveSEC on. An option for Openswan to allow a specification in one conn is planned, but has not yet been implemented. For each IP address you want to support, you will need a conn like this:

```
conn host51-to-world
    left=192.168.1.1          # IP of WaveSEC gateway
    leftsubnet=0.0.0.0/0      # all traffic
    right=192.168.1.51        # IP of potential client
    keylife=1h              # IP may be reused after 1 hour idle
    rekey=no                  # Let the client rekey
    auto=add
```

You can download a script from the WaveSEC website called gen-ipsec-conf.sh to generate these connections. The syntax of the script is:

```
./gen-ipsec-conf.sh baseIP low-IP high-IP wavesec-IP nexthop-IP
```

Catch 22 Traffic Setup

We need to run a script, for example through rc.local, that will create the necessary **holes** for DHCP, DNS, and ICMP echo traffic. We can use the following wavesec_hole.sh script:

```
iptables -A PREROUTING -t mangle -p udp -s 0.0.0.0/0 -d 192.168.1.0/24 --sport
53 -j MARK --set-mark 1
iptables -A PREROUTING -t mangle -p udp -s 0.0.0.0/0 -d 192.168.1.0/24 --sport
67:68 -j MARK --set-mark 1
iptables -A PREROUTING -t mangle -p icmp -s 0.0.0.0/0 -d 192.168.1.0/24 -j
MARK --set-mark 1
iptables -A OUTPUT -t mangle -p udp -s 0.0.0.0/0 -d 192.168.1.0/24 --sport
67:68 -j MARK --set-mark 1
iptables -A OUTPUT -t mangle -p udp -s 0.0.0.0/0 -d 192.168.1.0/24 --sport 53
-j MARK --set-mark 1
iptables -A OUTPUT -t mangle -p icmp -s 0.0.0.0/0 -d 192.168.1.0/24 -j MARK --
set-mark 1

ip rule add fwmark 1 table dhcpd
ip route add 192.168.1.0/24 dev wlan0 table dhcpd
```

In this example, the WaveSEC server uses eth0 for its uplink and wlan0 is its wireless device. Of course the wireless could also be a second Ethernet card connected to a wireless Access Point in bridging mode.

Building a WaveSEC Client

Setting up the client is relatively easy. However, you will need to install a patched version of dhclient, and properly configure Openswan for WaveSEC.

DH Client Setup

First, we need to put the Openswan public key in /etc/dhclient.conf. Some distributions already ship a dhclient.conf file, or use separate dhclient.conf files based on the interface name, such as dhclient-eth0.conf. Add the output of the following command to the appropriate dhclient.conf file:

```
ipsec showhostkey --dhclient
```

The resultant file will look something like this:

```
# this is a comment
option oe-key      code 159 = string;
option oe-gateway code 160 = ip-address;

send oe-key = "0x4200 4 1 AQOGxn6v9uF2Y26Ddir...AaRvf1AEW+KoIfKi9";
```

The dhclient program needs to be restarted before it will read the changed configuration file. You can use your Linux distribution's method of restarting the network subsystem, or you can just restart dhclient manually. Assuming your wireless interface is eth0, run the following:

```
killall dhclient
dhclient eth0
```

If everything worked correctly, your public key should now appear in the reverse DNS zone that belongs to your IP address. For instance, if the DNS server is 192.168.1.1 and your IP address obtained from DHCP is 192.168.1.51, then try this command:

```
dig @192.168.1.1 51.1.168.192.in-addr.arpa. ANY
```

The answer section should look something like:

```
;; ANSWER SECTION:
51.1.168.192.in-addr.arpa. 1200  IN      PTR     paul.wavesec.openswan.org.
51.1.168.192.in-addr.arpa. 1200  IN      KEY     0x4200 4 1
AQOGxn6v9uF2Y26Ddir...AaRvf1AEW+KoI
```

Openswan Setup

Because NETKEY does not yet support proper packet caching for dynamic IPsec tunnels, as required by OE (and thus WaveSEC), you must use KLIPS on the client. Add the following conn to /etc/ipsec.conf:

```
conn wavesec
    left=%defaultroute
    right=192.168.1.1              # Substitute your WaveSEC gateway here
    rightsubnet=0.0.0.0/0
    leftrsasigkey=%dnsondemand
    rightrsasigkey=%dnsondemand
    auto=add
```

Disable OE by including /etc/ipsec.d/examples/no_oe.conf in /etc/ipsec.conf.

Either restart Openswan or manually add the connection with the following command:

```
ipsec auto --add wavesec
```

Testing the WaveSEC

If your key has been successfully added to the DNS, you can now try and bring the WaveSEC connection up:

```
ipsec auto --up wavesec
```

If you are using KLIPS on the client, you can run tcpdump in one window, and ping a random machine on the Internet in a second window. You should only see encrypted packets with tcpdump. Remember that you should not test the encryption by pinging the gateway itself, since the gateway is part of the local subnet, which is not protected by WaveSEC unless you duplicated the 'routing trick' for the LAN by splitting those in two half routes into the ipsecx interfaces as well. If we are able to use NETKEY in the future, it should work for both LAN and remote addresses, but you would have to run tcpdump on another machine, to snoop the traffic.

Starting the WaveSEC Connection

When dhclient has finished all its work, it checks for the existence of a file called /etc/dhclient-exit-hooks. If it exists, it will execute it. We use this script to fire off our changes into the DNS and to fire up the WaveSEC connection.

```
if [ -n "$new_oe_gateway" ]          then
    export new_oe_key
    #. /etc/ipsec/wavesec_setup.sh $new_ip_address $new_oe_gateway
    $new_routers
fi
```

Known Issues with WaveSEC

First of all, there is nothing we can do to prevent a user from associating with a rogue AP. Until APs get cryptographically signed beacons, the risk of such an active attack will remain.

Another possible active attack is a man-in-the-middle attack on the DHCP protocol. Instead of connecting to the real DHCP server, we accept a rogue DHCP server's offer and encrypt everything to the attacker's key. The IETF DHC working group is currently working on securing the DHCP protocol. This will likely involve using DNSSEC.

WaveSEC cannot coexist with Opportunistic Encryption, and this is true for both the WaveSEC server and client. This happens because in choosing the outgoing packet path, two eroutes would conflict, and neither connection will work. Passive OE may not cause the same problems.

In inline mode, IPs once used for WaveSEC are not recycled cleanly. In particular, the IPsec tunnel remains routed from the server's perspective. For this reason, once you have set up WaveSEC on your laptop, you must continue to use it. The problem has several potential solutions, as yet unimplemented.

The biggest problem though, is the steep learning curve in setting up WaveSEC. We hope to provide distribution packages in the future that greatly simplify setting up WaveSEC. This should become easier as more distributions move to more flexible, though complex, DHCP client setups using the **Zeroconf** protocol.

WaveSEC for Windows

The problem with Windows is that we do not control any part of the DHCP or IPsec subsystem on the clients. We cannot hook Openswan additions into Windows, so we are left with the normal features of this OS.

The WaveSEC for Windows solution consists of two parts. The first part securely obtains an X.509 Certificate generated on the fly. The second part negotiates an IPsec tunnel to the default gateway, which will carry all the traffic.

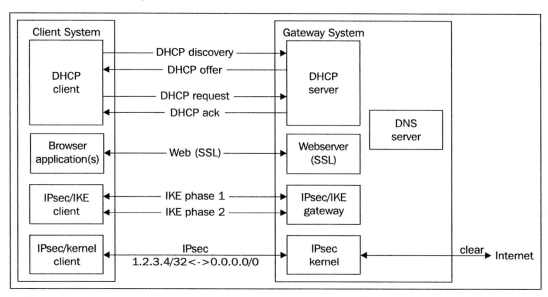

We use a redirect to a web server using SSL for this part, similar to how hotspots redirect you to their login page. To make things easier, we provide a tool to import the X.509 Certificate called certimport.exe. We also use a tool to make configuration of the Windows IPsec tunnel easier. This freely available tool, called lsipsectool.exe, is available on SourceForge.net. It provides a clear interface, and a tray icon, and takes care of shutting down the connection for us.

This solution of adding software onto the Windows machines is far from ideal, since it requires that the user installs software from an unknown source, but Microsoft really left us without any better alternative.

Design Limitations

This version of WaveSEC is really a better than nothing solution. The user has to install untrusted software. Worse, because Microsoft can only use IPsec X.509 Certificates for the 'Computer Account', installing the X.509 Certificate requires Local Administrator privileges. Not everyone with a company laptop actually has these privileges

This solution also clashes with any other running IPsec software, such as Nortel, Cisco, or other third-party products.

As with Full WaveSEC, this solution is vulnerable to rogue APs and rogue DHCP servers, although not using anything is of course also vulnerable to those active attacks.

The worst part is that this solution requires manual intervention and installation from the end user, rather than being fully transparent.

The most satisfactory alternative would be a port of the Openswan userland to Windows, with hooks into the Windows kernel IPsec stack using the ipsec2k library. The Openswan userland has already been ported to Windows using Cygwin (as opposed to the native Windows winsock API) and is already available in CVS HEAD, which will become the Openswan 2.5 branch. Hopefully, we will soon be able to offer Full WaveSEC on the Windows platform as well. A port of Openswan to Mac OS X has also recently started. For now, using an SSL web server with a specially downloadable client is the best we can offer for Windows and MacOSX.

Building a WaveSEC for Windows Server

A prototype WaveSEC for Windows server has been written using PHP. This is really no more than a proof of concept, and should not be rolled out in production environments. For example, no security has been added to prevent one client from downloading another client's generated certificate. The prototype can be downloaded from our FTP server at ftp.openswan.org.

The setup for this server is much easier than the Full WaveSEC variant. First you need to create the CA and the WaveSEC server's own IPsec certificate. In our prototype, this is done when you initialize the WaveSEC server over its SSL web interface.

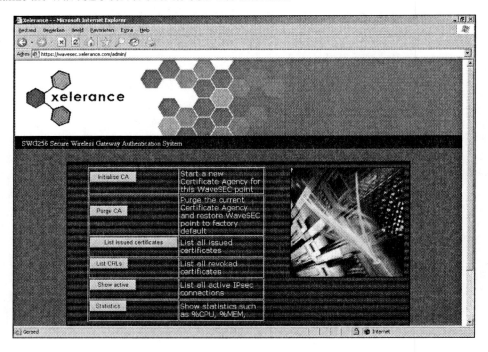

The SSL X.509 Certificate is also used for Openswan. On the WaveSEC server, we only need to configure one WaveSEC for Windows connection. Assuming our wireless network is 192.168.0.0/24 and our default gateway (and WaveSEC server!) is 192.168.0.254, our conn would look like:

```
conn wavesec-for-windows
    left=192.168.0.254
    leftrsasigkey=%cert
    leftsubnet=0.0.0.0/0
    leftcert=/etc/ipsec.d/certs/gateway-cert.pem
    right=%any
    rekey=no
    rightca=%same
    rightrsasigkey=%cert
    auto=add
    authby=rsasig
    pfs=yes
```

If you are using this machine with more than one type of IPsec tunnel, you will need to add a leftid= option with the DN of your gateway-cert.pem X.509 Certificate.

In ipsec.secrets, we would have the corresponding private key for this certificate:

```
: RSA /etc/ipsec.d/private/gateway-key.pem "ThePassphraseIsGlowingWhispers"
```

If you are not using lsipsectool.exe (which we recommend) but the older ipsec.exe tool, then your corresponding ipsec.conf would look like:

```
conn roadwarrior-net
    left=%any
    right=192.168.0.254
    rightsubnet=*
    rightca="C=NL, L=Amsterdam,O=Xelerance,CN=WaveSEC
CA,E=postmaster@xelerance.com"
    auto=start
    pfs=yes
    network=auto
```

The rightca= line varies according to how you initialized the WaveSEC server earlier on. lsipsectool.exe can be installed with a pre-recorded configuration file.

Obtaining the Certificate and Client Software

Once a client connects to the WaveSEC server website, the server will generate an X.509 Certificate in PKCS#12 format, which the client can then download:

Our prototype code detects the client connecting from the HTTP USER_AGENT string, and will redirect the client to the respective pages for Windows 2000, Windows XP, Linux, or 'Unknown'. The reason for the difference between 2000 and XP is that different DLLs were needed for our prototype WaveSEC client using the ipsec.exe tool. This tool is based on the Microsoft Resource Kit DLLs, which are different for Windows 2000 and Windows XP. This difference is not relevant with lsipsectool.exe.

The files for the client have been bundled using the NullSoft Installer Software (NSIS) for Windows. The .nsis file used is also available at ftp.openswan.org.

Unfortunately, this means we cannot bundle the client as an EXE file with the X.509 Certificate, since we cannot rebuild the client executable using NSIS on our Linux-based WaveSEC sever.

Our Prototype Experiences

We found a few oddities when deploying WaveSEC at the BlackHat security conferences and at the DefCon hacker conference.

Openswan Issues

Openswan ignored some Delete/Notify requests from Windows. This bug has since been fixed, but still, when someone closes their Windows laptop, there will be no Delete/Notify, and the IPsec tunnel to that IP address stays up. No one will be able to use that IP address until the conn expires. Therefore, short keylifes (keylife= and ipseckeylife=) should be used in combination with uniqueids=yes, which will cause old connections to die if the same X.509 Certificate (meaning the same laptop) shows up later on another IP address. This is the same reason why we use rekey=no on the server side. If the client is not there, we assume it left or died, and we tear down the tunnel, making the IP address available for a future client. Unfortunately, Microsoft does not support the Dead Peer Detection extensions to the IPsec protocol, which would be ideal for this situation.

Windows Client Issues

The ipsec.exe tool led to a few further problems. Sometimes running ipsec -off to kill the IPsec connection did not work properly. Some people closed their laptop when the tunnel was up. When they got home, they probably spent some time wondering why their laptop did not work, until they realized that all their traffic was still being sent to an unreachable WaveSEC server at the conference center. Worse, if they de-installed the WaveSEC client while the IPsec tunnel definitions were still active, they could no longer easily remove them using the ipsec -off command. And they likely did not know how to delete them using MMC. And yes, these definitions do survive a reboot too.

We hope that these issues will not happen with lsipsectool.exe, since that application has much better Windows integration, and features things like a tray icon that could act upon events such as closing the lid, or shutting down the machine.

Windows Kernel Issues

We encountered two important problems with the Windows IPsec implementation, though these issues could be due to how ipsec.exe interfaces with the Windows kernel IPsec stack.

The first problem occurs when the WaveSEC server is not the default gateway, when some Windows systems do not properly tunnel all traffic through the WaveSEC server, but instead try to send traffic to the default gateway. This unfortunately means that the WaveSEC server has to be in an inline position, instead of being in an appendix position, and therefore becomes part of the critical infrastructure.

The second problem also appears when an appendix mode setup is used, and the upstream router sends packets directly to the WaveSEC clients instead of via the appendix mode WaveSEC server. Windows then receives plaintext packets, since these packets only get encrypted on the WaveSEC server that is being bypassed now, and to our surprise, does NOT drop them. Of course, if a host has an IPsec SA up, it must never allow (possibly spoofed) plaintext packets. Again, this could be a bug in the ipsec.exe client setting up the Windows kernel IPsec stack, or a bug in Windows itself. We have not recently verified this issue with either an updated Windows machine or with the preferred lsipsectool.exe client.

Summary

Our WaveSEC solutions are prototype solutions for encrypting the LAN. They are really prototypes, and you should set aside a couple of days to get the code working in your setup. Even if you do not end up using any of the WaveSEC-specific code, you can use it as a starting point to secure your wireless network for Linux and Windows machines. In the near future, Xelerance hopes to find the time and resources to build on this prototype to make it into a turn-key offering that people can use to easily secure their wireless network.

11

Enterprise Implementation

Integrating VPNs into an existing large enterprise can be quite difficult. This chapter looks at the hardware and software limitations, network topology issues, and methods of obtaining enterprise-grade reliability from your Openswan VPN. The following key topics will be covered:

- Speed and Performance
- Integration into large existing networks
- Optimizations for dealing with large numbers of tunnels
- Use of GRE to create **Super Tunnels**
- Dynamic routing (OSPF and BGPv4)
- Fail-over between Openswan nodes to create **High Availability IPsec**

Many administrators are concerned about the speed and performance of devices on their network—especially if the device carries out cryptographic work. However, the single largest limitation you will run into on modern machines is network bandwidth, not processor speed. Usually your IPsec gateway will be able to encrypt and decrypt faster than your ISP can move your traffic.

Cipher Performance

A 2.8 GHz x86 class processor can saturate a 100 Mbps network link using 3DES, and sustain 300 Mbps using AES without hardware acceleration. Note that these benchmarks were performed without any additional requirements. Most notably, no firewall rules were defined. If you do need to deploy firewall rules, there are a few rules of thumbs that will help you optimize.

Try to branch often, so that you traverse through less firewall rules. Do not use a single top-down list of rules.

Use the *related* keyword somewhere at the top of your ruleset, so those connections that do not need to traverse the whole tree (again) are accepted.

Put those types of packets that you get most of at the top of your rulesets. Depending on the server, this could be ESP packets, UDP 4500/500 packets, HTTP packets, FTP packets, DNS packets, or even database packets.

Optimizing your firewall is outside the scope of this book, but you should realize it could impact heavily on the performance of your VPN gateway.

We have included two tables for those interested in sizing their IPsec gateways. Both are calculated using $B * \# = C$, where B is bandwidth, $\#$ is a constant indicating the speed of the algorithm, and C is the CPU speed required.

The following table shows performance of 3DES on the x86 architecture. In this case, the value for $\#$ in the above rule is 25.

Topology	Speed	CPU Needed
Cable modem/DSL	1 Mbps	25 MHz
Ethernet	10 Mbps	250 MHz
Fast Ethernet	100 Mbps	2.5 GHz
ATM OC3	155 Mbps	3.8 GHz
Gigabit Ethernet	1000 Mbps	22.5 GHz

This table shows performance of AES on the x86 architecture. The value for $\#$ is now 9.

Topology	Speed	CPU Needed
Ethernet	10 Mbps	90 MHz
Fast Ethernet	100 Mbps	900 MHz
ATM OC3	155 Mbps	1.4 GHz
Gigabit Ethernet	1000 Mbps	9 GHz

On x86 architectures, assembler code is used directly for 3DES and AES. On non-x86 architectures, compiled C code is used for these ciphers, which is not as optimal and therefore will be slower. For example the Linksys WRT54g (v1) which has a 100 MHz MIPS CPU can only do 7 to 8 Mbps on AES, which is less than the 10 Mbps that the 90 MHz x86-based chip can do.

With NETKEY, the CryptoAPI ciphers are used, only some of which have been written in assembler. Check the latest kernel source to see if the cipher you desire is in C or assembler.

If more performance is required, there are several crypto accelerator cards on the market from vendors such as Hifn, Cavium, and SafeNet. Support for these cards on Linux is practically non-existent, so verify this with the vendor before you purchase a product. Many vendors promise 1000 Mbps speeds for their PCI cards.

Handling Thousands of Tunnels

Openswan has been tested to scale to over a thousand concurrent tunnels with no technical problems. There are, however, two operational issues when managing many tunnels: dealing with the configuration file and reducing the Openswan startup time.

Managing Large Configuration Files

When you have an `ipsec.conf` file with hundreds, or even thousands, of tunnels defined, it can be quite difficult to manage. The following three tips should make this easier.

Standard Naming Convention

If you use standard names or abbreviations in your configuration files, they will be much easier to visually check and modify. It will also make it much easier to write custom scripts around common operations you might want to execute.

For example, to remove all connections you have described with KEYWORD as part of the connection name, you can use the following:

```
for conn in `grep "^conn .*KEYWORD.*" \
/etc/ipsec.conf|awk '{print $2}'`;
do
    ipsec auto --delete $conn
done;
```

The also= Parameter

The `also=` parameter ensures that you do not enter duplicate information anywhere in your configuration files. You only need to update one entry if some topological change needs to be made.

The include Parameter

Use the `include=` parameter to separate administrative or geographical boundaries. This makes it easy to make a change in all configurations for a certain location.

Openswan Startup Time

The length of time the script-based system takes to read `ipsec.conf` can become excessive past about 100 tunnels. The following graph shows the speed of the shell/awk-based parsing system:

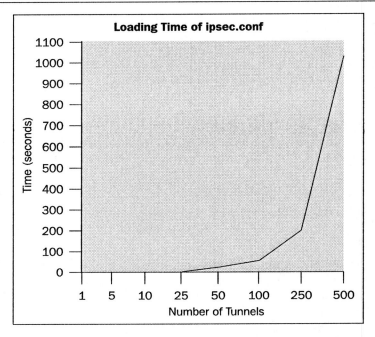

As can be seen from this benchmark, this is far from ideal for large-scale deployment on concentrator machines. The reason for the poor performance with a large number of tunnels is due to the startup scripts. Openswan will only start the tunnels sequentially. Currently, there are two solutions for avoiding this connection loading problem:

1. Configure all of your tunnels as `auto=ignore`, start Openswan, and then use a script, similar to that used in the *Standard Naming Convention* section above, to run through `ipsec.conf` executing `ipsec auto -add $conn` to load each connection. These connections are then loaded in the background, resulting in all connections being loaded in parallel, greatly reducing the start-up time.

2. Use the new C configuration parser written by Arkoon Networks—`ipsec starter`. Starter parses the `ipsec.conf` directly and spawns any Pluto and whack processes as needed, bypassing the scripts. The only downside of `starter` is that development lags behind regular Openswan development, so not all features that you can set in `ipsec.conf` are currently supported by `starter`.

Limitations of the Random Device

The other issue at startup is entropy from `/dev/random`. In July 2004, 1006 IPsec Tunnels were established in 205 seconds (~3.5 minutes), giving a rate of 5 tunnels/sec. This scales linearly, if the tunnel initiation rate does not increase. The CPU load during the test was always around 60% to 90% (very low).

The main problem we found was that there was a bottleneck in the Linux kernel random number generator. Switching from /dev/random to /dev/urandom increased the set-up rate to 10 tunnels per second, at the risk of being slightly less secure due to not-as-random numbers being used for the Diffe-Hellman calculations.

Note that both versions 1 and 2 of Openswan already use /dev/urandom, which is safe enough for generating the session keys that normally only last for an hour anyway. When the ipsec newhostkey command is used to generate long-term RSA keys, Openswan explicitly uses /dev/random to generate these keys.

If you are using a VIA CPU with the PadLock feature, such as some of the C3 chips and the Nehemia chips, and have compiled the Linux 2.6 kernel with CONFIG_HW_RANDOM support, then you can use these CPUs' hardware random generator. Just set the option USE_HWRANDOM=true in Openswan 2's Makefile.inc and it will use /dev/hw_random instead of /dev/random. You might also be able to use the PadLock's AES or 3DES functions through the Linux kernel CryptoAPI interface, with either NETKEY or KLIPS, but we have not yet researched whether this works and what speed benefits it brings.

There are a few other hardware random devices available on the market, but most seem to be a bit old. They are based on serial or parallel ports, or ISA slots, when PCI or miniPCI slots would be preferable. Some crypto accelerator cards also have hardware random support, but lack Linux support. We have also tried a few USB tokens but these were clearly not suitable for generating more random numbers than their own single key. However, we expect to see various new products and Linux drivers hitting the market in the coming year.

Other Performance-Enhancing Factors

There are a number of other tweaks that can assist in improving performance for Openswan that are not related to the startup time.

Logging to Disk

Depending on the plutodebug= and klipsdebug= settings, you might be logging so much data through syslog that the disk activity actually becomes a big limiting factor. In some benchmarks, we even found the minimal logging (plutodebug=none) to cause a possible bottleneck. A feature is planned to enable a minimal logging level that avoids this bottleneck. Ensure you are using 32-bit I/O on the disk where your logs are written. You can verify this, for /dev/hda in our example, using:

```
# hdparm -c /dev/hda
    /dev/hda:
    IO_support  = 0 (default 16-bit)
```

Here the 32-bit IO support is not enabled. Use the following command to enable it:

```
# hdparm -c 1 /dev/hda
    /dev/hda:
        setting 32-bit IO_support flag to 1
        IO_support  = 1 (32-bit)
```

Similar commands can be used to view and set DMA hard disk transfers, but with the options -d and -d 1. RAID or LVM can also influence the speed with which log files can be written to disk, though this is often not in use on VPN servers, since in general people build entire fail-over servers for VPNs rather than a simple disk fail-over scheme, since the disks in the VPN servers normally contain no user data apart from log files.

Disable Dead Peer Detection

You might want to consider whether or not DPD is a feature that you want to run on a busy VPN server. We have heard reports that DPD can cause a big slowdown in certain deployment scenarios. On the other hand, DPD is a nice feature for kicking out roadwarriors that have left without nicely closing down, something that might also impact on a large VPN server negatively. Play with these settings if you are encountering performance issues to see what works best in your scenario.

Reducing the Number of Tunnels

As each network combination requires a tunnel be established, in large networks with non-contiguous network blocks this can quickly add up to hundreds of tunnels between only a few IPsec peers. This is not ideal, and fortunately there are ways to reduce the number of tunnels, provided both ends are running Openswan.

Depending on your network topology, you may be able to reduce the number of tunnels down to one—a single host-to-host tunnel. You must set up a GRE (Generic Routing Encapsulation) tunnel between the two IPsec peers, and then either use static routes, or run a dynamic routing daemon, such as Quagga, Zebra, or GateD, to manage the network routing.

Packets are then encapsulated into GRE packets, which are in turn placed into the ESP packets exchanged between peers. The resulting packet as it goes over the wire looks like this:

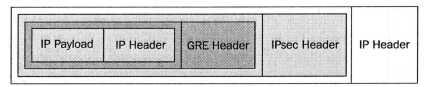

Once you bring up your IPsec tunnel, you will need to add a GRE tunnel on top of it. This is best done by hooking into the _updown scripts.

The following sample script will bring up a GRE tunnel:

```
#!/bin/sh
# $remote_ip = External IP of remote Gateway
# $local_ip = External IP of local Gateway
# $local_tun_ip = Local IP for the GRE tunnel (Usually RFC 1918 based)
# $remote_tun_ip = IP address on the other side of the GRE tunnel (usually
#   RFC1918 based)

ip tunnel add myGREtunnel mode gre remote $remote_ip local \ $local_ip ttl 255
ip link set myGRELtunnel up
ip addr add $local_tun_ip dev myGREtunnel
ip route add $remote_tun_ip dev myGREtunnel
```

Once your GRE tunnel is established, you can route as many networks as you want over your GRE tunnel. Here we will route some 192.168.x.x networks and the 172.16.0.0/18 address space over the tunnel.

```
ip route add 192.168.0.0/24 $remote_tun_ip
ip route add 192.168.5.0/24 $remote_tun_ip
ip route add 192.168.6.0/24 $remote_tun_ip
ip route add 172.16.0.0/16 $remote_tun_ip
```

Taking this a step further, you can use dynamic routing protocols such as OSPF or BGPv4 to automatically set up the routing for you. Three options currently exist for doing this—Zebra, Quagga, and OpenBGP. Quagga is actually a fork of the GNU Zebra project, so both share the same configuration syntax. OpenBGP has just been released at the time of writing and the authors have no operational experience with it as yet.

OSPF Setup

The following configuration uses OSPF to propagate all local routes (including directly connected networks, as well as static routes) to the remote peer.

```
interface    myGREtunnel
  ip ospf network point-to-point

router ospf
  ospf router-id 192.168.0.1
  redistribute kernel
  redistribute connected
  redistribute static
  network 10.1.20.1/32 area 0
```

BGPv4 Setup

The following sample Zebra/Quagga config stanza shows a configuration for BGPv4 between two peers, who are willing to send any RFC 1918 traffic between them.

```
! Use private AS numbers for this
router bgp 65432
! Our local GRE tunnel IP address
  bgp router-id 192.168.0.1
! Networks we are willing to share
  network 10.0.0.0/8
  network 172.16.0.0/18
  network 192.168.0.0/16
! Same AS as us
  neighbor 192.168.0.2 remote-as 65432
! Important - sets our GRE address as the next-hop
  neighbor 192.158.0.2 next-hop-self
  neighbor 192.168.0.2 distribute-list 101 out
  neighbor 192.168.0.2 distribute-list 101 in

! Permit RFC1918 networks to be shared.
access-list 101 permit 10.0.0.0/8
access-list 101 permit 172.16.0.0/18
access-list 101 permit 192.168.0.0/16
```

High Availability

When an IPsec gateway fails, the remote peer is not notified of the failure. Dead Peer Detection can help in this regard, but ideally we want a backup system that will take over the IPsec (and probably other duties as well). Since all IPsec tunnels are bound to either DNS host names or IP addresses, if we keep the old IP address (now known as the Service Address), taking over the tunnels is simple.

The solution is to use two systems, a primary and a backup. During regular operation, all traffic passes through the primary server. In the event of any network card/system failure, the backup server takes over the IP address(es) and starts up Openswan to renegotiate the tunnels and keep traffic flowing.

Heartbeat, from the Linux-HA-Project, is required for this. Heartbeat takes care of taking over the IP addresses, and will stop or start services as needed. You can add Zebra or Quagga to the heartbeat configuration if you need to take care of any dynamic routing.

Heartbeat

Heartbeat is the basic heartbeat subsystem from the Linux-HA project. It will run service scripts (using `service <name> start`) when it starts up, and when a system changes state (that is, from being a backup to a primary). It will also perform IP address takeover using gratuitous ARP. It works correctly for two-node configurations, and probably larger configurations.

Heartbeat is based on resources, and an IP address is a resource just as services (`ipsec`, `named`, `xinetd`) are resources. When the decision is made to change state, for example from backup mode to primary mode, each of the resources is *acquired*, and a notification is sent out to the other nodes in the HA cluster.

Heartbeat uses a protocol based on UDP (or a serial line, though this is not a very common setup) to send keepalives and notifications to other nodes in the cluster. These keepalives may also be MD5 or SHA1 hashed for security, to prevent a rogue node from taking over resources, though this security measure can be disabled if a dedicated network segment or crossover cable is used.

The master node, which has all the shared services for the cluster, will be monitoring the services as well. If at any time there is a problem with a service, it will shut that service down on the master and transfer it to a slave node that is still working. If a backup node detects that the master has gone down, it will attempt to acquire all resources, by taking over the IP addresses and starting all the services listed in the config file.

After installing Heartbeat, you can add Openswan in quite quickly. Simply add the **ipsec** resource to the resources in your `/etc/ha.d/haresources` configuration file:

```
# We have 2 IP addresses to takeover, the outside (206.1.1.1) and inside
(192.168.1.1)
# And 1 service (ipsec) to takeover
VPNGW1 206.1.1.1 192.168.0.1 ipsec
```

Next, configure Openswan. If you are using KLIPS, you will need to tell Openswan to bind `ipsec0` to the aliased interface, for example `eth0:0`. This is done in the `config setup` section of the `ipsec.conf` file:

```
config setup
    interfaces="ipsec0=eth0:0"
```

Lastly, copy `ipsec.conf`, along with `ipsec.secrets` and any X.509 Certificates, to all other nodes in the HA cluster.

Xen Migration

Another upcoming development is Xen VM technology. Xen allows the migration of live servers, which could be used to keep a continuous mirror state of the kernel's entire internal state, including all session information about IPsec not saved to disk. In case of a failure of the main server, the second Xen image could be told to 'go live'. Xen migration, however, is still very much on the bleeding edge of development, and the authors hope to be able to invest some time in exploring the options that it has to offer.

Using Anycast

Combining anycast with Openswan can be interesting in two scenarios. The first scenario is when you are moving a certain network and server farm that is announced by BGP from one physical location to the other, using just a single redundant Openswan router.

Let's say you have ColoA and ColoB. ColoA hosts most of the infrastructure, and ColoB has a copy of the Openswan router from ColoA. Depending on the shortest BPG prefix, clients trying to reach the network that is being moved will connect to either ColoA or ColoB. However, there is an IPsec tunnel using PA space from ColoA and ColoB that connects these two Openswan machines that share the same public IP address. By adding or removing tunnels for one machine (/32) or a few machines (e.g. /28), it is possible to tunnel the packets to wherever the physical server is at that point in time. If the server has not yet moved from ColoA to ColoB, and a packet for it reaches ColoB, it will be tunneled to ColoA. When the server is moved, the tunnel is updated to its reverse policy, and packets that still arrive at the old ColoA can be forwarded to ColoB.

You can extend this scheme. Imagine you are anycasting your VPN gateway worldwide. Wherever your roadwarriors are, they will be routed via the shortest prefix. This usually means over peering routes, instead of transit routes. By having most of your roadwarriors come in over peering instead of transit, you will achieve better network connectivity and save substantially on the traffic bill for your VPN service. Moreover, if one location should go down, the roadwarriors will just connect to the shortest prefix path location of the anycasted IP of the VPN server.

The same trick can also be used to set up an IPsec tunnel from the main office network to the particular VPN server the roadwarrior is connected to. There is one catch in this scenario. The different VPN front ends do not know about each other's state, so if a roadwarrior vanishes from one VPN server, and appears at another, some tunnels might need to be torn down or changed. This can, however, all be configured using custom _updown scripts.

Summary

Hopefully this chapter has given you some insight into sizing your IPsec gateway, and how to manage hundreds, or even thousands of IPsec tunnels. We have also covered the basics for a High Availability IPsec fail-over setup, with IP address takeover and IPsec tunnel takeover.

12

Debugging and Troubleshooting

IPsec can be very difficult to debug. In the first place of course it is not possible to capture too much data over the network to see what is wrong, since the first thing the IPsec protocol does is start a Diffie-Hellman key-exchange, guaranteeing privacy. Another issue is that when an IPsec policy is loaded, it prevents any packets from being sent between those machines in the clear. This security feature can be quite annoying to the system administrator who is present on one location, and who is using an SSH connection to configure the other end of the tunnel. The SSH connection will no longer work. Other failures can be the result of intermittent network problems, or even the network architecture.

This chapter aims to help you gather the information needed to diagnose a problem. If you have any doubt about your understanding of IP addresses, netmasks, CIDR notations, and gateways, please read Appendix B.

Do Not Lock Yourself Out!

To prevent losing access to one of your two IPsec endpoints, it is strongly recommended to have access to a third host, that is in no way related to any IPsec policy, and from which you can SSH into both IPsec endpoints. This will prevent you from locking yourself out of your own machines.

Note that if you did not configure Opportunistic Encryption (OE) properly in the DNS, or you forgot to disable OE, you may experience a loss of connectivity for up to 1-2 minutes upon restarting one gateway.

Narrowing Down the Problem

All problems can be categorized into four sections. They are either **host** system issues, **configuration** mistakes, **network** issues, or **software bugs**. For each type of problem, a different method of gathering information works best.

Host Issues

Most problems on the host itself become apparent when installing or starting Openswan. Openswan logs precise details of anything that goes wrong. If Openswan suddenly fails to start, check whether some automated update has changed something.

For example, a new kernel could have been installed that does not support KLIPS, where you had previously compiled KLIPS for the kernel. Perhaps someone changed a few firewall rules, some IP address on the host changed, or you are using a `nexthop` value, and your ISP has changed your default gateway. These problems should all have very clear error messages in the log files, and should be very obvious, though fixing them might involve some work.

A more subtle error can be related to the host clock. Especially when X.509 Certificates are used, which have a time-limited validity, accurate time becomes important. A clock skew can suddenly cause something to fail that worked before for months. The best defense is to set up an NTP service on the machine, in combination with an `ntpdate` command executed during the host's startup sequence. Be aware that you cannot run the `ntpdate` command when the NTP daemon is running. And the NTP daemon will not allow a large time correction (where large means more than a few seconds). So if your clock is off by a few hours, it will take a *very long time* for the NTP daemon to drift towards the proper time, and you might need to expedite things by stopping the NTP daemon, running `ntpdate` once, and then restarting the NTP daemon again.

If your new certificate does not work and complains about validity despite an accurate clock, you may be the victim of localization. If you live in a time zone that has a negative GMT offset (for example North America), and the host on which your certificate is generated lives in GMT or GMT+x (for example Europe or Japan), then your certificate will not yet be valid. The easiest solution for this is to just go to bed and try again tomorrow.

Configuration Problems

Most of the time, when Openswan fails to correctly set up a tunnel, you will see IKE errors in the system logs, and a configuration error is at fault.

A configuration error in this context does not necessarily mean an error in the Openswan configuration files, it could simply be that the two IPsec endpoints do not agree. If the connection has Openswan at both ends, this can be fairly easily verified, since most if not all parameters will be the same on each side. If you control both ends, which is often the case for Openswan-to-Openswan connections, then configuration errors are fairly easily spotted and corrected by reading and comparing the log entries on both ends.

> Do not enable debugging in `ipsec.conf` to debug configuration issues.

Connection Names

When the first packet of an IKE exchange is received, it is not always clear which connection definition applies to it. Pluto will pick a connection name that could match. Once it knows more about the connection being attempted, it could change the connection name, which can look confusing in the logs.

Interoperability

When the other end of the IPsec connection is not an Openswan machine, things are a little bit more complex. First of all, it is likely that you have no control over the other endpoint. You are also likely to be crossing an administrative domain, where you will need to talk to another system administrator, one who likely favors the IPsec vendor used by their end, and might even look down on this *free software thing*. Try to avoid getting drawn into a debate about why one is better than another, but of course do not hide the fact that you are using Openswan either. Remember that without a proper interop between system administrators, two devices will never achieve interoperability themselves. Put some effort into getting along with the other system administrator.

Often, there is also confusion about terminology. No one outside the Openswan world will know what left or right signifies. In other products, these are usually called **local** and **remote**. Some do not name the local part explicitly, and call the remote **the domain** or the **security domain**. Some products call Authentication Header 'Medium' security, some call Perfect Forward Secrecy anti-replay protection. The shared secret (PSK) probably has the largest number of different names, such as **password**, **passphrase**, **secret**, **netgroup**, **groupsecret**, or combinations of these words. When talking to the other system administrator, try to use the same terms. It might even be worth checking the Openswan website or Wiki, or using a search engine, to find out what terms are used by the vendor you are trying to interoperate with.

Hunting Ghosts

Another common mistake is failing to realize that the current configuration files no longer represent the current state of Openswan. This can happen if someone has edited a file, but did not restart the connection or the Openswan subsystem. If there is any doubt, restart Openswan before trying to debug the problem.

Remember that if a change is made in the 'config setup' section, Openswan must be restarted completely. Changes in the conn definitions, ca definitions, or in any of the other files do not require a complete restart. A changed connection can be reloaded using ipsec auto –replace connname. A changed secret can be re-read using the ipsec secrets command. See the relevant chapters for a full list of commands.

Most hardware routers never reset their Phase 1 if you change their configuration, and still try to re-use the current ISAKMP SA. Using ipsec auto --delete connname may or may not successfully terminate the Phase 1 connection. If possible though, always reboot these hardware routers after making any changes in their IPsec configuration, to prevent accidentally re-using an old ISAKMP SA (Phase 1).

Another ghost hunt could result from the other end changing its configuration, or some router somewhere on the path between the two endpoints suddenly behaving differently, for instance due to a new firewall rule, or a change in maximum packet size of some intermediate router. A phone call to the other administrator can save you a lot of time in debugging these problems.

Rekey Problems (After an Hour)

A more subtle type of error is one where initially things seem to work but after a while the system goes down. Which endpoint is responding and which is initiating is clear when you start the connection, but the responding end might just start the next rekey a little bit before the initiator, and thus become the initiator itself. You can try and trigger these kind of errors by setting the `ikelifetime=`, `rekeyfuzz=`, and `lifetime=` options to very short periods of time, such as one minute, and waiting for a few rekeys to occur.

If you have determined that the switching of initiator and responder at rekey time is the problem, you can resolve this by lowering the IKE and IPsec key lifetimes on the initiator end, ensuring that the initiator stays the initiator. See the man page of `ipsec.conf` for help on the options `lifetime=`, `ipseclifetime=` and `rekeyfuzz=`. If you are the responder, and do not control the initiator, you can also set `rekey=no` to prevent becoming an initiator. After changing these parameters to fix these issues in the future, you will need to reload the currently stuck connection. If you want to be the responder, a simple `ipsec auto -replace connname` will do. If you want to set yourself as the initiator, you will also need to `ipsec auto -up connname` the connection.

Openswan Error Messages

People using Openswan for the first time find it very hard to read the error messages provided, which are rather technical in their description of the problem. People are quick to try to solve this by getting more debugging information using the `plutodebug=` and `klipsdebug=` flags, but this is not necessary and in fact, often makes things much harder for the user, as well as helpful people on the mailing list, if your message is not rejected by the mailing list for being too big to begin with.

Even in the standard configuration without any debugging enabled, Openswan logs all the information needed to debug a configuration issue. Just make sure to look at the proper log files. Usually, the startup and shutdown messages go in the general log file (often `/var/log/messages`), while most other log entries go to a different log file for somewhat more serious errors (usually `/var/log/secure` or `/var/log/auth.log`).

> Do not enable `klipsdebug=` or `plutodebug=` until you are pretty sure your problem is not a configuration error but a software bug.
>
> These debug options are for developers, or for when developers ask you for logs with debugging enabled. They are only meant to help find software errors and debug protocol issues. If you enable all this debugging on a busy production server, you will likely bring the machine down by overloading its CPU and I/O disk bandwidth. If this is a remote machine and you were using SSH, you now have two problems.

IKE: Unknown VendorIDs

If you see unknown VendorIDs, it is likely that the other IPsec endpoint is requesting or notifying something unknown to Openswan. Usually VendorIDs are MD5 hashes of some option, for example:

```
Feb 13 16:11:23 SpainkMe pluto[6383]: "east-west"[1] 193.110.157.131 #1:
ignoring unknown Vendor ID payload
[47bbe7c993f1fc13b4e6d0db565c68e50102010102010310313131302e312e3120...]
Feb 13 16:11:23 SpainkMe pluto[6383]: "east-west"[1] 193.110.157.131 #1:
ignoring unknown Vendor ID payload [da8e937880010000]
```

This last unknown VendorID for example is sent by the WatchGuard Firebox VPN servers, the SafeNet SoftRemote client, and some derivatives of these, but we do not yet know what these VendorIDs mean. Unknown VendorIDs we have seen before but whose meanings are still unknown are listed in `programs/pluto/vendor.c`.

If you encounter unknown VendorIDs, see if there is a newer version of Openswan available. If not, please report them to the developer mailing list, preferably with as much information as possible about the client connecting to the Openswan server. If possible, enable full debugging on the client side, since it will likely tell us what VendorID it is sending, and we might be able to figure out what it is trying to tell Openswan.

Often VendorIDs are MD5 hashes of a certain string. You can verify this by running the string (ignore any newline characters) through the `md5sum` command:

```
# echo -n "Vid-Initial-Contact" | md5sum
  26244d38eddb61b3172a36e3d0cfb819 -
```

This is indeed the VendorID for 'initial contact' that some vendors send through IKE.

Since VendorIDs are often used to announce a certain capability, an unknown VendorID could very well point precisely to your problem. Try to see if you can figure out what it means. Even just Googling the VendorID might throw up some pointers to previous problems people have had with that VendorID. Since these MD5 hashes are pretty unique (that is the whole point of them), this is a very convenient way to find people who have had similar problems.

Network Issues

The most common network problems are related to firewalls, MTU issues, and NAT rules. Some of these can be determined by using the `ipsec verify` and `ipsec livetest` commands, as described in Chapter 4.

Firewalls

To ensure your own firewalls are not the problem, temporarily disable them, or insert rules to allow all traffic between the two IPsec endpoints. Another way of debugging your firewall is to try to determine which firewall rule is hit by a packet. For this, you need to run a rather verbose `iptables` view command twice in a row, and compare the output:

```
# iptables -L -n -v > before.txt
```

Quickly start Openswan and run the command again to a different file:

```
# iptables -L -n -v > after.txt
```

The `diff` command can be used to tell you which rule number(s) matched the packet:

```
# diff before.txt after.txt
```

MTU and Fragmentation Issues

MTU issues normally produce intermittent or flow problems. Simple things, such as a ping or an SSH login will work, but more intense tasks, such as an `ls -alg /` after log in, FTP, HTTP, or Windows file-sharing fails. In general, connections will seem to stall or hang. You can test this by using `ping` with small or big packet sizes:

```
# ping -s 500 ip-at-end-of-the-tunnel
# ping -s 2000 ip-at-end-of-the-tunnel
```

If using KLIPS, you can force a lower MTU for a tunnel with `overridemtu=`. Values to try are 1400 or even 1000. This option is not available with NETKEY as it does not have separate virtual `ipsecx` interfaces, but you can set the MTU for a particular route. By setting a route to your remote IPsec endpoint, you can effectively lower the MTU for your inner tunnel. This is done using the `ip` command:

```
# ip route replace 1.2.3.4 via x.x.x.x dev eth1 mtu yyyy
```

Here, `1.2.3.4` is the address of the remote gateway, `x.x.x.x` is your `nexthop` gateway, and `yyyy` is the new MTU for packets destined for the remote IPsec endpoint.

You can also try to set the MTU of your physical device (`ppp0` or `ethx`) to a lower value, although that would affect all packets on that interface, not just tunneled packets.

Another workaround, discussed at the end of Chapter 7, is TCP MSS clamping. Be aware that this only fixes protocols based on TCP. There is no similar fix for UDP. If you cannot get a Windows Logon working through the VPN, but you can ping, then your MTU issues might be preventing the Kerberos protocol from working properly, as it uses UDP by default. You can try to force Kerberos to using TCP. See the Microsoft Knowledge Base article Q244474, *How to force Kerberos to use TCP instead of UDP in Windows Server 2003, in Windows XP, and in Windows 2000*. You can also try to set the MTU on Windows, though this might cause you a lot more grief than pleasure. Do not do this lightly. You can find this information in Microsoft Knowledge Base article 826159, *HOW TO: Change the Default Maximum Transmission Unit (MTU) Size Settings for PPP Connections or for VPN Connections*.

Debugging IPsec on Apple Mac OS X

To view the logs in **Internet Connect**, select Window | Connection Log. You can also look at the Racoon log file in `/private/var/log/system.log`. Note that IPSecuritas for Mac OS X places all its Racoon logs in `/tmp`.

Debugging IPsec on Microsoft Windows

For a detailed overview of how to enable Microsoft Windows debugging, see the Microsoft website. Currently, the following URL works:

```
http://www.microsoft.com/resources/documentation/windows/xp/all/proddocs/en-
us/sag_ipsec_tools.mspx
```

Oakley Debugging

In essence, you want to enable oakley.log. This is the file where all IKE debugging information will end up. You need to add the following key to the Windows Registry:

```
HKEY_LOCAL_MACHINE\System\CurrentControlSet\Services\PolicyAgent\Oakley\Enable
Logging
```

and set it to the value 1. Then either reboot the machine, or just restart the IPsec IKE daemon using these commands at a command prompt:

```
net stop policyagent
net start policyagent
```

If you are running Remote Access, you will also need to restart the Remote Access Service.

If you are using Windows XP SP2 or higher, and have installed ipseccmd.exe from the Resource Kit, you can execute the following command to enable debugging:

```
ipseccmd set logike
```

To disable logging, you can use:

```
ipseccmd set dontlogike
```

The logike and dontlogike commands do not require you to explicitly restart the policy agent.

All IKE debugging information appears in %systemroot%\Debug\oakley.log. With later updates to 2000 and XP, oakley.log has become quite readable. Here's a typical excerpt:

```
[...]
> 5-10: 10:00:50:777:1fc entered kill_old_policy_sas 2
> 5-10: 10:00:50:777:1fc entered kill_old_policy_sas 2
> 5-10: 10:01:07:501:544 Acquire from driver: op=00000006 src=192.168.1.2.0
dst=192.168.2.234.0 proto = 0, SrcMask=255.255.255.255, DstMask=255.255.255.0,
Tunnel 1, TunnelEndpt=193.110.157.131 Inbound TunnelEndpt=192.168.1.2
> 5-10: 10:01:07:511:1fc Filter to match: Src 202.149.x.x Dst 192.168.1.2
> 5-10: 10:01:07:551:1fc MM PolicyName: 2
> 5-10: 10:01:07:551:1fc MMPolicy dwFlags 2 SoftSAExpireTime 28800
> 5-10: 10:01:07:551:1fc MMOffer[0] LifetimeSec 28800 QMLimit 1 DHGroup 2
> 5-10: 10:01:07:561:1fc MMOffer[0] Encrypt: Triple DES CBC Hash: SHA
> 5-10: 10:01:07:561:1fc MMOffer[1] LifetimeSec 28800 QMLimit 1 DHGroup 2
> 5-10: 10:01:07:561:1fc MMOffer[1] Encrypt: Triple DES CBC Hash: MD5
> 5-10: 10:01:07:561:1fc MMOffer[2] LifetimeSec 28800 QMLimit 1 DHGroup 1
> 5-10: 10:01:07:561:1fc MMOffer[2] Encrypt: DES CBC Hash: SHA
> 5-10: 10:01:07:561:1fc MMOffer[3] LifetimeSec 28800 QMLimit 1 DHGroup 1
> 5-10: 10:01:07:561:1fc MMOffer[3] Encrypt: DES CBC Hash: MD5
> 5-10: 10:01:07:571:1fc Auth[0]:RSA Sig C=CA, S=Ontario, L=Ottawa,
O=Xelerance, OU=IT, CN=Phb, E=phb@xelerance.com AuthFlags 0
> 5-10: 10:01:07:571:1fc QM PolicyName: Host-roadwarrior filter action dwFlags
1> 5-10: 10:01:07:571:1fc QMOffer[0] LifetimeKBytes 50000 LifetimeSec 3600
> 5-10: 10:01:07:571:1fc QMOffer[0] dwFlags 0 dwPFSGroup -2147483648
> 5-10: 10:01:07:571:1fc   Algo[0] Operation: ESP Algo: Triple DES CBC HMAC:
MD5
> 5-10: 10:01:07:571:1fc Starting Negotiation: src = 192.168.1.2.0500, dst =
202.149.x.x.0500, proto = 00, context = 00000006, ProxySrc = 192.168.1.2.0000,
ProxyDst = 192.168.2.0.0000 SrcMask = 255.255.255.255 DstMask = 255.255.255.0
> 5-10: 10:01:07:571:1fc constructing ISAKMP Header
> 5-10: 10:01:07:571:1fc constructing SA (ISAKMP)
> 5-10: 10:01:07:571:1fc Constructing Vendor MS NT5 ISAKMPOAKLEY
> 5-10: 10:01:07:581:1fc Constructing Vendor FRAGMENTATION
> 5-10: 10:01:07:581:1fc Constructing Vendor draft-ietf-ipsec-nat-t-ike-02
> 5-10: 10:01:07:581:1fc Constructing Vendor Vid-Initial-Contact
[...]
```

271

The most common errors on Windows are wrongly imported certificates and incorrect settings in ipsec.conf when using ipsec.exe. These will usually result in an error in the Openswan log similar to the following:

```
Jan 24 09:54:45 FenAtHome pluto[16979]: "west-roadwarriors"[1] 193.110.157.131
#1: encrypted Informational Exchange message is invalid because it is for
incomplete ISAKMP SA
```

This is because Windows seems to think the encryption for ISAKMP (Phase 1) already succeeded, while Openswan does not agree. Therefore Windows sends an encrypted packet, and Openswan drops this invalid packet. But the root of this problem is usually that Windows rejects a certificate. You can see the corresponding Windows error in oakley.log when Openswan sends an unencrypted notification to the Windows machine:

```
8-30: 15:58:48:865:714 Receive: (get) SA = 0x000fea00 from 193.110.157.131
8-30: 15:58:48:865:714 ISAKMP Header: (V1.0), len = 188
8-30: 15:58:48:865:714   I-COOKIE 72db281985c1bc2a
8-30: 15:58:48:865:714   R-COOKIE 1830a6b579ac5c77
8-30: 15:58:48:865:714   exchange: Oakley Main Mode
8-30: 15:58:48:865:714   flags: 0
8-30: 15:58:48:865:714   next payload: KE
8-30: 15:58:48:865:714   message ID: 00000000
8-30: 15:58:48:865:714 received an unencrypted packet when crypto active
8-30: 15:58:48:865:714 GetPacket failed 35ec
```

But Openswan does not always blindly send notification messages, because that could result in two systems sending endless ignored notification messages, a so-called **notification war**.

If Windows gets stuck slightly further into the IPsec SA set-up procedure before it fails, then it will actually send a delete for the ISAKMP SA:

```
Jan 24 10:15:48 EphemeralTruth pluto[25023]: "west-roadwarriors"[2]
193.110.157.131 #4: received Delete SA payload: deleting ISAKMP State #4
```

This happens either because of a wrong DN, or because the Root CA or X.509 Certificate is not found. See Chapter 8 to properly generate and import certificates on Windows. These problems can also be seen in the oakley.log file on Windows.

```
8-13: 02:28:36:250:d20 Looking for any cert
8-13: 02:28:36:250:d20 failed to get chain 80092004
8-13: 02:28:36:250:d20 ProcessFailure: sa:000D9EC0 centry:00000000 status:35ee
8-13: 02:28:36:250:d20 isadb_set_status sa:000D9EC0 centry:00000000 status
35ee 8-13: 02:28:36:250:d20 Key Exchange Mode (Main Mode)
8-13: 02:28:36:250:d20 Source IP Address 192.168.13.13 Source IP Address Mask
255.255.255.255  Destination IP Address 193.110.157.131 Destination IP Address
Mask 255.255.255.255 Protocol 0 Source Port 0 Destination Port 0 IKE Local
Addr IKE Peer Addr
8-13: 02:28:36:250:d20 Certificate based Identity. Peer IP Address:
193.110.157.131
8-13: 02:28:36:250:d20 Me
8-13: 02:28:36:250:d20 IKE failed to find valid machine certificate
8-13: 02:28:36:250:d20 0x80092004 0x0
8-13: 02:28:36:250:d20 ProcessFailure: sa:000D9EC0 centry:00000000 status:35ee
8-13: 02:28:36:250:d20 constructing ISAKMP Header
8-13: 02:28:36:250:d20 constructing HASH (null)
8-13: 02:28:36:250:d20 constructing NOTIFY 28
8-13: 02:28:36:250:d20 constructing HASH (Notify/Delete)
```

Note the line saying "IKE failed to find valid machine certificate". The certimport.exe tool can help here; you can find it on the Openswan website or FTP site.

If you cannot start the policy agent, and get this error:

```
Windows cannot start the policyagent
Could not start the IPSEC Services service on Local Computer
Error 123: The filename, directory name, or volume label syntax is incorrect
```

then your Windows machine cannot start the IKE daemon, lsass.exe. Go to the *IPSEC Services* service in Administrative Tools and view the properties window to verify the path to executable. If it starts with \SystemRoot\C:\Windows, then you need to remove the \systemRoot\ part.

Debugging ipsec.exe

If using the e.bootis VPN client (aka ipsec.exe), you can also run the command in debug mode to see exactly what it will do.

Be aware that Windows will only start IKE negotiation when it receives traffic destined for the other end of the VPN connection, so you should run a ping first. Often, that one ping command, which sends three consecutive ping packets, is enough to trigger the VPN to establish, but those three ping packets are almost always lost. Always issue the ping command at least twice to see the response packets confirming your IPsec connection has come up. If your ping commands do not even trigger the message "Negotiating IP security", then you might have accidentally used auto=add instead of auto=start in your Window's ipsec.conf file. To fix this, run ipsec --delete, edit the file, and rerun ipsec.exe.

If ipsec.exe on Windows XP gives you the error:

Error converting policy: 0x7b

then the Windows IKE daemon could not start for some reason. This could be because another VPN client is running (such as Cisco, or Nortel).

You can also run the IPsec monitor through MMC to see these loaded policies. See Chapter 8 for how to enable the IPsec monitor.

Microsoft L2TP Errors

The following section summarizes common errors related to Windows and L2TP. The error message you might see is given, followed by an explanation of the cause and how to fix it.

```
chalresp_avp: Challenge reply found
control_finish: Invalid authentication for host 'XENU2005'
call_close : Connection 27 closed to 193.110.157.131, port 1701 (Invalid
challenge authentication)
```

You have enabled L2TP authentication instead of PPP authentication. Windows does not support this mode of authentication. Remove the auth file and challenge parameters from l2tpd.conf.

```
Jun 29 03:34:18 aivd pppd[24014]: Connect: ppp0 <--> /dev/pts/1
Jun 29 03:34:20 aivd pppd[24014]: peer refused to authenticate: terminating
link
Jun 29 03:34:26 aivd pppd[24014]: Connection terminated.
Jun 29 03:34:27 aivd pppd[24014]: Exit.
Jun 29 03:34:27 aivd l2tpd[14785]: network_thread: tossing read packet, error=
Bad file descriptor (9). Closing call.
```

Windows then shows the error:

```
Error 734: The PPP link control protocol was terminated
```

This tells you that there was a disagreement about the authentication method to use. For instance, you might have forgotten to change the L2TP encryption option on Windows from encryption required to encryption optional. Windows then insists on L2TP encryption, which l2tpd on Linux does not support, and does not need because IPsec already takes care of encryption. Another cause behind this could be if the Windows L2TP connection is configured to only use CHAP MS-v2, and you forgot to add regular CHAP, or you changed it back after the bogus Windows message about CHAP resulting in unencrypted connections. Change this in L2TP Properties | Security | Advanced Settings.

```
Error 732: The PPP negotiation is not converging
```

This usually means that you have specified an incorrect local IP in your l2tpd.options file. It should be the local (private) IP address of the Openswan server, not the public IP address.

```
Error 734: The PPP link control protocol terminated
```

This error happens when for some reason 'call back' is set on the Windows L2TP connection. Disable it by selecting the Networking tab and then open the Settings option in the properties window of your L2TP connection and disable LCP extensions.

```
Error 781: Encryption failed because no valid certificate was found
```

The X.590 Certificate was not properly imported, or does not work in combination with the Openswan server. Check your X.509 Certificate and CA certificate using the MMC, or use certimport.exe to re-import the certificates properly.

```
Error 789: The L2TP connection attempt failed because the security layer
encountered a processing error during initial negotiations with the remote
computer
```

This message is a nasty one, because it basically means "something went wrong", and there could be many reasons for it. The most common is that the Microsoft Windows native IPsec subsystem has been disabled, for instance by installing a third-party IPsec client such as NCP/Astaro, SoftRemote, or SSH-Sentinel. To re-enable it, find the IPsec service in the Services item in Administrative Tools, and change from Disabled or Manual to Automatic. Start it as well.

If that does not help, double-check the certificates again. Note that this error also happens if you try to combine IPsec connections with Terminal Service sessions on Windows 2000.

```
Mar 4 01:38:03 BlueElf pluto[21324]: "west-l2tp"[2] 216.59.238.100 #1: cannot
respond to IPsec SA request because no connection is known for
193.110.157.131:17/1701 ... 216.59.238.100 [10.0.1.2] :17/56352===10.0.1.2/32
```

This indicates that you might have added a leftsubnet= statement in the L2TP connection. L2TP uses IPsec in host-to-host transport mode, rather than in host-to-subnet tunnel mode. Remove any leftsubnet= line completely.

Another reason could be that you have not specified rightproto=17/%any, but instead used rightprotoport=17/0 or rightprotoport=17/1701, and the connecting client is either using a high random source port (Mac OS X) or the incoming connection is from a Windows XP server without Service Pack 2. Another reason could be there is NAT-T involved and you did not specify a rightsubnet=vhost:%no,%priv option.

```
Jun 29 03:16:24 mi6 pluto[11872]: "west-l2tp-patched-windows-cert"[4]
193.110.157.155 #4: IPsec SA established {ESP=>0xc83a62af <0x7cb7f18c
xfrm=3DES_0-HMAC_MD5 NATD=none DPD=none}
```

If you get this success message, but you still did not manage to get the L2TP/IPsec tunnel working, and you are connecting from behind a NAT router, then double-check the NATD= setting in the above line. If it says NATD=none, then you are missing NAT-T support in the client. For XP, install at least SP2. For Windows 2000 first install SP4, then the Windows Update will list a patch in the 'Recommended updates' that adds IPsec NAT-Traversal support.

You Suddenly Cannot Log in Anymore over the VPN

Sometimes a Windows Update can cause a sudden failure of the VPN authentication. One user reported on the mailing list that his VPN broke after some security updates. After many days of tinkering, he finally solved it by applying Microsoft's Knowledge Base article Q244474, *How to force Kerberos to use TCP instead of UDP in Windows Server 2003, in Windows XP, and in Windows 2000*.

Obviously, the issue here was one of UDP, packet sizes, and fragmentation. Switching to TCP helped in this case, though of course it does not address the underlying problem.

Software Bugs

Software bugs can occur in the userland, such as in the startup scripts or the Pluto daemon, or in the kernel IPsec stack. Most software issues happen in the IKE daemon and if you can reproduce these errors, they can usually be fixed quickly. Kernel errors are more difficult to address, since finding the exact cause of a lock-up can be hard, and often the UML-based kernels do not exhibit the same problems as real kernels do.

Userland Issues: Assertion Failed or Segmentation Faults

When you hit a serious bug, Openswan's IKE daemon Pluto will terminate with either a *segmentation fault* or with an *assertion failed* error. When this happens, the plutorun script will automatically restart Pluto. All connections will automatically reload or restart, which could cause the same crash, resulting in a repeating loop.

A segmentation fault always indicates a problem that needs to be addressed by the Openswan development team. The code is simply wrong and needs to be fixed.

An 'assertion failed' error means that Openswan ended up in an unexpected state it should never end up in, and it will also die—although in a somewhat more controlled way—with an error message that usually pinpoints a single line of code referring to one particular state. The decision to have the daemon die on some issues, which sometimes seem fairly innocent, is controversial, but it is vital to the security of Openswan. 'Assertion failed' errors happen when we are reaching a state we should never reach. This normally only happens when handling IKE packets and the internal state of the loaded and active connections are somehow corrupted. If Openswan just logged a warning, and continued to try to work despite this, some serious security breach could be the result. Such breaches could include a flawed encryption state, but also a failure to process an IKE exchange. These assertion failures could be the result of a bad remote IPsec endpoint, but if we create a workaround for this, we want the workaround to be known, and a message to be logged. Ideally there would also be some define option or connection parameter to enable or disable such a workaround.

If you experience segmentation faults or assertion failures, the first thing to do is upgrade to the latest version of Openswan. If that does not help, report back to the Openswan community, preferably to either the bug tracker at http://bugs.openswan.org, or to the developer mailing list (dev@openswan.org). If you are somewhat familiar with the GNU debugger (gdb), then it would help if you could provide information about the internal state of Openswan at the moment of failure by using gdb on the Pluto core file. To enable core files, add the following option to the config setup section of ipsec.conf:

```
dumpdir=/tmp
plutorestartoncrash=no
```

This will cause Pluto to dump a core file and abort without restarting again on an assertion failure. Depending on a kernel tuning option, usually defined in /etc/sysctl.conf, core files might have a process ID number attached to their filename, for instance core.31337 to prevent old core files being overwritten if Pluto does restart.

Go to Openswan's source directory, for example /usr/src/openswan-2, and start gdb. Here is an example of roughly how this would look:

```
# gdb programs/pluto/pluto /tmp/core.31337
    GNU gdb Red Hat Linux (5.3.90-0.20030710.41rh)
    Copyright 2003 Free Software Foundation, Inc.
    GDB is free software, covered by the GNU General Public License, and you are
    welcome to change it and/or distribute copies of it under certain conditions.
    Type "show copying" to see the conditions.
    There is absolutely no warranty for GDB. Type "show warranty" for details.
    This GDB was configured as "i386-redhat-linux-gnu"...Using host libthread_db library
    "/lib/libthread_db.so.1".
```

Core was generated by `/usr/local/libexec/ipsec/pluto --nofork --secretsfile /etc/ipsec.secrets --
ipse'.
Program terminated with signal 11, Segmentation fault.
Reading symbols from /usr/lib/libgmp.so.3...done.
Loaded symbols for /usr/lib/libgmp.so.3
Reading symbols from /lib/libresolv.so.2...done.
Loaded symbols for /lib/libresolv.so.2
Reading symbols from /lib/i686/libc.so.6...done.
Loaded symbols for /lib/i686/libc.so.6
Reading symbols from /lib/ld-linux.so.2...done.
Loaded symbols for /lib/ld-linux.so.2
0 0x08076a59 in informational (md=0x8111740) at demux.c:1047
1047 if(st->st_connection->extra_debugging & IMPAIR_DIE_ONINFO) {

(gdb) bt

0 0x08076a59 in informational (md=0x8111740) at demux.c:1047
1 0x08078dd0 in process_packet (mdp=0x80e4a94) at demux.c:2247
0000002 0x08076cfd in comm_handle (ifp=0x8104340) at demux.c:1167
3 0x0805d72b in call_server () at server.c:1124
4 0x0805a616 in main (argc=8, argv=0xbffff154) at plutomain.c:747

(gdb) bt full

0 0x08076a59 in informational (md=0x8111740) at demux.c:1047
        disp_len = 135337912
        disp_buf = '\0' <repeats 12 times>, "\034\000\000\000\001", '\0' <repeats 23 times>,
"\fïÿ¿\000\000\000\000Ù\02
7\021\bðñ\r\bÕí\r\bPz\r\b\001\000\000\000\000\000\000\000øí\016\b°ñ\r\bÌÝ\021\bÃ\027\021\b
(ïÿ¿óÑ\n\b \201\r\b\004\000\0
00\000\000\000\000\000ðñ\r\bÍ\000\000\000\000\000\000\000\000\004\000\000\000\f", '\0' <repeats
11 times>, "\bïÿ¿\004\000\0
00\000Ðø\r\b\000\000\000\000üÝ\021\b\000\000\000\000\004\000\000\000üíÿ¿T\027\021\b\00
2\000\000\000\002\000\000\000t¦\0
17\bT\027\021\b`9åD \220ÑD\200ïÿ¿"
        n_pbs = (pb_stream * const) 0x8111824
        n = (struct isakmp_notification * const) 0x8111844
        st = (struct state *) 0x0
        n_pld = (struct payload_digest * const) 0x8111824
 . . .

In this case, we can see that the function informational from the file demux.c seems to have
become corrupted on line 1047.

If possible, also describe the brand, model, and firmware version of the remote endpoint, and any
relevant information from ipsec.conf. With this information, we should be able to pinpoint the
problem and resolve things on our end, and perhaps contact the vendor of the remote endpoint
about their bug. Please mail this information to dev@openswan.org.

Kernel Issues: Crashes and Oopses

If the problem lies in the kernel subsystem (KLIPS or NETKEY), then things are much harder to debug and get information on. Your system will probably either hang, reboot, or remain in an unknown dangerous state. The dmesg command might still work, giving you a hint as to what happened. When reporting these bugs, it is of course vitally important that we know which kernel stack you are using. The output of ipsec --version will tell us exactly what we need to know about the versions. Be aware that if you are using NETKEY, and you are not using the latest kernel, that we will more than likely ask you to try the latest kernel version first. These days, since the 2.6 kernel is such a rapidly moving target, we may even ask you to try the latest testing version, for example 2.6.12-rc3. If possible, give us the kernel 'oops' message. If it only shows numbers and no function names, run it through the ksymoops utility. For this you might need to specify the exact location of your system.map file. These are commonly found in /boot/ for distributions, or in the root or your Linux kernel source tree if you compiled the kernel yourself. Also ensure you are using the latest kernel utilities, either kernel-utils, modutils, or module-init-tools, depending on your kernel and distribution.

You can also try to eliminate some of your kernel issues by compiling the kernel subsystem (KLIPS or NETKEY) directly into the kernel, instead of as a module.

As of Linux 2.6, module unloading is not encouraged, and the kernel developers suggest that module unloading should not be attempted by end users. Module unloading on 2.4 kernels should work without any problem. If you are experiencing a 99% CPU load upon module unloading, you need to upgrade your module tools.

A lot of IPsec-related fixes went into release 2.6.8.1 and 2.6.11. Do not run anything older than 2.6.11. At the time of writing, some vendor kernels based on 2.6.13, and the official 2.6.14 kernel, have issues that have not yet been completely resolved in the latest version of Openswan, 2.4.0. This is due to massive code changes in the networking stack of those Linux kernels.

Memory Issues

If you are experiencing memory problems, which are more likely to happen on small embedded devices, then you should enable the -DLEAK_DETECTIVE option in Pluto's Makefile and recompile Pluto. Restart Openswan and let it run for a while so that the memory issues occur. Before the entire system runs out of memory, shut down the IPsec subsystem (gracefully, using the proper initscript). Upon shutdown, Pluto will log a lot of memory debugging information that will help us to find out which parts of the daemon are actually leaking the memory. Report these issues to the developer mailing list at dev@openswan.org. If you are an experienced software developer, then you could also help us by using valgrind.

Memory issues for the kernel stacks are a bit more difficult to trace. lsmod allows you to at least monitor how much memory a certain kernel module is using. If this keeps growing, then it signifies some kernel-level memory leak.

Common IKE Error Messages

Some errors are quite common, and are often asked about on the mailing list. Chances are high that if you have a problem, it is listed in this section. Probably the most common and feared error is a variation of this one:

```
cannot respond to IPsec SA request because no connection is known for .....
```

This error message is usually the first error you will see for a lot of problems that can be encountered. It basically says, "The incoming IKE request does not match any of my loaded connections, I cannot respond to this IKE request." However, the reason behind the mismatch could be down to the local Openswan machine, but also it could be due to the remote machine. Read the line very carefully, and then read the connection definition in ipsec.conf looking for any difference.

```
May 18 16:33:54 isi pluto[1917]: "west-l2tp-unpatched-windows-psk"[2]
69.196.174.6 #1: cannot respond to IPsec SA request because no connection is
known for 193.110.157.131:17/1701...69.196.174.6[@testxp]:17/1701
```

This example is caused by trying to use Windows combined with L2TP, NAT, and PSK. After the ISAKMP SA (Phase 1), Windows suddenly switches to use its host name (in our case "testxp") as identifying ID for the IPsec SA (Phase 2). Openswan has no idea who "testxp" is supposed to be. It cannot find a matching loaded connection and fails with the above error. Another example of this error is this:

```
July 24 02:00:00 AntonySquared pluto: "roadwarrior"[2] 192.168.1.111 #1:
cannot respond to IPsec SA request because no connection is known for
192.168.1.0/24===192.168.1.35[S=C]...192.168.1.111[0.0.0.0,S=C]
```

The problem for this connection is that the other end is asking the equivalent of:

```
left=192.168.1.111
leftsubnet=0.0.0.0/0
right=192.168.1.35
rightsubnet=192.168.1.0/24
```

Of course, this is not going to work. You cannot tunnel a subnet (as defined by rightsubnet) through a server (defined by right) that is part of that subnet. In this case, someone attempted to encrypt the LAN for all connections (hence the leftsubnet=0.0.0.0/0). If you run into this type of mistake, check Chapter 10 about WaveSEC, or check Chapter 8 on how to make this work using L2TP.

```
Apr 21 23:02:41 ussa-hd pluto[7739]: "zywall" #3: cannot respond to IPsec SA
request because no connection is known for
192.168.2.0/24===192.168.0.104[S=C]...192.168.0.187[S=C] ==192.168.10.34/32
```

In this example, the other end is asking for 192.168.10.34/32 instead of 192.168.10.0/24. This can be caused by an improper netmask on the rightsubnet= parameter (such as /32 instead of /24). In this case, the remote end was a ZyXEL ZyWALL, configured with:

```
Local: Addr Type= SINGLE
```

instead of:

```
Local: Addr Type= SUBNET
```

We were not kidding when we said this type of error is the most common one.

```
pluto[26541]: "es-to"[2] 192.168.0.146 #2: cannot respond to IPsec SA request
because no connection is known for 0.0.0.0/0===192.168.0.254[C=US, ST=CA,
L=Los Angeles, O=None, OU=None, CN=gateway,
E=yaro@xs4all.nl]...192.168.0.146[C=US, ST=Berkshire, L=Newbury, O=My Company
Ltd, CN=Tao White, E=tao@xs4all.nl]
```

There could be two reasons for this failure. You can see the request includes 0.0.0.0/0, which means the client might be asking to tunnel all its traffic through the VPN connection, while the server offers only its own subnet through the VPN. Windows and Mac OS X have well-hidden options to switch this off. See Chapter 8. In this example, however, both endpoints are in the same network, and it is actually more likely that this was meant as a VPN tunnel to encrypt the local LAN, probably a wireless network. In that case, the Openswan connection definition is missing a leftsubnet=0.0.0.0/0. The other reason could be an error in the certificate names. For instance, in this example the Location fields are different, which might not be what it says in the certificates.

```
022 "conname": We cannot identify ourselves with either end of this
connection.
```

When you start Openswan, or ipsec auto --up a connection, Openswan will automatically try to determine whether it is left= or right=. If it cannot determine which end it should be, you will see this error in the log. This could be something as simple as a typo in the IP address of this end of the connection. It could also be that you have dynamic IP addresses that have changed. Openswan does not (yet) support using multiple IP addresses that are configured using advanced routing. If you want multiple IP addresses on a single interface, you should use IP aliases. This can be done with the following commands:

```
# ifconfig eth0:1 1.2.3.4
# ifconfig eth0:2 5.6.7.8
```

If using KLIPS, you should add these new interfaces to the interfaces= line as well:

```
interfaces="ipsec0=eth0 ipsec1=eth0:1 ipsec2=eth0:2"
```

A related error where there is no proper connection found is indicated by the following log entry:

```
Mar 19 22:09:00 peace pluto[7946]: "west-raodwarriors"[1] 193.110.157.17 #6:
Main mode peer ID is ID_DER_ASN1_DN: 'C=CA, ST=Ontario, O=Xelerance,
OU=Support Staff, CN=east.xelerance.com, E=east@xelerance.com'
Mar 19 22:09:00 peace pluto[7946]: "west-raodwarriors"[1] 193.110.157.17 #6:
no suitable connection for peer 'C=CA, ST=Ontario, O=Xelerance, OU=Support
Staff, CN=east.xelerance.com, E=east@xelerance.com'
```

This could possibly be a conflict in the number of RDNs. This can be verified with openssl:

```
# openssl x509 -in /etc/ipsec.d/certs/westCert.pem -subject -noout
    subject= /C=CA/ST=Ontario/O=Xelerance/OU=Support Staff/ CN=west.xelerance.com/
    emailAddress=postmaster@xelerance.com
```

```
# openssl x509 -in /etc/ipsec.d/cacerts/caCert.pem -subject -noout
    subject= /C=CA/ST=Ontario/L=Toronto/O=Xelerance/OU=Support Staff/CN=Xelerance Root
    CA/ emailAddress=ca@xelerance.com
```

Note that one has the RDN of L=Toronto and the other does not. This can happen when openssl.cnf is edited after creating the root CA, but before creating the host certificate.

On the subject of openssl, another common mistake when generating more certificates results in the following output:

```
Certificate is to be certified until Jan 13 21:31:37 2006 GMT (365 days)
Sign the certificate? [y/n]:y
failed to update database
TXT_DB error number 2
```

In this case the administrator is trying to sign a certificate with a CN that already exists and which has already been signed by that CA. You cannot sign multiple certificates with identical Common Names.

```
May  9 21:31:51 jansen pluto[32188]: "west-l2tp"[2] 194.228.117.3  #1: cannot
respond to IPsec SA request because no connection is known for
193.110.157.131:17/1701...213.84.21.108[193.110.157.60]:17/%any
===193.110.157.60/32
```

This error is again one where one of the left/right parameters was wrong. In this case the local network was using a non-private IP space as private IP space. It will be NATed, but it is not part of the standard virtual_private line. In this case 193.110.157.58/29, the network containing 193.110.157.60, should have been added to the virtual_private= parameter, since it was used behind a NAT router. More often though, 10.0.0.0/8 or 192.168.0.0/16, or the entire virtual_private= line, is missing from the config setup section of ipsec.conf.

```
003 "cat2311" #1: we require peer to have ID '193.110.157.131', but peer
declares 'C=CA, ST=Ontario, O=Xelerance, OU=Support Staff,
CN=newwest.xelerance.com, E=newwest@xelerance.com'
```

In this case either there was no rightid= declared, or the right side of the connection on this server is not set up to use certificates, while the incoming connection has been set up to use them. Some gateways, such as Cisco and NetScreen, also use their IPv4 address as their ID, often with a subjectAltName of ipAddress=a.b.c.d. Openswan does not support currently this, since it provides no way to find a certificate from an IPv4 address. You can interop with these devices by just specifying an ID, and then Openswan will not use the DN= of the certificate.

```
Jan 13 22:21:02 GlowingWhispers pluto[7946]:   X.509 certificate is not valid
until Mar 19 21:34:55 UTC 2005 (it is now=Mar 19 21:21:02 UTC 2005)
```

The machine using the certificate and the machine used to generate the certificate are not using the same time. At least one of these machines is not using NTP, with the result that, in this case, the certificate is not yet valid for another 13 minutes.

```
ipsec_auto: fatal error in "": (/etc/ipsec.conf, line 104) did not find conn
section(s) "nana-vesna"
```

Unfortunately, the ipsec.conf parser is not very advanced. You must start a new connection definition at the start of a new line, and all subsequent options for that conn must be indented with a tab character. Sometimes, using a mouse with cut and paste can turn tabs into spaces, causing this error. Similar things can happen when a file uses MS-DOS end-of-line sequences, for instance if it has been copied through a Windows machine.

```
Jul 27 19:45:00 pa pluto[9365]: OAKLEY_DES_CBC is not supported. Attribute
OAKLEY_ENCRYPTION_ALGORITHM no acceptable Oakley Transform
```

The remote end is proposing 1DES only, which is rejected by Openswan unless it has been compiled with USE_WEAKSTUFF (see Makefile.inc). If no other proposals are sent, the connection is rejected with the no acceptable Oakley transform message. This happens on some hardware routers and on Windows 2000 without Service Pack 1 (or higher). Either install the High Encryption Pack, or the latest service packs.

```
Sep 10 00:00:37 silvia pluto[1968]: we require PFS but Quick I1 SA specifies
no GROUP_DESCRIPTION
```

Another example that seems to happen regularly is disagreement about PFS. This might be obvious when you initiate a connection that does not work, but Openswan will allow PFS even with pfs=no, because it is much safer. However, this can lead to the strange situation where if you have a connection between two Openswan machines with different PFS settings, things will work as long as the pfs=no endpoint is responding. However, if the pfs=no endpoint initiates the connection, it will be refused by the other end, which insists on pfs=yes. As stated above, responders can turn into initiators after a number of rekeys, so this could happen hours later without any apparent reason, due to rekey fuzz (randomness in the rekey times). This PFS confusion can also happen when connecting to other IPsec software.

```
Jan 6 03:015:43 Idaho001 pluto[3497]: only OAKLEY_GROUP_MODP1024 and
OAKLEY_GROUP_MODP1536 supported. Attribute OAKLEY_GROUP_DESCRIPTION
```

Here, the other end only proposes DH groups that are not supported by Openswan. Usually this means the other end only proposes 1DES. This can also happen later at rekey when talking to an IPsec host that accepts all DH groups, but only proposes one, the wrong one. Some Symantec machines show this behavior.

```
Jun 16 09:00:00 ams-yyz pluto[2005]: peer requested 64800 seconds which
exceeds our limit 28800 seconds. Attribute OAKLEY_LIFE_DURATION
```

Older versions of Openswan set a hardcoded upper limit for the IPsec SA lifetime that was lower than that proposed by other vendors, such as Cisco, Symantec, and Check Point. Current versions of Openswan accept lifetimes up to 64800 seconds, so if you see this error, you should upgrade Openswan.

```
Dec 31 23:59:59 PHkade pluto[1999]: packet from 193.110.157.17:500: Quick Mode
message is for a non-existent (expired?) ISAKMP SA
```

This end of the IPsec connection (in this case Phase 1, ISAKMP) has been restarted, but the other end does not know about this and is attempting to use a Phase 1 that no longer exists on this end. Either the remote end ignored a Delete/Notify packet, or more likely, this end crashed and never sent it. Either restart the remote end, or just initiate again from this end to replace the Phase 1 on the other end.

```
May 18 18:13:44 LinuxChildren pluto[7113]: "testme" #1: Signature check (on
193.110.157.17) failed (wrong key?); tried *AQOkF1Ggd
```

This error means that the RSA key loaded with leftrsasigkey= or rightrsasigkey= is not correct. This usually happens when you mistakenly use the right key as left and the leftkey as right. Sometimes this information is sent by email, or cut and pasted, and newlines or whitespace have accidentally been introduced. Sometimes it is missing the "0s" part when the key is copied from a DNS record. Once you have repaired the key statements on both ends, reload the connection and try again.

```
May 18 09:53:34 gnu-toad pluto[3012]: "mikes-paul": route-host output:
/usr/local/lib/ipsec/_updown: doroute `ip route add 193.110.157.131/32 via
193.110.157.131 dev ipsec0 ' failed (RTNETLINK answers: Network is
unreachable)
```

This is usually the result of a bug in Openswan when it does not recognize what your default gateway is. This mostly happens with NETKEY, and a lack of an interfaces="%defaulroute" line. In this case it incorrectly tries to route traffic for the remote through the remote. Openswan adds this route for KLIPS, as KLIPS will only process packets when they are routed into the ipsecx interfaces. These routes should not be attempted on NETKEY though.

A workaround for this is to specify a leftnexthop= setting of your default gateway. You might also have mixed up the leftnexthop= and righnexthop= setting, or you might have specified it, but your ISP changed default gateways on you, so now the nexthop entry has become incorrect.

```
May 18 19:11:41 BrianFBI pluto[7922]: packet from 70.196.174.6:500: initial
Main Mode message received on 193.110.157.131:500 but no connection has been
authorized
```

Either the connection did not load at all, and an error was logged, or there is another reason why it is refusing the conn you thought should match. Double-check that both ends have NAT traversal enabled or disabled, depending on whether this connection goes through a NAT router. This error can also occur if the incoming connection requires PSK instead of RSA, or if there is no connection with either PFS or Aggressive/Main mode. Or it could mean that you do not have any loaded connection at all.

```
ipsec_auto: fatal error in "south-park": ID "%any" cannot have RSA key
```

If you use RSA keys for both left and right, then Openswan can not distinguish between multiple instances of these connections from the first message exchange. You will explicitly need to specify a leftid= and/or a rightid=. If you use certificates, this error should not happen, as the certificate's DN is automatically used as the ID.

```
ipsec_auto: fatal error in "mikes-paul": unknown authby value "rsasigkey"
```

The authby= option should be either secret or rsasig.

```
Nov 11 00:13:40 west pluto[2748]: "road-warrior" #14: up-client command exited
with status 1
```

The last thing run by the _updown script probably failed, so that the exit code of _updown indicated failure. This could possibly be a bug in a custom _updown script that has an incorrect return code.

Some versions of Openswan showed this behavior if they could not properly determine the default gateway. In such cases, explicitly setting the leftnexthop= setting to the default gateway works around this bug. This error can also happen when using old versions of Openswan that still support the firewall= option. This option was only necessary for Linux 2.0 kernels, and has been since removed from Openswan.

```
Mar 12 13:23:17 Manojlovic l2tpd[30898]: getPtyMaster: No more free pseudo-
tty's
```

You are using a kernel without 'legacy (BSD) PTY support' (CONFIG_LEGACY_PTYS=y). Fedora Core 2 and 3 ship without this support. The L2TP daemon generating this error needs these legacy-type PTYs. Either recompile the kernel, or use a more modern version of l2tpd with support for modern Unix PTYs.

```
protocol/port in Phase 1 ID Payload must be 0/0 or 17/500 but are 17/0
```

You are trying to connect a Windows client without the latest service packs, or to connect an old broken Cisco PIX to an old version of Openswan. Upgrade the Windows clients or replace the old unsupported Cisco PIX, or upgrade Openswan and add `rightprotoport=17/%any`.

```
Question: I want to use AH+ESP, with Racoon/setkey I can, but with Openswan it
does not work?
```

NETKEY (and Kame) are quite happy to permit you to configure completely bogus encapsulation combinations, and seem quite happy to accept them as well. So your odd stacked encapsulations will work with an interop with Kame/NETKEY/Racoon only. Note that these are both silly (it wastes 20 more bytes for AH + ESP) but worse, they are quite insecure too—ESP without AH/AUTH in the same layer of encapsulation is insecure and vulnerable to known attacks.

```
Question: I have troubles with the VPN-passthrough feature of my modem...It
de-capsulates the ESP traffic encapsulated in UDP 4500 packets and sends ESP
packets with its own SPI number.
```

Some modems and routers exhibit this behavior. In this case, it was a Conexant modem, but many small devices offer "IPsec passthrough support" that cannot be disabled. There is no solution for this problem other than throwing the hardware away.

```
Oct 7 05:23:17 ooievaar pluto[23652]: "fenrir-managers" #5: ERROR:
asynchronous network error report on eth0 for message to 193.110.157.17 port
500, complainant 193.110.157.131: Connection refused [errno 111, origin ICMP
type 3 code 3 (not authenticated)]
```

A firewall (193.110.157.131) is rejecting UDP 500 for the machine behind it (193.110.15.17).

```
Apr 1 12:54:32 4u-e pluto: "wlan"[2] 192.168.1.111 #1: cannot respond to IPsec
SA request because no connection is known for
192.168.1.0/24===192.168.1.35[S=C]...192.168.1.111[0.0.0.0,S=C]
```

Indeed, this configuration is impossible. You cannot have a `left=` that is part of `leftsubnet=`. How could you reach left without having a connection to the leftsubnet, which requires left? You can't, just as you cannot run a firewall on `193.111.228.254` to protect the entire `193.111.228.0/24` network. This person is probably trying to secure a local wireless LAN. Instead, a configuration similar to the following should have been used on the server:

```
conn wlan
    left=192.168.1.35
    leftsubnet=0.0.0.0/0
    right=%any
    [...]
```

and on the client:

```
conn lwan
    left=%defaultroute
    right=192.168.1.35
    rightsubnet=0.0.0.0/0
    [...]
```

See the WaveSEC section of Chapter 10 for a detailed description on how to accomplish this.

Another reason why people sometimes make this 'left in leftsubnet' mistake is that their ISP has given them a subnet without a single point of entry. In other words, the entire customer subnet is reached directly from the ISP's router. In this situation, how could you set up a VPN tunnel to a single machine from that subnet to reach the entire subnet?

You could set up an IP alias on 1.2.3.1, for example:

```
# ifconfig eth0:1 192.168.1.244
```

Now you can build a tunnel from the remote end to 1.2.3.1 for the subnet 192.168.1.0/24. If you add aliases to your machines in the /24, you could reach them directly on their internal IP addresses over IPsec. Do not use the `ip` command to add IP addresses to the interface, since Openswan cannot handle that way of IP addressing. You could also run some NAT rule using the latest `iptables`, which supports the NETMAP target to allow you to NAT a whole subnet onto another subnet.

```
Nov 25 12:00:13 Reina "cert"[1] 169.254.0.100 #21: encrypted Informational
Exchange message is invalid because it is for incomplete ISAKMP SA
```

It seems that Windows is the only client that somehow thinks it can encrypt information messages before the Phase 1 is complete. This always means that the configuration on Openswan and the Windows machines does not match. What happens is that one end (Windows) thinks it has successfully started an ISAKMP SA, but Openswan does not agree with that. One end sends a message, and the other end will drop it because either it is encrypted when it should not be, or it should be encrypted but is not. This error often happens when there is no valid certificate on the Windows machine. In this case, it was due to a bad clock setting, causing the certificate to become invalid.

```
030 ignoring message from whack with bad magic 1869114144; should be
1869114140; probably wrong version
```

The Openswan programs whack and pluto do not come from the same compile. Re-install the package or compile yourself from source. Also make sure there are not two versions of Openswan installed, one in /usr and one in /usr/local.

```
Question: My gateway-subnet ping does not work on debian
```

The Debian `netkit` package, which contains the `ping` command, is broken and does not properly support the `-I` option. It accepts this option, but then ignores it. This results in pinging from the default outgoing address, likely not covered in the IPsec tunnel definition (unless `leftsourceip=` is used). A solution is to install a better ping program using `apt-get install iputil-ping`.

```
May 18 11:38:04 domoor pluto[23206]: "roadwarrior-l2tp"[21] 193.110.157.17
#20: end certificate with identical subject and issuer not accepted
May 18 11:38:04 domoor pluto[23206]: "roadwarrior-l2tp"[21] 193.110.157.17
#20: X.509 certificate rejected
```

The root CA that signed the X.509 Certificate of the incoming connection has the same Common Name (CN=) as the root CA itself. This is a security problem and is not allowed, and the certificate will be rejected. You can prevent this by adding the string "Root CA" in the CA's CN.

```
Mar 27 14:11:32 reggestraat pluto[16339]: ERROR: asynchronous network error
report on ppp0 for message to 193.251.9.130 port 500, complainant
62.4.10.15: Message too long [errno 90, origin ICMP type 3 code 4 (not
authenticated)]
```

When sniffing the interface with `tcpdump`, you see something like:

```
14:11:32.076807 193.251.9.130.500 > 80.65.1.2.500: isakmp: phase 1 I
ident[E]: [encrypted id] (frag 5721:1472@0+)
14:11:32.079680 193.251.9.130 > 80.65.1.2: (frag 5721:236@1472)
```

A router between this machine and the destination of the packet (in this case the router 62.4.10.15) does not seem to be able to handle the UDP packet size of the IKE packet. This behavior is mostly seen on connections involving lots of NAT and possible bad ISPs with tunnels within tunnels, for instance using PPTP over PPPoE. Adding another layer of packets (IPsec) then finally causes this problem. You can try to play with MTU sizes, or talk to the ISP that owns that particular router and ask for advice.

```
104 "GroupVPN" #1: STATE_MAIN_I1: initiate
003 "GroupVPN" #1: received Vendor ID payload [draft-ietf-ipsec-nat-t-ike-00]
106 "GroupVPN" #1: STATE_MAIN_I2: sent MI2, expecting MR2
003 "GroupVPN" #1: ignoring unknown Vendor ID payload [da8e937880010000]
003 "GroupVPN" #1: ignoring unknown Vendor ID payload [404bf439522ca3f6]
003 "GroupVPN" #1: received Vendor ID payload [XAUTH]
003 "GroupVPN" #1: NAT-Traversal: Result using draft-ietf-ipsec-nat-t-ike-
00/01: i am NATed
108 "GroupVPN" #1: STATE_MAIN_I3: sent MI3, expecting MR3
004 "GroupVPN" #1: STATE_MAIN_I4: ISAKMP SA established
117 "GroupVPN" #2: STATE_QUICK_I1: initiate
010 "GroupVPN" #2: STATE_QUICK_I1: retransmission; will wait 20s for response
```

This is an example of an incoming client that tries to negotiate an XAUTH connection, but Openswan has not been configured with leftxauthserver=yes and rightxauthclient=yes. In this case, Openswan was talking to a SonicWALL machine and XAUTH was not supposed to be negotiated.

```
023 authentication method disagrees with "ian-nikita", which is also for an
unspecified peer
```

This is a situation where the administrator tried to load more than one connection without uniquely identifying them. That is, you are using multiple connections with right=%any and the same authentication method, so that Pluto is not able to distinguish for which of those two connections an incoming connection is intended. The second connection that coincides with the first connection is refused by Pluto. This often happens if you use multiple PSK-based connections on dynamic IP addresses. You will have to use leftid= and rightid= options to clearly distinguish these connections, for example leftid=@YourName and rightid=@theirname.

Common Kernel-Related Error Messages

If the NAT-T patch fails with something like:

```
1 out of 2 hunks FAILED -- saving rejects to file include/net/sock.h.rej
1 out of 3 hunks FAILED -- saving rejects to file net/ipv4/udp.c.rej
```

you are trying to patch the kernel with the KLIPS NAT-T patch, but the kernel contains conflicting NETKEY code. This is either because there is a NETKEY backport in your kernel (such as RHEL3 and Debian/Woody), or this is Openswan 2.3.x, which did not automatically pick the proper 2.4/2.6 NAT-T patch.

You can try to override the automatic detection using make nattpatch24 or make nattpatch26. If your kernel contains NETKEY code, it should always try the 26 version of the patch. The 24 version is only for 2.4 kernels without the NETKEY backport.

```
Aug 8 19:37:51 kbantoft pluto[3154]: "kb-to-bp-38" #3: sent QI2, IPsec SA
established {ESP=>0x489df436 <0xb7093be3 NATOA=0.0.0.0}
Aug 8 19:38:16 kbantoft pluto[3154]: packet from ##.##.109.70:4500: recvfrom
##.##.109.70:4500 has no Non-ESP marker
Aug 8 19:39:01 kbantoft last message repeated 14 times
```

This was a NAT-Traversal bug in the NETKEY code that was fixed in Linux kernel 2.6.8.1.

```
003 ERROR: "cm-vpn" #13: netlink write() of XFRM_MSG_ALLOCSPI message for Get
SPI esp.0@192.168.0.13 failed. Errno 111: Connection refused
```

This kernel has no support for XFRM_USER. Recompile the kernel with CONFIG_XFRM_USER.

```
Unable to handle kernel NULL pointer dereference at virtual address 000000ec
d08bdcf6
*pde = 00000000
Oops: 0002
CPU: 0
EIP: 0010:[<d08bdcf6>] Not tainted
Using defaults from ksymoops -t elf32-i386 -a i386
EFLAGS: 00010246
eax: 00000000 ebx: cd675f68 ecx: 00000000 edx: cd675f04
esi: 00000000 edi: cd675f14 ebp: cf003000 esp: cd675ef4
ds: 0018 es: 0018 ss: 0018
Process snmpd (pid: 2436, stackpage=cd675000)
Stack: cd675f04 cd675f64 cfe43800 cf154ea0 da0110e9 00000000 00000000 00000000
     000089f0 cf003000 cd675f54 cd675f54 c021ec5f cf003000 cd675f54 000089f0
     00000000 000089f0 00000001 00000000 c021ee8a cd675f54 000089f0 00000020
Call Trace: [<c021ec5f>] [<c021ee8a>] [<c0216576>] [<c0144ef9>]
[<c010729b>]
Code: ff 0d ec 00 00 00 0f 94 c0 84 c0 75 0a b8 fa ff ff ff e9 fd
```

There was a conflict between KLIPS and the net-snmpd package if both used SIOCDEVPRIVATE. This has been fixed, so if you see this error you are running an old version of Openswan and you should upgrade.

```
Various KLIPS kernel panics on a multi-processor SMP machine (or a Pentium-IV
with hyperthreading)
```

When forwarding between tunnels on two (or more) ipsecX interfaces, KLIPS locks up the kernel and everything is frozen until you hit the reset button. This bug is only triggered when a packet comes in on one ipsecx interface, and goes out another ipsecx interface, which is quite rare. There is also still a bug with a missing spinlock() call, but this has been difficult to track down. This bug is present at least up to Openswan 2.4.4.

```
Jul 2 15:57:30 xenu pluto[29579]: "BRU" #3: ERROR: netlink response for Add SA
comp.661a@hhh.hhh.hhh.158 included errno 12: Cannot allocate memory
```

Old versions of NETKEY contained some bad memory allocation code for decompressing compressed packets. This has been fixed in recent 2.6 kernels. Either upgrade your kernel or add compress=no (on both ends!) as a workaround to disable compression.

```
003 "north-pole" #3: ERROR: netlink_get_spi for comp.0@xxx.xxx.xxx.xxx failed
with errno 22: Invalid argument
```

A race condition in the netlink_get_spi function. Notably the RHEL3 kernel, which contains an old NETKEY backport, still features this bug. A workaround for this was released in Openswan 2.3.2. A configuration workaround exists by disabling compression on both ends of the connection using compress=no. Note that setting compress to no only causes Openswan to not advertise the compress capability. It will still respond to requests for compression, so if you keep seeing this error even though you have disabled compression on this end, the other end is still asking for it.

```
Apr 27 01:05:22 south-park pluto[3448]: "phenome--extrude" #3: ERROR: netlink
response for Add SA esp.98650ce8@213.84.21.108 included errno 38: Function not
implemented
```

This error is returned when the kernel's crypto API functions are needed, but not loaded. Either the kernel is compiled without crypto API support, or the modules failed to load. Try:

```
# modprobe aes_i586 des sha1
```

For a list of crypto API ciphers, see /lib/modules/`uname -r`/kernel/crypto.

Common Errors when Upgrading

There are some common errors people run into when upgrading from an old FreeS/WAN or Super FreeS/WAN to Openswan, or when upgrading from Openswan 1 to Openswan 2.

```
"We only support version 2 of ipsec.conf"
```

If your ipsec.conf does not start with a line "version 2", then Openswan 2 will not start because it assumes an old version 1 configuration file is actually used. Apart from adding this line, you should remove the following two lines:

```
plutoload=
plutostart=
```

If you are not using Opportunistic Encryption, add the following line after the config setup and config default sections:

```
include /etc/ipsec.d/examples/no_oe.conf
```

If in this upgrade you also switched from KLIPS to NETKEY, you should be aware that you just lost your ipsecx interfaces. This will require a rewrite of your firewall and NAT rules. If you see errors similar to:

```
May 31 14:56:09 Noordwest pluto[13329]: "thuis-best" #4: ERROR: netlink
response for Add SA esp.b11cbf@193.111.228.3 included errno 2: No such file or
directory
```

then some of the NETKEY modules might have failed to (automatically) load. You can modprobe these modules manually:

```
# modprobe af_key esp4 ah4 ipcomp xfrm4_tunnel
```

If you are going to upgrade, first stop Openswan. Since the locations of some lock and pid files have changed, a newer version of Openswan will not be able to stop an older version of Openswan that is still running. If you have already installed the new version, you will have to manually kill the processes. Look for processes with 'pluto' in the name. For the new installed version, you should first run the initscript with 'stop' to clean up the dirty run and pid files, otherwise when you start you will see the following error:

```
# service ipsec start
    ipsec_setup: Openswan IPsec apparently already running, start aborted
```

Once you have killed all processes, check /var/run and remove the files related to Pluto or IPsec.

Also be careful not to install two versions in different locations. Most distributions will put the package in /usr, while your own compile will put things in /usr/local. However /usr will appear in your path first.

The behavior of rpm can also bite you. If installing a new RPM of a major new version, check for .rpmnew and .rpmsave files being created when you run the update command.

If you switched from KLIPS to NETKEY, you might suddenly be seeing ICMP redirect messages. This is because NETKEY does not use a separate virtual ipsecx interface like KLIPS. So now if you receive a packet on an interface through an IPsec tunnel, and the decrypted packet has to go back out over the same interface, it will send an ICMP redirect packet. Worse, it even sends these if such an IP address would fall outside the netmasks involved. In other words, the redirect packet can be completely bogus. Thankfully, you can disable ICMP redirect packets using:

```
# echo "0" > /proc/sys/net/ipv4/conf/all/send_redirects
```

Or you can add an entry into /etc/sysctl.conf:

```
net.ipv4.conf.all.send_redirects = 0
```

Path MTU discovery with NETKEY is broken, so lowering the MTU on the machine that you just upgraded will not help, since the other end is still talking to a broken Path MTU discovery machine. But once you lower the MTU on the **remote** end, Path MTU failure does not matter, since the MTU is now small enough not to trigger the need for Path MTU discovery. So once you lower the MTU on the remote machine, the one you did *not* change, then suddenly things start working again. This is a bit counterintuitive.

Another issue to be aware of is how the internal matching of IPsec policies within the kernel stacks works. While KLIPS sorts its tunnels like a routing table, meaning it uses the *most specific match first*, NETKEY matches based on destination for the incoming packets, and based on source for the outgoing packets. As a result NETKEY does a strange match of *most generic first*. This causes problems for a setup where a local IP range from a teleworker (such as 192.168.1.0/24) is part of a bigger range from the entire company (such as 192.168.0.0/16). With KLIPS, you can define one normal tunnel for this setup; with NETKEY you need to poke holes in the policies on the teleworker side to avoid having your local IP range considered as on the other end of the tunnel.

```
conn bypass
     left=192.168.1.1
     rIf you have another systemight=1.2.3.4
     type=passthrough
     authby=never
     auto=route
```

If you see many hanging ip xfrm state processes in D state, then you have a bad combination of Openswan and NETKEY. Openswan switched from using the external setkey command to using the ip xfrm command as of version 2.3.1. However NETKEY had a bug in the xfrm code, which was fixed in Linux kernel 2.6.11.7. Either downgrade Openswan or upgrade the kernel. Or change the _realsetup program to override the test for the ip xfrm capability.

Using tcpdump to Debug IPsec

As an example, let us assume that we have an Openswan-Openswan connection, where we have got IKE working fine, so we see an IPsec SA established, but when we try to use this IPsec connection, all packets seem to get lost.

We will use tcpdump to look at the network, but one could also use ethereal or tethereal in more or less the same way, since they also use libpcap, and therefore use the same expressions.

In general, tcpdump needs to run as root. Some distributions have customized versions of tcpdump, including options that mean the opposite from those in the official tcpdump package from tcpdump.org. If an option does not work for you, and the man page is no help, try to install tcpdump and libpcap from the original source yourself.

In our examples, we will assume that eth0 is the internal interface, and eth1 is the external interface. If PPPoE or PPTP is involved, then one should dump on the ppp0 interface rather than the eth1 interface: this will permit the selection expressions to work. tcpdump can decode PPPoE or PPTP packets, but cannot select based upon the encapsulated UDP port numbers within these packets.

The first thing to do is to observe the initiator's startup. If there is a NAT involved, remember that the system behind NAT always needs to be initiator—we will call this system **sg1**. After all, that machine cannot be reached behind its NAT. (Using port forwarding makes things immensely more complex and prone to failure.)

The ipsec auto –replace connname command removes any previous state, and reloads the definition of the conn from /etc/ipsec.conf. This is how it should look:

```
# ipsec auto --replace sg1--sg2-net
# ipsec auto --up sg1--sg2-net
    104 "sg1--sg2-net" #796: STATE_MAIN_I1: initiate
    003 "sg1--sg2-net" #796: received Vendor ID payload [Dead Peer Detection]
    106 "sg1--sg2-net" #796: STATE_MAIN_I2: sent MI2, expecting MR2
    108 "sg1--sg2-net" #796: STATE_MAIN_I3: sent MI3, expecting MR3
    004 "sg1--sg2-net" #796: STATE_MAIN_I4: ISAKMP SA established
    117 "sg1--sg2-net" #797: STATE_QUICK_I1: initiate
    004 "sg1--sg2-net" #797: STATE_QUICK_I2: sent QI2, IPsec SA established
    {ESP=>0xaa6fa19a        <0xa2f3b68d xfrm=3DES_0-HMAC_SHA1 NATD=none
    DPD=enabled}
```

There are four possible failures here:

	Symptom	Typical Cause
Situation A	No messages are ever received (only STATE_MAIN_I1)	Usually due to a firewall, some other blockage, or because the responder is not running (and ICMP messages are blocked by an overzealous system administrator).
Situation B	Message MI2 is repeated (MR1 and MR2 are received)	Often due to failure to authenticate, but can also be due to a firewall on port 4500, when NAT-T is involved.
Situation C	QUICK mode initiates, but never completes	Often due to a mis-matched policy.
Situation D	All of the IKE messages occur, but traffic does not flow.	Can be due to a number of things, including: firewalled ESP packets, firewalled port 4500 packets, Path MTU issues, local or remote system misconfiguration such as a missing ip command, errors from the _updown scripts, miscompiled kernel modules, and so on. Apart from firewall and MTU issues, all these problems should clearly show up in the log files on either the initiator or the responder.

Let us have a look at how tcpdump can assist in these situations.

Situation A: No Communication on Port 500

Use tcpdump on **sg1** and on **sg2** at the same time:

```
# tcpdump -i eth1 -n -p udp port 500 or udp port 4500
```

The following table explains the options used here.

-i eth1	Only look on this interface. Some distributions include support for dumping on all interfaces. Avoid using that, as it will confuse.
-n	Do not perform reverse DNS resolution.
-p	Do not use promiscuous mode. We only want to see packets for this host.
udp port 500	Only look for UDP packets with a source or destination port of 500.
or udp port 4500	Or look for UDP packets with a source or destination port of 4500. This happens with NAT-Traversal.

Now repeat the --replace and --up commands mentioned before the previous two tables. If there are no problems, then each packet leaving **sg1** should be seen arriving at **sg2**. If one of these gateways has many tunnels, you will want to limit tcpdump to only show the packets for this particular **sg1-sg2** combination. You can do this by extending the tcpdump filter we used above:

```
sg1# tcpdump -i eth1 -n -p ip host 1.2.3.4 and '(' udp port 500 or udp port 4500 ')'
sg2# tcpdump -i eth1 -n -p ip host 5.6.7.8 and '(' udp port 500 or udp port 4500 ')'
```

1.2.3.4 is the IP of **sg2** and 5.6.7.8 is the IP of **sg1**. Note each system filters for the IP of the opposite system.

You may be tempted to just look at all traffic from the opposite security gateway. This can be done, but be careful if you are SSHed into one security gateway from another. You will dump port 22 traffic, which is your SSH session with your tcpdump running. Since capturing these packets shows up in tcpdump, this will be transferred to you by SSH, using port 22. This will create more port-22 traffic for tcpdump, leading to an endless loop. You can, however, also listen to everything and just exclude the port-22 traffic using:

```
sg1# tcpdump -i eth1 -n -p ip host 1.2.3.4 and not port 22
```

What we are looking for are packets that start at **sg1**, and do not get to **sg2**. It may be helpful to include the -v option to tcpdump, which will decode the initial main mode proposal, since those first two exchanges are not encrypted.

There are two possible outcomes:

A1: All Packets Arrive on sg2

If all the packets arrive on **sg2**, but the Pluto running on it does not acknowledge them, then the problem is likely firewalling on **sg2**. You can confirm this by enabling plutodebug=all, and checking that Pluto does not receive a single packet. Or you can temporarily add an ACCEPT rule for all packets from and to **sg1** using:

```
sg2: # iptables -I INPUT -s ip_of_sg1 -j ACCEPT
sg2: # iptables -I OUTPUT -d ip_of_sg1 -j ACCEPT
```

A2: No Packets Arrive on sg2

This most likely means there is a firewall somewhere in between that is filtering your packets, or there is a NAT involved that you do not know about.

Situation B: Failure at Third Exchange

First, examine the logs on **sg2**. If it is complaining about being unable to find the appropriate keys, then the problem is not a communication failure. It will log that it received MI3 and complain about a failure to authenticate when RSA keys are used. If this conn uses PSK (authby=secret) then this error will appear as a failure to decrypt properly.

Assuming that there are no log entries on **sg2**, then the third packet may not be received. There are a number of possible reasons for this. Use tcpdump on both ends again, but include -v:

```
sg1# tcpdump -i eth1 -v -n -p udp port 500 or udp port 4500
sg2# tcpdump -i eth1 -v -n -p udp port 500 or udp port 4500
```

Look for the third exchange; it will be marked as [E].

The first exchange will look like:

> 11:14:25.516187 IP (tos 0x0, ttl 64, id 0, offset 0, flags [DF], proto 17, length: 320)
> 205.150.200.247.500 > 205.150.200.252.500: isakmp 1.0 msgid : phase 1 I ident: [|sa]

> 11:14:25.537388 IP (tos 0x0, ttl 64, id 0, offset 0, flags [DF], proto 17, length: 128)
> 205.150.200.252.500 > 205.150.200.247.500: isakmp 1.0 msgid : phase 1 R ident: [|sa]

And the second exchange will look like:

> 11:14:25.547023 IP (tos 0x0, ttl 64, id 0, offset 0, flags [DF], proto 17, length: 272)
> 205.150.200.247.500 > 205.150.200.252.500: isakmp 1.0 msgid : phase 1 I ident: [|ke]

> 11:14:25.772504 IP (tos 0x0, ttl 64, id 0, offset 0, flags [DF], proto 17, length: 272)
> 205.150.200.252.500 > 205.150.200.247.500: isakmp 1.0 msgid : phase 1 R ident: [|ke]

And the third exchange will look like:

> 11:14:25.781501 IP (tos 0x0, ttl 64, id 0, offset 0, flags [DF], proto 17, length: 232)
> 205.150.200.247.500 > 205.150.200.252.500: isakmp 1.0 msgid : phase 1 I ident[E]:
> [encrypted id]

> 11:14:25.865700 IP (tos 0x0, ttl 64, id 0, offset 0, flags [DF], proto 17, length: 360)
> 205.150.200.252.500 > 205.150.200.247.500: isakmp 1.0 msgid : phase 1 R ident[E]:
> [encrypted id]

The above is what it should look like: you should see the same thing at each end. Variations that one might see are:

- the packet may have been fragmented
- traffic on port 4500
- the IP addresses may also have changed if a NAT is involved
- any combination of the above

Fragmentation Problem

If certificates are involved, and they are being sent inline, that may lead to I3/R3 packets that are larger than 1500 bytes, which requires that the packet be fragmented. This will be indicated by having a non-zero 'id' field, and the flags will include '[+]'. The above filter will not show the fragments.

If you are seeing fragmentation, then adjust the filter to show all packets going to the other end. Be careful, as this may result in a lot of traffic:

```
sg1# tcpdump -i eth1 -v -n -p ip host 1.2.3.4 and not port 22
sg2# tcpdump -i eth1 -v -n -p ip host 5.6.7.8 and not port 22
```

Very carefully check for fragments leaving one system and not arriving at the other system. Note that Linux sends the fragments *before* the initial fragment.

It is also possible that the local system is filtering the fragments itself; in which case, no packet will emerge at all. This can be due to local firewalling, but can also be due to UDP on the 2.6 kernel having the *Don't Fragment* bit set.

If you enable partial logging for Pluto using plutodebug=emitting, the logs will show you how big the UDP packet is that is being sent. This way you can confirm that large packets are being sent, and that receiving these packets is the problem.

The most common situation is ISPs, poorly designed routers, or over-zealous firewall admins who have filtered out fragments. Often they will claim that they have not done that. Test the situation with:

```
sg1# ping -s 5000 1.2.3.4
```

You may also want to try this using the hping2 utility:

```
sg1# hping2 -2 -x -y --destport 500 1.2.3.4
```

A way to determine that this is in fact the problem is to omit the certificate payload by putting leftsendcert=never. Copy the certificate to **sg2**, and point the conn at it. While you may not want to operate like this permanently, it can help to diagnose the problem.

Port 4500 is Closed

If NAT was detected, which will be logged by Pluto when you use the --up command, and you see the I3 packet leaving **sg1** to port 4500, but not arriving at **sg2**, then the likely reason is that port 4500 has been blocked. If you see the packet arrive, but Pluto on **sg2** never sees it, then the problem is probably firewalling on **sg2** or on a firewall in front of **sg2**, or the fault of **sg2**'s ISP.

Be careful with firewall rules: port 4500 traffic, unlike port 500 traffic, does not always originate on port 4500. For example:

```
# iptables -I INPUT -s 0.0.0.0/0 -d 0.0.0.0/0 -p udp --sport 500 --dport 500 -j
ACCEPT
```

This rule will work fine for plain IKE traffic when there is no NAT involved, but you cannot use a similar rule for UDP 4500, since the source port might be a random high port instead of 4500. Instead, you need rules like:

```
# iptables -A INPUT -s 0.0.0.0/0 -d 0.0.0.0/0 -p udp --sport 4500 -j ACCEPT
# iptables -A INPUT -s 0.0.0.0/0 -d 0.0.0.0/0 -p udp --dport 4500 -j ACCEPT
```

However, this is a rather liberal rule set. For example, it would permit traffic from port 4500 *to* port 138, which is not the intended behavior. Either place these firewall rules after all your other firewall rules (and use -A to append, not -I to insert, the rule), or further tighten the IP address of the machines you are willing to talk IKE with. Of course if you have roadwarriors, then you will need to open up IKE to the world.

Situation C: QUICK Mode Initiates, but Never Completes

This situation can be diagnosed from the logs on **sg2**. tcpdump does not help at all in this case.

Situation D: All IKE Messages Occur, but no Traffic Flows

If you are using KLIPS, you have access to the ipsecx interfaces. You can run tcpdump on them to see if encrypted packets on the Ethernet device are being decrypted properly and sent out on the ipsecx device. First start tcpdump again on both machines, but now on the ipsecx device:

```
sg1# tcpdump -i ipsec0 -n -p
sg2# tcpdump -i ipsec0 -n -p
```

Then, send some traffic. Do you see the traffic you are sending? If **sg1** is a very busy IPsec machine, then you might want to add some additional filters to limit the decrypted traffic you want to see.

If you see traffic, but the traffic does not get through to its final destination, then you could have a firewall problem on **sg2**, or perhaps a routing problem. Alternatively, you might not have enabled **IP forwarding** in /etc/sysctl.conf.

If you see no traffic on **sg1**, then you may have a firewall problem there. Also read the logs on both ends. Was the SA set up properly? Look for errors from the ip or route commands.

If you see traffic on **sg1**, but none on **sg2**, then you need to investigate if the session layer ESP traffic is getting through.

Third, is there NAT involved? It could be that a NAT device will try to be *helpful*. As a result, the two gateways may not detect that there is a NAT involved, and may not switch from using port 500 and protocol 50 (ESP) packets to UDP port 4500 packets with encapsulated ESP as payload.

As of version 2.3.0, Pluto will log what it is going to do:

```
004 "sg1--sg2-net" #797: STATE_QUICK_I2: sent QI2, IPsec SA established
{ESP=>0xaa6fa19a <0xa2f3b68d xfrm=3DES_0-HMAC_SHA1 NATD=none DPD=enabled}
```

If it says "NATD=none", and you think that there is NAT, then you may have to set forceencaps=yes in the conn definition.

If this is not the case, then on each end issue the following:

```
sg1# tcpdump -i eth1 -v -n -p ip host 1.2.3.4 and ip proto 50
sg2# tcpdump -i eth1 -v -n -p ip host 5.6.7.8 and ip proto 50
```

You should see ESP packets with SPI 0xaa6fa19a leaving **sg1** (this the => in the log entry), and ESP packets with SPI 0xa2f3b68d arriving on **sg1**. On **sg2**, you should see the opposite.

Ensure that you do not only see traffic going in one direction.

Go back and confirm whether or not you see traffic sent from **sg1** on **sg2**'s eth0 (the internal interface). If you see the response traffic, then the problem is in the reverse flow. Repeat this last step, but with **sg1** and **sg2** swapped.

A Final tcpdump Example

The following tcpdump output shows an unfortunately common case:

```
19:22:18.002772 216.59.238.100.34242 > 216.191.140.38.4500: udp 1 (DF)
19:22:20.331001 216.191.140.38.4500 > 216.59.238.100.34242: udp 84
19:22:22.330900 216.191.140.38.4500 > 216.59.238.100.34242: udp 84
19:22:22.330962 216.191.140.38.4500 > 216.59.238.100.34242: udp 100
19:22:30.330702 216.191.140.38.4500 > 216.59.238.100.34242: udp 84
```

What is happening here is that the server on 216.191.140.38 is seeing really odd UDP packets on port 4500. The sizes of these packets, 1, 84, and 100, are just completely bogus. This is often the result of either broken NAT routers that do **IPsec passthrough**, or a broken NETKEY or KLIPS stack.

User Mode Linux Testing

User Mode Linux (**UML**) is a way to compile a Linux kernel such that it can run as a process in another Linux system (potentially as a *BSD or Windows process). See http://user-mode-linux.sourceforge.net for more information about UML.

UML is a good platform for testing and experimenting with Openswan. It allows several network nodes to be simulated on a single machine. Creating, configuring, installing, monitoring, and controlling these nodes is generally simpler and easier to script with UML than with real hardware. There are other virtual machine implementations, such as Xen and VMware, but these are not supported by the UML test suite.

You will need about 2 Gigabytes of free disk space for a full setup of seven to nine UMLs. You can possibly get this down by 130Mb if you remove the Sunrise/Sunset kernel build. If you just want to play around, then you can even remove the East/West kernel build.

Nothing needs be done as superuser, and we encourage people to run the UMLs as a regular user. UML seems to use a system-wide /tmp/uml directory so different users may interfere with one another. Later UMLs use .uml instead, so multiple users running UML tests should not be a problem, but note that a single user running the UML tests will only be able run one set. Be aware that sometimes UMLs get stuck and hang, taking up a lot of resources. These 'zombies' (most will actually be in the 'T' state in the process table) will interfere with subsequent tests. It might require a reboot of the host at times to resolve this, though often killing the hanging UMLs will work too.

> Use a dedicated or spare development machine to run tests with UML. Do not use a production server.

Preparing the Openswan for the UML Build Process

The UMLs we will be using will run our custom-build UML kernel, the latest Openswan, and a very basic 'Linux distribution'. Since we are creating many hosts based on UML to talk to each other, and we do not want to create separate file-trees for all these hosts, a complex system of hardlinked directories is part of the UML setup. It is important to keep all of these locations on one hard disk, which allows hardlinks.

In our examples, we create everything in /umls. First create the base directories to hold the kernel, Openswan, and the root file system:

```
# mkdir /umls
$ cd /umls
$ mkdir umlrootfs kernel Openswan tools results
$ cd umlrootfs
$ wget ftp://ftp.openswan.org/openswan/umlrootfs/umlswanroot-22.tar.gz
$ tar zxvf umlswanroot-22.tar.gz
```

Download the Linux kernel and UML patch. Linux 2.6.11 or above has integrated the UML patch. If you use this kernel or a newer version, you do not need to apply a UML patch.

```
$ cd /umls/kernel
$ wget ftp://ftp.ca.kernel.org/linux/kernel/v2.4/linux-2.4.27.tar.bz2
$ tar jxf linux-2.4.27.tar.gz
$ wget ftp://ftp.openswan.org/openswan/umlfsrootfs/uml-patch-2.4.27-1.bz2
```

> The exact path to the Linux kernel tree varies according to the mirror site.

To report an error (and to submit a UML test to document this error), it is best to try to reproduce this error in a UML with the latest CVS version of Openswan 2, since some problems might have been fixed in the latest release of Openswan even if a new version incorporating this fix has not yet been released. To download the latest CVS HEAD Openswan 2 version, issue the following commands, using **anoncvs** as the CVS login password:

```
$ cd /umls/openswan
$ cvs -d :pserver:anoncvs@anoncvs.openswan.org:/public/cvs login
$ cvs -d :pserver:anoncvs@anoncvs.openswan.org:/public/cvs co openswan-2
```

If your Linux distribution does not have a binary package for **uml_utilities**, build and install this now:

```
$ cd /umls/tools
$ tar xjvf uml_utilities_20040114.tar.bz2
$ cd tools
$ make all
$ su -c "make install BIN_DIR=/usr/local/bin"
```

Now we are ready to configure the build script. First we need to copy it to the main Openswan directory.

```
$ cd /umls/openswan/openswan-2
$ cp testing/utils/umlsetup-sample.sh umlsetup.sh
```

Edit the script according to your setup. Our example has been used in the table below:

Variable	Usage
UMLPREFIX=/umls	The base UML tree to use for everything.
KERNPOOL=$UMLPREFIX/kernel/linux-2.4.27	Location of the kernel source. This tree should be **unconfigured!**
UMLPATCH=$UMLPREFIX/kernel/uml-patch-2.4.27-1.bz2	Location of the UML patch. Set to /dev/null if using a kernel tree that already has UML support (2.6.11 or higher, or when using certain vendors' kernel trees).
OPENSWANDIR=$UMLPREFIX/openswan/openswan-2	The directory where the unpacked Openswan 2 directory was created.
BASICROOT=$UMLPREFIX/umlrootfs/root-22/	The directory used for umlswanroot.
POOLSPACE=$UMLPREFIX/umlbuild	Build location. This location should have at least 500Mb of free disk space and should be on the same physical hard disk partition as $BASICROOT so it can use hardlinks.
KERNVER=24	Set the kernel version, either 24 or 26.
NONINTPATCH=none	Whether the non-int patch should be applied.
NATTPATCH=true	Whether the NAT-T patch should be applied.
SHAREDIR=$BASICROOT/usr/share	This should be set to /usr/share for Debian potato users, or to $BASICROOT/usr/share for everyone else.
TCPDUMP=/usr/sbin/tcpdump	The location of your tcpdump binary.
REGRESSRESULTS=$UMLPREFIX/results	(Optional) Should be set to the location where you want the results (pass or fail) of each test stored.

Make sure that umlsetup.sh contains an entry for OPENSWANHOSTS. Versions prior to 2.3.2 mistakenly used FREESWANHOSTS.

You should now be able to build the entire UML system with all hosts using:

$ make uml

If you get an error about lndir not existing on your system, install the appropriate X Server package (xorg-x11 or xFree86). On Fedora Core 3, and other systems using gcc-3.4, there is a problem with the 2.4 kernel's use of FASTCALL. Please check the Openswan Wiki pages for updates on whether this problem still exists.

If the build fails with the error "*The following defaults are missing:*", containing a few new kernel options, you will need to add these options to openswan/openswan-2/testing/kernelconfigs/uml*.

Always remove the entire $POOLSPACE directory if your build failed and you change something in the kernel tree, otherwise your build tree will be a combination of kernel versions due to the use of hardlinks.

Running the UMLs

You can now start a machine, for example East, by running;

```
$ $POOLSPACE/east/start.sh
```

Or you can start up a few xterms with a Linux box in each of them:

```
$ for i in sunrise sunset east west
  do
      xterm -name $i -title $i -e $POOLSPACE/$i/start.sh &
  done
```

You can login as root, with the password "**root**". The UMLs are all networked together, so East can talk to West, when they have both been started, but there is no connectivity on East or West to the outside world. The following figure shows an overview of the entire Openswan UML-based test network.

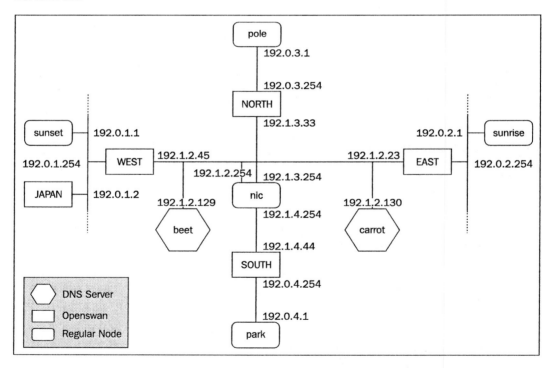

To run all test cases in the various UMLs, run:

```
$ cd /umls/openswan/openswan-2
$ make check
```

This will take a few hours, depending on your hardware. To present the results, run:

```
$ source umlsetup.sh
$ perl testing/utils/regress-summarize-results.pl $REGRESSRESULTS
```

This will produce `results/testresults.html` which is a hyperlinked summary of the entire test run.

You can also run a single test. For example, to just run the `xauth-pluto-09` test, you would use:

```
$ cd testing/pluto/xauth-pluto-09
$ ../../runme.sh
```

If you find an error in Openswan, creating a test case such as those that exist in the testing directory, and mailing that back to the Openswan developer list (dev@openswan.org) is by far the best way to report a bug. And once it is fixed, the test will remain part of Openswan, and all subsequent versions will test this specific case that went wrong once. If you write extensions to Openswan, then adding a test case is mandatory for the developers to incorporate the new code.

Writing a UML Test Case

Writing your own test case is not that difficult. Usually you can take an existing test, copy it, and then slightly modify it to represent the scenario you know causes a software error or kernel panic. Determine what type of test case you are writing—KLIPS, pluto, packaging, kernelconfig, utils, or something else. Create a new subdirectory under the proper subdirectory of testing/.

Populate that directory with the test files. Find an existing test that does something similar to what you are trying, and copy the files in and modify them. Add your test to testing/TEST-TYPE/TESTLIST.

Edit the description.txt file to explain what your test case is actually testing, and possibly what problem you have encountered that you are trying to trigger with this test. Use ASCII-art drawings if it will make things clearer.

Then edit testparms.sh, which is largely self explanatory:

```
#!/bin/sh

# There are two main purposes, regress, or goal.
# goal: something that must pass for a release
# regress: a feature we always want to test, in case new code breaks it
TEST_PURPOSE=regress
TEST_PROB_REPORT=0

# There are several 'types' of tests
# umlplutotest - Testing pluto under UML
# klipstest - Test KLIPS
# ctltest - ?
# mkinsttest - Test of 'make install'
# kernel_patch_test - Test patching of a kernel
# module_compile - Test building of the ipsec.o module
# umlXhost - Test involving several UML hosts
```

```
TEST_TYPE=umlplutotest

# The name of the test. Must not be duplicated elsewhere in the testing tree.
TESTNAME=dpd-01

# UML virtual 'hosts' you want to run
EASTHOST=east
WESTHOST=west

# Output files for each hosts's console
REF_EAST_CONSOLE_OUTPUT=east-console.txt
REF_WEST_CONSOLE_OUTPUT=west-console.txt

# Scripts to run against the console.txt files. These remove specific version
#s, or # other variable strings and swap in CONSTANTS.
REF_CONSOLE_FIXUPS="kern-list-fixups.sed nocr.sed"
REF_CONSOLE_FIXUPS="$REF_CONSOLE_FIXUPS cutout.sed"
REF_CONSOLE_FIXUPS="$REF_CONSOLE_FIXUPS east-prompt-splitline.pl"
REF_CONSOLE_FIXUPS="$REF_CONSOLE_FIXUPS ipsec-look-esp-sanitize.pl"
REF_CONSOLE_FIXUPS="$REF_CONSOLE_FIXUPS klips-debug-sanitize.sed"
REF_CONSOLE_FIXUPS="$REF_CONSOLE_FIXUPS ipsec-setup-sanitize.sed"
REF_CONSOLE_FIXUPS="$REF_CONSOLE_FIXUPS pluto-whack-sanitize.sed"
REF_CONSOLE_FIXUPS="$REF_CONSOLE_FIXUPS host-ping-sanitize.sed"

# Initialization scripts. Usually one per host. Use these to start ipsec, load
# a conn
EAST_INIT_SCRIPT=eastinit.sh
WEST_INIT_SCRIPT=westinit.sh

# These are the scripts that normally run your test
# Note1: These do NOT run in parallel. They are run one at a time.
# For play-by-play, interaction, use EAST_RUN2_SCRIPT=eastrun2.sh, etc...
# Note2: East is run before west
#
EAST_RUN_SCRIPT=eastrun.sh
WEST_RUN_SCRIPT=westrun.sh

# Scripts to run at the end. Useful to tail /tmp/pluto.log, or
# 'ipsec auto --look' to get a final look at the state of things.
EAST_FINAL_SCRIPT=final.sh
WEST_FINAL_SCRIPT=final.sh

NETJIG_EXTRA=debugpublic.txt
```

> There is a timeout to catch when a process does not return to a prompt for the *init.sh,
> *run.sh scripts. For this reason, do not do things like 'sleep 60'—instead, use 'sleep 10'
> six times.

Now your test is ready to run, and to be submitted to the developer mailing list for inclusion in Openswan.

Debugging the Kernel with GDB

With User Mode Linux, you can debug the kernel using GDB.

See http://user-mode-linux.sourceforge.net/debugging.htm.

Typically, you will have one test failing with a kernel crash, so you want to run just that one test. First start GDB. Tell it to open the $POOLSPACE/swan/Linux program. Check the PID of GDB:

```
$ ps ax | grep gdb
    1659 pts/9   SN    0:00 /usr/bin/gdb -fullname -cd /umls/umlbuild/east/  linux
```

Set the following in the environment:

```
$ UML_east_OPT="debug gdb-pid=1659"
```

Then start the UML in the test scheme you wish:

```
$ cd testing/klips/east-icmp-02
$ ../../utils/runme.sh
```

The UML will stop on boot, giving you a chance to attach to the process:

```
(gdb) file linux
Reading symbols from linux...done.
(gdb) attach 1
Attaching to program: /mara4/openswan/kernpatch/UMLPOOL/swan/linux, process 1
0xa0118bc1 in kill () at hostfs_kern.c:770
```

At this point, break points should be created as appropriate. If you are running a standard test, after all the packets are sent, the UML will be shut down. This can cause problems, because the UML may get terminated while you are debugging. The environment variable NETJIGWAITUSER can be set to 'waituser'. If so, then the testing system will prompt before exiting the test.

Asking the Openswan Community for Help

There are various sources of information about Openswan available on the Internet. Apart from the documentation that comes with Openswan, there is an Openswan Wiki at http://wiki.openswan.org. Using a search engine or browsing the user mailing list archive can also be very helpful. Or you can try IRC.

Internet Relay Chat (IRC)

You can ask your question on the #openswan IRC channel on FreeNode (irc.freenode.net). When asking questions through IRC, do not ask for permission to ask a question, just ask it, even if people are idle for hours. Some of the developers are often lingering idly on the channel, and might not notice your question immediately. Ask your question and hang around for a while, and you will be surprised how helpful that can be. Many people who join the #openswan channel for the first time ask a question on IRC and leave within five minutes because they think no one is listening. Have some patience; most developers have a day job, and will not be able to respond in seconds.

The Openswan Mailing Lists

If you believe your issue is rather specific, then it is time to organize your information and ask for help on the Openswan mailing lists. There are currently four mailing lists for Openswan. For a complete overview, please see http://lists.openswan.org/.

Openswan Mailing List	Description
announce	A very low volume announce-only mailing list. New versions and important information about security issues with other software is announced here.
users	Mailing list for system administrators trying to build and set up Openswan.
dev	Mailing list for developers and for reporting software bugs. This list is not meant for configuration issues. If you are unsure whether your issue is a configuration issue or a bug, please use the users list.
cvs	This is an announce-only mailing list of every code change in the CVS repository. This is useful for developers who want to closely track Openswan development, and those who have their own fork of our code.

If you are not subscribed to the list you are trying to send email to, your message will be held for the moderator to approve. This can take a few hours to a few days.

Posting to the Lists

Use a proper subject line describing the problem. A subject with "help" or "Openswan fails to work properly" will not get as much attention as "Openswan fails to rekey a roadwarrior connection" or "Openswan responds with 'no connection is known' message". Start your email with a short description of your setup. If you are using some 'ASCII art', ensure it does not take up more than about 70 characters, so it does not wrap and break when someone hits 'Reply' to your message. Also be aware of 'flowed messages'. Some mail programs assume that for any line ending with a space, the next line should be appended, and wrapped according to the reader's screen size. This does not work well with ASCII art drawings. An example of a proper configuration overview would be:

```
+------+
| RW   | 10.0.1.101 eth0
+--+---+
   |
   | 10.0.1.254 lan
+--+---------+
| NAT router |
+--+---------+
   | 193.111.228.42 wan
internet
   |
   | 193.110.157.131 eth1
+--+------------+
| VPN2 Openswan |
+--+------------+
10.0.2.2 eth1
   |
10.0.2.0/24
```

If your situation is simple enough, you can probably display it horizontally as well.

Then give a very brief summary of the problem, and what you believe is the relevant log error. For example:

```
The roadwarrior (RW) machine fails to connect to the VPN2 server, which
displays the error:
Cannot respond to...........[insert]
```

Then provide a link to a website that contains the output of the `ipsec barf` command. Do not run this command before the problem has occurred. If possible, clean out the log files (and perhaps restart the syslog service) so that all old log entries that are no longer appropriate will not become part of your report. Right after the error occurred, run `ipsec barf > rw-vpn2-barf.txt`. Depending on your setup, this might take from a few seconds to up to a minute to complete.

Do not send `barf` files to the user mailing list, since they can be huge. Also do not send configuration problems to the developer mailing list, unless you are sure that you are bitten by a software bug. If your problem turns out to be a software bug, the developers will bounce it to the developer mailing list when responding to your message. Do *not* CC your message to both the `dev` and `users` lists.

> Do not send `barf` output or core dumps to the lists!

Research First, Ask Later

It should be unnecessary to say this, but the bulk of the Openswan user mailing list still relates to a handful of common configuration mistakes, and people not taking the time to research properly before asking for help. Remember that the mailing list is a community effort. Demanding a quick answer, or informing the list that you will lose your job if you do not get it working before tomorrow, will not help you getting your issue resolved. You will have much more luck getting a quick answer if you properly provide a brief overview of your problem, the relevant error message, and a link to the bulk of your information gathered on a web page. Asking questions like, "Can someone help me get this working with Windows?", or "I cannot get this to work, please help" also will not get you much help. (Yes, these types of questions without any configuration or log message are unfortunately very common.)

Free, as in Beer

Support through IRC and the mailing lists is free. It is given as a courtesy. Please treat it as such. Do not ask 20 questions per day. If you need 20 questions, then you have not done enough research. Do not repeat your question every day if you did not receive an answer. Do not demand response times. Do not try to give the community a guilt trip about you losing your job if you cannot get this to work now. Do not email the people who answer to the mailing lists privately for more. The whole idea is that this free support is shared by the community. Various people can help you if you post to the list, and if the answer appears on the list, others will be able to find it when running into the same issue, reducing the workload for the developers who answer these questions.

Do not Anonymize

Obfuscating your information by replacing your (private and sensitive) IP addresses with letters is another good way of discouraging people from helping you. Without the proper information people cannot provide assistance. People are often willing to share information if you make it easy for them to do so. Providing them with an unreadable puzzle will not encourage them.

If your information is too sensitive to ask a question in public, you should consider hiring a professional consultant to assist you.

Summary

The most common errors have been explained in this chapter, with the intention of giving a good idea of how to read error messages for less common errors as well. Additional problem scenarios were discussed for when the developers should be contacted because of an obvious software bug. The chapter should also have taught you how to safely use tcpdump to trace certain network issues.

A

Unresolved and Upcoming Issues

This appendix lists some of the latest developments and issues that will be relevant to users of Openswan.

Linux Kernel Developments

Both the Linux networking stack and the IPsec transformation code (XFRM) are undergoing major changes as of kernel version 2.6.12, up to and including the latest version. Some of these changes keep on breaking KLIPS on every major and minor release. The Openswan developers cannot keep up with every minor version, so we advise you to stick to full releases such as 2.6.14, and not releases such as 2.6.14.7 or 2.6.15-rc1.

For each item in the networking code that has changed, you will find a define in the file `openswan-2/linux/include/openswan/ipsec_kversion.h` that switches between the old and the new behavior.

Kernel API Changes between 2.6.12 and 2.6.14

The following table lists relevant changes to the kernel API:

Version	ipsec_kversion.h define	Description
2.6.12+	HAVE_SOCK_ZAPPED	`sk->sk_zapped` changed to `sock_flag(sk, SOCK_ZAPPED)`
2.6.12+	NET_26_12_SKALLOC	`sk_alloc` argument order change
2.6.13+	HAVE_SOCK_SECURITY	`skb->security` vanished
2.6.13+	HAVE_SKB_NF_DEBUG	`skb->nf_debug` vanished
2.6.14+	HAVE_TSTAMP	`skb->stamp` changed to `skb->tstamp`
2.6.14+	HAVE_INET_SK_SPORT	`tcp_tw_bucket` vanished for `inet_sk()`
2.6.14 (only?)	HAVE_MISSING_IP_DEFAULT_TTL	`sysctl_ip_default_ttl` vanished (by accident?)

If you send the developers patches for newer kernels, please try to use this method of creating a define in `ipsec_kversion.h` and using that define in the actual KLIPS code.

Normally, these defines should work fine. If you have problems with these defines, or think your problems are related to these, you can override them either in `ipsec_kversion.h`, or better by setting a proper define for `MODULE_EXTRA_INCLUDE`.

Red Hat Kernel Developments

The problem described above is the prime reason why recent Red Hat kernels have been so unstable when used with KLIPS. Red Hat kernels tend to incorporate the above kernel features one version before they appear in the Torvalds Linux kernel. For instance, `sk_alloc()` was already changed in one of the 2.6.11-based Fedora kernel versions, but appeared in 2.6.12 in the Torvalds Linux kernel. The spec file, as shipped with Openswan in `openswan-2/packaging/Red Hat/openswan.spec`, shows the proper use of `MODULE_EXTRA_INCLUDE`.

Fedora Kernel Source/Headers Packaging Change

Fedora has changed where the kernel source can be found on a few occasions. First it was in a `kernel-source` binary RPM, then moved to a `kernel` source RPM, and is now in the `kernel-devel` binary RPM package.

To build KLIPS, some kernel header files are needed. Usually, there is a softlink in `/lib/modules/`uname -r`/build` that points to the proper location. Fedora has changed this a bit, with a new scheme to save on disk space that hardlinks all the kernel source files that did not change between kernel revisions in `/usr/src/kernels/`. This is mostly noticeable by the extremely long time it takes to post-process the `kernel-devel` package installation. It will take at least several minutes. We have had mixed results when adding and removing those `kernel-devel` packages, ending up with no proper kernel headers in any of the kernel trees installed.

MD5 Insecurities

Every few months, a new article appears on the "holes" in the MD5 hashing algorithm. It is true that some uses for MD5 are now far less secure than originally thought. SHA-1 is affected in a similar way. However, these hashing algorithms are vulnerable for hashes stored long-term, for instance, MD5 hashes of binary files, such as those used to check file integrity by `tripwire` and the RPM package manager (for example when invoked with `rpm -V openswan`).

However, IPsec uses keyed MD5, also called HMAC. This means that an attacker would have to break an MD5 hash *PER PACKET*. And on top of that, all the mathematical shortcuts that these MD5 vulnerabilities are based on do not work for HMAC-MD5.

The greatest danger of MD5 and SHA-1 being broken is in their use within X.509 certificates, though even those are still considered to be safe for quite a while. The official IETF view is "walk, not run, to another secure hashing algorithm". Whether this will be SHA-256 or another algorithm is not yet known.

Discontinuation of Openswan 1 by the End of 2005

By the time this book becomes available, Openswan 1 will have been fully discontinued. That means no new versions will be released, not even for grave security vulnerabilities. Since Openswan 1 itself was the continuation of Super FreeS/WAN, neither should be deployed, and current deployments should be phased out. Items specific to Openswan 1 have been left out of this book completely.

Update on UML Testing Suite Installation

Some additional scripts have been added to the contrib/ directory to greatly simplify the building of the UML-based test harness. If you run into problems and want to assist by showing us test results or adding new tests, please see the new UML scripts in the contrib/ directory.

Openswan GIT Repositories

The developers of Openswan might be moving from CVS to GIT. Currently, repositories are kept both in CVS and GIT. If you wish to use the GIT trees instead of the CVS trees, you should install the appropriate software: git and cogito. Run the following commands to check out a copy of the latest Openswan 2 development tree:

```
# mkdir git
# cd git
# cg-clone http://git.openswan.org/public/scm/openswan.git/.git
```

To update a previously checked-out tree, run:

```
# cg-fetch
```

For more information about git, see docs/HACKING/GitSOP, docs/HACKING/HowToGit, and docs/HACKING/PostToYourOwnGitTree. For up-to-date information on development tools used by Openswan, see http://www.openswan.org/development/.

For general information about git, see http://git.or.cz/.

Openswan on Windows and Mac OS X Updates

The Openswan userland currently runs on both Windows (using cygwin) and on Mac OS X (using Xcode). Both can only run with the "NO_KERNEL" kernel interface at this point. We hope to continue our porting efforts by porting the appropriate kernel hooks to those platforms. On Windows, this will likely happen by using the free **ipsec2k library**. This library is available on SourceForge.net. For Mac OS X, the kernel_netkey interface will need to be ported to the Apple KAME interface. Since NETKEY itself is a port of KAME, this should not be an impossible task.

Both these tasks require commitments for which Xelerance currently has no resources. If you wish to sponsor these projects by submitting code or by making a financial contribution, please contact Xelerance.

Known Outstanding Bugs

There are currently a few unresolved bugs that might affect your Openswan installation. You should make sure that the latest release of Openswan has not fixed these issues and also check any open issues listed at `http://bugs.openswan.org/`.

- Some people encounter very short UDP fragments on TCP or SYN packets after updating their Openswan from 2.3.x to 2.4.x. This was due to a bug in KLIPS in versions 2.4.0 to 2.4.4. Please upgrade or specify `fragicmp=no` as workaround.

- It seems that SMP machines might still experience crashes when KLIPS is used. There is a fix in Openswan 2.4.4 which might have resolved this issue.

- There are still some Mac OS X interoperability problems with NAT-T because Apple did not correctly implement the NAT-T specifications. Currently, the initial connection will work fine, but at rekey time, the connection will fail.

- Multiple roadwarriors behind the same NAT router cannot establish transport mode (L2TP) connections to the same Openswan server. A patch is currently being worked on to resolve this.

- There have been reports that using an AMD64 (x86_64) kernel with a 32-bit Openswan userland fails with NETKEY errors.

- Some minor NAT-T issues were reported where Openswan would use the wrong source port or incorrectly detect double NAT.

- `type=transport` and `rightsubnet=vhost:%priv` should work together but give a bogus error. (Workaround: remove `type=transport` and it will still use transport mode.)

Vulnerability Fixes in Openswan 2.4.4

(or "*A week in the life of the Openswan developers*")

When this book entered the final edit stage, we were at version 2.4.1. Two weeks later version 2.4.4 was out. With Openswan releases normally going out every few months, this is rather odd. We decided to write up our clarification in this appendix, as these events are truly the latest developments, and we could no longer update the texts in the regular chapters, as they had already gone into the final publishing stage.

On August 31 2005, Xelerance was notified by the UK's National Infrastructure Security Coordination Centre (NISCC) that a cross-vendor vulnerability had been found in various implementations of the IKE protocol. They could not tell if Openswan was vulnerable, since they did not test it. They required us to sign a "*Social Contract*" that included terms that the Openswan developers could not agree to.

The biggest problem was that the Openswan developers could not disclose any information about this vulnerability, until NISCC chose to go public themselves, yet no deadline was given for a publication date. This limitation meant that developers could not even fix the bug until the announcement, since Openswan is open-source software. Any change in the code is automatically published, and would disclose the vulnerability information. NISCC said they would likely publish the vulnerability on October 31 2005 but could not make any hard guarantees. No contract was signed.

October 31 came and passed. Then we were told this vulnerability would be disclosed in January, since a large vendor needed more time to repair its IPsec devices. Meanwhile, Openswan developers still did not know whether they were vulnerable or not.

On November 14, NISCC and CERT-FI, the Finnish CERT department, released the vulnerability information including a substantial test suite written by the University of Oulu, Finland. This was probably the worst timing they could have done, since the week before a lot of IPsec developers, including some of the Openswan developers, had been at the IETF meeting in Vancouver, Canada, and were still traveling back home. Even worse was that Openswan developers were not notified beforehand (nor in fact, afterwards). They were given a "*0-day exploit*" by a National Security organization who had been sitting on this bug for months.

The developers scrambled to run the test suite, which alone took over three hours to run, since it consisted of 5000 test cases that had to run sequentially. They then decided to release Openswan 2.4.2 late that same day, even though it only fixed one of the two bugs that had been encountered. A day later, Openswan 2.4.3 was created, but it turned out to be a dud—the second bug was not properly fixed, and this version was pulled from the web and FTP servers. On November 18, Openswan 2.4.4 was released that properly fixed the second bug.

Looking back after the events, the vulnerabilities were not as shocking as first assumed. The Openswan code actually caught the bogus packets in a controlled matter, in the '*assertion*' functions, meaning no buffer overflows or other methods to inject malicious code were ever possible with these exploits. Furthermore, it turned out these two bugs were only triggered in Phase 2, meaning one had to know the shared secret (PSK) to perform an attack. Furthermore, one of the two bugs required Aggressive Mode as well. Aggressive Mode is really only used to talk to Cisco routers, and is hardly used with Openswan at all. The only attack vector for a malicious attacker could be someone from within the organization, severely limiting the impact of these bugs. None of this is discussed in the vulnerability release, nor in the updates that NISCC has since issued.

For more details, see the announcements of Openswan 2.4.3 and Openswan 2.4.4 and our public response to the NISCC vulnerability announcement. These texts can be read at:

http://www.openswan.org/niscc2/

http://lists.openswan.org/pipermail/announce/2005-November/000008.html

http://lists.openswan.org/pipermail/announce/2005-November/000009.html

B
Networking 101

The Internet has become a big place, with many different kinds of individual computers as well as LANs connected to it. Sometimes a group of LANs have special interconnections, making a Wide Area Network (WAN). Though these networks used to operate using a variety of network protocols, these have all more or less died out in favor of one, the Internet Protocol, or IP. Protocols that did not make it to the Internet include IPX, DecNet, NetBEUI, LAT, and X.25. This book focuses only on the IP protocol. Many of these obsolete protocols can be encapsulated in IP packets if they really need to travel over the Internet. Sometimes the entire Internet Protocol is called TCP/IP, although technically speaking this is a very bad name.

The OSI Model and the IP Model

The Internet Protocol defies the old **OSI network model** from the ISO committee. For those of you who still try to believe in this model, think about it for a bit. You might be able to match some things, such as 802.3 to layer 2, IP to layer 3, TCP to layer 4, TLS to layer 5, HTTP to layer 6, and HTML to layer 7. But ICMP is also layer 3, IPsec ESP is layer 2, 3, and 4, since ESP can live on top of layer 3 (therefore it must be 4 also), and it can have layer 4 in it (so it must be layer 3), and it can have a layer 3 in it (so it must be layer 2). We will try and prevent using anything from this old model, and we encourage you to rip your OSI model poster off the wall and focus on the properties of IP. Welcome to the real world...

No Layers, Just Packets

The IP protocol has no concept of layers. It consists simply of packets. When people talk about layers (often layer 2 or layer 3) they are actually talking about how to stuff IP packets into some transport medium such as coax cables, fiber, WiFi, or Ethernet. We will hardly have to worry about those layers, since IPsec deals with IP packets, and not the physical medium of sending those packets.

If you connect from one machine to the other, you are sending and receiving packets. A **connection** is nothing more than two machines remembering the state of the packets sent and received. An IP packet consists of an IP header, and the IP body. The header contains information that ensures the packets are passed along until they reach their destination. The header also describes what kind of data is inside the packet. The body is the actual data, or the payload.

Each IP packet's header contains the source address, the IP address of the machine that created the packet (and later on perhaps expects an answer). It contains the destination IP address, the place where this packet is intended to go, and a protocol number. Most protocols also require a port number. The IP header has further space for a bunch of other options or flags that can be set.

The Protocol

Without going into too much detail about all the different kinds of protocols and options, Internet communication today mostly consists of two protocols, TCP and UDP. Note that technically we should be talking about sub-protocols of the IP protocol, but the fact that to do so would actually make things more confusing is only proof that the OSI model is dead.

These two IP protocols, TCP and UDP, have ports, which are simply a way of sub-addressing an IP address. Ports go from 1 to 65535. TCP and UDP connections are therefore characterized by four properties: source address, source port, destination address, and destination port. You can either listen or send on a certain address and port, but you can not use them for both sending and receiving at the same time.

These ports are separate 'entries' into the host. For instance, email is sent using the SMTP protocol, which consists of a TCP connection to the IP address of a mail server on port 25. A DNS server listens on UDP port 53 for questions about translating a hostname to an IP address.

Another well known IP protocol is ICMP. This protocol is used to send error or informational messages. The ping command uses an ICMP packet. The ICMP protocol has no ports. Actually, this protocol is a bit special, as it is a control function of the IP protocol, and not a sub-protocol of the IP protocol.

IP Network Overview

Most people are familiar with IP address notation and netmasks, but in our support work and on the mailing lists we often see people using impossible configurations. Usually, this is because they have not fully understood the meaning of netmasks, the CIDR notation, or the concept of the gateway. We will give a quick explanation of these concepts for IPv4. If you are familiar with these, you can skip this part, but be aware that if you do not fully understand netmasks and gateways, you will run into problems later.

If you connect a computer to the Internet, you have to ensure that its address is unique, or else you cannot distinguish it. This is done by assigning the computer (which becomes a **host** on the network) an Internet Protocol address, or IP address.

An IPv4 address is a unique 32 bit number. Because humans are not fluent in binary notation, we write them in a special way, four bytes separated by dots. For example, 193.110.157.77 is the IP address of the mailing list server of the Openswan project.

IP Address Management

These addresses are handed out in chunks by a few central organizations. This registration started with Jon Postel, who started the **IANA**, the **Internet Assigned Number Authority**. After the Internet hype and commercial and government interests in the Internet increased, this technical process became a political process. Currently, the authority for these numbers formerly resides at ICANN, though in practice the three Regional Internet Registrars (RIRs) control and hand out the address space. ARIN hands out IP addresses in North and South America, RIPE hands them out in Europe and bits of Africa and the Middle East, and APNIC gives out addresses to the Asian and Pacific regions.

The Old IP Classes

In the early days, these chunks of addresses were split up in classes. The smallest class was the Class C, which would have 256 IP addresses. For example, 193.111.228.*, where * can be any number between 0 and 255. Bigger organizations such as universities would receive a Class B, for example 131.174.*.*. They could then split that class B into smaller class C networks for internal use. Some organizations were lucky enough to receive a huge pool, a class A. Stanford University used to have 36.*.*.*.

We will not go into the political discussion of the IP space shortage, but when it was deemed that this was a problem, people wanted to replace this system of network classes with something else. The problem of these classes was that a lot of IP addresses were wasted. If you needed 300 addresses, you could not use a class C, so you would get a class B, which contained 256*256= 65536 addresses, of which 65000 would be wasted. The difference between a class B and a class A is even worse.

Classless IP Networks

The concept of classes was replaced as ISPs needed to hand out smaller chunks of IP addresses to their customers. Instead of giving every customer 256 IP addresses, they would receive much smaller chunks. This could be any power of two between 4 and 256.

The Definition of a Subnet

Every Internet-connected network has two sides, the inside and the outside. Hosts on the inside can be reached directly, without the help of another host. The inside network is often called the LAN, which stands for Local Area Network. Sometimes people distinguish the LAN from a remote network according to who administers the hosts. An organization can have several *local* networks that fall into the larger corporate network. If you look at the corporate network as a whole versus the Internet, then you can call that corporate network the LAN too. We will be focusing on the technical aspects of networks. When we say local network, we mean this from the technical point of view. Two machines are in the same local network if they can communicate to each other without the help of a third host, even if they are five buildings and six kilometers apart, or end up belonging to a different company department and system administrator. The entire local network of all machines that can talk to each other without a third host is also called a **subnet**. The term subnet originates from the old days when we still spoke about classes. If you had a class B network, you could subnet this class into C classes and give separate buildings or departments their own subnet. These days we still speak of subnets, but more in a sense that every network on the Internet is a subnet of that Internet.

Calculating with Subnets: The Subnet Mask

Because subnets can have different sizes, we need to have a method for hosts to *know* what they should consider as their subnet. You do not want the host to try and *find* the host in the local subnet when the host it is trying to talk to is on the other side of the planet. Remember that an IP address is just a 32-bit number. The IP address 193.110.157.77 can be written in bits as 11000001 01101110 10011101 01001101. What do we know about these bits for the subnet that contains all the addresses in 193.110.157.*? Well, we notice that some of the bits, in our case the first 24, are always the same. The last 8 bits change, depending on the number we want that "*" to be, as anything from 0 to 255. This is exactly what the subnet mask (also called the **netmask**) tells us. It is also a series of 32 bits, but now the bits do not represent a number, but the property of a bit in the IP address.

> For each bit in an IP address range that will never change, the corresponding bit in the netmask will be 1. If changing a bit in an IP address would indicate a different host in the *same* network, the netmask bit corresponding to the address bit would be 0.

Let us visualize this in a table, because it sounds a lot more complex than it really is. Let us write down our IP address, but also the first and last address possible in our subnet. The parts in bold in the table below never change, and are part of the subnet, and thus receive a 1 in the netmask.

IP address	Binary notation			
193.110.157.0	**11000001**	**01101110**	**10011101**	00000000
193.110.157.77	**11000001**	**01101110**	**10011101**	01001101
193.110.157.255	**11000001**	**01101110**	**10011101**	11111111
Netmask	11111111	11111111	11111111	00000000

As expected, the only difference between IP addresses in the 193.110.157.* range are the last 8 bits: the first 24 bits (3 bytes) are always the same. We can also see another property of the netmask. It will always start with 1s and at one (and only one) point, it will switch to zeros. This is because our subnets will always be a continuous set of increasing numbers, e.g. from 0 to 255.

So if we want to describe our IP address and its subnet, we could use the decimal syntax **193.110.157.77/255.255.255.0**. This gives us all the information we need. Our host's IP address is 193.110.157.77, and all the IP addresses that fall within 193.110.157.* can be reached directly.

But since sysadmins are inherently lazy, they do not want to write all these netmask numbers every time they need an address. Instead, a shorthand notation is used. For instance, for '255.255.255.0' we count the number of 1s in the netmask, and write that. So, the most common notation for our machine here would be **193.110.157.77/24**. If we want to describe the entire subnet instead of a single host in a subnet, we would use the lowest address in that subnet. Our subnet would be written as **193.110.157.0/24**. This is called the **CIDR** notation, the **Classless Internet Domain Routing** notation.

Let us now see how this works with a second range, often used elsewhere in this book, and go from CIDR to a full network description. The CIDR notation is **205.150.200.223/28**. First, we rewrite the full netmask. 28 bits is 8 bits + 8 bits + 8 bits + 4 bits. So we have a netmask of **11111111 11111111 11111111 1111**0000, which in decimal is 255.255.255.240.

IP address	205.150.200.223	11001101 10010110 11001000 11011111
Netmask	255.255.255.240	11111111 11111111 11111111 1111**0000**

So, the bits in the netmask that are zero are those that can be changed for this subnet. Again, to get the lowest address, we write zeros in the IP address for which the netmask has a zero, which means that bit can be changed. To get the highest address, we write ones in the IP address for which the netmask has a zero.

The following table might help make this clear:

	IP address	Netmask	IP address AND netmask
Lowest IP	205.150.200.223	11001101 10010110 11001000 1101**0000**	205.150.200.208
Highest IP	205.150.200.223	11001101 10010110 11001000 1101**1111**	205.150.200.223

The lowest address is also called the **network address**, the highest address is also called the **broadcast address**, as this is used to send messages that need to reach all the hosts in the subnet. It is important to realize that a netmask does not mean anything *on its own*; it must be used in conjunction with an actual IP address.

The Rest of the Network

Now we have a method for determining what is a local directly reachable host, and what is not directly reachable. We only need one last piece of information. If we cannot communicate to a host directly, because it is not in our local subnet, where do we send packets for that host to? We send it to a special host called the **gateway**. A host can have different gateways it uses for different remote subnets, and usually a host also has one gateway that it uses for all the unspecified subnets. This gateway is called the 'default gateway'. Obviously, this gateway *must* be in the local subnet, or we would need a gateway to reach the gateway! Since a gateway is also part of the remote LAN in the remote subnet, you can already deduce that such a gateway machine is in two different subnets, and that it will have two different IP address for that one host. Since an IP address is therefore no longer something that we can unique identify a host with, we need another qualifier to denote a host. This is called the **Autonomous System** number (**AS**). Only hosts that need to make dynamic routing decisions tend to get an AS assignment.

Linux Networking Commands

To see the IP address and netmask of a machine, you can use the `ifconfig` command. To see what a host knows about other subnets and gateways, you can use the `route` command. Technically speaking, however, both these two commands are obsolete. On Linux, they have been obsoleted in favor of the less friendly and almost completely undocumented but more powerful `ip` command.

Old Style	New Style
`ifconfig`	`ip iface listen`
`route -n`	`ip route list`

Routing

In essence the Internet is nothing more than a lot of these local subnets and gateway machines connected to each other. An important difference between a leaf node of the Internet and a core host in the Internet is the **default route**. A leaf node can just send packets upstream using the default gateway. But giving a packet to a default gateway is really just postponing making a decision in the hope that the default gateway knows what to do with the packet. And our default gateway itself might have its own default gateway defined, or it might keep a big table of subnets and gateways. There are various routing protocols that facilitate learning and updating these lists of routes. Some older routing protocols are RIP (which is really R.I.P.) and **Open Shortest Path First (OSPF)**. Mostly, modern day routers use the **Border Gateway Protocol (BGP)**.

Routing Decisions

So far we have made decisions on where to send packets to based on where they need to go to. This is called **destination-based routing**, and is the most common type of routing on leaf nodes. Routing decisions can, however, be made based on many criteria. Another common type of routing is **source-based routing**. For those familiar with the '*funny routes*' with Openswan, these two half default routes into the IPsec network device make sure all packets are processed by Openswan to get encrypted. This mechanism predates proper source routing and will be replaced soon. Linux source routing is performed using the `ip rule` command.

Routing of packets to non-local machines is a rather dynamic process. Hosts on the Internet keep changing locations from a network topology point of view. If there is an outage, a different route will be taken. But there are more things to consider when routing packets, and the most common criterion on backbone routers these days sadly is money. Packets will be routed based on the cost. Some call this **hot-potato routing**, which means "get rid of the packet as soon as you can", because that is most often the cheapest solution.

Peering

The concept of peering is that you have a few 'network routes' or subnets and that you are willing to exchange traffic with them. Two networks exchanging traffic like this are called **peering partners**. Internet Exchanges are locations where many peering partners get together to lower the costs of running cables to too many peering partners. Instead, everyone gets together on a few big switches and exchanges routing information using BGP. If the relationship between two ISPs is rather asymmetrical, that is one end has a few networks or routes and the other has "most or all of the Internet routes", one usually speaks of transit traffic. Transit traffic is much more expensive than peering traffic.

Network Address Translation

Every host on the Internet has to have a unique routable IP address, or else it would not be considered a host *on the Internet*. For various reasons, people have started to use tricks to get more IP addresses. ISPs often give an end user only one IP address, while those end users want to connect more than one computer. The trick mostly deployed now is **Network Address Translation (NAT,** sometimes also called NAPT). The end user connects these computers together using internal IP addresses. On the machine that is actually connected to the Internet, which could be a phone, cable or DSL line, the real globally routable IP address is configured. This is the IP address that everyone on the Internet can talk to. The address is given out by the ISP.

This computer, technically speaking now acting as a router, takes incoming packets from the LAN's private IP addresses, and rewrites these packets so they appear to come from its own real IP address. It remembers which local machine these packets were translated for. When the remote machine it were trying to reach answers, that machine thinks it is talking to the router. Once the router receives the response packet, it matches it with the list of local computers and their network connections, and translates the destination IP address back to the local machine's private IP address and sends the packets onto the local network.

Of course, there is one problem. A remote machine cannot reach the local machine behind the router, since it has no public routable IP address. It cannot just connect to the public IP address either, because the router would have no idea for whom this packet was intended, since no local machine has initiated the communication.

People began to see this as more than a shortcoming. After all, this setup is ideal for protecting those internal machines. Since the world cannot reach them, no hackers or viruses could ever reach them either. It sort of works like a firewall, and this is why you often see NAT and firewalls combined on one device. All common DSL and cable modem routers can do NAT and firewalling.

Port Forwarding

A trick to allow more direct access to those machines behind a NAT host is to listen on certain ports, for example port 80 which is used for HTTP web servers, and any packet received for this port can be forwarded to a predefined 'internal' machine. Once the web server with its private IP address answers, the router rewrites the source address to itself, and sends it back to the machine on the Internet. The machine on the Internet never knows its packet was actually sent further into the network than the machine it contacted. This trick is also used to create load balancing or fail-over configurations.

C

Openswan Resources on the Internet

Openswan Links

Openswan website	`http://www.openswan.org/`	Main website for Openswan
Xelerance website	`http://www.xelerance.com/`	Maintainers of Openswan
Openswan Wiki	`http://wiki.openswan.org/`	Community-based documentation
WaveSEC website	`http://www.wavesec.net/`	Encrypting wireless using IPsec
Openswan FTP site	`ftp://ftp.openswan.org/`	Main repository for Openswan binaries
Openswan bug tracker	`http://bugs.openswan.org/`	Report and search for known bugs
Openswan mailing lists	`http://lists.openswan.org/`	Mailing lists for announcements, support, developers, and CVS commits
FreeS/WAN	`http://www.freeswan.org/`	The (closed) FreeS/WAN Project
XS4all FTP server	`ftp://ftp.xs4all.nl/pub/crypto/freeswan/`	The FreeS/WAN main repository

Community Documentation

Jacco de Leeuw's documentation on IPsec with L2TP	`http://www.jacco2.dds.nl/networking/`
Nate Carlson's documentation on configuring Openswan with Microsoft Windows	`http://www.natecarlson.com/linux/ipsec-x509.php`
Openswan Wiki	`http://wiki.openswan.org/`
Collection of DNSSEC-related websites and information	`http://www.dnssec.net/`

Generic Linux Distributions Containing Openswan

Red Hat Enterprise Linux (RHEL)	`http://www.redhat.com/`
Fedora Linux	`http://fedora.redhat.com/`
GNU/Debian	`http://www.debian.org/`
SuSE / Novell	`http://www.novell.com/linux/suse/`
Mandriva	`http://www.mandriva.com/`
Gentoo	`http://www.gentoo.org/`
Centos	`http://www.centos.org/`

Specialized Linux Distributions Containing Openswan

IPcop	`http://www.ipcop.org/`
SnapGear	`http://www.snapgear.org/`
Arkoon	`http://open-source.arkoon.net/gpl.php`
MaraSystems	`http://marasystems.com/download/freeswan/`
OpenWRT	`http://www.openwrt.org/`
PePLink MANGA	`http://www.peplink.com/`
SmoothWall	`http://www.smoothwall.org/`
Gibraltar	`http://www.gibraltar.at/`

D

IPsec-Related Requests For Comments (RFCs)

All RFCs can be downloaded from http://www.rfc-editor.org/ or one of the many mirror sites.

Overview RFCs

RFC 2401	Security Architecture for the Internet Protocol
RFC 2411	IP Security Document Roadmap
RFC 4301	Security Architecture for the Internet Protocol

Basic Protocols

RFC 2402	IP Authentication Header (AH)
RFC 2406	IP Encapsulating Security Payload (ESP)
RFC 4302	IP Authentication Header
RFC 4303	IP Encapsulating Security Payload (ESP)

Key Management

RFC 2367	PF_KEY Key Management API, Version 2
RFC 2407	The Internet IP Security Domain of Interpretation for ISAKMP
RFC 2408	Internet Security Association and Key Management Protocol (ISAKMP)
RFC 2409	The Internet Key Exchange (IKE)
RFC 2412	The OAKLEY Key Determination Protocol
RFC 2528	Internet X.509 Public Key Infrastructure
RFC 3526	More Modular Exponential (MODP) Diffie-Hellman groups for Internet Key Exchange (IKE)

RFC 3664	The AES-XCBC-PRF-128 Algorithm for the Internet Key Exchange Protocol (IKE)
RFC 4109	Algorithms for Internet Key Exchange version 1 (IKEv1)
RFC 4210	Internet X.509 Public Key Infrastructure Certificate Management Protocol (CMP)
RFC 4304	Extended Sequence Number (ESN) Addendum to IPsec Domain of Interpretation (DOI) for Internet Security Association and Key Management Protocol (ISAKMP)
RFC 4306	Internet Key Exchange (IKEv2) Protocol

Procedural and Operational RFCs

RFC 1750	Randomness Recommendations for Security
RFC 1918	Address Allocation for Private Internets
RFC 1984	IAB and IESG Statement on Cryptographic Technology and the Internet
RFC 2144	The CAST-128 Encryption Algorithm
RFC 3457	Requirements for IPsec Remote Access Scenarios
RFC 3585	IPsec Configuration Policy Information Model

Detailed RFCs on Specific Cryptographic Algorithms and Ciphers

RFC 1321	The MD5 Message-Digest Algorithm
RFC 1828	IP Authentication using Keyed MD5
RFC 1829	The ESP DES-CBC Transform
RFC 1851	The ESP Triple DES Transform
RFC 1852	IP Authentication using Keyed SHA
RFC 2085	HMAC-MD5 IP Authentication with Replay Prevention
RFC 2104	HMAC: Keyed-Hashing for Message Authentication
RFC 2202	Test Cases for HMAC-MD5 and HMAC-SHA-1
RFC 2403	The Use of HMAC-MD5-96 within ESP and AH
RFC 2404	The Use of HMAC-SHA-1-96 within ESP and AH

RFC 2405	The ESP DES-CBC Cipher Algorithm With Explicit IV
RFC 2410	The NULL Encryption Algorithm and Its Use With IPsec
RFC 2451	The ESP CBC-Mode Cipher Algorithms
RFC 2521	ICMP Security Failures Messages
RFC 3566	The AES-XCBC-MAC-96 Algorithm and Its Use With IPsec
RFC 3602	The AES-CBC Cipher Algorithm and Its Use with IPsec
RFC 3686	Using Advanced Encryption Standard (AES) Counter Mode With IPsec Encapsulating Security Payload (ESP)
RFC 4196	The SEED Cipher Algorithm and Its Use with IPsec
RFC 4106	The Use of Galois/Counter Mode (GCM) in IPsec Encapsulating Security Payload (ESP)
RFC 4305	Cryptographic Algorithm Implementation Requirements for Encapsulating Security Payload (ESP) and Authentication Header (AH)
RFC 4307	Cryptographic Algorithms for Use in the Internet Key Exchange Version 2 (IKEv2)
RFC 4308	Cryptographic Suites for IPsec
RFC 4309	Using Advanced Encryption Standard (AES) CCM Mode with IPsec Encapsulating Security Payload (ESP)

Dead Peer Detection RFCs

RFC 3706	A Traffic-Based Method of Detecting Dead Internet Key Exchange (IKE) Peers

NAT-Traversal and UDP Encapsulation RFCs

RFC 2709	Security Model with Tunnel-mode IPsec for NAT Domains
RFC 3715	IPsec Network Address Translation (NAT) Compatibility Requirements
RFC 3947	Negotiation of NAT-Traversal in the IKE
RFC 3948	UDP Encapsulation of IPsec ESP Packets

RFCs for Secure DNS Service, which IPSEC May Use

RFC 2137	Secure Domain Name System Dynamic Update
RFC 2230	Key Exchange Delegation Record for the DNS
RFC 2535	Domain Name System Security Extensions
RFC 2536	DSA KEYs and SIGs in the Domain Name System (DNS)
RFC 2537	RSA/MD5 KEYs and SIGs in the Domain Name System (DNS)
RFC 2538	Storing Certificates in the Domain Name System (DNS)
RFC 2539	Storage of Diffie-Hellman Keys in the Domain Name System (DNS)
RFC 3007	Secure Domain Name System (DNS) Dynamic Update
RFC 3008	Domain Name System Security (DNSSEC) Signing Authority [obsoleted]
RFC 3130	Notes from the State-Of-The-Technology: DNSSEC
RFC 3225	Indicating Resolver Support of DNSSEC
RFC 3226	DNSSEC and IPv6 A6 aware server/resolver message size requirements
RFC 3757	Domain Name System KEY (DNSKEY) Resource Record (RR) Secure Entry Point (SEP) Flag [obsoleted]
RFC 3845	DNS Security (DNSSEC) NextSECure (NSEC) RDATA Format [obsoleted]
RFC 4025	A Method for Storing IPsec Keying Material in DNS
RFC 4033	DNS Security Introduction and Requirements
RFC 4034	Resource Records for the DNS Security Extensions
RFC 4035	Protocol Modifications for the DNS Security Extensions
RFC 4322	Opportunistic Encryption using the Internet Key Exchange (IKE)

RFCs Related to L2TP, Often Used in Combination with IPsec

RFC 2341	Cisco Layer Two Forwarding (Protocol) "L2F". (A predecessor to L2TP)
RFC 2637	Point-to-Point Tunneling Protocol (PPTP). (A predecessor to L2TP)
RFC 2661	Layer Two Tunneling Protocol "L2TP"
RFC 2809	Implementation of L2TP Compulsory Tunneling via RADIUS

RFC 2888	Secure Remote Access with L2TP
RFC 3070	Layer Two Tunneling Protocol (L2TP) over Frame Relay
RFC 3145	L2TP Disconnect Cause Information
RFC 3193	Securing L2TP using IPsec
RFC 3301	Layer Two Tunneling Protocol (L2TP): ATM access network
RFC 3308	Layer Two Tunneling Protocol (L2TP) Differentiated Services
RFC 3355	Layer Two Tunneling Protocol (L2TP) Over ATM Adaptation Layer 5 (AAL5)
RFC 3371	Layer Two Tunneling Protocol "L2TP" Management Information Base
RFC 3437	Layer Two Tunneling Protocol Extensions for PPP Link Control Protocol Negotiation
RFC 3438	Layer Two Tunneling Protocol (L2TP) Internet Assigned Numbers: Internet Assigned Numbers Authority (IANA) Considerations Update
RFC 3573	Signaling of Modem-On-Hold status in Layer 2 Tunneling Protocol (L2TP)
RFC 3817	Layer 2 Tunneling Protocol (L2TP) Active Discovery Relay for PPP over Ethernet (PPPoE)

RFCs on IPsec in Relation to Other Protocols

RFC 2207	RSVP Extensions for IPSEC Data Flows
RFC 2521	ICMP Security Failures Messages
RFC 3104	RSIP Support for End-to-end IPsec
RFC 3554	On the Use of Stream Control Transmission Protocol (SCTP) with IPsec
RFC 3776	Using IPsec to Protect Mobile IPv6 Signaling Between Mobile Nodes and Home Agents
RFC 3884	Use of IPsec Transport Mode for Dynamic Routing

RFCs Not in Use or Implemented across Multiple Vendors

RFC 2522	Photuris: Session-Key Management Protocol
RFC 2523	Photuris: Extended Schemes and Attributes
RFC 3456	Dynamic Host Configuration Protocol (DHCPv4) Configuration of IPsec Tunnel Mode

Index

iVPN. *See* TauVPN client

K

KAME/Racoon, 233
keepalive packet, 98, 208
kernel
  compile options, 66-68
  configuration, 65, 71, 72
  debugging, GDB, 300
  errors, 278
  Fedora, 306
  patching, 69, 72
  prerequisites, 64
  Red Hat, 306
kernel API, 305
kernel mode
  Authentication Header, 33
  Encapsulated Security Payload, 34
  encryption, software, 36
  IPsec mode, 35
  manual keying, 36
  packet handling, 32
  protocols, 37
  transport mode, 34
  tunnel mode, 34
key, 29, 37, 107
KEY record, 135, 141
KLIPS
  about, 50
  activation, 70
  compile, 66, 68, 69
  drawbacks, 52
  features, 51, 52
  firewall, 151
  installation, 64
  interface, 89
  ipsecX, 51
  packet caching, 51
  patching, 67, 72, 74
  Path MTU discovery, 51, 52
KLIPS installation
  binary package, 63, 64
  Linux kernel, 71
  source package, 64

L

L2TP. *See* **Layer 2 Tunneling Protocol**

L2TP daemon
  securing, 162
  selecting, 163
L2TP/IPsec
  client configuration, 159, 176
  Linux kernel runtime parameter, 161
  Openswan, configuration, 160
  server configuration, 159, 175
  setup, types, 158
l2tpd daemon
  about, 163
  configuration, 164, 165
LAN. *See* **Local Area Network**
Layer 2 Tunneling Protocol
  about, 157
  configuring in Mac OS X, 173-175
  configuring in Windows 2000, 169-173
  configuring in Windows XP, 165-169
  disadvantage, 158
  encryption, 236
  errors, 274, 275
  options, 68
  properties, 157
  PSK, 158
  setup, types, 158
  VPN server, 156
  X.509, 158
leap of faith, 31
Leeuw, Jacco de, 159, 202
link layer, protection, 238, 239
Linksys, VPN setup, 231
Linsys IPsec tool, configuration, 179-181
Linux kernel runtime parameter, L2TP/IPsec,
  161
Linux kernel, developement, 305
listall command, 118
Local Area Network
  definition, 313
  Opportunistic Encryption, 236
log file, debugging, 268
lsipsectool, 179-181
Lucent Brick, 232
lwdnsq application, 134

M

Mac OS X, 155, 156
main mode, 38, 39
manual keying, 36, 75

Maximum Segment Size, 153
Maximum Transmission Unit
    packet size, 152, 153
    troubleshooting, 270
MD5
    hash algorithm, 29
    security holes, 306
Message Digest 5. *See* MD5
Microsoft certificate store, 176
Microsoft IKE daemon, X.509 IPsec, 176
Microsoft IPsec, implementing, 177
Microsoft Management Console, 176
MMC, 176
ModeConfig extension, 40, 157
MODP group, 206
MS IKE daemon, 176
MS Windows, 155
MSL2TP, 155
MSS. *See* Maximum Segment Size
MTU. *See* Maximum Transmission Unit
Müller, Marcus, 177

N

NAP, 235
NAT. *See* Network Address Translation
NAT-T. *See* NAT-Traversal. *See also* IPsec
    NAT-Traversal, 43
NAT-Traversal
    about, 43, 149
    checking, 97
    enabling, 96
    IP packet, encapsulation, 44
    IPsec passthrough, 43
    limitation, 44, 96
    patching, 69, 72
    subnetwithin= syntax, 97
NATworks, 42
NetGear, 233
NETKEY
    about, 18
    drawbacks, 53
    firewall, 151, 152
    stack options, 66, 67
netmask, 314
NetScreen
    issues, 227
    VPN, configuring, 226
Network Access Protection, 235
network address, 315

Network Address Translation
    IP address, rewriting, 317
    IP address, swaping, 41
    IPsec passthrough, 43
    NAT-Traversal, 43, 44
    NATworks, 42
Nortel Contivity
    about, 212
    local network, adding definition, 213, 215,
        216

O

Oakley.log file, 271, 272
OCSP. *See* Online Certificate Status Protocol
OE. *See* Opportunistic Encryption
OE DNS record, 136
Online Certificate Status Protocol, 128
open-source software, 16
OpenSSL
    certificate authority, creating, 122
    certificate generation, commands, 115, 116
    configuration, 114
openssl.cnf file, 114, 115, 123
Openswan
    agreements, 21, 22
    bugs, 308
    client, 205
    client setup, 247
    community, 301
    compile, 57
    configuration, 59-62, 80-82
    copyright, 20
    GIT repository, 307
    help, 301
    history, 17, 18
    installation, 55, 56
    L2TP/IPsec, 160
    legalities, 21
    license, 20
    Linux distribution, choosing, 45-48
    mailing list, 301
    NETKEY, 18
    Pluto, testing, 48
    server setup, 246
    startup time, 257
    testing, UML, 295
    troubleshooting, 265
    tweaks, 259
    UML, script building, 296, 298

client, supplicant side, 105
drawbacks, 104, 105
gateway, server side, 105
PSK, 104
rekeying, 104
Xelerance, 142, 177, 308
Xen, 263

Z

zeroconf protocol, 248
Zyxcel
  bug, 217
  configuring, 217, 218

Thank you for buying Building and Integrating Virtual Private Networks with Openswan

Packt Open Source Project Royalties

When we sell a book written on an Open Source project, we pay a royalty directly to that project. Therefore by purchasing *Building and Integrating Virtual Private Networks with Openswan*, Packt will have given some of the money received to the openswan project.

In the long term, we see ourselves and you—customers and readers of our books—as part of the Open Source ecosystem, providing sustainable revenue for the projects we publish on. Our aim at Packt is to establish publishing royalties as an essential part of the service and support a business model that sustains Open Source.

If you're working with an Open Source project that you would like us to publish on, and subsequently pay royalties to, please get in touch with us.

Writing for Packt

We welcome all inquiries from people who are interested in authoring. Book proposals should be sent to authors@packtpub.com. If your book idea is still at an early stage and you would like to discuss it first before writing a formal book proposal, contact us; one of our commissioning editors will get in touch with you.

We're not just looking for published authors; if you have strong technical skills but no writing experience, our experienced editors can help you develop a writing career, or simply get some additional reward for your expertise.

About Packt Publishing

Packt, pronounced 'packed', published its first book "*Mastering phpMyAdmin for Effective MySQL Management*" in April 2004 and subsequently continued to specialize in publishing highly focused books on specific technologies and solutions.

Our books and publications share the experiences of your fellow IT professionals in adapting and customizing today's systems, applications, and frameworks. Our solution-based books give you the knowledge and power to customize the software and technologies you're using to get the job done. Packt books are more specific and less general than the IT books you have seen in the past. Our unique business model allows us to bring you more focused information, giving you more of what you need to know, and less of what you don't.

Packt is a modern, yet unique publishing company, which focuses on producing quality, cutting-edge books for communities of developers, administrators, and newbies alike. For more information, please visit our website: www.PacktPub.com.

Printed in the United States
50422LVS00004B/13

9 781904 811251